THE HANGING OF

EPHRAIM WHEELER

IRENE   QUENZLER   BROWN

The Hanging of Ephraim Wheeler

RICHARD   D.   BROWN

A Story of
Rape, Incest, and Justice
in Early America

THE BELKNAP PRESS OF

HARVARD UNIVERSITY PRESS

Cambridge, Massachusetts

London, England

2003

Library of Congress Cataloging-in-Publication Data
Brown, Irene Quenzler.
The hanging of Ephraim Wheeler : a story of rape, incest, and justice in
early America / Irene Quenzler Brown, Richard D. Brown.
p.   cm.
Includes bibliographical references and index.
ISBN 0-674-01020-5 (alk. paper)
1. Wheeler, Ephraim. 2. Rape—Massachusetts—Berkshire County—History—
19th century—Case studies. 3. Incest—Massachusetts—Berkshire County—History—
19th century—Case studies. 4. Hanging—Massachusetts—Lenox—History—
19th century—Case studies. 5. Problem families—Massachusetts—Berkshire County—
History—19th century—Case studies. 6. Interracial marriage—Massachusetts—
Berkshire County—History—19th century—Case studies. 7. Capital punishment—
Massachusetts—Berkshire County—History—19th century—Case studies. 8. Berkshire
County (Mass.)—Social conditions—19th century. 9. Berkshire County (Mass.)—
Social conditions—18th century. I. Brown, Richard D. II. Title.

HV6565.M4B76 2003
364.15′32′097441—dc21   2002038266

FOR

JOSIAH AND NICHOLAS

AND THEIR GRANDPARENTS

CONTENTS

ILLUSTRATIONS

THE HANGING OF

EPHRAIM WHEELER

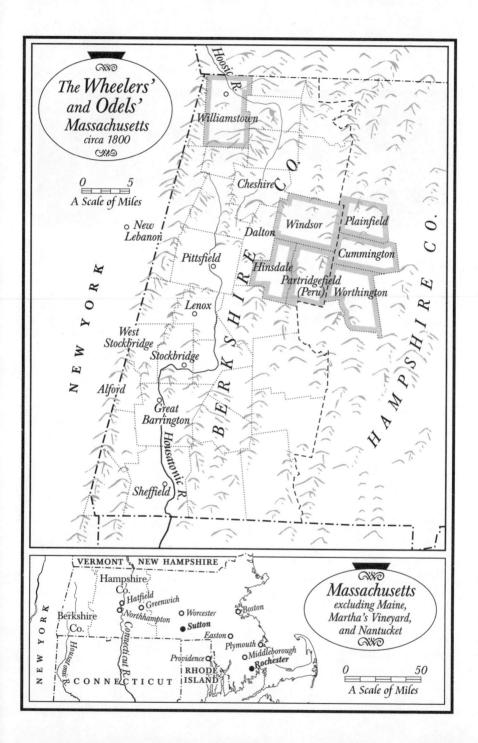

The Wheelers' and Odels' Massachusetts
circa 1800

0   5
A Scale of Miles

Massachusetts
excluding Maine,
Martha's Vineyard,
and Nantucket

0   50
A Scale of Miles

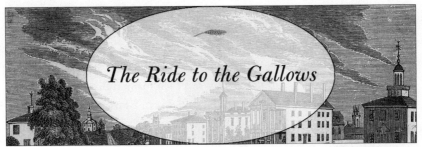

The Ride to the Gallows

The Reverend Samuel Shepard's words on the rainy afternoon of February 20, 1806, had been aimed at him: "EPHRAIM WHEELER . . . Your heaven or hell may hang suspended on the present moment. . . . Look back on a life, all covered with pollution! . . . Fly . . . to the ark of safety."[1] Hundreds of people—women, men, children—had prayed for his salvation; and now, chained by his wrists and his ankles, he was the center of attention. He rose from his seat on the coffin so that the sheriff's deputies could carry the pine box out. Then the deputies led him from the new meetinghouse atop Lenox hill. They lifted both Wheeler and his coffin into the cart that would carry the forty-three-year-old condemned man through the village to the gallows that stood waiting under the gray, rainy sky.[2] One hundred fifty-nine days earlier, on another gloomy day, Ephraim had listened and wept when Judge Simeon Strong sentenced him "to be hanged by the neck until he be Dead."[3] Now the moment for his execution had arrived. The authorities had ordered that he be "launched into eternity" within the hour, to dwell in hellfire or heaven forever.

The country folk of Berkshire County could only imagine Ephraim Wheeler's thoughts during the jolting, chain-clanking cart ride down the hill and along the muddy road as he passed among the

1

throng that gathered by thousands to watch his execution. A few of the spectators knew that, in telling his life story the night before, Wheeler had said, "I declare myself to be innocent." Possessed by anger and self-pity, Wheeler blamed the prosecutor, jury, and judges, indeed the whole standing order of church and state, "for the destruction which they have brought upon me." He blamed his wife and his two oldest children for their deadly betrayal of him as husband and father. And he blamed his fate as a poor, abused orphan boy, stalked forever by misfortune.[4]

In his gloom, Wheeler's only glimmer of hope was that the petitions asking to spare his life, petitions that he and over one hundred others had signed and sent to the governor, might yet be granted.[5] In that case he would live out his days in hard labor at the state prison. But prison was better than hanging. Wheeler had known hard labor and coarse food all his life. He had survived the miseries of Revolutionary war service and the dangers of shipboard life. He would escape from prison if he could (two weeks earlier he had escaped briefly from the Lenox jail); but if he must be in prison, he would survive. He would be grateful, in fact. His only other ray of hope, that he would experience a last-minute conversion on the scaffold, would not stop the execution; but at least his soul would be free in heaven. Yet thus far, though clergymen had been praying and preaching with him for days, he remained unmoved spiritually.[6]

As he rode along looking out at the sea of upturned, mostly silent faces, he might have thought back to the bright June day eight months earlier, when he had been arrested on the charge of raping his thirteen-year-old daughter, Betsy. At the time, his arrest had taken him by surprise and a trial seemed unlikely. But when Betsy, backed by his wife, Hannah, accused him before a justice and then stuck to her story throughout the summer, the Berkshire grand jury indicted him. When Wheeler came to trial in September, he knew he was in deep trouble, because rape was a capital crime in Massachusetts in 1805. No one in Berkshire County had ever been convicted for this offense, however, and no one in the entire state had been executed for rape in a generation.[7] Wheeler faced a jury trial before a three-member panel of the state's highest tribunal, the Supreme Judicial Court. True, the court had appointed two skilled attorneys to defend him, but they had been up against the Massachusetts attorney general, James Sullivan, a lawyer and politician who in fifteen years of prosecutions before juries had seldom lost a case.[8]

Wheeler had hoped, perhaps even expected, that this panel would acquit him. His lawyers might have assured him that the odds were in his favor, since jurymen rarely convicted defendants of rape, especially when those charged were white Yankees like themselves. Jurors preferred to find prisoners guilty of the lesser charges of attempted rape or lewd and lascivious behavior, crimes that at most carried penalties of a year or two in prison and sometimes only an hour on the pillory plus a fine. But Wheeler's accuser was not just any young serving woman; she was his own daughter. That was why the Lenox courthouse had overflowed with hundreds of spectators, and that was why a nearby printer had hired a man to attend the trial to compile an exact report for publication and sale. The printer believed there was a market for Wheeler's life story. The charge of incestuous rape was shocking, and made Wheeler the subject of press coverage all over New England and even as far away as Richmond, Virginia.[9]

After the verdict was brought in and the sentence pronounced, Wheeler had gone back to jail, where he had plenty of time to nurse his sense of injury. From his *Narrative* we know that above all he blamed his wife and his daughter for putting his life in jeopardy. Hannah, his wife of fourteen years, had never been the love of his life. But she had borne him five children, and she was a good worker and a frugal housewife. Her family, some of whom were recognizably black, were capable people who managed to scrape by as independent farmers and laborers.[10] But now, aided by her kinfolk, Hannah was Wheeler's chief enemy. Instead of submitting to his rule, as was proper, he was convinced she had schemed with his children to get him out of the way. And, he raged silently, she had succeeded. The fact that Hannah and the children had petitioned Governor Caleb Strong to spare his life did not allay his anger.[11] Even if the governor were to commute his sentence, Wheeler knew he would be locked up for the next twenty-five years at least. His wife would triumph, and he was as good as dead.

In fact, however, neither Wheeler nor the thousands who watched him on his ride to the gallows as yet knew his fate. Wheeler's attorneys had drafted a petition for him to mark (he could not write his name), and they had also sent their own carefully argued pardon petition to the governor. In addition, over one hundred men, including over seventy from Wheeler's own town of Windsor, had petitioned to save his life. Most of them believed that rape should not be punished by death. Two Congregational pastors, the county sheriff, and leading Federalists and Republicans had all signed to save him. They knew, as did Wheeler's attorneys, that just four years earlier, Governor Caleb Strong had pardoned a black man from India who had been sentenced to die after raping a white girl.[12]

During the five months between Wheeler's sentencing and the February date for his execution, no pardon had come, and Wheeler's desperation had mounted. Yet he continued to hope right up until the last minute. It was generally understood that in order to dramatize the power of the state to punish, the sheriff was sometimes directed to wait until he had placed the rope around the subject's neck before proclaiming a last-minute pardon. Twenty years before, when Berkshire leaders of the Shays' Rebellion stood convicted of treason, the state had enacted precisely this drama at the Lenox gallows. And

4

spectators who read the local papers knew that barely seven months earlier the governor of New York had ordered a last-minute stay of execution for Stephen Arnold, a schoolmaster convicted of murdering his six-year-old niece. Some in the crowd that waited patiently in the rain at the Lenox gallows were hoping that such a scene would again be enacted so as to prevent the killing of a fellow citizen. Even as the cart rolled toward the gallows and the crowd of 5,000 people swelled around him, Wheeler's fate remained in doubt.[13]

This is a book about Americans who were caught up in a shocking criminal case two hundred years ago. Confronted with a capital crime, they tried to find the path of justice. Their statutes and procedures were clear enough: but in addition they relied on discretion and judgment. Victims had to decide whether to complain and testify. Witnesses had to choose their words. And court professionals and public officials had to fulfill their prescribed duties under the scrutiny of their peers and the public. Indeed the stakes were high for participants of all ranks, living as they did in a small society under their neighbors' surveillance and acting without the confidentiality supplied by impersonal bureaucracy or the privacy that accompanies metropolitan life.

Inspired by Natalie Zemon Davis's *Return of Martin Guerre*, we have undertaken the close analysis of an exceptional trial report and of the equally remarkable autobiography of its central figure.[14] By setting the evidence these documents supply in context, we reveal the moving and provocative story of a family in crisis. In the story of Ephraim Wheeler, we explore subjects, both repellent and fascinating, that reflect deeply rooted American beliefs about right and wrong. *The Hanging of Ephraim Wheeler* provides a careful examination of a sordid event and its aftermath in full context so as to deepen readers' understanding of both past and present-day responses to family violence. Assessing this account of rape and Ephraim Wheeler's subsequent trial and execution from the distance of two centuries allows us to reflect with a measure of detachment on a horrifying story, in which a brutally violated girl confronted her attacker and so began a process that led the state to take her father's life. Though these events happened long ago, the actions, the politics, and the emotions they generated resonate across time.

Much of what happened seems far away. Executions, for example, are today hidden from view in the death chambers of distant prisons. Consequently, the execution-day ritual of New England two centuries ago appears grotesque, even frightening, in its public, communal character. In the present day we find it strange to yoke Christianity, a religion of forgiveness as well as judgment, to didactic, ceremonial killing in the manner of Islamic fundamentalist states. Nowadays, though the tabloid media feature executions, American officials do not bring prisoners into churches for display and use their executions to awaken individual and public consciousness of sin, mortality, and the necessity of commitment to Christ. Today we think it strange for whole families to pray publicly, and for citizens to shed tears of pity for someone they are about to execute. Authorities no longer invite the public to witness the gallows spectacle. Such ritual killing is alien; yet all these things were customary in the founding era of the American republic. Good and sensitive men and women joined in execution ceremonies and brought their children along to witness the convict's death throes. Why, we wonder? What did such an exercise signify for them and their society?

More particularly we wonder why in 1806 Massachusetts authorities would actually execute a husband and father for the crime of rape. Citizens of Massachusetts, leaders especially, thought of themselves as enlightened and progressive. Like citizens of other states, they had been seeking to reform—and to moderate—their system of criminal punishment. In the very year of Ephraim Wheeler's trial, Governor Strong had signed laws that removed sodomy from the list of capital crimes and abolished corporal punishments such as whipping, branding, cropping ears and cutting off fingers. Legislators even put an end to the stocks and the pillory because they were convinced that prison time and hard labor were more humane methods of punishment—and better suited to improve a convict's behavior and morals. The death penalty, a hallmark of the British monarchy's criminal code, had become a particular target of Republican reformers, and in Massachusetts, as in other states, reformers argued that only murder and treason should be punished at the scaffold.[15]

Moreover, in the county where the trial was held, people expressed doubts about the rightness of Ephraim Wheeler's conviction, both because of defects in the evidence presented in court and because Wheeler always and absolutely denied that he had committed rape, even when he stood with clergymen at the gallows. If it had been seen as just for Governor Strong to grant conditional pardon to a black rapist in 1802, and proper to stay the execution of child murderer Stephen Arnold (whom the New York legislature later incarcerated), what did Wheeler deserve? Other men around Massachusetts were punished with prison or fines when convicted of assault with attempt to rape, incest, or lewd and lascivious carriage. Did justice truly require Wheeler's death?

The meaning of justice is, of course, so abstract that in particular cases it can only be determined in context. Here the intensive study of a single episode, one that is confined in time and place, enables us to explore large questions of policy and principle at the level of actual people and specific experience. This approach, often called "microhistory," allows us to understand the entire episode in light of the longer histories of the participants and their community and in relation to the surrounding events that shaped their outlook and behavior. Microscopic examination of a case where laws and institutions confronted life-and-death questions of crime and punishment—as well as issues of class, gender, and race—enables us to appreciate important realities in early republican society.

Our book tells a tale of real people who, though separated from us by time, engage our emotions. At the center of the story are Ephraim Wheeler and his wife, Hannah Odel, who came to Berkshire County in their late twenties and joined in an unlawful interracial marriage. We describe their personal histories and how they made their way at the margins of Berkshire's economy and society. Over a fourteen-year span their troubled marriage brought them five children and three separations as they labored to become an independent farm family. Their failure was only one among the countless small tragedies of Americans in the early republic.

Ours is also the tale of James Sullivan, the brilliant attorney general who prosecuted Wheeler while simultaneously running for governor. Sullivan, a family man in love with the wife who bore him eight children before her early death, had risen from frontier poverty to build an extensive legal practice. Though suffering from lameness and epileptic attacks, in the Revolutionary era he had been a founder of the new state of Massachusetts. Later he was a champion of Jeffersonian democracy and religious freedom—and also an advocate of capital punishment. Though Sullivan came to live the life of a Boston grandee, he was as comfortable with artisans as with aristocrats. When traveling the court circuit, this gentleman who had often dined at the table of John Hancock was known to offer a farmer a place in his bed. This was the prosecutor who brought Betsy Wheeler's charge to the grand jury and whose eloquence helped convict her father before the Supreme Judicial Court.

This is also the story of Wheeler's judges, among them Theodore

Sedgwick, a friend of George Washington and a baron of Berkshire Federalism. Although Sedgwick had worked with Sullivan in leading the Revolution in Massachusetts, his elitist, pro-British politics would later set the two apart. An advocate of enlightened paternalism generally, Sedgwick challenged the legality of chattel slavery in a celebrated case in the 1780s, where, by winning freedom for Elizabeth Freeman, he also won the lifelong loyalty of a housekeeper and mother-surrogate for his children. On the night before he and his colleagues sentenced Wheeler to hang, Sedgwick went home from the courthouse to his own teenage daughter in Stockbridge. When she grew up, that daughter would write a story based on the Wheeler case.[16]

The drama of Wheeler's trial and execution also included a score of lesser participants—clergymen, lawyers, jurors and other officials, and Betsy Wheeler's racially mixed aunts and uncles. Among the clergy, Samuel Shepard and Thomas Allen stand out. Shepard, a young revivalist, would use the sermon he delivered at Wheeler's execution as an opportunity to evangelize, and would later be selected by the Federalists to preach the annual election sermon to the state government in Boston. Allen, an aging Revolutionary firebrand and at the time of the Wheeler affair a staunch Jeffersonian, led the anti-capital punishment forces in Berkshire County, circulating a petition on Wheeler's behalf and attacking the Federalists for supporting this "sanguinary, . . . monarchical" punishment.[17] A year later, when James Sullivan was elected governor, Jeffersonians would honor Allen by choosing him to give the election sermon at the opening of the new legislative session in the State House.

Equally important were Wheeler's politically ambitious court-appointed lawyers, John W. Hulbert and Daniel Dewey. Both had trained as clerks in Sedgwick's office, and they brought respectability to Ephraim's side. Fashioning an imaginative defense for their pauper client, and advocating clemency after the conviction, they did their best to save Ephraim Wheeler's life. Taking a less prominent but still notable role was Simon Larned, the Jeffersonian county sheriff and militia colonel. This Pittsfield merchant and onetime United States congressman petitioned to save Wheeler's life, but was officially required to conduct the hanging—something he had never done before. No wonder that on the scaffold Larned treated Wheeler "with marks of great sensibility, tenderness, and compassion."[18] Wheeler had recklessly broken the taboos against rape and incest; but now, while others could stand by and watch, Larned must coolly, deliberately, and as a matter of duty, take the life of a fellow man.

Our book probes forbidden subjects—rape, incest, hanging—primal acts that rouse our curiosity and engage us emotionally because of their painful, abhorrent, even terrifying character. Ephraim Wheeler's case was not simple, emotionally or intellectually—not for his contemporaries and not for us. Throughout this book we sometimes speculate as to the thoughts and feelings of the participants. We do so in order to understand better the meaning of the events for the participants as well as to appreciate the motives that propelled them to act as they did. Though there is much in our story we can establish as fact, there are gaps in the record. And in key parts of the narrative, there can be no single "true" version. What "really" happened in 1805 and 1806 was not the same for any of the major protagonists. In our speculations, we try to offer judgments that are both informed and plausible.

The chapters that follow present the story of how Ephraim Wheeler came to stand at the gallows in Lenox, Massachusetts, on February 20, 1806. Each chapter begins with an extended quotation from a primary source, which we then interpret in the context of the history of the subject and a broad social and cultural perspective. We invite you to imagine Wheeler's story from the different viewpoints of his wife and daughter, of the prosecutor and the court, of the community and the press, and of Ephraim Wheeler himself. We also invite you to imagine yourself a juror, to weigh the evidence and consider your verdict. By considering Wheeler's case in the context of the pardoning process and other serious crimes of the period, we encourage you to ponder whether, guilty or not, Ephraim Wheeler received justice. We close with our own assessment of the tragedy and its significance for the early republic and our own time.

The Setting

This county may be regarded as composed of a very intelligent and moral, and relatively considered, religious population. The literary and pious institutions and customs of our fathers have sent down a blessed influence, which has reached until the present time, notwithstanding the evil moral tendency of the Revolutionary war and Shays insurrection, the party politics that have sometimes raged, and other unhappy events. Our scattered settlements and general employments are favorable to good morals. The repeated revivals, affecting many of the influential men & families, and very many of the substantial yeomanry, have had a mighty and most beneficial effect upon the whole community.

[David Dudley Field and Chester Dewey],
A History of the County of Berkshire, Massachusetts . . . (1829)

D ramas of good and evil, of crime and punishment can be enacted anytime, anywhere; but each one is shaped by its own time and place. The story of Ephraim Wheeler, his wife Hannah, and their children belongs to Massachusetts' westernmost county of Berkshire in the decades after the American Revolution. The roughly thirty thousand people of this hilly region of farms and forests were struggling toward prosperity as they cleared and cultivated a landscape that had been largely Indian country prior to American independence. Indian warriors killed a handful of Berkshire settlers and carried several more into captivity less than twenty years before the battles of Lexington and Concord. Only the British victories over the French and the Indians in 1759 and 1760 enabled English families to settle the central and northern parts of the county.

The settlement drive accelerated after 1761, when the Massachusetts legislature formally organized Berkshire County, a twenty-mile-wide strip that ran between Massachusetts' southern and northern borders. Lying more than a four-day horseback ride (120 miles) west of Boston, but only a single day's ride from Hudson and Albany, New York, the new county was bounded to the east by the 1,500- to 2,500-foot Green Mountain barrier that it shared with Hampshire County, and to the west by the 2,000- to 3,000-foot Taconic Mountains that spread into New York. Lacking any great, fertile and navigable river valley such as the Connecticut to the east or the Hudson to the west, Berkshire did boast the narrow but productive Housatonic valley, which meandered through the central and southern portions of the county on its way to Connecticut and Long Island Sound. To the north, the smaller Hoosic River, a tributary of the Hudson, ran north and west.[1]

At the beginning of the 1760s, except for the few settlements in the south that lay along the Housatonic River, the region was heavily forested. Because Berkshire possessed good (though often shallow) soils, moderate rainfall (36 inches annually), and a growing season (about 150 days) long enough to support deciduous trees as well as conifers, a great variety of plant and animal life flourished in its hills and valleys, swamps and hollows, ponds and streams. During the first half of the eighteenth century the forest had sustained hundreds of Indians, people who chose to clear only small patches of land. They had, however, embraced European trade goods and so had exterminated the beaver for the sake of their pelts. Now their English successors would attack bear, wolves, and rattlesnakes for safety's sake, and deer and turkeys for meat, hunting so avidly that within a generation or so—certainly by 1800—large game and rattlesnakes would become a rarity. But in 1760 these animals, as well as foxes, wildcats, woodchucks, raccoons, and skunks, thrived wherever they found suitable habitat. Rodents, large and small—from porcupines, rabbits, and squirrels to weasels, muskrats, and minks—were also abundant. Field rats and mice foraged mostly in the meadows created by the natural filling in of old beaver ponds.[2]

Life also thrived in Berkshire's chilly waters. Downstream waterfalls blocked the entry of migratory fish such as salmon and shad into the region, but there were perch and trout, bullhead (catfish), dace and suckers, sunfish, eels, and shiners. These, together with crawfish, freshwater clams, and several kinds of turtles, snakes, frogs, and salamanders, fed the mammals and birds that hunted them.

Beneath the forest canopy and around Berkshire's meadows, swamps, ponds, and rivers several dozen kinds of birds passed at least part of their year. In 1760 wild turkeys were still numerous, and eagles occasionally scoured the region's waters, where loons and gulls, black ducks, and Canada geese sometimes nested. In daylight when hawks hunted, blue jays and crows called out warnings. At night, when searching for prey, owls screeched and hooted to each other through the darkness, their calls both territorial and triumphant. In the springtime the woods hummed with the songs of thrushes and wrens, mockingbirds and phoebes. Near dusk, as the calls of other birds died away, the rhythmic song of whippoorwills and the hammering of woodpeckers stood out. As years passed and meadows and pasturelands multiplied, so also did blackbirds and robins, doves and woodcocks, martins and swallows, as well as an abundance of flies, grasshoppers, butterflies, and moths, and the magical fireflies of early summer.

To the farmers who cleared Berkshire valleys and hillsides the forest was not the sylvan paradise that later generations envisioned. For them it was a rough wilderness, an obstacle to their prosperity. When they looked at the great oaks, chestnuts, sugar maples, ash and beech trees, white and yellow pine, and spruce trees that grew 70 to 100 feet into the air, they saw timber, firewood, and fencing. Most of the other trees—aspens, poplars, hornbeam, black alder, elms, cherries, balsam firs, hemlocks, and hackmatacks—were simply obstacles to be destroyed in order for the settlers to raise crops and livestock.

No one in the 1760s or later expected Berkshire to be a land of milk and honey, where farmers would grow fat; so much of the land was sloping, and the growing season was too short. But because southern New England was filling up, its farmland becoming scarce and expensive, Berkshire seemed attractive. The closest Berkshire ever came to a land rush was in the 1760s and 1770s, when the legislature incorporated twenty towns. Thereafter, not new arrivals but the children of the settlers—mostly English, with small numbers of Scots, Irish, and Hudson River Dutch—accounted for most of Berkshire's growth.

By the eighteenth century, Berkshire's Indian population was much diminished. In the 1730s Massachusetts clergymen, with English support, created a mission that brought nearly all the Indians to villages in Stockbridge. Here the Reverends John Sergeant, Jonathan Edwards, and Stephen West converted several hundred native people to Christianity. But as white settlers multiplied after the Revolution, the Native Americans fell prey to alcohol and debt. To halt their further decline, groups of Indian families moved out of Berkshire County to settle on a large tract in New York, a gift of the Oneida people that they named New Stockbridge.[3] During the same decade, as the Indians departed, scores of newly free African Americans came into Berkshire, augmenting the handful of ex-slaves once owned by county gentlefolk. Berkshire's white Yankee residents were not especially welcoming to black or mixed-race people, but those who worked hard and behaved decently could be accepted on their own merits. Indeed, sixty miles to the north, at Rutland, Vermont, the Congregational church was even willing to install a mulatto, Lemuel Haynes, as its clergyman in 1788.[4] No such recognition was accorded to any people of color in Berkshire, but by the time of the first United States census in 1790 over 300 blacks had settled in the county. Among this group was a family of seven headed by Ichabod Odel. His daughter Hannah would later marry Ephraim Wheeler, a white Yankee who had arrived in the region in the 1780s.[5]

By 1790 the inhabitants of Berkshire's twenty-four towns had reached the 30,000 level, and their number would continue to grow modestly to a peak of 36,000 in 1810. Then, in the decade that followed, repeated cold seasons, soil depletion, and erosion on hill farmlands led to bad harvests and a slight population decline, as young men and some farm families sought more and better land in New York and Ohio. Hereafter Berkshire's growth would no longer depend on the multiplication of traditional Yankee farmsteads that produced most of their own food, fuel, and clothing, but on commerce, manufacturing, extractive industries such as timber and quarrying, and farms that specialized in sheep or dairying.[6]

Around 1800, however, the county seemed prosperous. The European warfare that had begun in the early 1790s and would continue until the defeat of Napoleon in 1815 brought high prices for farm products; so, in a region where more than nine out of ten families depended on the land, times were good. Never before had the people of Berkshire enjoyed such protection from physical danger, privation, and want. But the blessings of peace and prosperity did not bring tranquility to everyday life. Though nearly all were Yankee Protestants with southern New England roots, Berkshire people argued vigorously over matters of this world and the next.

That they did so verbally and legally—in the courts, at town and parish meetings, in the press, and at the ballot box—contrasted with the turbulent, dangerous past that many adults remembered. During the independence movement and Berkshire's subsequent protest against independent Massachusetts' "unconstitutional" government in the Revolution, the Reverend Thomas Allen of Pittsfield had led hundreds of Berkshiremen to seize control of the county, arguing that they were empowered by "natural law" to run their own affairs.[7] Similarly, but on a much broader scale, during the farmers' Shays' Rebellion of 1786–1787 some in Berkshire County had resorted to extralegal measures, including military action.

In the southern part of the county, in skirmishes at West Stockbridge and Sheffield, hundreds of pro- and antigovernment Berkshiremen had fired on each other, wounding three dozen men, five fatally. In the West Stockbridge action Theodore Sedgwick, then the Speaker of the Massachusetts House and later a Federalist congressman (and one of Wheeler's judges), exposed himself to rebel gunfire before talking scores of the insurgents, some of whom he knew personally, into laying down their arms. In the neighborhood of Sheffield and Stockbridge, Berkshire's two oldest towns—both were incorporated in the 1730s—the conflict between gentlemen creditors and mortgaged farmers was often personal. Soon after Sedgwick's victorious West Stockbridge confrontation, a group of rebels retaliated by raiding his home while the master was away in Boston. They seized Sedgwick's two apprentice law clerks and stole his clothing, his linens, and a horse.[8] These lawbreakers escaped punishment. However, John Bly and Charles Rose, two Shaysites who went on a rampage of violent burglaries after the rebellion had ended, were captured, tried, and executed at Lenox in 1787.[9]

When the uprising collapsed in the spring of 1787 the state recoiled from bloody political reprisals. The leaders of the rebellion were tried for treason, convicted, and sentenced to hang; but when John Hancock was swept into the governorship in May 1787 his mandate was moderation. So although he let the prisoners mount the scaffold as a mark of state authority, when they stood at the brink of execution he pardoned them. This gesture of reconciliation was intended to ease the enmities surrounding the conflict.[10]

Despite these attempts at peacemaking, however, alienation from the state government and its court system remained widespread. One Berkshire-bred recent Yale graduate, Barnabas Bidwell, reported that "the majority" in Berkshire were "disaffected to Governmental measures." Whereas the few "Gentlemen of learning and the liberal professions, especially the Clergy, are universally for Government," Bidwell observed that "Debtors are generally on the other side; and this class comprehends more than half the people." He disdainfully concluded that "Rhode Island Emigrants and almost all of the denomination of Baptists; men of warm passions and but little reason; men of fickle minds, fond of every new scheme and proud of an enterprising spirit—such have generally engaged in the Insurrection." In addition the rebellion had gained strength from the "ignorant, uninformed, but well-meaning common people, who hearing such a dreadful outcry against Government" naively embraced the cause. Now that the rebellion was finished, Bidwell found that "almost all, with whom I have conversed, acknowledge that they took a wrong method to get redress, by resorting to arms and stopping Courts." Now they realized they could have achieved reforms "by instructing their [state] Representatives or changing them" at the annual election.[11] Against this backdrop, with anarchy and bloodshed so immediate in local memory, the rule of law was no mere abstraction, especially among property owners, men who voted and served on juries. Experience had taught them that social order was an achievement attained by blending consent with coercion.

By 1800 social conflict in Berkshire was more orderly, but still intense. The state and national contests between Federalists and Jeffersonians divided the county elite. Though Sedgwick and Bidwell had been on the same side during Shays' Rebellion, now Sedgwick led the Federalists in Congress as Speaker of the House and Bidwell, who would win the same seat for the Jeffersonians five years later, represented Berkshire in the state senate as a Republican. Like their learned and wealthy neighbors, farmers too displayed divided loyalties. The fact that local, legislative, and gubernatorial elections took place every spring made party competition virtually continuous, and for some it was deadly serious.

Berkshire, moreover, was especially contentious because neither the Federalist party of Washington, Adams, and Hamilton nor the Republicans of Jefferson and Madison could wholly dominate. Countywide, Republicans generally achieved only narrow majorities, and in particular communities competition was so intense that party leaders like Sedgwick counted every last vote and, on occasion, brought residents who were away on business back to town on horseback so as to secure their votes.[12] In one election Jeffersonians complained that Federalists "brought out their last man," including "four negro votes."[13] Because Berkshire was among the state's more agrarian and less commercial and cosmopolitan regions, it was unlikely to warm to the Federalist agenda of a strong, procommerce central government. In addition, Republican arguments in favor of separation of church and state were popular in a county where the officially preferred Congregationalists faced challenges from dissenting Baptists and Methodists. And although Episcopalians, Quakers, and Shakers, as well as unchurched residents, differed with each other in religion, the issue of religious establishment often brought them to support the Republicans at the polls.

The two centers of Berkshire's political geography in 1800—

Stockbridge with 1,260 people, and Pittsfield with 2,260 inhabitants—lay along the Housatonic River near the middle of the county. At the older town of Stockbridge, Heman Willard, a twenty-five-year-old native, published the ardently Federalist weekly paper, *The Western Star*. At Pittsfield, Phinehas Allen, the twenty-four-year-old native and nephew of activist parson Thomas Allen, published *The Pittsfield Sun, or Republican Monitor,* a resolutely Jeffersonian weekly. With each paper circulating to some 500 subscribers, roughly one household in six took either the *Star* or the *Sun*. In addition, one or the other, rarely both, were kept in most public houses, taverns where like-minded men routinely gathered to talk and carry on their personal and public business.[14]

Both papers looked almost the same; both followed the journalistic conventions typical of the American press of the period. Beneath their boldface titles, the first page displayed four columns of small print that usually included commentary in the form of an essay or letter signed with a pseudonym. In addition, the papers carried official news from Washington, Boston, and foreign capitals that might cover the second page or even part of a third. The third page, which presented news from around the United States, also ran a column dedicated to Berkshire county affairs headed, respectively, "STOCKBRIDGE" or "PITTSFIELD." Here Heman Willard and Phinehas Allen offered their own unsigned comments together with a miscellany of local news, ranging from notes on crops and the weather to reports of accidents, fires, crimes, and court judgments. Here, too, notices of marriages and deaths among the county elite appeared. The fourth page might include a short poem, humorous lines, or an essay, usually by a local author; but this final page contained mostly commercial notices from county shopkeepers and craftsmen, as well as advertisements—for real estate, for horses at stud and livestock, for help wanted and runaway apprentices—and legal notices. Here one found reports of marital conflict by wives who were suing for divorce and by deserted husbands (usually) notifying the public that they would no longer pay their wives' debts.

Though there were variations in format depending on the season, the electoral cycle, and the ebb and flow of national and international news in this era of recurrent European warfare, subscribers to the *Star* and the *Sun* knew what they might and might not find in their papers. They understood that they might best seek local news and information in face-to-face encounters with family and neighbors at church and in their work and business activities. Living in small, interconnected communities, townsfolk formed their opinions of each other and events according to their own and others' judgments. That was one reason why people in Berkshire County, as in other parts of America in 1800, were so often sociable. When men called on a neighbor to borrow a tool or walked to the store to trade, there was always time for talk beyond the immediate task at hand. When women gathered to exchange work or to help at a sickbed or a lying-in, they shared experiences and information. Most often men and women spoke about weather and health, prices and trade, kinsmen and neighbors; but annual elections encouraged political talk among men, and in years of Christian revival, religious conversation was common among both sexes. Extraordinary events, too, commanded attention—whether it was a lightning strike that set fire to a barn, or a robbery. In a region where more than 80 percent of households did not take a newspaper, news was a valuable commodity, savored not only for its usefulness, but also as entertainment.[15]

The advent of locally printed newspapers, from 1787 in Pittsfield and 1789 in Stockbridge, was a measure of the commercial development of Berkshire County and a sign that its people were becoming more urbane. By 1790 a string of six comparatively wealthy Housatonic Valley towns (Pittsfield, Lenox, Stockbridge, Lee, Great Barrington, and Sheffield), together with Williamstown in the north, had emerged as centers of trade and high culture. All seven had been settled by the early 1760s, largely by Connecticut migrants, and all possessed Congregational churches headed by Yale- or Harvard-trained ministers. Two, Lenox and Great Barrington, also possessed small Episcopalian churches.

By 1800 these towns had moved away from their colonial frontier past into an era of civilized republican refinement. In their centers new two-story, eight-room, wooden mansions with center hallways announced the cosmopolitan standards of village residents. One of the earliest of these impressive new structures belonged to Ephraim Wheeler's judge, Theodore Sedgwick, who had it constructed when he moved to Stockbridge from nearby Sheffield in 1786, the year of Shays' Rebellion. Located on rising ground beside the Housatonic River plain on the opposite side of Stockbridge's main street from the old dwelling of Stockbridge's Indian missionary clergymen, John Sergeant and Jonathan Edwards, the new mansion displayed the genteel features then in vogue. Unlike the fifty-year-old Sergeant-Edwards house that stood near the street, the Sedgwick home facing it was set back forty yards, away from traffic. Designed with a hipped roof, a fanlight over the doorway, and moldings over the windows and under the eaves, the house proclaimed gentility to all who passed by. To Sedgwick's law clients and visitors the wide center doorway and hall declared welcome, while permitting each of the large, high-ceilinged downstairs rooms to be self-contained. Unlike the older center-chimney houses, the rooms in the Sedgwick mansion no longer served as passageways; and on the second story the center hallway provided new privacy for the bedchambers of family and overnight guests. Sedgwick's home, like others of the rural gentry, was modest by the standards of Boston and Salem—where mansions often rose three stories in brick. But in contrast to the finest Berkshire dwellings of the

22

colonial era, which followed the center-chimney design, places like Sedgwick's made an important statement of village wealth and aspiration. During the decades from 1790 to 1820, in all the major Berkshire townships from Sheffield on the Connecticut border to Williamstown abutting Vermont, prosperity enabled the village gentry to erect scores of these houses to accommodate and to display their increasingly refined and respectable lifestyle.[16]

The hallmark of this aspiring Berkshire culture was a blend of the seemingly contradictory tendencies toward provincialism and cosmopolitanism. They showed their cosmopolitanism in an ebullient consumerism: village gentry and their imitators purchased fancy fabrics, polished and decorated furniture, clothing and carriages, and painted portraits, books, and musical instruments. The pages of the *Star* and the *Sun* were full of advertisements for these goods, which were usually brought up the Hudson River from New York City and were said to reflect the latest fashion. On the outside at least, the respectable men and women of Berkshire wanted to appear to be the equals of their counterparts at centers of material refinement such as Boston or New York.[17]

But aspiring Berkshire people were also insular and assertively provincial in important ways. Though they were ready to defer to Boston or New York on standards of consumer culture and polite refinement, on questions of theology and morals they believed they knew best. Their standard was proudly old-fashioned. Berkshire's orthodox Christian majority was rooted in the evangelical Calvinism of influential county clergy, from Jonathan Edwards (Stockbridge, 1751–1756) and Samuel Hopkins (Great Barrington, 1743–1769) to Stephen West, who served Stockbridge from 1759 to 1818; Alvan Hyde, who held the Lee pulpit from 1792 to 1833; and Samuel Shepard, the Lenox pastor from 1795 to 1846 (and Ephraim Wheeler's jailhouse counselor). Emphasizing Great Awakening themes, such as the omnipotence of God and the depravity of man, week after week these ministers preached that only sincere recognition of personal sin and repentance could lead to genuine conversion and the hope of salvation, and that this life on earth was merely a preparation for eternity.[18] Their own congregations generally shared these convictions; and by means of the Berkshire ministerial association—which controlled the ordination of new clergy—these ministers' version of Calvinism became the county standard. In 1793 Calvinist clergy and laymen (including Theodore Sedgwick) even won incorporation of their own doctrinally sound Williams College, at Williamstown.

The founding of the college represented more than just the renewed vitality of old-style Calvinism. It also demonstrated the enterprising, activist, elevating dimension of genteel republican culture. At Williams the region's elite hoped to polish and refine the county's rising generation of leaders by introducing them to the cosmopolitan ideas and values of the Enlightenment while indoctrinating them against the corrupting influences of aristocratic libertinism and Deists.[19] In their college they would train gentlemen of virtue, both Christian and civic. Combining Christian morality and refined sensibility, they would breed men of strength and feeling whose heartfelt sense of duty would lead them to defend the weak and friendless. Such gentlemen would also endorse the idea that "the civilization of a country may fairly be estimated by the degree of respect which is paid to its women."[20] And they would contrast the beastly appetite of lust with the inspiring sentiment of love. "Lust, like a rav'nous tyger, springs with savage gust, upon its prey," a newspaper poet declared, while "Love, like the genial sun of May, Emits its kind, refreshing beams."[21] To gentlemen and farmers who cultivated this virtuous sensibility and sought to enforce it on their less pious and refined peers, crimes against women and children especially violated their social code, and rape was tantamount to murder.

Confronting the new nineteenth century, Berkshire's leaders, whether college bred or not, shared in the village enlightenment that spawned the creation of numerous voluntary associations in Berkshire as elsewhere in Massachusetts. For Congregationalists, who were used to being part of the ruling majority and who possessed a traditional commitment to a vision of community well-being, voluntary associations such as Williamstown's Auxiliary Society for Promoting Good Morals and its Female Charitable Society provided opportunities to do the Lord's work and improve the quality of Berkshire life, both moral and material.[22]

Four kinds of overt objectives—religious, cultural, occupational, and economic—guided the chiefly male villagers who founded the voluntary associations that enriched civil society in Berkshire in the decades between 1790 and 1820. Clergymen took the lead in 1798 by founding the Berkshire and Columbia County (New York) Missionary Society, an organization that raised money from churchgoers to support missionaries—not to distant continents, but to fellow Yankees. Indeed, one of their missionaries was Lenox's Reverend Samuel Shepard, who made a nine-day, eighty-mile tour of northern Berkshire in 1808, delivering thirteen sermons, making ten family visits, and bringing back $3.63 in contributions to support further efforts.[23] Concerned by the number of heathenish unchurched settlers as well as by the rise of Universalism, the competition of Methodists, and the efforts of the Baptist John Leland from the hill town of Cheshire (and later the town of Peru), the orthodox promoted their message at every opportunity. In addition to the missionary society, they organized at local and county levels to promote good morals by curbing swearing and sabbath-breaking and by distributing Bibles and tracts.[24]

Many of the same people, though here following lay rather than clerical leadership, also organized to support academies for their sons at Lenox (1803) and daughters at Pittsfield (1807); and later, in 1818, they founded a County Education Society to provide college scholarships for pious but poor young men.[25] That elite aspirations came first was not merely selfish, it followed from the widely shared belief that improvement must begin at the top of society and flow down to ordinary people. This outlook was evident in the formation of social libraries during the 1790s at Sheffield, Great Barrington, Lee, and Pittsfield, in addition to the Berkshire Republican Library, which was organized at Stockbridge in 1794, largely through the leadership of Jonathan Edwards' eldest son, the merchant and shopkeeper Timothy Edwards. This social library set its dues at $2 per share, the same price as an annual newspaper subscription.[26] Its members included gentry from several of the leading towns, both future Federalists like Sedgwick and future Jeffersonians like Bidwell. The library's 150 or so titles were divided among well-known works in history, travel, biography, and philosophy, and works by such controversial transatlantic Enlightenment authors as Rousseau, Voltaire, and feminist Mary Wollstonecraft. If the Berkshire Republican Library possessed a distinctive regional character, it was sobriety, as the collection possessed few literary titles—works of poetry, satire, or fiction. Gentry families did purchase belles lettres and novels for their personal libraries; but in Stockbridge, at least, they did not choose to buy and use them as a community.

The earnest, improving motive connected to male sociability among the gentry was manifest in their enthusiasm for the benevolent brotherhood of Freemasonry. This fashion encompassed Berkshire as it did the rest of New England, New York, and much of the north in the decades from 1790 until the widespread anti-Masonic reaction of the 1820s. Freemasonry, a moralistic, ecumenical, secret club, first appeared in Berkshire at Stockbridge in 1779, but by the early 1800s it was spreading into rural towns like New Marlborough in the south and Lanesborough in the north. Both Calvinists and more liberal

Christians came together in Masonry; and both the Federalist Heman Willard of Stockbridge and his Jeffersonian counterpart, Phinehas Allen of Pittsfield, printed and sold local Masonic sermons.[27] With elite men contesting each other ever more sharply in town and church affairs and in the press, Masonry helped define membership in the gentry class and encouraged congeniality among the clergy, lawyers, merchants, artisans, and prosperous farmers who led each locality.

Another way that leaders reached across partisan divisions was through occupational groups. The oldest of these, the county ministerial association, dated back to the colonial era. The Berkshire association was partisan with respect to religious doctrine—it was Calvinist—and included only orthodox pastors, not Baptists; but although most of its roughly twenty members were Federalists, the Reverends Thomas Allen of Pittsfield and Ephraim Judson of Sheffield were both Republicans.

Physicians, too, formed a nonpartisan medical association, and lawyers reached across political and religious divisions by creating a bar association and, in 1815, a law library at Pittsfield. Most inclusive of all was the nation's first county agricultural society, formed at Pittsfield in 1810 by Elkanah Watson with the express intention of serving common farmers as well as the gentry. In addition, Berkshire men created business corporations that sought profit and development through turnpike companies and banks. Since Berkshire remained overwhelmingly agricultural, such business ventures lagged behind the rest of Massachusetts, but the same ambitions that propelled entrepreneurs elsewhere were evident in Berkshire County. Altogether, by around 1800 Berkshire's voluntary associations helped to make the county's leading 500 to 1,000 families (10 to 20 percent) a community in important respects. Though they were sharply divided in politics and differed in religion, they had much in common as newspaper readers, as churchgoers, and as respectable, active citizens of town and parish. Living in a society that was largely village centered, they expressed the cosmopolitanism of the province that lay between the Green Mountains and the Taconics.

Integrally related to this lowland, village-centered Berkshire, and supplying one-third of its population, was upland Berkshire—more recently settled, more rural, less refined, more down-to-earth. The 10,000 people who dwelled in the hill towns that bordered the two mountain ranges were also mostly white Yankees, but they were generally poorer, more agricultural, more often Shaysites alienated from village elites, and more generally provincial. In these communities relatively few houses rose a full two stories, and those that did mostly retained the older center-chimney style that made up in economy of construction and heating costs what they lacked in household privacy and the genteel lifestyle. These towns—Windsor, Partridgefield (after 1806 named Peru), Hinsdale, Washington, and Savoy, to name several—mostly organized in the 1770s or later, scarcely had villages. Most of their families lived in isolated farmsteads scattered over uneven slopes of meadows, pastures, and woodland. Though nearly every Berkshire town possessed a meetinghouse by 1800, few enjoyed other amenities. District schools were unheated, dirt-floored cabins sided with sawmill slabs. Children aged four years to eighteen years attended school irregularly, depending on the availability of teachers, the demands of outdoor labor, and the willingness and ability of parents to spare them from work and buy them textbooks. These are the towns where Ephraim Wheeler and his African American kinsmen, the Odels, made their way, however precarious and close to the margin.

Virtually all the elements of the material, secular, and religious culture of the wealthier towns were in evidence in the hills—the fine fabrics, furniture, books, and even a sprinkling of voluntary associations. But in the hill towns, except for the culture of Calvinism, these cultural assets were always fewer, lesser, unexpected. Possessing less capital from the beginning, and often in debt for their land to gentlemen of the older, richer towns, the settlers of the hill towns cleared and farmed land that was naturally less productive and accessible than that of their Housatonic Valley neighbors. But when crop prices were up and the weather cooperated, they could meet their obligations and accumulate some wealth. Men raised wheat, rye, oats, barley, corn (maize), and buckwheat in their fields; and women grew peas and beans, potatoes, carrots, turnips, pumpkins, and cucumbers in their kitchen gardens. By 1800 farmers throughout the county grew apples, and some cultivated pears and plums.

The crops were the same in the hills and the valleys, with the advantage sometimes belonging to the hills, where late spring and early autumn frosts were less frequent than on lower ground. Because much of the uplands was too sloping for repeated cultivation, more of the hill country was devoted to pasturing cows and sheep for dairy and wool, as well as for meat and hides. In the woods, lean, long-legged swine foraged for themselves before their owners fattened them a little and converted them to pork and leather.[28] When winter closed in, farmers turned to their woodlots, cutting timber to haul to local water-powered saw mills, splitting firewood for home use and sale to the villagers, and producing the charcoal consumed by the region's tiny ironworks. Women and girls fortunate enough to own spinning wheels made woolen thread; and the most prosperous, who owned looms, used home labor to weave the thread into homespun cloth. By raising a variety of marginally profitable products and processing food and fiber, farm families could cushion themselves against the fluctuations of marketplace and weather and come out ahead.[29]

When individual farmers felt prosperous they could indulge their wives in fine fabrics or invest in a new team of oxen. When a community felt prosperous, farmers might join together to remodel the meetinghouse, or even build a new one. In the Baptist farming town of Cheshire there was so much enthusiasm for Thomas Jefferson's inauguration in 1801 that farm women agreed to donate all their cheese curds on a single day so as to make the President a great wheel of cheddar. Using the press of a cider mill, the farm families of Cheshire made a 1,450-pound cheese, thirteen feet in diameter. Their church elder, John Leland, an old ally of Jefferson's from the 1780s battle for religious freedom in Virginia, drew national press coverage when he transported the *"Mammoth Cheese"* to Washington, D.C. He presented it to President Jefferson on January 1, 1802—in a ceremony intended to celebrate Republican prosperity and Cheshire's belief in religious freedom.[30]

No other group of townspeople expressed their optimism and sense of well-being so playfully, but at the beginning of the nineteenth century in both the hill and the valley towns of Berkshire material and cultural expectations were rising. Their world was divided and competitive, and temptations to sin were as pervasive as ever, but when men and women recalled the experiences of past decades—the Revolutionary War, Berkshire's civil turmoil, and their own daily struggles to create homes and turn forest into farmland while they were founding churches and communities—they felt hopeful. New buildings and new voluntary associations testified to their belief in improvement, material and spiritual, individual and collective.

The village of Lenox, where Ephraim Wheeler would be tried, exemplified the new era as much as any in Berkshire. Organized in 1767 and settled mostly by Connecticut emigrants, the Revolution had generated broad support in the town: 110 householders, the great majority, had signed a boycott petition against British policy in July 1774. But independence also "occasioned very bitter animosities among the people"; and Shays' Rebellion, which followed soon after, "was productive of much evil" in Lenox.[31] No local memoir of the era preserves the details of the town's conflicts, but one controversy concerned the successful efforts of Lenox's leading men to bring the county seat from Sheffield, on the Connecticut border, to their own village, which stood at almost the exact midpoint between the north and south of the county.

As a project for Lenox development, bringing the county courts to town would be a major feat. It would attract business to the village, enhance the local market, and provide more convenient access to government for Lenox people and everyone else in central and northern Berkshire County. But to woo the courts at precisely the time when many in Berkshire were most alienated from those very courts made some people angry. In November 1786 delegates from many Berkshire towns had convened in Lenox to call for reform of the county courts. They sought more power for the towns, changes in the legal profession and lawyers' fees, and an end to imprisonment for debt.[32] Simultaneously the village elite wanted to bring the county courts—to Shaysites the emblems of oppression—into the town. Competing with four other valley towns (Great Barrington, Stockbridge, Lanesborough, and Pittsfield) to win the courts, Lenox leaders pledged that they would donate £800 worth of materials to help construct the courthouse and jail. Inasmuch as the benefits of the court project were concentrated among merchants, lawyers, innkeepers, and tradesmen of the village, together with the few who owned land in the center, most townspeople believed it would have been unfair to tax everyone to come up with the subsidy.

When the 1786 Massachusetts legislature chose Lenox, and when the courts held their first sessions in Lenox in 1787, using the church meetinghouse for a temporary courtroom, not everyone was pleased. But as time passed and village leaders secured their ascendancy, prosperity came to Lenox, and the rancor subsided as the village was gradually transformed. Construction on the new county buildings, where Wheeler would be jailed and tried, began in 1788, and as they took shape they brought a new urbanity to the settlement. The two-story, forty-foot-square courthouse provided an elegant statement of the dignity, even the majesty, of the law and the state. Rising twenty-five feet to the roof from a three-foot-high, three-foot-thick cut stone foundation, and topped by a domed cupola, a needle spire, and a weathervane, the courthouse at Lenox was the most impressive secular building in the county. Its interior, graced by an arched, twenty-two-foot ceiling and illuminated by two rows of large windows, created an impressive stage for the public officials and professional attorneys who entered through its pedimented doorway to carry on the work of justice.[33] A few years later, in 1793, the proprietor of the Lenox tavern expressed villagers' fashionable aspirations by renaming his establishment a "coffee house."[34]

The county jail was built one-half mile south of the courthouse, and completed more urgently because Lenox had no substitute building. Only half as large as the courthouse, it was a massive monument to "strength and security."[35] Enclosed by stone walls three feet thick, with eighteen-inch stone interior partitions and three-inch-thick white oak planks for flooring, the two-story jail was built to withstand jailbreaks from within or without. In contrast to the light, airy courthouse interior, the four-room jail had only eight small windows, all secured by wrought iron grates inside and out on the ground floor. The exterior doors were eight inches thick, constructed of white oak planks laid double and inlaid with hardened steel bars. When the state locked someone up, the Berkshire jail aimed to proclaim, there was no escape.

Adjoining the jail was a two-story, painted wooden jailhouse. Connected to the jail itself by a covered walkway, this service building matched the jail in size but did not have the same provisions for security. Whereas the jail was heated by stoves to prevent an escape through a chimney, the jailhouse had fashionable end chimneys, and half of its ground floor was devoted to a kitchen and buttery for storing liquor and other provisions. The jailhouse provided a residence for the jailer, William A. Whelpley, and his family, and supplied the prisoners' victuals as well as refreshments for visitors such as the sheriff and his deputies, attorneys, and the clergy. Whelpley essentially served as innkeeper for people on both sides of the law.[36]

As soon as the Lenox jail was ready in 1790, the sheriff brought the inmates up ten miles from the old jail at Great Barrington. The courthouse was not ready until 1792, when, with some fanfare, it opened for business. Altogether the three structures had taken over three years to build, at a cost of £3,441 5s. 3d.—the largest project in the town's thirty-year history. Although prosperous townspeople had contributed £800 worth of local stone, timbers, and planking, more than three-quarters of the bill was paid by the state government. The benefits for Lenox were only beginning.[37]

A lawyer's description of the scene in Lenox in the 1830s during court days would have been apt for the 1790s and for the decades in between, since Berkshire grew only slowly. "Lenox is alive during the administration of Justice," he wrote; "our Village has abounded with Judges and Jurors, lawyers, and litigants, prosecutors and prosecuted." In addition there were "witnesses of all orders and descriptions . . . spectators trading horses in the street, and politicians smoking over government affairs in the bar room." Like a market-day fair, court days meant business for the entire county. "Our boarding houses have their long tables lined on both sides with earnest applicants," he reported, "and all expect more business, more calls, more conversation, and more cheerfulness.—Messages are sent, and errands done between one end of the county and the other; business accounts are settled, plans laid, caucuses, conventions, and singing schools agreed upon; news-papers subscribed for and distant matters in general arranged."[38] For a county where farming spread people out over a landscape intersected with hills and valleys, rivers and streams, bringing the courts to Lenox gave the bucolic community of 1,100 people an urban dimension, which the village elite eagerly cultivated.

In the first years of the new century Lenox people created an even more impressive landmark on their own by constructing a new meetinghouse—which, like the courthouse and the jail, would be a key site in the Wheeler drama. They placed the new church beside the old one, on the hill overlooking the main village street. For generations to come the people of the village would literally look up to the church. Unlike the earlier courthouse and jail projects, the meetinghouse was completed within a matter of months during 1805.

Church leaders sought to display republican refinement at its best. They modeled their new building largely on the 1793 plan that Charles Bulfinch, Massachusetts' most prominent architect, had drawn for the Congregational meetinghouse in neighboring Pittsfield. Bulfinch, the Bostonian who had designed a number of the capital city's most elegant churches, was widely known as the architect for the statehouses of both Connecticut and Massachusetts. His understated neoclassicism made his work especially appealing to New England gentry. The Lenox deacons did not feel so wealthy or adventuresome as to hire Bulfinch himself, but they paid his design the sincerest compliment by imitating it directly, as had their near neighbors in the congregations at Richmond and Lee. In each of these communities the yearning for cosmopolitan urbanity rested on a conservative, provincial foundation. Once Pittsfield leaders had imported Boston style, it became tried and true in Berkshire, and neighbors were happy to follow Pittsfield's lead—thus achieving elegance carefully and economically.

In the case of the new Lenox meetinghouse there was an additional borrowing in that the deacons hired the builder of the similar church in the neighboring town of Richmond.[39] For their steeple, however, they followed an illustration in Asher Benjamin's 1797 architectural manual, a work that was widely used to achieve the new elegance in rural New England. Indeed the deacons' contract with the builder specified "the steeple and the workmanship of it to be made conformable to the plan laid down in . . . Benjamin's *Country Builder's Assistant*."[40] Conformity to an established model for a genteel house of worship was their goal, not innovation.

The church, which still looks out over Lenox village, fulfilled that goal. A two-story clapboard rectangle, at fifty feet by eighty feet it was more than twice as large as the courthouse. Like the courthouse it had a lofty interior lighted by many large windows. The floor, as was traditional, was laid out with the high-walled box pews that had been sold to help finance the $6,619 construction cost. Above the pews on three sides of the room, roman-style columns supported galleries that were set with benches. The circular pulpit, which faced the doorway, was elevated on a fluted column almost level with the gallery and accessible by its twin flights of stairs. This lofty, isolated perch underscored the pastor's uniquely authoritative voice in the parish.[41]

From the exterior, the meetinghouse's most notable features were its Bulfinch-style, gabled and enclosed front "porch" and the Asher Benjamin bell tower and steeple—cupola really—that rose above the whole structure. Three entry doors supplied access; the middle one, framed by classical pilasters and an arched pediment, stood beneath a grand Palladian window. In all, the meetinghouse blended the traditional rectangular box of previous generations with a luminous, discreetly ornamented interior and a bold new porch and bell tower. The building suggested what the pastor and his deacons believed: they must stand fast for the good old religion, while simultaneously embracing present-day refinement and enlightenment. The Berkshire elite's eagerness to move forward was unmistakable in Pittsfield's importation of the new Bulfinch style and in the imitation of it by the village gentry of Richmond, Lee, and now Lenox. Yet evident too was a hesitancy, perhaps born of ambivalence toward enlightened urbanity, that made Berkshire's—and Lenox's—embrace of the modern awkward. However cosmopolitan professional and mercantile leaders might be in their aspirations, Berkshire, with its mix of religious sects, its rustic farmers and laborers, its African Americans and Indians, was a diverse place where varied traditions and old and new ideas pulled in different directions.

Exemplifying this tension is a curious episode that troubled Sheffield in November 1801. One night between ten and eleven o'clock a man and two boys in a village clothier's shop were startled by a rain of small, hard objects that flew through the windows, breaking the glass. This assault continued through the night and on two successive evenings, even during an hour of daylight, before switching to the home of a man who lived outside the village. In all, almost sixty windowpanes were broken by projectiles of wood, charcoal, stone, and mortar. As one witness reported, "nothing could be seen coming till the glass broke, and whatever passed through, fell directly on the window-sill, as if it had been put through with a person's fingers, and many pieces of mortar and coal were thrown through the same hole in the glass in succession." This was a great mystery to the people of Sheffield and their neighbors, and as reports of this strange phenomenon spread, "many hundreds of people assembled to witness the scene, among whom were clergymen and other gentlemen." Yet even when these local leaders inspected the scene firsthand, they could not fathom "the source of the mischief." The enlightened, rational conclusion, which most people reached, was that the projectiles had been launched against the two buildings by a handful of pranksters. But even in 1802 there were some "more credulous" people who "readily believed it to be witchcraft."[42]

Clearly, a certain vernacular culture of supernatural belief, including witchcraft, persisted. Several years before the Sheffield episode a physician's wife at Cummington, just over the county border from Windsor where the Wheelers lived, noted that a neighbor's house was "bewitched." The local clergyman visited the house, but no record survives of how the learned gentleman dealt with this "witchcraft."[43] Such events were unusual, of course, but they signaled a cultural division between some of the common people and the village gentry that the latter found disturbing. For although the gentry earnestly wished that most of their neighbors were guided by faith and reason, they feared that some of the common folk, including perhaps blacks and Indians, were superstitious and might be misled by the devil and their own irrational desires. The elite wanted to believe that their country was "composed of a very intelligent and moral, and relatively considered, religious population." But gentlemen always viewed social order as a top-down achievement whereby the piety of "influential men & families, and very many of the substantial yeomanry" could triumph over ignorance, irreligion, and vice.[44] In this context the Sheffield and Cummington episodes, and the supernatural way some chose to interpret them, were, like other violations of the community's moral order, unsettling. They were reminders of the reality of human weakness and depravity and the ways these human flaws could undermine the structures of piety, refinement, and civility that community leaders were working so hard to establish. At the same time, for common folk who were wary of the new, Enlightenment confidence in reason, local leaders' dismissal of their concerns cannot have been reassuring.

For most Berkshire inhabitants, however, a bewitched house or the seriocomic enigma of Sheffield's glass-shattering projectiles was far less disturbing than the tide of criminal activity that news reports suggested was sweeping over the land. During lulls in Napoleonic warfare, newspapers in Berkshire County and all over the nation filled the void in military news with human-interest stories, often dwelling on crime. By the late summer of 1805, the eve of Wheeler's trial, people in Berkshire could think back on a horrifying array of violent crimes—in the prior six months alone the local press had reported fourteen murders and three suicides. Most had occurred in faraway places—London, South Carolina, Maryland. But some of the violence was committed frighteningly nearby—across the New York border, down in Connecticut, up in New Hampshire, and even in Berkshire, where a Pittsfield married man with a wife and five children hanged himself just three weeks before the court met.[45] Though press accounts were not necessarily sensational, just the bare facts created a palpable sense of the fearsome possibilities of human derangement and depravity. For Calvinists reared to believe in original sin, there seemed to be a heightened interest in crime as current events supplied confirming chapter and verse on mankind's fallen state.

Three kinds of violent behavior engaged Berkshire's immediate attention in the spring and summer of 1805. Killers who were outsiders, typically drunken brawlers or criminals who assaulted each other, and suicides, who often displayed signs of depression or madness before taking their own lives, were disquieting but not shocking. But the third type of violence—seemingly ordinary people who acted brutally against members of their own households—was profoundly alarming because it unexpectedly violated the system of trust on which every household, regardless of class and occupation, was founded. Because the people of Berkshire, as elsewhere, believed in a system of household governance—patriarchy—in which fathers and masters ruled for the mutual benefit of all family members, news of such incidents was especially disturbing. Ideally, everyone had a place in the domestic hierarchy; by fulfilling their roles, fathers and mothers, children and other kin, as well as servants, enabled families to flourish in good times and to endure in times of sickness and want. But in 1805 a worrisome succession of stories from the Stockbridge *Western Star* and the *Pittsfield Sun* suggested that domestic peace was under siege.[46] Hovering in the consciousness of people in Lenox and throughout Berkshire County, these stories made the Wheeler case appear to be part of an alarming pattern suggesting that household government was in such disarray that government must intervene.[47]

This seeming wave of evil had been evident in March of 1805 with the report of a "horrid act of barbarity" forty miles away in Suffield, Connecticut. Here, on a cold night, a poor householder in charge of a twelve-year-old boy had sent the lad, covered only by "a few rags," away from the hearth to sleep in an unheated garret. When the boy's crying reached "the master of the house, . . . [he] beat and mangled him, till all complaints were effectually silenced." The next morning the child "was found apparently lifeless" and later died.[48] Even more grisly, perhaps, was a case reported from a Philadelphia court in which a master, Samuel Depui, had repeatedly assaulted another twelve-year-old, an apprentice girl. Depui suspected her of stealing "some chestnuts and a few apples" and asserted that "sometimes she would not answer when she was called." His cruelty, which included suspending the girl by her heels and beating her, compelling her to eat excrement, tying her up to freeze, and forcing her to rub lime juice and pepper in wounds he had inflicted with his whip, had drawn a ten-day jail sentence, a $15 fine, and the removal of the apprentice girl to another master. Berkshire journalist Phinehas Allen apologized for offending the sensibility of his readers by publishing this story; but, he explained, "when the offender has been suffered to escape almost with impunity" justice required that he should be made into a public "object of horror and detestation."[49] Moral purpose justified such lurid news.

An even more frightening story came from Otsego County, New

York, eighty-five miles to the west in a region connected to Berkshire by migration. Early in 1805 a transplanted Yankee schoolmaster had, while his wife and a servant girl stood by, whipped his six-year-old adopted daughter Betsey, his own niece, so mercilessly for mispronouncing a word that she died soon after. Throughout 1805 and on into 1806 the story of this man, Stephen Arnold—his crime and his flight, his incarceration and trial, his death sentence and its commutation—would be woven into the consciousness surrounding Ephraim Wheeler's case.[50] Once more, as in the Suffield and Philadelphia cases, Arnold's abuse of his patriarchal power reminded people that evil could break out anywhere, anytime, even at home between a master and a servant or a parent and a child.

Complementing these shocking cases of abuse were other horrendous reports of violence in families. In April the Berkshire press published a story from South Carolina of a wife who conspired with a man to kill her husband, and from Virginia the account of a stranger who entered a home while the parents had gone to church and attacked their three children, two fatally.[51] In the following month the *Pittsfield Sun* reported a familicide from Hollis, New Hampshire, eighty-five miles away. John P. Kendrick, a thirty-year-old man who had shown "symptoms of insanity" but was usually "able to conduct his business, with propriety;—and, when well, was sober and regular in his deportment," had gone berserk and killed the older sister and mother who kept house for him and doted on him.[52] Only one week later word came of a filicide in London. Samuel Mitchell, a sixty-year-old silk-weaver, had slain his nine-year-old daughter, Sarah, to stop his estranged wife from taking custody of the girl. This story, reprinted from a London paper, consumed nearly three full columns and read like a tragic novella. Indeed when Mitchell's trial ended, the press reported that "the Jury, the Counsel and all present, were melted into tears." Later, at the gallows, spectators wept again as the repentant, "unhappy man" met his duly ordained end. Though these events were five months old and had occurred in a foreign capital thousands of miles away, local journalists played on universal themes to make the story immediate and affecting.[53] Inasmuch as most Berkshire marriages had not been made in heaven, the idea that a husband's rage against his wife could be so monstrous as to actually kill his own daughter was a cautionary tale.

Then, at the end of August, just before the court was to meet, stories of intrafamily violence reached a crescendo when two cases of family murder were reported in a single week. One involved Peter Shaver, a forty-four-year-old man from forty miles away at Rhinebeck, New York. Shaver had murdered his sister ten months earlier, and the *Sun* reported his execution. Shaver had turned penitent and both joined in prayer with the pastor who preached from his scaffold and sang a hymn with the vast crowd who had gathered to watch him "launched from vigorous life into the unknown regions of boundless eternity."[54] This account of Shaver's execution, unlike his crime, provided a reassuring sense of closure on a hideous event. After all, justice was done.

But the other story, imported from South Carolina, was deeply upsetting, not only for relationships of trust within families, but for the whole natural and social order. "SHOCKING MURDER!" the paper proclaimed in a frankly sensational appeal to readers: twenty-three-year-old Richard Maples had ambushed his father, Thomas Maples, reputedly "an honest, industrious, and good man," and shot him in the back at a distance of fourteen paces. Both the young man's mother and his brother were also jailed "as accessories to the murder."[55] Evidently this grown child, with the assistance of his mother and brother, had attacked patriarchy directly. Like the Arnold and Mitchell filicides, the Maples patricide violated people's understanding of the most fundamental natural laws and Biblical prescriptions governing relations between parents and children. Unlike Kendrick's matricide, there had been no mitigating evidence of insanity to explain the deeds of Arnold, Mitchell, and Maples. Instead they seemed to personify the infinite power of evil. When churchgoers reflected on such stories they were forced to recognize the abyss of depravity in this world that served as the gateway to hell.

The contemplation of such horrifying events was accepted, even prescribed in Anglo-American Christian culture; indeed, publishing certain crime stories had a long and respected history.[56] Execution sermons, which included criminal narratives and pleas of repentance from the gallows, had been a staple in New England culture for over a century. In these accounts a clergyman served as intermediary and interpreter, assuring that the Christian message and judgments of taste prevailed in the printed pamphlet. But newspaper accounts spoke in a secular voice; and recently, in imitation of English practices, American printers had begun to publish detailed and authentic trial reports. Such trial reports were not wholly new at the end of the eighteenth century, but until the 1790s they were rare. The few trial reports that had come from American presses earlier were almost exclusively reprints of London works that recounted the misdeeds of aristocrats, such as Frederick Calvert, Baron Baltimore, whose 1768 trial for rape was the only rape trial report published in America until the 1790s.[57]

In that decade, however, printers turned to the trial report with new interest. Usually their subject was murder, but in Boston the 1798 reprint of an English work, *Cuckold's Chronicle: Being Select Trials for Adultery, Imbecility, Incest, Ravishment, &c.*, displayed the obscene possibilities of trial reports. Contained in this "inexhaustible fund of amusement" were four contemporary English rape trials that included explicit testimony describing the rape of ten- and fourteen-year-old girls.[58] A year earlier the same subject matter had appeared in New York when a printer took the innovative step of choosing a local case among common people—the rape of ten-year-old Unice Williamson—as the text for an eight-page trial report.[59] There is no evidence that connects such sexually explicit material to Berkshire's two print shops; but, following common practice, Phinehas Allen and Heman Willard exchanged their newspapers with fellow printers around New England and the nation. They could readily follow the doings of other printers through their advertisements in the press. By the time of Wheeler's trial, both men were familiar with the trial report genre.

Indeed, the up-and-coming Federalist and orthodox Christian, Heman Willard, had even made his own foray into the trial report market by reprinting for Berkshire subscribers the most commercially successful case of the era, *Report of the Trial of Jason Fairbanks, on an Indictment for the Murder of Elizabeth Fales.* Demand for this 1801 report of a genteel Dedham, Massachusetts, romance gone wrong had generated four Boston editions in addition to Willard's reprint. Willard's ten-town subscription network must have enabled the printer to turn a profit, because when the Wheeler trial came along in 1805 he decided that an original trial report would be profitable as well.[60] Willard hired either an attorney or a law student to attend the Wheeler trial, make detailed notes, and prepare a report. Willard promoted sales by advertising for a month in nearby Hampshire County as well as in his own paper, and by sending letters previewing the report to printers as far away as Richmond, Virginia.[61] Later he would arrange for a second, Newburyport, Massachusetts, edition as well.

To boost sales, Willard exploited the sensational character of the crime explicitly on the title page and by advertising that "the particulars of this unnatural transaction are so shocking in their nature that public utility . . . demands a publicity of the facts."[62] Yet Willard's *Report of the Trial of Ephraim Wheeler,* the first original trial report published in western Massachusetts, was primarily didactic. Willard declared in his preface that the report aimed to instruct readers and to deter crime, and unlike the *Cuckold's Chronicle* Willard excluded graphic sexual description entirely.[63] Though the subject was sensational, the substance of the Wheeler trial report was generally accepted as standing securely on the moral side of the boundary with licentiousness. Indeed, Attorney General James Sullivan inscribed a copy of it with a Latin quotation in praise of public service and presented it to his Boston pastor.[64] Reminders of human depravity and of the efforts of society to prevent and to punish it were not only legitimate, they were essential for the preservation of moral order. The alternative, of concealing evil deeds—even in the name of delicacy and taste—was to deny their ever-present threat, lulling people into a dangerous complacency.

This was the setting for the trial of poor, ex-Shaysite farm laborer Ephraim Wheeler—an uneducated, unruly man whose unsettled way of life contrasted with both the polite village standard and the rustic, upland ideal of hardworking, manly independence. Wheeler, a man who barely scraped out a living in a hill town, would be put on trial in the valley by people whose lineage and discipline—with God's blessing—had enabled them to earn respectable places in Berkshire society. These officials were not without pity, and they sought to be guided by reason. Impartial justice was one of their highest ideals. But they lived in a time of anxiety over violence and depravity. Whether they could achieve impartiality in judging a rough, poverty-stricken man charged with the rape of his own daughter would test their own integrity and the values of their society.

CHAPTER TWO

The Trial

A man (I may with more propriety say a *monster* in human form) by the name of Ephraim Wheeler, of Windsor, this day received the dreadful sentence of DEATH, at the Supreme Judicial Court now sitting at Lenox, for committing the abominable, disgraceful, unnatural, and unheard of crime, of *Rape!*, on the body of *his own daughter!!!* a girl of only 13 years of age!—it appeared in evidence, that this was the third time that he had attempted the same crime, the two latter times he succeeded—the first he did not. I attended the trial—it lasted 14 hours—the crime was fully and substantially proved to the satisfaction of almost every one—(there were at least 1000 spectators) though Wheeler yet persists in his innocence. The jury without leaving their seats pronounced him GUILTY. This is, probably, the only instance of the kind that has ever occurred since the world began—well might the Judge exclaim, when pronouncing the sentence of the law, that he (Wheeler) "had added a new crime to the catalogue of crimes," or words to this effect. The gentleman whom I employed to take minutes of the trial has just informed me that he believes he can make out a complete "report of the trial" for publication—if he does, I shall publish the whole proceedings soon—it will make a pamphlet of 100 octavo pages, *more or less.*

Letter from Heman Willard to the *Richmond (Virginia) Enquirer,*
October 8, 1805

It was still summertime, and the weather was fair and in the seventies during the second week of September 1805 when the Supreme Judicial Court came to Lenox for its semiannual session.[1] To farmers who were hurrying to bring in their grain and hay before the first frost, the blue skies with intermittent clouds were a blessing, and for the villagers the comfortable weather meant customers, filling shops and overflowing Lenox's inns and public houses. In a county where public opinion forbade professional theater, the courtroom drama attracted spectators by the hundred to watch both trained and amateur performers bring real stories to life. When life and death hung in the balance, as was often true before the Supreme Judicial Court, since it alone tried capital cases, courthouse crowds watched intently for signs of the ultimate outcome. Prisoners, witnesses, lawyers, juries, and judges all played their roles with the utmost seriousness.

According to ancient custom, county officials led by the sheriff, in 1805 Simon Larned of Pittsfield, welcomed the three-man panel of the state's highest court, as well as accompanying state officials and a phalanx of attorneys and clerks, by meeting them on the road and escorting them into the town in a parade of justice. This was an occasion for pomp and ceremony as well as camaraderie, since many of these gentlemen were old acquaintances. Though divided by partisan allegiance—Judges Theodore Sedgwick, Samuel Sewall, and Simeon Strong were all Federalists, and Attorney General James Sullivan and county officers like Larned were Jeffersonians—they had spent many days and nights together over the years, not only doing the public's business, but taking refreshment together, sharing victuals at country inns, and even bedding down together. As they rode into Lenox Village, they were greeted by the stares of strangers and the smiles of friends. The arrival of the Supreme Judicial Court and its entourage inaugurated the court-week festival that would make some folks richer and others poorer, bringing joy and relief as well as pain and disgust.[2] When the week was over, some would be set free and others locked up, to face months or years in prison. A man might even be sentenced to hang.

Curbing human vices was the task of social institutions, families, communities, churches, and the state. The last barrier, in practical terms, was the criminal justice system—the statutes, the courts, and the punishment regime that sought to block vicious behavior. When justices Sedgwick, Sewall, and Strong rode into Lenox they saw themselves not only as judicial professionals charged with clearing a docket, but also and preeminently as agents of the moral and social order who must pursue justice according to law. Who the judges were and how they understood their tasks were crucial for the operation of their court and the character of the justice it dispensed.

All three had been born into New England's elite and were among the tiny fraction (less than one percent) of the population who had attended college. The eldest, Simeon Strong, was a 1736 Northampton, Massachusetts, native who had graduated from Yale in 1756 and was now in his seventieth year. After studying law with the powerful, aristocratic John Worthington of Springfield, Strong settled in Amherst, Massachusetts. A longtime Hampshire County attorney, Strong served local and state government in a variety of offices before and after the Revolution, but not during the war, when he had been suspected of being a loyalist. Unlike his colleagues on the bench, when Strong was appointed in 1800 his career was wholly provincial—he had lived and served only in Massachusetts.[3]

Ten years younger than Strong was Theodore Sedgwick, the most prominent of the judges and a resident of Lenox's neighboring town, Stockbridge. Born in Hartford, Connecticut, in 1746, and raised on a farm in Cornwall on the Connecticut frontier just south of Berkshire, Theodore and his five siblings were orphaned by the death of their father during the time of the French and Indian War. John, the oldest son, took over the farm when he was fourteen and saw to it that Theodore would be prepared for Yale, which he entered in 1761. During Theodore's senior year, however, the nineteen-year-old was expelled for some "boyish" misconduct; so after first trying ministerial training under an evangelical Calvinist, he turned to the study of law. A second cousin who was practicing at the county seat of Great Barrington made a place for him, and in the following year, 1766, the twenty-year-old Sedgwick was admitted to the Berkshire bar. Moving his practice to Sheffield in 1767, Sedgwick—who was as much a self-made man as a son of privilege—moved up dramatically. Tall, broad-shouldered, and energetic, his powerful mind and forceful argument brought him success as an attorney and recognition as a public official. A friend to the Revolution, he served in the disastrous 1776 expedition to Canada. Later he went on to extended service in the Massachusetts legislature, where he helped draft several penal laws, including two—rape and arson—that prescribed the death penalty.[4] Serving in both the Massachusetts House and the Senate (as had Simeon Strong), as well as being elected to serve in the Continental Congress during its last several years in the 1780s, he became a prominent leader in public affairs. A foe to Shaysites and a supporter of the new United States Constitution, Sedgwick helped ratify that document in Massachusetts and then went on to serve in both the United States House and Senate during the Washington and Adams administrations. Before taking up his seat on the Supreme Judicial Court in 1802, Sedgwick had served two years as Speaker of the nation's House of Representatives (1799–1801). In contrast to his colleagues, Sedgwick was a national figure acquainted with the likes of George Washington and John Adams. By 1805, with the Jeffersonians in charge of the national government, the fifty-nine-year-old Sedgwick was in eclipse. But his own sense of authority remained strong.[5]

The third justice, Samuel Sewall, was a Boston native, a 1776 Harvard graduate, and a scion of Puritan Massachusetts' most distinguished families. Boasting a genealogy studded with clergymen, magistrates, and merchants, he was the great-grandson and namesake of the judge who convicted the Salem witches and later recanted his part in that miscarriage of justice. Sewall was also the nephew of Stephen Sewall, who had served for twenty years on the colonial predecessor of the Supreme Judicial Court. At the time of his own appointment in 1801, Sewall was forty-eight years old and a leading attorney in the commercial and maritime county of Essex. Like Sedgwick, with whom he had served in the United States Congress, Sewall was a firm Federalist and a veteran representative to the state legislature. Indeed, when he traveled to Lenox in September 1805 he had just published a report to the legislature recommending reforms in the state's criminal code so as to abolish cropping ears, branding, the ducking stool, and the pillory, as well as providing regulations for the brand-new state prison. Dwelling in Marblehead, just a day's travel away from Boston, Sewall, who was twenty-one years younger than Strong and eleven years Sedgwick's junior, was active as an adviser to both the legislature and the Federalist governor, Caleb Strong, who had appointed all three to the bench.[6]

One cannot know just why Governor Strong selected these men for the court. All were mature, experienced lawyers and public figures; all were Federalists; and all were pious Christians, two orthodox Congregationalists and the third (Sewall) an Episcopalian. These were basic requirements. In addition Strong or any governor would have wanted to appoint men who would bring their own earned and inherited stature to add dignity to the bench. Outside the courtroom such men were entitled not merely to respect but to deference from ordinary citizens. Inside the court they were magisterial personages, learned, astute, commanding.

These judges embodied the patriarchal ideal in their personal as well as their public lives. All were husbands and fathers, to all appearances exemplary married men. The two older judges, Strong and Sedgwick, were in their second marriages. Strong's first wife, Sarah Wright, had died in 1784 after twenty-one years of marriage and giving birth to eight children. Of Strong's seven surviving children in 1805, his five sons had all followed him to become lawyers. Strong's second wife, Mary Whiting Barron, herself a widow, had married him four years after Sarah's death.[7] Everything about Strong's own marital history suggested fulfillment of the Christian ideal of marriage.

Much the same was true of Sedgwick, although his own experiences displayed both a more romantic and a more tragic cast. He had married his first wife, Elizabeth Mason, in 1768 when he was only twenty-two years and she twenty-four. But their marriage was cut short within three years when, late in pregnancy, Elizabeth suddenly died from smallpox, which Theodore believed she had caught from him. Sedgwick married again three years later; with Pamela Dwight, his second wife, he fathered ten children, seven of whom survived into adulthood.[8] But the memory of his first wife never left him, and each year he dreamed of a visit from her in "every-day dress," surrounded by "a heavenly radiance," in which she looked at him from the foot of his bed, "her face lit with love and happiness." As long as Sedgwick lived, this recurrent vision awakened a tender nostalgia in him.[9] It was not that his subsequent marriage to Pamela was without love—they were devoted to each other—but their relationship was clouded by her depressed spells. By the early 1790s Sedgwick had come close to resigning from public life so as to assist his wife. But he could not give her solace; and in 1804 she was so severely depressed as to be judged insane. By September 1805 she had recovered somewhat, but remained an invalid. Their one child who was still at home for extended periods was fifteen-year-old Catharine Maria, the future novelist, a comfort to her father and on occasion a companion when he traveled the court circuit.[10] When Sedgwick considered the relations between husbands and wives and between parents and children he, like Strong, could draw on personal experience as well as knowledge gleaned from decades of observation in and out of court.

Sewall, too, was married and a father. In Marblehead he had taken the lead in improving public schools and in helping to found an academy to prepare boys for college. Sewall was also active on behalf of the local poor, whose ranks swelled periodically owing to the vicissitudes of fishing and trade. Conscious of his lineage of Puritan and public-spirited leaders, Sewall, the Episcopalian, guarded his reputation for rectitude, and made sure that he was the bestower rather than the recipient of gifts. Deferential to his senior colleagues Strong and Sedgwick, he was not always entirely candid. Within the year he would earn Sedgwick's resentment by supporting his brilliant Essex County colleague Theophilus Parsons for the position of Chief Justice, after first leading Sedgwick to believe he was backing him.[11] But when the Supreme Judicial Court opened for business in Lenox on Tuesday, September 10, 1805, that conflict lay ahead; on this day the judges presented a united front of learned, patriarchal authority. In keeping with the republican spirit of the age, they dressed in black simply as gentlemen; unlike their colonial predecessors they needed neither snowy periwigs nor crimson robes to enhance their dignity.[12]

Representing the state in arguments before them, they knew, would be the familiar face and voice of the attorney general, James Sullivan. For nearly thirty years Sedgwick had known and worked with Sullivan; and Sedgwick's colleagues Strong and Sewall had known the attorney general almost as long. But long association had not made them friends. Sullivan, the champion of religious liberty, manhood suffrage, and Thomas Jefferson, was the regular target of Federalist invective—he was dubbed a "Francophile" and a "Jacobin"—and in addition to partisan differences, Sullivan and Sedgwick had old personal grievances. Back in 1787 they had differed over Governor John Hancock's pardoning of convicted Shaysites. Though Sullivan had lost his eldest son to disease in the campaign against the rebels, he urged that traitors be pardoned so as to heal the body politic; whereas Sedgwick, a victim of Shaysite marauders, argued that those convicted of treason should hang.[13] When Sedgwick spread derogatory stories about Sullivan in the legislature, Sullivan confronted him, daring Sedgwick to air the facts publicly in the press. Sedgwick, though proud and combative like Sullivan—especially on points of honor—accepted Sullivan's rebuke; but he did not forget it.[14] Though outwardly civil, both men had long memories.

The judges and the attorney general were well acquainted, but they had traveled different paths to Lenox. Sullivan had risen to his position by a singular route. He was no college-educated scion of Puritan founders, but the son of Irish indentured servants who had come penniless to the Maine coast in 1723. His father, John Sullivan, was from a genteel family and possessed a European humanistic education. But a failed courtship and a family quarrel set him adrift, and when he arrived in York, Maine, the local pastor, on seeing that Sullivan was the master of seven languages and thus a gentleman, loaned him payment for his indenture and set him up as a schoolmaster. Thereupon John Sullivan borrowed more to purchase the indenture of a young shipmate, the vivacious nine-year-old Margery Brown. Little Margery became Sullivan's housekeeper, and in 1735, when she reached twenty-one years, the now forty-three-year-old schoolmaster, farmer, and scrivener, who drew wills and deeds for his neighbors, married her. Nine years and four sons later, James was born into this unusual family, headed by a father who was "averse to physical labor" but whose wife was energetic and ambitious.[15] In the Sullivan household the father taught the boys English, French, and Latin, and their mother set them to work outdoors. Ever after, James Sullivan was an outdoorsman as well as a scholar—ready with an ax, a saw, or a shovel and comfortable walking behind a plow. Even as a young lawyer, one of his neighbors remembered, Sullivan "would fell a tree equal to any, and lift as much."[16] James's legal education came from an apprenticeship with his older brother John, who had settled twenty miles down the coast at Durham, New Hampshire. The story was told that when the Sullivans came to Durham, John was visited by townsmen who declared they were much better off without lawyers, so he had better depart. Taking up the challenge, James offered to fight the antilawyer champion for the right to settle in the town. Though James had a permanent limp, the legacy of a tree-felling accident, and though he was subject to epileptic seizures throughout his life, James won the fight and the Sullivans stayed.[17] John, who was close to James and something of a mentor to his younger brother, would go on to become a general in the Revolutionary War as well as the governor of New Hampshire. James returned to Maine to practice law, but he came back to Durham to marry Mehitable ("Hetty") Odiorne in 1768. They moved to Biddeford, in York County, Maine, and set up housekeeping and lawyering in a one-story, two-room dwelling.[18]

By the eve of the Revolution in 1774, when Sullivan was barely thirty years old, he had emerged as a local leader. John Adams, nearly ten years his senior, reported enviously on Sullivan's success when, following the court circuit, he visited him: "He began with neither learning, books, estate, not anything but his head and hands, and now is a very popular lawyer, and growing rich very fast, purchasing great farms, and is a justice of the peace and a member of the General

Court [legislature]."[19] In addition Sullivan was King's Counsel for York County and John Hancock's agent, trading on behalf of Boston's richest merchant and handling his local legal work. Sullivan's ability to do several things at once was already well developed.[20]

Soon after Adams's visit the Revolutionary crisis closed the courts, so Sullivan turned to clearing land in a frontier township in which he had acquired a share and named Limerick, to honor his father's birthplace.[21] When Massachusetts mobilized resistance, Sullivan became a patriot workhorse. Anonymously he wrote articles for the press as well as the legislature's official account of the Battle of Lexington and Concord.[22] He drafted state papers and regulations, serving almost continuously throughout the war. Sullivan prosecuted the traitor-spy Benjamin Church, went on a mission to Fort Ticonderoga to instruct Benedict Arnold, raised and supplied troops, and helped draft Massachusetts' new constitution. In addition, the legislature appointed Sullivan to serve on the state's highest court, on which he served from 1776 to 1782.[23] No wonder, then, that in 1805, more than twenty years later, the sixty-one-year-old Sullivan was at ease arguing before a court where he had once sat, and which was operating according to laws that he himself had drafted.[24]

At war's end in 1782 Sullivan resigned from the Supreme Judicial Court because he was in financial straits and, as the father of five children (with a sixth on the way) he felt he must recoup by practicing law. For this reason, though his colleagues in the legislature elected him to the Continental Congress in 1782 and 1783, he declined. He was willing to hold public office, but not if it would remove him from his law practice and his family, whom he brought to Boston in 1783. During the 1780s he was active in Boston, serving on town committees, in the legislature, and as a member of the Governor's Council that urged Governor Hancock to pardon convicted Shaysites. He was also judge of probate. Then in 1790 his friend Hancock appointed him attorney general. He was free to carry on his private practice as time permitted as he followed the traveling court doing state business. In this way Sullivan both developed unparalleled trial experience and, bringing his Federalist son William into his office, built up Massachusetts' most extensive legal practice.[25]

Sullivan had become a leading citizen. Joining the fashionable Brattle Street Church, he brought his family to services where a succession of governors—James Bowdoin, John Hancock, and Caleb Strong—also worshipped. By 1792 his fortunes had so recovered that Sullivan built a three-story brick mansion. The middle-aged man who had long ago thrashed an antilawyer bully back in New Hampshire now "dressed with great care and elegance" and was "noted for the refinement and elegance of his manners."[26] He had arrived, handsomely.

But while the Berkshire magnate Theodore Sedgwick pursued his ambitions on the national stage at the Continental Congress in Philadelphia, Sullivan made his mark in Massachusetts as a leader in law, public affairs, and economic development. While others might pass the time casually during procedural delays and courtroom arguments, Sullivan seized every moment for drafting legal documents and composing articles for the press. Using at least fourteen different pseudonyms, from "Plain Truth" and "Honest Republican" to "Americanus" and "Democracy," Sullivan engaged in dozens of debates over foreign and domestic policies, usually taking a partisan stance. When one of the princes of Boston Federalism, Harrison Gray Otis—a sometime courtroom adversary—denounced Irish immigration, claiming that the wild Irishmen would raise a rebellion, Sullivan, no friend to immigrant radicals, rejoined by listing Irish contributions to American independence and by demonstrating the legitimacy of Irish grievances against England.[27] Repeatedly Sullivan wrote on behalf of popular government, free speech, and freedom of religion, all key issues for Massachusetts Jeffersonians.

Sullivan's engagements in public projects were emblematic of his wide-ranging interests and usefulness in both elite and popular circles. Harvard had awarded him and his brother John honorary degrees in 1780 in recognition of their wartime service. Soon after, Sullivan joined in founding the American Academy of Arts and Sciences and the Massachusetts Charitable Congregational Society, which supported ministers. In the decade that followed, he was a founder and first president of the Massachusetts Historical Society, and active in the Humane Society for assisting mariners as well as in the Society for the Propagation of the Gospel among the Indians.[28] That Sullivan was also a leader in bringing Boston a public water supply and building a bridge across the Charles River to enhance Boston trade, as well as developing the Middlesex canal to join the Merrimack River and southern New Hampshire, did not surprise his friends.[29] With interests at once secular and Christian, learned and philanthropic, Sullivan's intelligence and energy were public as well as partisan assets.

In his private life, no less than the judges, Sullivan was a model patriarch. Like Strong and Sedgwick, he had married twice, and for the same reason. In January 1786 Hetty, the wife of his youth in Maine, had died suddenly in her thirty-eighth year. She had borne him eight children in eighteen years, six of whom survived into adulthood—and just six months before her death husband and wife had comforted each other when their last child, fifteen-month-old Nancy, had died. Sullivan struggled to accept Hetty's death: "On Thursday morning last I felt myself as happy as I wished. I breakfasted with a lady whom you know I adored. She was cheerful and gay, but before eight o'clock in the evening she was a breathless corpse." For the moment Sullivan's feelings overwhelmed his faith: "She for whom alone I lived, she who wished to live for me, is now no more. Religion points her out to me in the company of angels; but that form, in which she blessed me with every domestic happiness . . . is now mouldering in the tomb."[30] Management of the Sullivan household, a home with five boys aged three to seventeen years, fell on his fourteen-year-old daughter, Mehitable. For her sake and for the sake of her brothers, Sullivan felt he must remarry. His choice was Martha Langdon, an elegant Portsmouth, New Hampshire, widow and the sister of one of Governor John Sullivan's fellow New Hampshire leaders. As the year 1786 ended, they married; once more Sullivan's domestic affairs enjoyed expert management.[31]

The sentiments Sullivan expressed concerning his late wife reveal a romantic sensibility unexpected in a self-made man, a onetime Maine rustic. Yet this "soft" side of Sullivan's character ran deep and occasionally found unusual outlets. It was Sullivan, for example, who took the rare step of advertising a reward for the return of his lost "Spaniel Dog, having on his neck a brass collar, inscribed with the name of James Sullivan."[32] It was Sullivan, too, who as attorney general prosecuted a "truckman," George Johnson, for criminally abusing his horse. According to Sullivan's indictment, Johnson was "of cruel and inhuman disposition, and not minding and regarding the due and proper use of animals, which the great Creator of the universe has placed under the dominion of man . . . : but indulging a cruel disposition of heart, and in order to gratify the unlawful rage and cruel inclination of his depraved mind . . . did cruelly, inhumanly, outrageously and excessively, beat, bruise, mangle and torture a certain horse . . . by means of which . . . the said horse then and there instantly died." Sullivan did not claim legal protection for the horse, or what we now call "animal rights"; rather, he argued on behalf of the humane sensibility of Massachusetts society. By Johnson's "cruelty . . . an evil example was set before others, who will offend in like manner, and before the rising generation." By his flagrant abuse of one of God's creatures, Johnson had committed a sort of blasphemy, and so "hurt and injured . . . the feelings of the good citizens." To defend his absolute property rights, Johnson hired the great Federalist litigator Harrison Gray Otis. But the jury agreed with Sullivan and convicted Johnson.[33]

Sullivan was not opposed to whipping a horse any more than he was opposed to whipping a child, so long as it was done according to "the rational powers of the head." He had punished his own boys with a stick and, if necessary, he recommended that his daughter carry out this "painful task" on his own granddaughters.[34] At bottom, Sullivan's remarkable prosecution of George Johnson was a defense of the proper use of authority and power. It was Johnson's abuse of his legitimate authority over his horse that prompted Sullivan to act so as to shore up the barriers against depravity.

That the Massachusetts attorney general would undertake such a prosecution and win it in the absence of any statute specifically forbidding cruelty to one's livestock, like Judge Sewall's and the legislature's push to end Massachusetts' ancient corporal punishments, indicated that there were many in early republican Massachusetts who shared in the larger humanitarian outlook that was growing in societies touched by Enlightenment ideas. A new empathy toward victims of power, especially abusive power—including women and children, prisoners and slaves, even animals—was evident throughout the United States.[35] Its consequences for criminal justice were apparent even on such an obscure, backwater stage as the Berkshire County courthouse, where the influence of this new humanitarian sensibility was evident.

On Tuesday, September 10, when judges Sedgwick, Sewall, and Strong opened the court, they faced a docket of twenty-three cases.[36] Only one of these was widely regarded as a major public trial with important statewide consequences. That was the case of the Baptist elder Ebenezer Smith, who was appealing to the Supreme Judicial Court to force the town of Dalton to deliver to him the religious tax money collected by the town from his fellow Baptist, Samuel Whipple. In this civil action James Sullivan represented the Baptists as their private attorney. Though himself a Congregationalist, Sullivan was a prominent advocate for religious liberty who had fought similar cases repeatedly, though with mixed results. As far back as the 1780s Sullivan had defended the rights of Baptists and Universalists, and more recently in three separate cases he had defended the rights of Roman Catholic, Methodist, and Baptist clergy to receive their adherents' religious taxes. Now, arguing that even though the Baptist society was not incorporated, giving Whipple's taxes to Elder Smith was precisely what the constitution intended, Sullivan won the case.[37] The Jeffersonian press celebrated the court's ruling as a victory for religious liberty and for James Sullivan. According to the *Pittsfield Sun,* Sullivan, the most popular candidate for governor in Berkshire in 1804 and 1805, was "truly a prodigy of knowledge and every mental endowment that can adorn man; a star of the first magnitude, and every way worthy of being the first magistrate in this Commonwealth."[38] From a statewide political perspective this *Smith v. Dalton* ruling on religious liberty was the major event of the 1805 Supreme Judicial Court session in Berkshire.

Indeed apart from *Smith v. Dalton,* most of the twenty-two other cases were routine. There was, for example, the fraud committed by Stockbridge husbandman Eliphalet Whittlesey, who had deliberately taken the meat of a diseased swine, pickled it, and sold it. He drew a $20 fine (about three weeks' pay) and the costs of prosecution.[39] But there were other cases that were more unusual, and which echoed the disturbing family stories that people had been reading in the newspapers. One troubling illustration of vicious abuse of family trust was evident in the divorce petition of a saddler's wife, Phebe Eastman of

Sheffield, who claimed that her husband, Philip, had deserted her three years earlier and was now married bigamously to a woman in Worcester County. Because Phebe Eastman had properly advertised her charges in the press and Philip Eastman did not come forward to contest her claims, the judges granted Phebe a divorce as a matter of routine.[40] Every year divorce suits like Phebe Eastman's came before the Supreme Judicial Court as it made the circuit of Massachusetts counties; desertion and adultery by husband or wife were regularly judged sufficient grounds for a divorce decree.[41] When marriages failed, especially among people without much property, desertion and adultery were distressingly commonplace.

Much more rare, indeed shocking, were two sexual assault cases that the state brought against fathers accused of attempting to rape, or actually raping, their own daughters. The first of these concerned a Pittsfield laborer, Abner Durwin, who was charged with attempted rape and assault on his eleven-year-old daughter, Nancy, on October 20, 1804. According to the law any girl from ten years up was deemed capable of sexual consent, and Sullivan's indictment charged that Durwin had attempted both "carnally to know" Nancy, and that he "did beat and wound" her; in addition Durwin had "lewdly and lasciviously conducted himself towards her." As was expected in criminal cases, Durwin pled "not guilty" on all charges.[42]

After a short trial the jury, twelve men who had been randomly selected from the voters of twelve different towns, deliberated briefly and acquitted Durwin of the most serious charge, attempted rape. Had he been convicted of this crime, a term of up to five years in the new Massachusetts prison could have been expected. But the jury did not set Durwin free. He had, the jurors concluded, "lewdly and lasciviously conducted himself towards her in evil example to others." After conferring, Sedgwick, Sewall, and Strong sentenced Durwin to two years' imprisonment, with Durwin to pay the costs of his prosecution and to post bond for his good behavior after leaving prison.[43] Though Durwin's crime was unusual, the sentence was not. The fact that his victim was also his daughter was irrelevant legally.

Durwin had not been charged with raping his daughter nor, in the jury's judgment, had he tried to rape her; but the crime for which he was convicted was grave enough. The jurors, mostly yeoman farmers who were themselves parents, believed that as fathers they were properly the guardians and guides of their children. As clergymen and magistrates had explained for generations, they were intended by divine and natural law to direct their children in righteous paths only. Indeed just recently the Berkshire and Columbia County Missionary Society had purchased 400 copies of Heman Willard's new Stockbridge edition of an old Philip Doddridge sermon on family government, which the society intended to distribute in the region. These instructions to "the Master of a Family" counseled fathers "to suppress that turbulency of passion, which may now be ready to break out."[44] Though technically the law did not recognize Durwin's relation to his victim, his crime signified his own corruption and magnified it, since he had attacked the innocence and virtue of a child he ought to nurture and defend.

Yet as destructive of family and social order as Durwin's crime was, the fact that it went unnoticed in the press suggests that although people saw his case as despicable, it was unremarkable. Indeed crimes such as Durwin's almost never rose to the prevailing standard of newsworthiness in the early republic. Court proceedings were well-attended public events, but although they generated conversation, they could rarely command press attention unless they involved prominent gentry or some important principle, as in *Smith v. Dalton.* The only other circumstance that made court proceedings worthy of print coverage was the threat of capital punishment. The last item on the docket, *Commonwealth of Massachusetts v. Wheeler,* was just such a capital case; and though it had not yet been mentioned in print, it drew a huge crowd.[45]

All summer there had been talk of the charge against Ephraim Wheeler, so on Thursday, September 12, when Sheriff Larned and his deputies walked Wheeler up the road from Lenox jail through the center doorway and into the courtroom to be arraigned, they created a stir. It was a warm, sunny day and the great courtroom windows were propped wide open so that the crowd that clustered around the building could hear the attorney general read the words he had drafted for the grand jury's indictment:

> The Jurors for the Commonwealth of Massachusetts, on their oath, present that Ephraim Wheeler of Windsor, in the County of Berkshire, labourer, not having the fear of God before his eyes, but being moved and seduced by the instigation of the devil, on the eighth day of June, now last past, with force and arms, at Partridgefield, in the county of Berkshire aforesaid, in and upon one Betsy Wheeler, single woman and spinster, in the peace of God, and the same Commonwealth then and there being, violently and feloniously, did make an assault, and her the said Betsy Wheeler then and there did ravish and carnally know, against the law in such case made and provided, and against the peace and dignity of the Commonwealth aforesaid.

It was signed by the grand jury foreman, Levi Nye, a Federalist church deacon from the nearby town of Lee. Except for the names, the date, and the places that Attorney General Sullivan inserted, the language of the indictment was standard, a formula brought forward from the English and colonial past.[46] Legally speaking, Betsy's relationship to her assailant was irrelevant. Not everyone who listened to that formula believed literally that the devil himself had visited Berkshire and led Wheeler into crime; but most agreed that man's sinful nature was at the root of crimes like rape.

While Wheeler remained standing the court clerk, Stockbridge Federalist Joseph Woodbridge, asked him how he pleaded and, as expected, Wheeler replied, "Not Guilty." According to long-standing Anglo-American practice, all prisoners in capital cases were routinely encouraged to plead "not guilty" so as to forestall an automatic death sentence. Prosecutors agreed that the adversarial process of the courtroom was necessary to bring out information that might later serve to support commutation of the death sentence or even an outright pardon. Had Wheeler chosen to plead guilty, the judges would have rejected his plea and advised him that morally and legally he was not required to plead either guilty or not guilty. If Wheeler had insisted, the court would only have accepted his second attempt at a guilty plea if they were certain that he had been given sufficient time to reflect freely on the decision. In that case, after an examination under oath of the sheriff, the jailer, and the arresting justice of the peace, the judges would have allowed a guilty plea only if they were convinced that Wheeler was sane and that no improper influence, such as a promise of leniency or a hope of pardon, had led him to plead guilty.[47]

Following Wheeler's formal plea, Clerk Woodbridge asked: "Prisoner, how will you be tried?" To which Wheeler was coached to respond, "By God and my Country." Speaking now for the court and the authorities it represented, Woodbridge answered: "God send you a good deliverance."[48] From the outset, court officials, including the prosecutor, would emphasize that the purpose of this trial, like every trial, was not to win conviction but to secure justice.

The next step in assuring justice, one that had long separated Massachusetts criminal justice from its English counterpart, was Judge Simeon Strong's question to Wheeler asking whether he wished to have counsel assigned to defend him. In Massachusetts, in contrast to

Britain, ever since the Puritan era defendants in capital cases were normally allowed counsel and, if they were too poor to hire an advocate, one was supplied by the court.[49] When Wheeler responded to Judge Strong that he wished to have John W. Hulbert, Esq., assigned to him, it was so ordered. Now, for the first time, Hulbert spoke: he declared he would have the prisoner ready for trial the following morning at 9:00 A.M., and in the meantime he asked permission for another attorney to join him for Wheeler's defense. His associate was to be Daniel Dewey, Esq., who would be formally assigned first thing the next morning. Together Hulbert and Dewey would have less than one day to interview their client, gather information, collect witnesses, and prepare the prisoner's defense.[50] This, too, was routine.

Why Wheeler chose Hulbert to defend him, or whether he had any real choice, is not known; and the same is true of the assignment of Dewey to the case. During the years Wheeler had lived in Berkshire he would have heard some gossip about the Berkshire bar, and as a spectator he may even have watched some attorneys in action during past court sessions; but he had never before been represented by an attorney, and he was in no position to make a discriminating choice from among the seventeen men in the county qualified to practice before the Supreme Judicial Court.[51] Yet had he done so, John Hulbert and Daniel Dewey might have been high on his list.

Hulbert, a thirty-five-year-old native of Alford on the New York border, was married and the father of two daughters and a baby boy.[52] A 1795 Harvard graduate, he had trained in Judge Sedgwick's Stockbridge law office and now practiced from his home in that town. Like his former mentor, Hulbert was a Federalist who shared much the same outlook as the justices. Later described as "a man of brilliant intellect and keen wit," his courtroom oratory displayed such "pointed and incisive but polished" eloquence that his colleagues called him "silver tongued."[53] Less than a decade later Hulbert would represent

Berkshire in the United States Congress. Hulbert's preparation, talents, and ambition made him a weighty advocate. Even more immediately relevant to Wheeler than Hulbert's credentials, perhaps, was the fact that three years earlier, in front of Judges Strong and Sewall, Hulbert had successfully defended a shoemaker, Uriel Gleazen, who had killed a man and stood charged with murder. As a result of Hulbert's defense, instead of being hanged, Gleazen got off with a manslaughter conviction and six months in prison, a year of probationary good behavior, and court costs.[54] From the vantage point of the defendant's box, Hulbert's success was encouraging.

His co-counsel, Daniel Dewey, was four years Hulbert's senior, and also a family man, who had trained with Judge Sedgwick during the time of Shays' Rebellion. A native of Sheffield who had attended Yale but not graduated, Dewey gained admission to the bar in 1787 and had gone on to practice in Williamstown. There he became a pillar of Williams College, the Calvinist Congregational Church, and Federalism. He had been the Federalist nominee for Congress in the past four elections, always losing to the Jeffersonian—most recently Barnabas Bidwell. But within a decade his gentlemanly ambition would be rewarded with election to the Governor's Council as well as the United States Congress (immediately preceding Hulbert), and with appointment by Governor Caleb Strong to the Supreme Judicial Court. Of more direct significance for Wheeler was the fact that when the court had last met in Berkshire, Judge Sedgwick had chosen Dewey to serve as the state's prosecuting attorney in the absence of both the attorney general and the solicitor general.[55] Not only was this a sign of Sedgwick's continuing approbation of his former student, it also gave Dewey additional insight into how the present prosecutor might frame the case and argue it before the jury. Known for his "amiable temper" and his "exemplary piety," Dewey was valued by other lawyers for "his modest and retired manners [and] his diligence in business."[56] Together Hulbert and Dewey would be a talented, seasoned, and self-assured defense team—one that possessed a high level of credibility with both judges and jury.

When Wheeler walked back to jail Thursday afternoon the sky was still bright and the air warm from the sun. But next morning, when Sheriff Larned's deputies brought him back to court just before nine o'clock the weather had turned cool and rainy. For the first day in over a week, farmers could take time off from haying and the harvest to come watch the drama of Wheeler's trial. With John W. Hulbert and Daniel Dewey arrayed against James Sullivan before the Supreme Court, over the course of the day this life-and-death theater drew as many as a thousand spectators, most packed outside the courthouse windows, straining to hear the proceedings inside.

Inside the courtroom the first business was the judges' official assignment of Dewey as Hulbert's co-counsel. The next was to impanel Wheeler's jury. Evidently the court began with the same trial jury that had just acquitted Abner Durwin of attempted rape; but Wheeler's lawyers challenged four of Durwin's jurors, and four were replaced. No record explains why the defense viewed these four as problematic; however, Berkshire was small enough—only about 6,000 men were qualified as voters and jurors—that Hulbert or Dewey, or perhaps Wheeler himself, might have known something about these individuals that the defense felt made them likely to convict. It may be significant that one of the challenged jurors came from Wheeler's own community of Windsor, and another came from Partridgefield, a town where Wheeler and his family had lived some years earlier; a third had relatives in Partridgefield. Whatever the reasons for the defense's challenges, the original four were dismissed and four new jurors, none from Windsor or Partridgefield, were added immediately to the Durwin eight.[57]

Together the twelve men who would deliberate on Wheeler's fate represented the farmers of modest means who headed the majority of Berkshire households. Among the eleven whose occupations are known, ten were farmers—nine yeomen and one a mere husbandman—and one was a shopkeeper. They came from all parts of the county, from Williamstown and Cheshire in the north, to Pittsfield, Lenox, Washington, and Lee in the center, to Sandisfield and Great Barrington in the south. Most of the jurors were middle-aged, like Wheeler, having been born in the 1750s and 1760s. They remembered the Revolution and the civil unrest that had followed; and whatever their religion or politics, they all had a stake in social order as property holders and household patriarchs. A majority of the jurymen had children at home, several had daughters, and a few had grandchildren. And though none was highly educated in a formal sense, collectively they possessed a store of knowledge and experience that would enable them to put the testimony of the witnesses, the arguments of the lawyers, and the instructions of the judges into perspective.[58] Though we can only guess their preferences and prejudices, the record in Abner Durwin's trial suggests that eight of them, when faced with the choice of convicting a man for a major crime or simply letting him go free, preferred a middle course: delivering a guilty verdict for a lesser crime.

With preliminaries concluded, the trial began. Viewed from the spectators' benches that rose in stages on both sides of the door at the back of the room, the scene was theatrical. On the far wall at the front of the room behind a rounded enclosure sat the judges, facing the carefully defined space before them. Directly in front of them, seated at tables in their assigned places, were the court clerk, the attorney general, and the county barristers, including Hulbert and Dewey. On the left wall a grand jury box rose in three tiers of four seats, and on the right wall the petty jurors who were about to hear the trial were seated in a matching enclosure. Directly before the spectators on left and right were benches for witnesses, and in the center were boxes for the sheriff, other court officers, and the defendant. Surrounded by dozens of officials and an audience in the hundreds, Ephraim Wheeler went on trial.[59]

Clerk Joseph Woodbridge read the indictment once more while Wheeler, as ordered, identified himself by holding up his right hand. Though he would be defended by able counsel, his vulnerability was unmistakable. One commentator sketched a generic portrait of Wheeler's sort: "a criminal in his trial—squalid in his appearance, his body debilitated by confinement, his mind weakened by misery or conscious guilt, abandoned by all the world, he stands alone, to contend with the fearful odds that are arrayed against him."[60] Foremost among the obstacles to his acquittal was the attorney general, James Sullivan, whose breadth of experience and mastery of courtroom oratory were unsurpassed. Moreover, according to routine procedures, Sullivan would not only frame the case at the outset by setting forth the prosecution's account, he would also have the last word, presenting his final analysis only after Hulbert and Dewey had closed Wheeler's defense.

When Sullivan rose to speak at the front of the courtroom, his was a commanding presence. At first glance his black suit and snow-white linens gave him the appearance of the most urbane of old-school clergymen. Moreover, as he spoke, his gravity and style of reasoning directly from first principles resembled pulpit oratory at its rational best. Sullivan attacked no one. His stance was that of a solemn public servant, concerned only with instructing the court on the case within the broader context of upholding the law and society. Because rape was a capital offense and capital punishment for this crime was under attack—chiefly by Sullivan's fellow Republicans—his first objective was to defend the death penalty, even for rape.[61]

"May it please your Honors, and Gentlemen of the Jury," he began, "the continuance of life is an object of the first magnitude with the human race"; but it was not the only object.[62] Order, too, was essential. As most Christians recognized, "the human race is depraved, and man has become the prey of man"; consequently "we fly to the arms of civil society for protection." This civil society, Sullivan explained, required laws to sustain it, and those laws could only be maintained if they were "sanctioned by adequate penalties." Taking the broadest perspective, Sullivan invited his audience to recognize that although humans were indeed committed to preserve life, "nearly all" governments throughout history had employed the death penalty for "those high and aggravated offences" that threatened the community or damaged individuals irreparably. In Massachusetts, he reported, "there are but eight crimes punishable . . . with death." Though he never used the word "rape," this case, he said, was one of them.[63] The attorney general went on to define that crime as "carnal copulation . . . by force," emphasizing that it was the man's force and violence without the woman's consent that was criminal. As his brown eyes looked around the room, and perhaps at the crowd gathered outside the windows, Sullivan declined to go into the particulars, believing that to do so would offend proper standards of "delicacy" and "decency."[64] Acting as the jury's guide, he outlined the trial scenario that would follow, stressing that in this, as in all rape trials, the credibility of the victim's testimony was crucial, because other witnesses could only partially corroborate what she said. Then, as he had done a hundred times in a dozen courtrooms, he asserted control over the case by presenting his own recitation of the crime. Sullivan's narrative prepared the jury to understand events from the prosecution's perspective; and he would support it with the testimony of seven witnesses.

The account the attorney general provided was a grim tale of family conflict and abuse of authority. The father, Ephraim Wheeler, had decided to leave the mother, Hannah Wheeler, and take the children away. On June 8, 1805, he had "commanded" thirteen-year-old Betsy and her eight-year-old brother, Ephraim, Jr., to go with him to their uncle Isaac Odel's house, several miles away. Reluctantly the children mounted his horse while he walked before. When they came to a thick wood, Wheeler stopped and "commanded" Betsy to go into the wood with him to look for avens-root, a medicinal chocolate substitute. Though Betsy cried and said she did not want to go, and then asked if her brother could come too, "the prisoner directed" the boy to stay and hold the horse. When Wheeler and his daughter were fifty yards into the wood, "he commanded her to lie down on her back, which she refusing to do, he threw her down with violence; and with a cruel and savage force, committed the capital crime." With Betsy in tears they returned to the road; whereupon Wheeler now "ordered" the children to go back home and then come to him at Uncle Odel's the next dry day. Sullivan concluded his preliminary account by explaining that when the children got home, Betsy informed her mother of what had happened, and then Hannah Wheeler sent for Robert Walker, the local justice of the peace. Walker came and took the girl's statement, questioned other witnesses, and ordered the prisoner's arrest. As flat and understated as Sullivan's sketch was, Wheeler's guilt appeared certain. Now, the attorney general announced, he would call the witnesses to the events of June 8, "and examine them before you."[65]

The first person he called to the stand was the star witness, Betsy Wheeler, a girl who was at that point thirteen years and seven months old. We do not know Betsy's appearance—whether she was large or small for her age, mature or immature, dark or fair-haired. But since both the trial report and the newspaper coverage were silent as to her race, we may assume that she appeared to be a white girl, although at least one of her mother's siblings as well as her maternal grandfather were identified as black or negro in church and census records.[66] We may also guess that Betsy was a child who was used to working full-time the year round, because unlike most girls her age, she could not write her name. She appears from her testimony to have had the speak-when-spoken-to demeanor of a poor girl who was used to taking orders. But though Betsy's words were terse, and delivered in so low a tone that the people gathered outside the windows could not readily distinguish them, they were far more powerful and dramatic than Attorney General Sullivan's preface.

She began by recounting the events of June 8 substantially as Sullivan had reported them. But there were details the prosecutor had omitted. Her father, for example, had threatened to kill her if she did not lie down for him; and when she tried to scream he had struck her on the head, choked her, and held her mouth. Betsy further testified to the physical details of the rape, including penetration and emission, but the trial report suppressed her explicit testimony on grounds of modesty. After Betsy had disclosed the basic facts of the crime, Sullivan guided her through a series of questions designed to show her candor and innocence in revealing the rape, first to her mother and then Justice Walker.

The trial reporter reproduced this portion of the testimony:

Question by the Attorney General. What did you do after this affair took place?
Answer. We returned to the place where we had left the boy.
Q. Did your father tell you to keep secret what he had done?
A. Yes. When we were in the woods he said that if I ever told what he had done to me, he would kill me in the most cruel way he could think of.
Q. What did your father say when you returned to your brother?

A. He asked Ephraim if he had been asleep, he said no—he told us we might return home, but that we must meet him the next day if it was fair, and bring the baby with us, if it was not, we must come the first fair day.

Q. Did you tell your brother what your father had done to you?

A. I told him some.

Q. Did you tell your mother when you got home?

A. Yes.

Q. Did she examine you?

A. Yes.

Question by the Court [judges]. Was you injured much in your body?

A. Some.[67]

Compared with her statement of the crime itself, the importance of Betsy's answers here was secondary. But this testimony did advance two key prosecution points: the issues of consent and force. If she had consented to the sexual act, Wheeler would not have needed to threaten Betsy's life to assure her silence; nor would Wheeler have wondered whether his son was asleep if he had not been concerned that the noise of Betsy's resistance might have reached the boy. In addition, Betsy's testimony that her mother had examined her and that she had suffered injury also helped to verify the fact of the crime. Without testimony regarding physical examination and injury, a rape prosecution could scarcely succeed. Indeed on this point the state's case against Wheeler was weak, because Betsy's mother could not corroborate Betsy's statement in court. The rules of criminal procedure barred the state from calling Hannah Wheeler to testify against her husband.[68]

The next part of Betsy's testimony was surprising to the spectators, and potentially explosive for the prosecution's case. Sullivan asked Betsy: "Did he [Wheeler] ever have any thing to do with you before?" and she answered, "Yes, he attempted twice before."[69] Opening up this testimony could be hazardous for Sullivan because it might show that Betsy had been her father's sexual partner repeatedly and thus a consenting partner in the forbidden act. But the attorney general calculated that by revealing the ingrained depravity of Ephraim Wheeler, Betsy's own credibility would be enhanced. If Betsy put the whole incident in the context of repeated violations, the twelve fathers sitting in judgment a few feet away from the wounded girl would appreciate her impulse to report her father's crime, no matter what.

In response to Sullivan's questions, Betsy reported that her father's first attempt, almost a year earlier, had not succeeded but that the second time he did "partly." Now the attorney general asked the key question, and the judges finished his work by following up:

Q. Why did you not tell your mother when he made the attempt the first time?

A. I dare not, he said he would kill me if I did.

Court. Did you consent to his lying with you?

A. I did not.

Court. Was it against your will?

A. Yes.

Court. Did you ever tell any person of his attempt upon you before?

A. No.

Court. How came you to tell of this?

A. I thought I had as lieve [as soon] die one way as another.[70]

Thus, with the judges asking precisely the questions he would have asked, James Sullivan's first interrogation ended. Now John

Hulbert and Daniel Dewey, men about the age of Sullivan's eldest son, faced a severe challenge. They must cast doubt on a girl who, surmounting her despair at her father's abuse, had demonstrated a stoic, if doleful, courage.

John Hulbert's cross-examination tested Betsy by probing her account, hoping to find inconsistencies that could be used to challenge her testimony, and to uncover evidence of consensual sex. Failing that, Hulbert might at least elicit evidence that Betsy's resistance to his client had been so muted and passive as to be interpreted as consent. His tactics were standard in defending against the charge of rape; for without conspicuous evidence of resistance, such as screaming, running away, or striking back, juries—which were all male and normally reluctant to send a man to the gallows—gave the benefit of the doubt to the defendant.[71] Hulbert began by asking Betsy if she had tried "to run from your father while in the woods?" "Yes," she replied, "and he caught up a stone to throw at me."[72] Hulbert then turned to picking at the details of Betsy's account; and each time, from Wheeler's order to go home and return the next day, to Betsy's revealing the assault to her mother, Betsy's responses were consistent with her original testimony.

Hulbert went on to examine the previous sexual encounters that Betsy had just revealed in court. He knew this sordid testimony would be damaging to his client's moral standing, but the accusation had already been made in open court, and if his cross-examination could make the notion of Betsy's consent or nonresistance credible, he could save Ephraim's neck. So Hulbert plunged ahead, asking Betsy the details of Wheeler's "first attempt upon you." Betsy said that it had happened one evening: "He told me to get off the horse and get a stick, which I did, and then he got off and tried to persuade me to let him have *to do* with me." But on that occasion he did "not much" compel her, but instead "he offered me a gown and a petti-

74

coat."[73] Evidently this attempt had been more of a failed seduction than a rape.

Unfortunately for Hulbert's client, the account did not stop there. The second time, Betsy related, when they were going for firewood and passing through the bushes some fifty yards from their home, Wheeler had partially succeeded in raping her. "I began to scream," she said, "and he clapped his hand upon my mouth."[74] Hulbert stopped. Whether his disappointment with Betsy's testimony was visible or not, he decided to end his cross-examination. His questioning had not only failed to shake Betsy's testimony, it had strengthened it; and any attempt to bully her into an inconsistency would be even more dangerous for the defense.

Betsy's task was now finished, and she was directed to leave the witness stand and return to the witnesses' bench. Now Attorney General Sullivan called Betsy's little brother to testify, with the expectation that he would reinforce his sister's credibility by corroborating significant details of her testimony. But because Ephraim, Jr., was under ten years of age, Sullivan knew the defense would immediately challenge the boy as a witness. He had encountered such objections before, and knew how to respond. Sullivan began by asking Ephraim, Jr., "How old are you?" The boy, whom he had probably coached, replied: "I shall be nine years old the third day of next October." Sullivan asked one more question: "Can you read?" The answer was "No." At that moment Hulbert interrupted the interrogation with a formal objection: Ephraim, Jr., was underage and "incapable" of understanding the meaning of an oath. Hulbert cited two English precedents to support his objection; but Sullivan trumped them by pointing to a more recent English case, which held that "if an infant appears upon strict examination by the Court, to possess a sufficient knowledge of the nature and consequence of an oath, and of the danger and impiety of swearing falsely, which must be collected from his answers to questions, propounded to him by the Court, he may be sworn at any age."[75] In short, if the judges would conduct a simple catechism with Ephraim, Jr., the boy could be a witness. Simeon Strong, who was presiding, asked the questions:

Q. Who made you?
A. God.
Q. Do you expect ever to die?
A. Yes.
Q. What do you believe will become of you after death, if you are wicked here?
A. I shall be punished.
Q. Do you know that it is wicked to tell a lie?
A. Yes.
Q. Do you know you are more liable to be punished for telling a lie here at Court, when you are sworn, than you are at home, when you are not sworn?
A. Yes.

Thereupon Strong overruled Hulbert's objection and ordered that Ephraim, Jr., be sworn in.[76]

The attorney general asked the boy to tell what he knew. Ephraim, Jr., responded with a child's directness. If young Ephraim understood that God was his maker and that he would be punished if he lied, it appears from his testimony that he did not fully grasp the seriousness of the trial, or realize that what he said might help end his father's life:

My daddy said I must go with him to uncle Isaac's; Betsy and I rode together; when we got near to Mr. Dibbles, daddy told Betsy that she must get off and go with him and get *avens-root*. I asked him if I might not go with them, he said no, I must stay and hold the horse. After they had been gone a little time I heard Betsy make a noise, when they returned she was crying— daddy asked me if I had been asleep—he said we might go home and come again the next day, if it was fair. Betsy said if she must go she had rather go then. When we were going home Betsy said Daddy had pounded her head and pinched her throat.[77]

Except for a single detail—Betsy said that she had asked permission for her brother to accompany them into the woods, whereas Ephraim, Jr., reported that he had asked to go along—the boy's statement corroborated both the substance of Betsy's account of the circumstances and the sequence of events. It only remained for James Sullivan to question Ephraim, Jr., as to whether Betsy had revealed anything else about the rape in his presence. From the boy's responses it was clear that Betsy had concealed all but the head-pounding and throat-pinching from him. Though Ephraim, Jr., had seen the justice of the peace, Robert Walker, at the house that day, he did not know why he was there.[78]

When Sullivan finished, once more Hulbert faced a challenging assignment: he must cross-examine an eight-year-old boy whose father's life was at stake. Hulbert began by asking the lad about the circumstances of the events of June 8: When did he hear the noise from the woods, was there any cleared land or any house in sight, were there any passersby on the road? Ephraim, Jr.'s answers were straightforward, factual. The best that Hulbert could extract was the boy's statement that he had not heard "any threatening words" directed at Betsy. So at least Betsy's accusation of a death threat was not corroborated. But the rest of young Ephraim's testimony either confirmed what Betsy had said or had no bearing on the central question of rape. There was nothing here to challenge Betsy's truthfulness.[79]

Hulbert, who could not have been encouraged by his efforts with the first two witnesses, sat down.

Attorney General Sullivan stood. He had one more question for the boy, one that would start to fill in the family context of Wheeler's assault that he had sketched in his opening summary by depicting Wheeler as an angry, violent man. Both the question and the answer were simple:

Q. Had your father and mother quarreled that morning?
A. Yes.[80]

Just a few minutes later Sullivan would use the testimony of Wheeler's brother-in-law, Bill Martin, to drive home this point. Once more, however, one of the judges intervened, producing a colloquy that further illuminated the family crisis:

Q. Did you know that morning that your father was going away to live?
A. He said so.
Q. Did you hear him tell any person so?
A. Yes, he told my mother so.[81]

So ended the testimony of Ephraim, Jr., and he was now free to sit down next to his sister on the witness bench.

The next two witnesses James Sullivan called, Eunice Hart and Bill Martin, provided substantial information about the Wheelers' family situation, as well as the circumstances in which Betsy told her mother about her father's assault. The Wheelers, it became clear, did not have a house of their own, but dwelled in part of a house headed by Bill Martin, the husband of Hannah Wheeler's sister Lucy. Because Lucy Martin was in labor giving birth to a child on the day of the alleged rape, a neighbor, Eunice Hart, had come to the house to care for her. As a result Eunice Hart as well as Bill Martin had witnessed much of what had gone on in the Martin-Wheeler dwelling on June 8.

Eunice Hart described Betsy as unwilling to go with her father when he left in the morning "and cried," Eunice said. And in the afternoon when Eunice saw Betsy, the girl "was sitting with her head down."[82] Bill Martin reported that on the morning of June 8 the Wheelers' third child, a little girl, had come into his part of the house and asked him to come to the Wheelers'. There, Martin testified, he saw Wheeler "with a bayonet in his hand threatening his wife." Martin told Wheeler "he had better not strike her"; and when Wheeler "did strike" Hannah, Martin testified that he seized Wheeler and put him out of the house. Later that day, when Betsy and Ephraim, Jr., had returned, their mother, Hannah, asked Martin to go to Justice Walker's, "for something had happened worse than" Wheeler's blow with the bayonet. Martin asked what it was; "she said it was almost too bad to tell: I asked her to tell me—she said the prisoner [Wheeler] had had to do with Betsy."[83] Sullivan stopped there. Hart's and Martin's testimony, he believed, strengthened Betsy's account.

Hulbert began his cross-examination of Martin from a difficult position. His client had been depicted as a brute. Hulbert could not erase that; but he hoped to show that the conflict between Ephraim and Hannah Wheeler was chronic, and that Hannah harbored ill will, perhaps vengeance, toward her husband. Martin, in responding to Hulbert's queries, observed that the couple "repeatedly quarrel." To the question of whether Betsy was "much in fear" of her father, Martin replied: "I do not know, he is a violent man, and frequently treats his family ill." No doubt Hulbert would have preferred Martin to have cut off his response at "I do not know," since Martin's uninvited comment on Wheeler's violence toward his family could only damage the defense.[84]

Attorney General Sullivan concluded his presentation of evidence by calling three officials to testify briefly: Robert Walker, the justice of the peace in Windsor; Deacon Levi Nye of Lee, the foreman of the grand jury that indicted Wheeler; and Dr. Asahel Wright, a Windsor farmer turned doctor. Sullivan asked Walker and Wright to describe the scene of the crime, which they said was a swampy wood some fifty yards from the road and roughly one hundred fifty yards from the nearest house. Wright testified that the woods there were thick enough "to conceal" the assault, while Walker's testimony confirmed Martin's statement and part of Betsy's. Martin had indeed come to Walker's house on June 8 and asked him to return with him to the Wheelers' regarding a crime. "I went down," Walker said, and "took Betsy into a separate room; she immediately fell to crying, and I could get nothing from her. I then called the mother in, and she (Betsy) then related to me the same story that she has here." When asked by one of the judges to confirm that Betsy's testimony was the same then as now, Walker replied that it was, except that Betsy had not spoken of Ephraim's second, partially successful, rape attempt. When Levi Nye was called, he swore that Betsy's testimony in court and before the grand jury was "the same."[85]

Nye's testimony seemed to secure the prosecution case, and the defense did not cross-examine; but then Walker returned to the stand to reveal a startling error of omission, which opened a major breach in Sullivan's seemingly well-constructed case. Sullivan had allowed Walker to leave the stand without questioning him about Betsy's physical condition on June 8. Now the Windsor justice of the peace and leader of the "Sincerity Lodge" of Partridgefield Freemasons "recollected" that he ought to have testified about the girl's physical state: "there appeared to be marks of violence on the right side of her head; it looked red, and was considerably swollen. She said her father had beaten her, and that she was injured in other parts of her body, which from motives of delicacy" Walker had not examined.[86] Here was the omission that might acquit Wheeler of the capital crime. The prosecution could present no corroborating testimony to establish the fact of sexual contact, let alone sexual assault. Either Sullivan had blundered by failing to question Walker on this crucial subject or, as seems more likely, he had tried to contrive a way around Walker's clear failure to direct a physician, a midwife, or a jury of matrons to examine Betsy promptly for signs of a sexual assault, as was usual practice when investigating accusations of rape.

But Walker, to his credit—as well as his own embarrassment—volunteered this important information. Had he not done so, it is probable that Hulbert and Dewey would have raised the issue in making the argument for "reasonable doubt" regarding Wheeler's guilt. As it was, James Sullivan brushed off the question as if it was insignificant. He "observed to the Court and Jury, That the issue depended on no legal investigation." Compared to Betsy Wheeler's testimony, procedural issues were insignificant. Everything, he claimed, depended on her credibility. To the jurors he declared that if they did not believe her, "there was no crime proved against the prisoner." But, he advised them, if they did accept Betsy as truthful, then the crime of rape had been "fully proved," so "an application of the evidence could not be necessary."[87] Here Sullivan displayed the self-assurance he had ripened over thirty years in the courtroom and that made him so successful with juries. Plain yeoman farmers would likely agree that the core of the case was Betsy's truthfulness, even though there was a gap in the evidence owing to the blunder of an inexperienced local justice who had never before dealt with a rape accusation.

The weakness of Ephraim Wheeler's courtroom situation is suggested by the fact that when it was Hulbert's turn to call witnesses for the defense, he called no one. Usually in rape trials, where so much hinged on the credibility of the charge rather than hard evidence, the defense used witnesses to undermine the reputation and character of the accuser and to proclaim such virtues as industry, sobriety, peacefulness, and piety for the defendant. Indeed in Britain if a man of high rank would testify under oath that he knew the defendant to be a man of good character, acquittal often followed. But evidently Wheeler did not possess such high-ranking friends who could be brought to testify on his behalf, so Hulbert proceeded immediately to argument.[88]

Hulbert began by erecting psychological barriers against conviction by emphasizing the death penalty and the anxiety he felt conducting a defense under its shadow. By praising the humanity and mercy of the jurors, he sought to align them with him in a compassionate stance. Then Hulbert directly addressed the most difficult aspect of Wheeler's defense, that the prisoner was charged with one of the "blackest and most unnatural crimes," committing "a rape on the body of his own daughter."[89] Whereas James Sullivan had rhetorically isolated the charge of rape in his opening remarks, admonishing the jurors to put the father-daughter relationship out of their minds, Hulbert, knowing, like Sullivan, that this was impossible, tried to work the incestuous part of the accusation around to the defense's advantage. He aimed to use the jurors' own self-image as fair-minded, charitable men to gain a sympathetic hearing for his client. Acknowledging that the jury must surely have felt sympathy for the alleged victim and horror at the accused—"so great is our natural detestation of such abominable crimes"—Hulbert reminded the jurors that Wheeler had "put himself upon you for trial" and that "his life depends upon your verdict." Jurors must set aside all prejudices and "lean on the side of mercy."[90]

Precisely because the charge against Wheeler was so enormous Hulbert invited the jury to doubt it. "Never," he told the jurymen, "was a man accused of a more unnatural and improbable crime." In order to convict him, Hulbert argued, they must consider Wheeler the most evil of men, lacking in all "moral and religious sentiment," indeed "a monster wholly destitute of that natural affection, which so powerfully and happily binds the tender parent to the beloved child."[91] The accusation was so extreme, Hulbert said, echoing a point James Sullivan had made at the outset, that jurors should intensify their ordinary presumption of innocence. Hulbert wrapped up the introductory part of Wheeler's defense by quoting Lord Chief Justice Sir Matthew Hale, the seventeenth-century English jurist whose commentary on rape had been a staple for attorneys defending rape charges for generations: "rape is . . . an accusation easy to be made, hard to be proved, but harder to be defended by the party accused, though innocent." Still relying on Hale, Hulbert went on to report "many cases where false accusations have been made and directly sworn to, by the women pretending to have been injured."[92] This more or less standard rape defense was the choice of Ephraim Wheeler's defenders, John W. Hulbert and Daniel Dewey. Though Wheeler was silent in court, as required by law, this was precisely the defense Wheeler preferred, according to his later published narrative. His attorney would be required to attack Betsy's testimony as utterly false.

The question was how to employ the "Hale defense" so as to fit the facts of the present case and make Betsy appear a liar. Usually in a false rape scenario the accuser was motivated by either vengeance or the hope of gain, such as extorting money in exchange for dropping her charge. But it would have been absurd for Hulbert and Dewey to try to place Betsy in such a script, since there was nothing in the trial testimony to suggest that she was seeking either revenge or monetary gain. Nevertheless the defense team had discovered motives in their interviews with their client and in the trial evidence that could be adapted to Hale's standard defense. Conflict in a loveless marriage and competition for the "ownership" of children often ignited the deepest passions—anger, hatred, and revenge. Some in the courtroom, perhaps even jurors, would remember the recent newspaper account of Samuel Mitchell, the London silk-weaver whose passion for marital vengeance was so explosive that he had killed his own daughter to keep her out of his wife's custody. Hulbert and Dewey would seek to undermine Betsy's testimony by using the undisputed evidence that her parents quarreled and that Ephraim was taking the children away as the grounds for asserting that Betsy and Ephraim, Jr., were engaged in a conspiracy designed by their mother to stop their father by fabricating the rape accusation.

This was a daring strategy because the two attorneys had only a few ambiguities and discrepancies in the testimony on which to challenge the children's truthfulness and construct their narrative. But they knew that all the spectators would believe that back in June, on the day Ephraim assaulted Hannah with his bayonet, she and the children must have been desperate to find a way to block Ephraim from using his lawful authority to take "his" children. Furthermore, Hulbert and Dewey did not need to convince many people that their argument was sound; they only needed to persuade a single household patriarch among the dozen who sat in the jury box silently watching the proceedings. They aimed to make it appear reasonable to regard the accusation against Ephraim as a domestic insurrection—not so blatant, to be sure, as the South Carolina patricide against Thomas Maples that had just been reported in the *Pittsfield Sun*—but potentially just as lethal, and even more perverse, since the agent of death would be a state execution.

Their assault on Betsy's veracity had several parts. As gentlemen, no convention required Hulbert or Dewey to speak of a young, lower-class female with respect, but referring to Betsy as "a little ignorant girl" conveyed a measure of scorn intended to disparage her authority as a witness. By coupling the teenaged Betsy with the younger Ephraim, Jr., and speaking of "these little children," the defense attorneys hoped to undermine their testimony. To drive home the point, Hulbert and Dewey asked the members of the jury whether they would be confident entrusting a large sum of their own money to "these uneducated, these prejudiced children," then emphasized how much more doubtful it was to entrust them, through their testimony, with "the life of a human being."[93]

Moreover, Hulbert asserted that the entire substance of Betsy's story was "extremely unnatural and preposterous" and so should not be trusted. Shrewdly, he merged the unspeakable with the unlikely character of the charge so as to assert that it was not to be believed. Inviting jurors to accept his own assessment of Wheeler, Hulbert declared that "the prisoner appears to be a person of at least ordinary discernment," who would not be so foolish as to perform "such an abominable deed" under circumstances where he was so likely to be discovered. Nor was it reasonable to imagine, as Betsy claimed, that having "injured this girl" in so "shocking" a manner, Wheeler would then have returned the child to her mother.[94]

Betsy's entire story, Hulbert told the court, defied common sense. No man intent on raping his daughter would bring his son along on the outing, commit the act so close to a public road and near a neighbor's dwelling, and then send the abused, weeping child back to the wife with whom he was fighting. Moreover, even supposing a girl had just been raped by her father, surely she would not, having resisted going with him in the first place, then be willing to go with him afterwards. The behavior Betsy described was so contrary to both Ephraim's and Betsy's instincts of self-preservation—nature's first law—as to be incredible. The fact that she now claimed her father had committed a prior rape, Hulbert argued, made her story doubly suspicious. Having first, she said, concealed this rape, now she asked them all to believe her.[95] As Dewey pointed out, according to Hale and Blackstone, in order for a rape charge to be credible, the victim must attempt an outcry at the moment of the crime and then swiftly report the offense.[96] "This girl," they said, could not be believed.

In a final effort to buttress this point, Dewey called two witnesses. During Hulbert's argument Wheeler had realized that there were two men among the spectators who might help his cause. One was Michael Pepper, a laborer, husband of Hannah's sister, Releaf Odel; and the other was Hannah's older brother, Isaac Odel, a husbandman.[97] Evidently both of these uncles of Betsy's had said previously that she was untruthful. Though neither man may have wanted to assist Wheeler's defense, they had no choice. Wheeler was calling on them to help save his life, and his attorneys and the court compelled them to testify.

After Pepper was sworn in, Dewey asked him, "Do you know any thing about the general reputation of Betsy Wheeler for truth and veracity?" Here direct testimony of Betsy's readiness to tell lies, illustrated by specific examples, would have greatly strengthened Wheeler's defense. But Pepper's reply was vague: "She is not believed so well as some." Dewey did not push for an illustration of Betsy's falsehoods, evidently fearing that Pepper would have nothing to offer. Since Attorney General Sullivan chose not to cross-examine, Dewey went on to call Isaac Odel, who answered Dewey's question about Betsy's "veracity" in almost the same words as Pepper: "I believe she is not so generally believed as some." Once more Dewey did not follow up. But this time Sullivan did want to question the witness. He wanted to establish Odel's kinship to Betsy, so he asked, "Are you not uncle to this girl?" To which Odel replied, "I expect I am." Sullivan then asked him "how many years" Betsy had sustained her reputation as "not to be believed." Odel's response, like his earlier statement, was vague: "two or three."[98] Presumably Sullivan, recognizing that Odel had nothing concrete to report, wanted to underscore the haziness of the testimony against Betsy's truthfulness, as well as making explicit the possibility that Odel's kinship to Betsy may have given him an interest in the case, since Wheeler's conviction could saddle Odel with the financial responsibility of caring for his sister and her children.

At most the Pepper-Odel challenge to Betsy's truthfulness was inconclusive. Now the attorney general called back three of his witnesses to refute it entirely. He began with Odel's brother-in-law William Martin, "Uncle Bill," as Ephraim, Jr., had called him, the head of the household where Betsy lived. "Do you know anything against the general reputation of this girl for truth and veracity?" Sullivan asked. "I do not," Martin swore. Sullivan then put the same question to Dr. Asahel Wright and Justice of the Peace Robert Walker, who reported that they, too, had "heard nothing" against Betsy's reputation.[99] The prosecutor could not prove that Betsy's story was true, but he could defend her reputation to the extent that the positive assertions he drew out of Martin, Wright, and Walker outweighed the doubts raised by Pepper and Odel.

Wheeler's defenders, however, did not concede defeat. Instead Hulbert and Dewey launched an attack in which they accused Wheeler's wife, Hannah, as the true author of the false charge of rape. Drawing on common stereotypes of women, they claimed that Hannah's lies came naturally to a mother who had been cast aside by her husband and was about to be deprived of her children. Though there was no mention of Hannah in the indictment, nor could she testify in court, the defense attorneys evoked her presence. To her they would attribute the motives of revenge and personal advantage required by the Hale defense.

The portrait of Hannah Wheeler they painted was not a hardened, vicious schemer, but a vulnerable, desperate mother, impulsively driven to conspiracy by accumulated grievances and by Wheeler's immediate plan to take away their children. In Hulbert's version of events, when Betsy and Ephraim, Jr., returned home on June 8, they "must have" told their mother of their father's order to come to him again permanently. Here was the climax of the defense scenario: "It was at that moment that, alarmed with the fear of being separated from these children; struck with horror that a beloved infant would be torn from her arms, and fired with indignation at the prisoner, she resolved to sacrifice a man whom she hated and abhorred, to secure to herself these objects of her fond affection! It was then that she fabricated this cruel accusation!"[100] Inviting the jurors to deduce Hannah's motives from the common understanding of maternal instinct and female sentiment, Hulbert replaced Betsy with Hannah as Ephraim's false accuser, implying that the case was really a domestic relations conflict, not a capital trial for rape.

To buttress this construction of events Hulbert elaborated on his stereotype of female psychology: "the female heart is, generally, the sanctuary of truth, innocence, and love"—but not always. The relations between men and women prompted powerful passions, and when women's "affections have been engaged, and warmly placed on any one of our sex, and those affections have afterwards . . . been chilled and destroyed, the disgust, the resentment, the spirit of revenge which succeed, are stronger, and more implacable than can be found in our [male] sex." According to Hulbert, women's nature joined to the testimony of family conflict explained Hannah's motives. Betsy and Ephraim, Jr., who felt a "strong affection and partiality" for their mother and "dread" of their father, were merely her instruments when "the last spark of affection for her husband had long been extinguished in her heart, and the flames of malice and revenge were burning in its place!" The entire case against Wheeler rested on noth-

ing more than the "unnatural," uncorroborated story of "a little ignorant girl" that had been invented by her mother so as to end her abusive marriage and gain custody of the children.[101]

Notwithstanding all they had said to raise reasonable doubts in the
jurors' minds, however, the defense did not insist on an acquittal for
their client. While they emphatically denied that there had been any
sexual connection between Ephraim Wheeler and his daughter on
June 8, they invited the jury to consider the lesser, noncapital charge
of incest. If any fragment of Betsy's story was not invented, it was her
admission of prior sexual encounters with her father, encounters that
she had neither vigorously resisted nor reported. If the jury believed
this part of Betsy's testimony, Dewey explained, Wheeler was guilty
of "a crime of a different nature . . . a horrible crime, yet if committed
without force and violence and not against her will," not the capital
crime of rape.[102] Just as Hulbert had gotten Uriel Gleazen off two
years before with a conviction of manslaughter rather than murder,
now the defense hoped that an uncertain or divided jury might prefer
to convict their client of incest. Only the day before eight of these ·
very same jurors had made a similar judgment on Abner Durwin,
convicting the Pittsfield laborer of lewd and lascivious conduct rather
than attempted rape and assault on his daughter.

Hulbert and Dewey concluded their defense on a more positive,
judicious note. Recognizing the jury's duty, they acknowledged that if
the jury found the evidence "irresistible" they must convict. But,
Dewey assured the jurors, if they felt any "doubts arising from reasonable grounds," he believed they would "cheerfully acquit" the
prisoner.[103]

James Sullivan's awareness that the state could lose a conviction
owing to the jury's reluctance to impose the death penalty gave his
closing statement unusual breadth and power. In a county and at
a moment when reformers challenged the death penalty, Sullivan

pressed the case for conviction based on principles of law and order, and on the evidence of the trial. He began by admonishing the "Gentlemen of the Jury" to dismiss the defense's invitation to consider convicting Ephraim Wheeler of a lesser charge. No, the attorney general declared, "this cause admits of no different degrees of guilt; you are obliged, on your oaths, to acquit the prisoner entirely, or to find him guilty of the crime, with which he is charged in the indictment."[104] Technically, Sullivan was correct; but in actual practice juries were not bound by indictments, and they exercised a significant measure of discretion in criminal cases.[105] Sullivan would have to convince them that Wheeler had committed the crime of rape.

Before considering the evidence, however, the attorney general chose to reinforce the legitimacy of the death penalty by reviewing its relationship to mercy, the pardoning power, and justice itself. It was crucial, Sullivan argued, that jurors and society maintain a correct understanding of that "charming word" mercy, lest they extend mercy so promiscuously as to undermine all distinctions between virtue and vice. Mercy must not be used to escape the "pain and uneasiness" that suffering, whether just or unjust, naturally evoked. Duty and justice must be our guides. Bringing the jurors and the whole assembly of officials and spectators face-to-face with "the awful spectacle of one near the gibbet, ready to be launched into the unknown world," Sullivan asked, "what ought to be our wish, and our prayer?" His answer was orthodox, official: we should wish this execution to deter all others, so "that this may be the last victim to the depravity of morals which has brought him to the fatal tree." What we must not wish is the power to suspend the laws or to "snatch" the prisoner "from the hand of justice." To save him from suffering would not be mercy but sedition, and would destroy public justice.[106]

These same principles, Sullivan explained, applied to the governor's power to pardon, which must interfere with neither the laws nor the processes of justice. A pardon was legitimate only to protect the innocent. The existence of the pardoning power should no more encourage us to convict than our "pity" or objection to a law's severity should encourage us to acquit. To Sullivan, shaped by the founding experience of the republic and by challenges to its authority, jurors and all public officials were agents of the Massachusetts constitution, the social compact that stood as a bulwark against both arbitrary rule and disorder.[107]

There is no record of what the jurors were thinking as they took in the Boston gentleman's civics lesson. But it had been a long day. Already it was past six o'clock. Sullivan knew that his own closing statement could take an hour, and that the judges' summaries to follow might last as much as two hours beyond that. In the twilight of the cloudy afternoon, Sullivan felt the jurors' attention wandering, and he apologized for his "more tedious than entertaining" remarks. Now he returned "to the issue before us": Wheeler's innocence or guilt.[108]

The attorney general built his argument around Betsy Wheeler's veracity. Though this task would have been easier with physical evidence of a rape, Sullivan claimed there was sufficient corroboration of her surrounding account to win conviction. "The essential facts which constitute this crime must always depend, for proof," he argued, "on the testimony of the person injured." There was no need for two witnesses to the crime of rape, and in the present case "corroborating evidence" pointed to the prisoner's guilt. It was true that part of the evidence came from an underage boy, but the court had judged him competent. Whereas Hulbert and Dewey had described him as "uneducated," "prejudiced," and raised in "ignorance," Sullivan contended that Ephraim, Jr., was "a lad of good capacity" and unexpected "intelligence." The boy had shown that he understood the obligation of an oath and God's future rewards and punishments. "Many grown persons in this audience," Sullivan declared, could have done no better. The boy's simple narrative of what he had seen and heard, which did not include knowledge of any rape, had the ring of truth. Surely, if his story had been "fabricated," he would have reported that he had followed his sister and his father far enough into the wood to have witnessed the assault just as Betsy described it. Ephraim, Jr., was telling the truth; and there was no innocent explanation for what he had seen—a father taking his daughter alone into the woods for over half an hour, returning without avens-root and with the girl in evident distress, showing marks of abuse on her face.[109] Betsy's testimony concerning the whole day of June 8—excepting only the time spent alone with the prisoner in the woods—was confirmed not only by her brother's report, but by the testimony of William Martin, Eunice Hart, and (regarding Betsy's visible injuries) Robert Walker.

The only aspect of Betsy's testimony that possessed no corroboration was her report of the two prior sexual advances—one a rape. Although this evidence did not relate to the indictment and so could have been excluded from the trial, Sullivan had introduced it—at Hulbert's and Dewey's request, he said—so as to give the defense "every legal advantage." They had used this testimony to try to destroy Betsy's credibility owing to her failure to make a loud outcry and report the attempts. But Sullivan argued that her silence was based not on complicity, but fear, and so did not damage her credibility.[110] His narrative of Betsy's family situation did not rely on a simple calculus of self-interest, but on a deeper realization of conflicting motives.

Let the jurors consider, he said, that "one cannot complain unless there is somebody to complain to," and that Betsy, only twelve years old at the time of her father's first two assaults, was "dependent on the person who had injured her for her being and support." Wheeler had threatened her with "the most cruel death"; and from Martin's report it was clear that Wheeler was "terrible to his family" and that Hannah could not protect her. According to Sullivan's interpretation, after the assault of June 8 Betsy recognized that if she were forced to go with her father he "would prostitute her to his brutal lust when he pleased." That was why she had said she would "as lieve die one way as another." She had told her mother in the hope of escaping his grasp. The call to Justice Walker was no domestic insurrection; it was a cry for protection only. Fear accounted for Betsy's behavior in all three episodes; and so, according to the rules of law cited by the defense, Sullivan asserted, her credibility remained intact.[111]

To seal the case for Betsy's truthfulness, Sullivan dismissed the defense's references to her as a "little girl" too young to exercise discretion. According to Massachusetts law, he noted, a ten-year-old girl was "competent to consent to an intercourse with the other sex," girls of twelve years could marry, and there were even "women" of thirteen and fourteen years who were mothers and mistresses of households. Betsy was sufficiently mature to be reliable, and she did not offer her testimony as "one who has been taught her tale" in pursuit of revenge, but with "great reserve and reluctance." As to her uncle Isaac Odel's testimony, Sullivan suggested that since Betsy had lived in Odel's household for over a month after her father's arrest, if she were inclined to tell lies he could have convinced her to deny her story or to so alter it as to have destroyed its credibility.[112] But she held to the same testimony under all circumstances from June 8 onward—surely, Sullivan claimed, an indication of her integrity.

Four more issues that the defense had raised remained for Sullivan to address, but because he was concerned that he would "weary the patience" of the jury he would be brief. First, there was the suggestion that the actual crime had been incest, not rape. Sullivan reminded the jurors that the only evidence of any sexual connection came from Betsy, and if they did not believe her there was no reason to convict

Wheeler of anything—they should acquit. But if they believed Betsy, they must agree that the crime was rape. For if Betsy had consented she would not have asked permission for her brother to come into the woods, and she would not have come out crying, with "bruises on her face" and "marks of violence on her throat." That she returned home complaining to her brother and that she later tearfully reported her injuries to her mother were additional circumstances contradicting consent. Second, in response to Hulbert's argument that the crime site was unsuitable, Sullivan answered that Dr. Wright had viewed it and sworn otherwise. But the point was immaterial, since Wheeler's crime was not guided by caution or prudence but by "the rage of lust," and so might have been committed anywhere.[113]

Next, the attorney general took up Hulbert and Dewey's rival narrative of Hannah Wheeler's conspiracy to liberate herself and her children from a hateful, violent husband and father by inventing the rape story and instructing Betsy and Ephraim, Jr., to testify falsely. According to law, he explained, the burden of proof for this scenario lay with the defense, and there was no evidence in the record to support it. Certainly it was true that a woman could be so "filled with malice or resentment" as to murder her husband, but there was no evidence that Hannah Wheeler felt such rage or acted on it—even when Wheeler attacked her with a bayonet. Hannah's sole action that supported the defense's narrative was her decision to send for Justice Walker. But what her motives may have been was a matter of pure conjecture; and if she felt jealousy or vengeful emotions after learning of "the brutal injury" to her daughter because "her husband had laid" with her, that did not exonerate Wheeler from the charge against him. Since Hannah was "a poor, ignorant woman" there was no reason to believe she knew Ephraim's conviction might lead to his death. Sullivan maintained it was just as likely that she hoped only to "deliver the daughter from the power of her father, and seperate [sic] herself from a cruel and dangerous husband."[114]

The idea that Hannah invented the rape story and then instructed Betsy and Ephraim, Jr., in their differing testimonies so as to fit the facts was preposterous. To have fabricated and executed such a scheme, one that flawlessly mixed "the natural simplicity of truth" with perjurious inventions, would have demanded exceptional "ability," "artifice," and "more adroitness than the greatest lawyer." And even if that could be done, the defense could not deny that Betsy's tears and bruises had come from her father. If the jury believed "the violence offered induced her, finally, to consent," Sullivan emphasized that the act was "no less a rape than if she had resisted to the last moment."[115]

One point only of the defense argument remained to be answered: Hulbert's initial claim that the alleged deed was so atrocious and unnatural that Betsy's accusation was incredible. Sullivan dispatched this claim quickly. If "the sexual connection between a father and a daughter" was not part of human nature, then God would have had no need to prohibit "the incestuous intercourse," nor would states have enacted laws against it. Alluding perhaps to the previous day's Abner Durwin trial or to the conviction eight years earlier of Lenox yeoman Job Northrup for lewd and lascivious conduct with his daughter, Sullivan reminded everyone that "there have been convictions in this court, of fathers and daughters, for lascivious cohabitation." True, neither Durwin nor Northrup had been charged with actually raping their daughters, but their conduct had violated the community's moral and legal codes. Addressing the entire court and the spectators outside, the attorney general proclaimed the fundamental social principles that elevated the Wheeler case to high public significance: "the rage of habitual lust knows no boundaries, and the indulgence of the most depraved passions . . . can be checked by public opinion only." "Civil society," Sullivan asserted, was essential to the existence of public opinion; and the just execution of the law was necessary to make public opinion effective.[116] Law and morality relied for their survival on the opinions of Berkshire people. The Supreme Judicial Court's work in enforcing the law against Wheeler's crime was more than a matter of justice for Betsy; it was crucial for maintaining the blessings of civil society among Berkshire's thirty-four thousand people, both churched and unchurched.

Sullivan closed by addressing the jury directly. Now, he said, they possessed "the evidence, and the arguments for and against the prisoner." Praising his adversaries at the bar, Sullivan declared he was "happy" that Hulbert and Dewey had done everything possible for the prisoner. If he himself had erred in any way, the judges would correct him in their summaries of the case. Turning to the prisoner, perhaps, Sullivan apologized if anything he had said was "coloured with severity," for those were not "the feelings of my heart." Alluding once more to the dreaded death penalty, he proclaimed, "I seek the blood of no man." He had acted according to his official obligation to preserve and defend "the morals, and the safety of my fellow-citizens."[117]

Sullivan had been on his feet, gesturing, turning, raising his voice with practiced eloquence for nearly an hour. Now, with his characteristic limp, he returned to his seat at the prosecutor's table as judges Strong, Sedgwick, and Sewall took over. Each would take about thirty minutes to summarize the key points of the case, instructing the jurors on the law as it related to the evidence and the arguments before them. But Heman Willard did not report all of their statements in his trial report, since, he said, "there was but one opinion," and to have printed all three summaries would have added too many pages to his publication. The summation he selected to represent the judges' statements was that of his Federalist patron and Stockbridge neighbor, Theodore Sedgwick, who evidently supplied the printer with his notes.[118]

Following courtroom etiquette, the jurors rose as Judge Sedgwick stood to address them. But acknowledging their "fatigue"—it was now past eight o'clock in the evening—he asked them to be seated. The subject of their proceedings, he said, was indeed so "unnatural" as to "excite passion and agitate our feelings" that the task of the jurors, to render a judgment based on "cool and dispassionate" reason, was especially difficult. Still, he admonished, they must "subdue every sentiment" so as to guard against a verdict shaped by "indignation at the atrocity" of the alleged crime or influenced by compassion for the prisoner's "unhappy situation." Their duty was unavoidably "painful," and he advised jurors that only the "consciousness" that they had performed their duty with "integrity" could ease their minds. Like Sullivan, he wanted to acknowledge openly the propriety of their feelings, whether aversion, hatred, and revenge or sympathy for a defeated fellow man whose wife and children were now turned against him. By recognizing the jurors' emotions, Sedgwick hoped they could discipline themselves to be ruled by reason. He went on to ennoble their duty by praising the conduct of the trial and Massachusetts' criminal procedure, which was so protective of innocence "that our hearts should be impressed with gratitude for the blessings, derived from the government, which we enjoy."[119] If the jurors should decide to convict Wheeler, no one should doubt the justice of the proceedings or their verdict.

Concerning this critical judgment they were poised to render, Sedgwick reiterated the distinction between "reasonable doubt" and "any doubts . . . possible for the mind to conceive." The human condition was such that "certainty is almost never to be obtained," so in criminal cases, especially this one, we must assess "human testimony." This could, of course, always be false; and yet for society to operate we must place "a reasonable confidence" in such testimony. Since the line between doubt and confidence was impossible to define, it was up to the jury to make a judgment. Sedgwick went on to note key points in the testimony and to point out that Wheeler's conviction turned on the credibility of "the girl." Like his colleagues on the bench, Sedgwick leaned in favor of the prosecution, echoing Sullivan's assertion that, notwithstanding the defense arguments to the contrary, the "uncorroborated testimony" of a single victim could be valid in a case like this. Sedgwick further asserted that because of the "impossibility" of a motive for a "false charge" by the victim and the "strong motives" for a victim to "conceal" the crime, the woman's oath was "irresistible" for him.[120] Thinking perhaps not only of poor Betsy Wheeler who was before them in the courtroom, but also of his own teenaged daughter, Catharine, and her sense of privacy and self-respect, he could not imagine that any girl or woman would falsely swear to an episode that was so profoundly embarrassing, degrading, and destructive of her family.

On only a single point did Sedgwick reinforce the defense: Justice Walker's failure to procure an impartial physical examination of Betsy Wheeler on June 8. Though Walker had initially conducted the case "with great prudence and discretion, . . . he should have procured some reputable matron who might have been a witness to inspect such parts of the girl's body as it was not decent for him to view." Hannah Wheeler's statement concerning the matter was only "hearsay," and her direct testimony was inadmissible anyway, since she was "the prisoner's wife."[121]

With regard to the defense argument that Betsy might have consented to relations with her father, Sedgwick followed Sullivan's arguments almost verbatim; but he was even more dismissive than the prosecutor. Betsy's reluctance, her tears, her wounds, could not indicate consent. Indeed it was absurd to imagine that having engaged in "a voluntary incestuous intercourse" she would then reveal it to her mother and follow up with the present prosecution, which could lead to the death of her supposedly voluntarily chosen partner. Such a defense defied all logic and, the judge told the jury, "you will probably not dwell long on this point."[122]

Judge Sedgwick was more respectful of Hulbert's and Dewey's challenges to the reasonableness of the prosecution's scenario, and addressed it point by point. In one case he seemed to agree that Betsy's willingness to go with her father afterward, if he had just assaulted her, was, if not "incredible" as the defense claimed, then certainly "difficult to account for." Yet Sedgwick resolved this contradiction in the prosecution's favor by observing that "if her story is true" concerning the assault, then "the agitation of her mind would prevent all cool and temperate reflection" and would thus account for her behavior.[123]

As to Betsy's long silence concerning the first two attempts on her chastity, Sedgwick again outdid Sullivan. That she only reported them now was not a measure of her deceitfulness but of her "integrity." As to her previous concealment, Judge Sedgwick explained that in addition to the "threatenings" of her father—a fully sufficient reason for silence—she must have "felt an utter aversion for declaring circumstances so execrable, so horrible, so disgusting." Whatever feelings Betsy may have experienced, these clearly were Sedgwick's reactions to Wheeler's incestuous assaults. Here his own speech, not the prosecutor's, undercut his earlier admonitions to the jurors on behalf of reasoned detachment and his final reminders to weigh "the whole . . . cooly and dispassionately."[124] Sedgwick's instructions to the jury rhetorically paid homage to evenhanded objectivity. But no one who heard his summary could doubt how the judge would cast his vote if he were seated not on the bench but in the jury box.

When Judge Sedgwick had finished, a few minutes before nine o'clock, Judge Strong adjourned the court until ten, initially allowing the jurors an hour to decide Ephraim Wheeler's fate. Two officers, sworn to "take charge of the Jury," remained in their seats as the courtroom cleared so that the jurors could discuss the case in private. To hasten their decision-making, Massachusetts procedure forbade the jurymen from taking any refreshment during their deliberations.[125] When the courtroom again filled shortly before ten, they were ready. After Sheriff Larned brought Wheeler to the front of the courtroom to receive the verdict, Clerk Woodbridge called out the names of each juror and asked each one whether he had agreed on a verdict. Yes, they said. "What say you, gentlemen," Clerk Woodbridge asked, "do you find the prisoner at the bar guilty of the felony where of he stands indicted, or not guilty?" The jury's foreman, Elijah Gates, a Lenox yeoman and father of a grown daughter, announced: "Guilty of rape."[126] With that, Judge Strong adjourned until the following morning.

The judges, the jurors, the court officers, and the attorneys could now relax and take their rest. But Ephraim Wheeler could not have passed a good night. As he walked back to the jail with the deputies, the sky threatened rain. No moon, no stars, just the deputies' lanterns swinging in the dark as he retraced the ten-minute walk he had made early that morning, when he still hoped he would be freed. Now he had almost twelve hours until he was due back in court for sentencing—twelve hours to reflect on the trial and all the courtroom talk of the death penalty. Ephraim Wheeler returned to his bed in the Lenox jail with nearly seven hours of darkness stretching out before dawn. He was tired enough to sleep, but could he? Nearly twenty-five years before, feeling lonely and discouraged, he had weighed taking his own life.[127] Perhaps that would have been for the best. Even now he might seek to cheat the hangman by doing so. But as yet there had been no sentence; and no one in Berkshire had ever been hanged for rape.

When daylight dawned it was raining again. People crowded around as the deputies brought the prisoner back to the courthouse, and the room was full. The proceedings were ceremonious but simple. When the presiding judge, Simeon Strong, called the court to order Attorney General Sullivan rose to his feet and moved that the "sentence of death be pronounced against Ephraim Wheeler." Then Judge Strong stood to address the court. Most of his words were not recorded, but his judgment against Wheeler was evident in his assertion that the prisoner "had added a new crime to the catalogue of crimes."[128] Newspapers described Strong's remarks as "very solemn, impressive, and affecting."[129] And so they were, particularly for Ephraim Wheeler. For although he had sat "calmly" in silence the day before as the authorities disposed of his fate, now when he heard Strong declaring the "nature and enormity of his crime" and then pronouncing "the awful sentence of DEATH," Wheeler broke down: "he appeared much affected, and frequently shed tears."[130] Now that he was a condemned man, the deputies, "according to custom," placed his legs in irons.[131] Once more he would walk back to jail under cloudy skies, but this time in shackles and under sentence of death. For all Wheeler knew, the next time he walked out-of-doors, it would be to his execution.

CHAPTER THREE

The Daughter

Betsy Wheeler, was then called and sworn. She testified, that on the 8th of June last her father told her, that she and her brother Ephraim Wheeler must pack up their clothes and go with him to their uncle Isaac's in Cummington, about four and an half miles distant. She got onto the horse first, her brother rode behind her, and her father went on foot. After they had got about a mile from home, her father told her she must get off the horse, and go with him into the woods and get *avens-root:* she said she did not want to go—her father said she must: she asked if Ephraim might not go with them—he said no, he should stay and hold the horse. She went, and after they had got about ten or twelve rods [50–60 yards] into the woods, he told her to lie down—she said she did not want to; he said he would kill her if she did not, she still refused; he then took hold of her and threw her on the ground. *(A particular description of the scene that followed is too indelicate and too shocking to the feelings of modesty to be detailed. It will be sufficient only to observe, that every act necessary to complete the crime of RAPE, was directly and positively sworn to.)* She further testified, that she attempted to scream, that he struck her two or three times on her head, pinched her throat, and held her mouth so that she could not make much noise.

Report of the Trial of Ephraim Wheeler. . . . (1805)

etsy Wheeler woke up on an unseasonably cool, rainy morning, Saturday, June 8, 1805.[1] As she rose to go about her chores, helping her mother with breakfast and her baby sister, Betsy could have had no idea that this would be the most fateful day of her thirteen-year life. She could not know that before sundown her words—her accusation—would set the state against her father and put his life in peril. Nothing in Betsy's short life had prepared her for such an awesome exercise of power. Three months later, after she had had time to think over the events of that day, she would stand up in front of hundreds of men before the Supreme Judicial Court and tell what she remembered. That day, Friday, September 13, would also be critical for Betsy and her family. But to Betsy it was less crucial than June 8, the day when her father had plunged her into a crisis by forcing her to make a terrifying choice. On that day she defied Ephraim Wheeler's expectations; Betsy stood up for herself.

How it came to that cannot be established with certainty. Betsy kept no diary during the months leading up to the crisis, nor is there any body of her letters surrounding these events. Indeed, scarcely any papers of poor girls survive from this period. Moreover, since Betsy could not sign her name, she could not have left any written record to document her experiences.[2] Still, we are not wholly without resources for constructing an account of her life and addressing the key questions raised by her charges against her father. The trial record, her father's narrative, and scraps of personal and family history in public records all supply clues. When combined with what is generally known of childhood in the early republic, we can sketch Betsy Wheeler—the eldest child in a poor, mixed-race family that lived near the bottom of Yankee rural society and economy.

We know, for example, that Betsy, who was named for her mother's mother, was the Wheelers' first child, born in January 1792, probably at her maternal grandfather's house in the town of Worthington, which lay just east of Berkshire County, high among the hills at the western border of Hampshire.[3] We also know that her family moved frequently. Unlike the majority of local girls her age, the daughters of yeoman farmers, Betsy's father did not own land, and the lives of her parents and mixed-race kin were not woven into the fabric of community civic, religious, and commercial life as a by-product of settled residence and social standing. While Betsy was still an infant in 1793 her parents separated, and her father, as well as her mother's father and brother, were "warned out" of Cummington, the Hampshire hill town that lay just north of Worthington. This did not mean that the Wheelers and the Odels were required to leave the township, but "warning out" put them on notice that town officials had recorded their names as outsiders so that a future court could not require the town to provide them with welfare assistance. Warning out was often a sign that the individuals in question were poor: in making this designation the selectmen who administered town affairs had identified a family head and its members as potential claimants for support.[4]

In that same year, when she was little more than a year old, Betsy first became an older sister, a role that over time would grow into an important part of her identity. But in this year of hand-to-mouth poverty, when Betsy's mother, Hannah, pregnant again, took Betsy and left Ephraim for the first time, Betsy must have suffered owing to her parents' conflict and the strains her mother faced. The newborn sibling, born when Betsy herself was still a baby, died before Betsy's second birthday. Though the death of such an infant only "a few months old" was almost an ordinary event in families of all ranks in the 1790s, parents still grieved and siblings, too, were affected. Sheriff Larned had lost his first two baby Rebekahs this way, and John Hulbert his little Frederick at the age of thirteen months and nine days.[5] The fact that the Wheeler child's name, sex, and birthdate are nowhere recorded does not set the Wheelers apart either, although it was more common for the marriages and deaths of poor transients to pass without official notice.[6] But it would be wrong to conclude from the absence of records that the life and death of this infant were insignificant for the Wheeler family. To Hannah Wheeler, the loss of this nursing child may have relieved her of a burden, but it must also have been painful; and the infant's death probably strengthened the attachment between her and Betsy, as they struggled to make their way without Ephraim.

We have no record of how Hannah supported herself and Betsy in late 1793 and on through 1794 and into 1795; but, judging from the evidence of later years, Hannah probably earned food, shelter, and a few pounds annually for herself and Betsy by working as a domestic on a yeoman farm. Most likely she lived in, but she may have gone to live with relatives and earned her way by day labor. Womanly skills—preparing food, spinning and sewing, operating a kitchen garden and a family dairy, as well as caring for infirm and elderly householders—were always in demand, and Hannah, then in her early thirties, would have learned them at home or from experienced women in the households where she had worked.[7] That was the custom. Betsy, who went from being a toddler to a little girl who could speak and manage small chores, such as feeding chickens, sorting grains and beans, and fetching whatever was out of reach, formed her first sense of herself at her mother's elbow. Since her mother was an employee in another's household, Betsy would have early learned to do as she was told, sharing in her mother's experience and seeing that obedience was not only part of a girl's life, but part of a woman's too.

In 1795, when Betsy was three years old, her parents reunited, but not in a household of their own. They lived briefly at Hannah's brother Isaac Odel's house, a small dwelling at the corner of the Cummington township. Odel's property, which he had purchased two years before, was located on a twenty-four-acre parcel of land that straddled the Hampshire-Berkshire County boundary, with four acres (including the house) in Cummington and twenty acres in Partridge-field (later Peru). This location, literally on the outskirts of two townships and two counties, suggests social isolation. Though Odel, identified as "negro" in the 1800 census, paid taxes to Cummington (he was in the poorest 5 percent of taxpayers), he was not part of the Cummington community, and the only way for him to reach the village was by a circuitous route through the town of Worthington.[8] The Wheelers' and the Odels' only community, it appears, was supplied by their mixed-race kinship connections.

Before Betsy's fourth birthday she came to learn that her kinship community was not necessarily loving and protective. After only a short period together at Odel's, her parents had a falling out, and Hannah once more left Ephraim, taking Betsy with her. The separation was especially antagonistic this time, and involved Wheeler's failure to pay his debts. According to Ephraim, Bill Martin—the same man who would later testify against Ephraim at his trial—and Samuel Peters attacked Ephraim on the road in front of Odel's house, dragging him from his horse and beating him. Ephraim never explained the reason for the attack, but since he had a record of "hard drinking and quarrelling" as well as failing to keep his agreements, Martin and Peters were probably giving Wheeler a taste of vigilante justice. Afterward, when Ephraim complained of the assault to a justice of the peace, his attackers were punished lightly with fines. Ephraim believed his wife, Hannah, was behind the attack, plotting with Martin and Peters to injure him.[9] Though Betsy was still a little girl, she was old enough to be frightened by the grownups' fighting, and to feel her own vulnerability.

After this family fracas Hannah took Betsy, and once more they made their way on their own. But this time their separation from Ephraim was brief. Ephraim reported that at the end of 1795 or early in 1796 they all reunited and went to Williamstown to live on the farm of an old Revolutionary war veteran, Captain Absalom Blair. As live-in help the Wheelers enjoyed more security and stability than before. Moreover their domestic employment required that they maintain peace. Hannah and Ephraim's reunion at Captain Blair's was marked by the birth of a boy in October 1796. The decision to name the baby Ephraim, Jr., suggests his father's patriarchal yearnings.[10]

At this point Betsy, then almost five years old, became her mother's full-time assistant. Though she had grown to an age when most families sent girls to a district school or to a little home school run by a neighbor-woman in order to learn both reading and writing, poor serving children like Betsy might be kept home to do chores, and so remain illiterate.[11] Still, compared with the insecurity and turmoil she had already experienced, even if Betsy did not attend school she must have found her role in the Blair household, helping to tend her brother so that her mother could do her work, rewarding. But it came at the cost not only of her education, but also of forming relationships outside her family. Set apart from most other youngsters, Betsy's only opportunities to engage with them came when the farmer who employed the Wheelers had children. But whereas those children went to school and possessed stable roots in the community, Betsy was an outsider, always about to move on. The social isolation of her parents, starting with their mixed-race marriage and reinforced by their ongoing transiency and poverty, was becoming central to Betsy's own identity.

Life in the Blair household gave Betsy a taste of stability, but it did not last. After a year or so the Wheelers moved again, first briefly back with the Odels in Cummington and then across the Berkshire

County line to Partridgefield, where Hannah's sister Releaf and her husband, Michael Pepper, also settled. Here in 1797 Ephraim was able to buy an interest in a tract of land. Though his only collateral was his labor, that was sufficient for the remote, windswept, sloping piece of woods he obtained.[12] Either Ephraim Wheeler would succeed in making his payments by selling timber, firewood, and charcoal, or he would default—leaving behind as compensation the labor he had invested in clearing the land. For Betsy the move to Partridgefield when she was five years old might have meant less stability and security than she had enjoyed in the Blair household, and more conflict between her parents.

Yet in some respects this was a hopeful period for the Wheelers. Now, for the first time, they had the prospect of rising into the yeomanry with a farm of their own. For now they were their own bosses, and whatever their tensions, they had to work together. Betsy was most likely in charge of little Ephraim while her parents cleared land and constructed a house, and the little boy would have learned to walk and to talk while she was tending him on their Partridgefield farm. As her mother's deputy, Betsy was a key part of her family's economic adventure. But making a go of it without capital in the Berkshire uplands was nearly impossible, even for the most skilled, disciplined, and robust. To succeed, everything had to be just right, not only woodland and farm management, but seasonal weather, terms of credit, and market prices.[13] That the Wheelers failed was not remarkable. What is impressive is that they persisted beyond the first year.

But after two years of struggle Wheeler acknowledged defeat. He sold his meager interest in the Partridgefield property in 1799 and, as hired help, moved his family into the household of a more prosperous Partridgefield farmer, George Pierce. Betsy, now almost eight years old, may have welcomed the move, since it brought her and her family back into a more regulated and less isolated social environment where her parents would have to live in peace, if not in harmony. The fact that Mr. and Mrs. Pierce had a boy and girl under the age of ten meant that when Betsy was not working she and her little brother had playmates.[14] But from then on the Wheelers moved at least once annually: to Jonathan Ward's in Buckland, to Joseph Ripley's in Windsor, and to John Fobes's and to the Widow Converse's, also in Windsor. Betsy must have become increasingly conscious that her family was set apart. This kind of transient life was the ordinary experience of only the poorest agricultural workers, those who owned no land. Though such workers were more common in long-settled regions of New England, they could be found in every county, even Berkshire, where families usually either settled or moved on to frontier New York or Vermont.[15] For Betsy, who was growing up knowing that other children—such as the Pierces, the Wards, the Ripleys, the Fobeses—lived in settled homes and went to school several months a year, her consciousness of being an outsider must have strengthened with each passing season.

How Betsy explained her situation to herself is a matter of conjecture. She may, like many children, have considered her parents' conflicts as exceptional, and the reason for her transient life; or she may have linked her condition to her family's poverty. As the eldest child, she could also have imagined that some personal defect of her own was to blame. But though she and her mother appeared white, as she matured it is likely that she became increasingly conscious of her mixed racial lineage and of the stigma connected to black ancestry. Racism was not particularly intense in Massachusetts—the first state to abolish slavery—but black-white intermarriage was illegal and the common belief that blacks were morally and mentally inferior was pervasive, so Betsy could not have escaped being touched by such prejudice as she grew up among white Yankee families in Partridgefield, Buckland, Cummington, and Windsor. Though the Wheelers appeared as white as most Yankees, their continuing relationships with their Odel relatives, some of whom displayed black ancestry, made race mixture part of her outsider's identity.[16]

During these years, around 1800, Betsy gained another sibling to look after, when Hannah bore her fourth child. Like the infant who died in 1793, almost nothing is known of this child—including its name and sex—because it too died young. But the cause of the baby's death is recorded: the "child was scalded to death" in a household accident in 1803.[17] For ten-year-old Betsy this must have been a deeply traumatic event, even though such household calamities were by no means rare. Whether or not Betsy felt any personal responsibility for the accident that claimed the baby's life, this sudden death was a vivid reminder of mortality that most likely drew surviving family members closer together and reinforced the bond between Betsy and her mother.

About this time or soon thereafter, Hannah gave birth again, to a little girl, her fifth child with Ephraim.[18] For Betsy as for her mother the new baby might have provided some diversion from all the strains in the family; but Betsy must have seen her mother's trials as sobering previews of her own approaching womanhood. In 1804, as the time of Betsy's sexual maturity drew closer—though still two or three years away—Betsy's strongest bond was with the mother from whom she had never been separated, and with whom she had shared the deaths of two babies and a dozen or so changes in residence.[19]

The historical record does not provide much evidence for assessing how Betsy felt about her father or the nature of their attachment before his sexual assaults began in 1804. Her first real memories of Ephraim probably dated back to 1796, her fifth year, when she and her mother had resumed living with him at the Blair homestead in Williamstown. In spite of his drinking, his fights with her mother, and his occasional violence, an attachment to her father was virtually inevitable for Betsy. The fact that as an eight-year-old Ephraim, Jr., referred to him as "Daddy" suggests that Betsy, too, had seen him as her "daddy" when she was young.[20] It is also significant that during Ephraim's first sexual advance toward Betsy, when the girl was twelve, he had sought to use gifts to ingratiate himself with her; that he had accepted her rebuff, at least temporarily, is a further indication of complexity in Betsy's relationship with her father. Had Betsy accepted his gift in exchange for sex, she would have simultaneously ruptured her allegiance to her mother and created a secret bond with her father. When Betsy testified about this episode in court she asserted that the notion of yielding to him voluntarily was unthinkable; but if that first attempt by her father had come in the context of some serious disagreement between Betsy and her mother, to Ephraim, at least, it might have seemed plausible that she would consent. That he never again tried to purchase her compliance, but resorted instead to commands, threats, and violence, shows that Betsy's initial rebuff must have been definite. Although Betsy, like all daughters, had learned to obey her father, by her thirteenth year she also possessed a sufficient sense of herself to draw a boundary and to assert her own will.[21]

Well before her thirteenth birthday in 1805, it seems, Betsy had learned to keep her head down in the midst of family discord; and if, as two of her uncles testified, she did not always tell the whole truth, we should not be surprised. Betsy had been living in a family where selective concealment must have been a strategy for maintaining peace. Her father, after all, had threatened to kill her if she told the truth. Though Betsy was by no means sophisticated or worldly, having spent her entire life as an unlettered serving girl within twenty miles of her birthplace, she had learned key survival skills.[22]

It is for that reason, in part, that Betsy's charge of rape against her father was and is so astonishing. The usual path for survival was evasion or secrecy, not confrontation—especially for someone as lowly as a serving girl in early America's patriarchal world. Fifteen years earlier, in New Hampshire, when Phebe Bailey, daughter of respectable Yankees, had been seduced into a sixteen-month incestuous relationship with her father, Asa Bailey, both Phebe and her mother had hidden the truth from themselves for months and from the world for years.[23] This was an era when a Maine midwife "Begd" one of her adult patients, a clergyman's wife and rape victim, "never to mentin it to any other person" because of the almost certain ruin she would suffer. Indeed the victim herself "believed it was best for her to keep her troubles to her Selfe."[24] To pursue a charge of rape was rightly understood to be just as dangerous for the victim as the perpetrator, perhaps more so because, as Sir Matthew Hale had stated, the crime was "hard to be proved."[25] Whatever the outcome of the court proceedings, most women were subjected to a further trial in the court of community opinion, where humiliation and ostracism were often meted out to the victim.[26] Both in Britain and America these realities were sometimes acknowledged as the reason that rape prosecutions and convictions were so much less common than those for murder.

But if it was exceptional for a woman to accuse a man of rape, it was virtually unheard of for a daughter to pursue such a charge against her father. We have found only one other example in New England between the era of settlement and the Civil War—an eleven-year-old Maine girl who charged her father in 1802—but the case never came to trial because the child evidently retracted her accusation.[27] That was why so learned and experienced a judge as Simeon Strong declared at Wheeler's sentencing that the prisoner had "added a new crime to the catalogue of crimes" and Heman Willard, the printer of the trial report, could claim that "this is, probably, the only instance of the kind that has ever occurred since the world began."[28] This was hyperbole, of course; but at one level, that of the printed record, Willard's perception of the rarity of a father's rape of his daughter was close to being accurate. No one knows exactly how many such cases there had been in life or in judicial proceedings during past centuries, but incest cases went unpublished in the printed annals of American crime up through 1805. Wheeler's was the sole case of father-daughter rape among dozens of rapes and scores of murders. And in the published record of Britain, which included hundreds more capital cases, there was only a single father-daughter rape, that committed by Job Wells, a laborer who was convicted and executed for the rape of his sixteen-year-old daughter in Hertford-shire in 1753.[29]

But although rape charges against fathers were exceedingly rare, this is not to suggest that father-daughter sexual relations were unknown. In Lenox alone, within the decade Job Northrup had been charged with incest and Abner Durwin with the attempted rape of his daughter. Though both men had been acquitted of these charges, as James Sullivan argued in court, lawmakers had enacted statutes against these crimes because they were real.[30] Moreover, no one assumed that daughters initiated these couplings, so although such connections may not have been forcible in a legal sense, they were seldom voluntary either. Up and down the social spectrum unmarried daughters had been the legal dependents of their fathers for centuries, and they were all taught to believe that submission to superiors was a virtue. In situations where custom and habit dictated obedience—as seems to have been true for Phebe Bailey's relationship with her father, Asa—violent coercion may have been unnecessary. Moreover, as Judge Sedgwick had pointed out, the motives for concealment were powerful. Every daughter, he was sure, "felt an utter aversion for declaring circumstances so execrable, so horrible, so disgusting."[31] Such a profound violation of deeply ingrained taboos provoked an intense psychological and practical need to deny and hide the misconduct. For the victim as well as her relatives a conspiracy of silence was so compelling and expedient that incest accusations could only come to court in exceptional circumstances. In the case of father-daughter rape, only the daughter could bring the accusation, because, as any justice of the peace would explain, she alone could testify on the question of consent—the defining characteristic of the crime.

Judge Sedgwick had listed horror and disgust at the evilness of the crime as sufficient reasons for a daughter's concealment. But there were other reasons connected to the customary family power structure that raised even higher barriers to a daughter's accusation of her father. Because society placed fathers over their daughters as governors, both in law and in common experience, a dramatic inversion of family power was required to sustain a daughter's accusation. Fathers, after all, were entitled to beat their children, so who could say where the boundary lay between paternal discipline and coercion? In 1806 the governor of New York had argued that because it was lawful for a father to punish a child, Stephen Arnold's killing of his adopted daughter was not murder, but only manslaughter. And five years before the Wheeler trial James Sullivan, no patriarchal tyrant himself, would counsel his daughter to beat his own granddaughters so that they would learn to obey, a technique he had employed when raising his own children.[32] Fathers enjoyed wide latitude according to law and custom; they could deprive their children of food and amenities, lock them away, or work them mercilessly without public interference.[33] Had Stephen Arnold's child survived her beating, there is no reason to suppose that Arnold would ever have been prosecuted. As it was, when the little girl died, neither Arnold's wife nor his servant girl spoke out.[34] Paternal power was real, and family subordinates knew it; so it fell to local physicians to report Arnold's crime. Daughters, whether Phebe Bailey or Betsy Wheeler, could not find food and shelter on their own or succeed by running away. For them submission was almost always the rule.

But on June 8, 1805, Betsy chose neither submission nor concealment. Twice before when her father had meddled with her she had kept her head down and, like the Maine minister's wife who was raped, tried to keep "her troubles to her Selfe." This time, although she shielded her little brother from knowledge of their father's outrage, she decided to tell her mother. Yet from Betsy's testimony it is evident that she first considered concealment. On the mile or so trip back home from the spot where Ephraim left the children she had wept intermittently, but all she told her brother was that their father had "pounded her head and pinched her throat." Evidently this rough treatment at Ephraim's hands was not so unusual as to frighten the boy or prompt him to ask further questions. And when they arrived back at Uncle Bill's homestead, Betsy told her mother no more than she had told her brother. Perhaps reflexively, perhaps from shame, or perhaps in fear of Ephraim's death threat, she was still covering up the truth of what had happened. Hours passed; Eunice Hart, the neighbor who had come to nurse Martin's wife through childbirth, reported that she had seen Betsy "sitting with her head down . . . but [she] did not appear to be crying." That Betsy was reluctant to give up on concealment as her method of coping with her crisis is apparent from her extended delay in telling her mother and from the fact that she continued to hide Ephraim's prior rape some months before. Only after the midday meal, "she eat [ate] her dinner with us, then she and mother went into another room"—as her brother testified—did Betsy finally unburden herself, and even then only regarding the single assault she had that day sustained.[35] Hannah must have sensed that Betsy needed to speak privately, because despite the close confines of the crowded house, she went with her daughter into a separate room.

When Betsy told her mother what Ephraim had done that morning she set in motion the process that would lead to Ephraim's arrest. But at the moment when Betsy finally decided to tell her mother the awful truth there is no reason to believe that Betsy was thinking of calling on the law to protect her. Most likely she felt so hurt and so cornered that she urgently needed to confide in a sympathetic listener and find a way to escape from becoming her father's incestuous possession. Her mother, Hannah, with whom she had always lived and who had been her teacher and guide from infancy, was her closest friend in the world, but perhaps a strict one, too. Though she may have been fearful that Hannah would be angry with her, or that her mother might start a row with her violent father over the incident and that he might beat either or both of them severely, Betsy must have hoped that Hannah would give her comfort. Hannah might also find her a way to escape Ephraim's bondage.

The way out that Hannah proposed, calling on the authorities to protect them from Ephraim, meant the absolute end of concealment. However reluctantly, Betsy must have accepted this view, because that very afternoon she would be required to repeat the story of her humiliation to Robert Walker, the Windsor justice of the peace.[36] That Hannah, as well as Betsy, still shared the impulse to hide the rape is clear from the way that Hannah asked her brother-in-law, Bill Martin, to summon "Esquire Walker," as they called him. Though the whole story would soon come out, Hannah herself at first tried to conceal the reason Walker must come, explaining only that "something had happened worse than his striking her." Even when Martin insisted on learning why he was being sent on this errand, Hannah remained reluctant to reveal the truth: as Martin testified, "I asked her what it was—she said it was almost too bad to tell: I asked her to tell me—she said . . . [Ephraim] had had to do with Betsy."[37] Hannah seemed unable to name her husband's crime.

If Betsy felt relieved after unburdening herself of that morning's events, the anguish that her mother expressed cannot have been reassuring. Still, Betsy had made a start at confessing her dark secret; and instead of rejecting her, Hannah stood by her literally, staying with Betsy while Uncle Bill went off to fetch Esquire Walker at his home just half a mile away. While they were waiting Betsy might have chosen to reveal to her mother that in addition to this rape and the time she had turned down his offer of a gown and a petticoat, he had actually raped her some months back. That she did not suggests some combination of deep shame at what had happened, together with bewilderment, confusion, and feelings of guilt and fear connected to the earlier sexual contact and its concealment from her mother. On the afternoon of June 8, 1805, it seems that Betsy had not entirely given up on secrecy as a survival strategy; apparently she still feared her mother might judge her harshly or even abandon her.

Before Walker arrived to hear Betsy's account of the crime, Bill Martin told him "in part" what had happened, so Walker had a few minutes to consider how he would proceed. Walker, a fifty-two-year-old farmer and tanner, who was himself the father of a thirteen-year-old daughter (among his eleven children), knew the Wheelers not only as neighbors but also as the family who had lived in town with his relative, the Widow Converse.[38] Walker also knew that there was violence in the household because that very morning, on Ephraim's complaint, Walker had fined both Wheeler and Bill Martin for fighting. Though Justice Walker's record book does not survive, since no capital case had ever come to trial from Windsor most likely he had never dealt with an accusation that might be a capital crime.

When he arrived at Martin's house Walker's first decision was to take Betsy alone with him "into a separate room" so as to hear her testimony directly, and free from other influences and distractions. But this proved fruitless. Walker reported, "she immediately fell to crying, and I could get nothing from her." Only a short time earlier Betsy had screwed up her courage to the point where she could tell her mother; now she collapsed in tears when asked to repeat the painful, humiliating story of that morning's events to a gentleman whom she knew only slightly, an officer of the law. Walker could get nothing from her, though he did observe "marks of violence on the right side of her head; it looked red, and was considerably swollen."[39]

Justice Walker then decided to call Hannah Wheeler into the room to calm her daughter in the hope of getting Betsy to talk. Now, with her mother's reassurance, Betsy collected herself and "told the same story" she would later tell in court: how Ephraim ordered her to go with him into the woods for medicinal avens-root; how she had tried not to go, then had asked to bring her brother along; and how in the end her father assaulted her, penetrated her, and threatened to kill her if she ever told. Walker must have been chastened by her account and eager to avoid adding to Betsy's obvious suffering, because from "motives of delicacy" he neither examined Betsy himself nor did he order Eunice Hart, who was in the house, or any other woman to check for evidence of violent sexual contact.[40] Hannah, who was standing by, had said that she had examined Betsy privately when they were alone; and Walker, perhaps responding more to his neighbors' human drama than to the requirements of a court of law, either forgot that Hannah could not testify against her husband or failed to consider the legal importance of physical evidence—in any case, he let pass the best moment for acquiring such evidence. Betsy, no doubt, was unaware of such legal questions. It was enough for her that she had broken her silence and survived her second great ordeal that day.

When Walker got home, he wrote out a warrant for Ephraim's arrest and delivered it to a constable. The next day, the Sabbath, Constable Francis Cooppers seized Wheeler and held him under guard until Monday morning, June 10, when Cooppers delivered his prisoner to Justice Walker for arraignment. There, on the bright sunny day that Ephraim had expected Betsy and Ephraim, Jr., to return to him with the baby, Walker examined the accused man before "a Justices Court . . . at my Dwelling hous."[41]

For Betsy this first postrape confrontation with her father must have been agonizing, even though Justice Walker would have given her some advance knowledge of the procedure. Now the man who had threatened to kill her if she ever revealed the assault stood with her in the same room in Walker's house, while she, backed by her mother and younger brother, explained the awful injury he had done to her. Betsy had to listen, too, while Ephraim flatly denied her charge and asked to have her examined physically so as to prove she was lying. Justice Walker listened to the angry father's protests as he had listened just two days before to Ephraim's complaints about Bill Martin putting him out of the house. But this time Walker did not believe Wheeler. Initially, he had seized Wheeler "on a Complaint of Betsey Wheeler against Ephraim Wheelor [*sic*] her Father for having Carnol Knoledge of her Body—on the Eighth Instant." But now that Walker had a chance to question both Betsy and the accused, he decided to commit Wheeler to jail, not for "Carnol Knoledge," but for the far more serious crime of "a Rape on the Body of Betsey Wheeler his Daughter." Evidently, to Justice Walker, Betsy was more convincing than her father. He ruled against his neighbor and immediately committed Wheeler to jail in the valley at Lenox, twenty miles away.[42]

The proceedings were over. Walker would earn $2.02 for his labors, and Betsy and Ephraim, Jr., would each be compensated 33 cents for their attendance and 4 cents more for their travel. This was all routine. But, for Betsy, standing up against her father had been harrowing—even though her mother's judgment to seek protection from Esquire Walker seemed vindicated. Now, it was true, Betsy could walk the half-mile back to Uncle Bill's knowing that for the present Ephraim could not attack her. She, who had lived in dread of her father for two days, also knew that he would not take her away from her mother, Ephraim, Jr., and her little sister. In addition, her face and her body were starting to recover from Ephraim's violence. Still, each night when she lay down to sleep, the scene in the woods or the confrontation in Walker's house might come back to frighten her.[43]

Even her daytime respite was temporary and incomplete. The hard challenges she had faced on June 8 and June 10 in telling her mother and Esquire Walker would lead to further tests where concealment and keeping her head down were forbidden. Betsy's testimony to Esquire Walker accusing her father of forcible "Carnol knoledge" of her would place the girl at the center of a capital trial where she would have to repeat her account to the prosecutor, James Sullivan, to the grand jury, and in the open forum of the Supreme Judicial Court. Moreover, Betsy might have had mixed feelings as she came to recognize that her parents might not only be separated permanently by her "complaint," but that her father's life might actually be taken as a result. And if her accusation failed and Ephraim were to be acquitted of her charges, he might punish her brutally.

We do not know how Betsy felt about these new realities in the summer of 1805, during the three months between her accusation of Ephraim Wheeler in June and his trial in September. But several facts are clear, and passages in her September trial testimony provide clues as to how we should interpret those facts. The first and most important fact is that all through the summer while her father was languishing in the Lenox jail, Betsy stood by her original testimony. She had not known the full consequences of her disclosures at the time that she made them on June 8 and June 10, but by July and August she had had ample time to consider what had transpired and to consult with her mother, Uncle Bill, and the Odel family as to what might happen in the future, and what she—and they—must do.

Betsy could still undercut the public proceeding that her accusation had launched. If she changed her story and dropped the charge the prosecution would have nothing to bring to the grand jury, the case against Ephraim would collapse, and Wheeler would be free to rejoin his family. A more likely alternative, based on the threats he had made and the enmities within the family, was that Betsy and Hannah, and perhaps also Bill Martin, could require Ephraim to agree to leave them forever in exchange for dropping the charge. Some years earlier Abigail Abbot Bailey and her brothers had followed a similar path after discovering Asa Bailey's incest, and they used the threat of criminal charges against Asa Bailey to compel his permanent departure for the west and his acquiescence in a divorce.[44] In the Wheeler case, Betsy would bear the brunt of humiliation in such an extralegal scheme because the authorities were already involved. She would have to tell a new story and allow herself to appear to be mentally unstable, hysterical perhaps, or even a liar.

If Ephraim had been a potential source of property, as Asa Bailey was, such a plan might have been attractive to Hannah and her family, and they might have pressured Betsy to go along. That Betsy never attempted any such revision in her account of June 8 does not mean that a like strategy was never contemplated in the family. A similar tactic might have been considered and rejected for many reasons, not the least of which was Ephraim's unreliability as a breadwinner, and his record of broken promises and of calling on his Odel in-laws for assistance. Betsy, Hannah, and the others may have doubted either that Ephraim would hold up his side of the bargain or that they would be able to refuse him assistance under any and all circumstances. Moreover if Betsy dropped the public charges there was no legal way to prevent Wheeler from reclaiming paternal control.

Betsy, and Hannah too, must have thought long and hard about the prosecution Betsy was pursuing against her father. Betsy's fear of Ephraim's abuse, her hatred of him, and his threat to her and her siblings all helped to stiffen Betsy's resolve. But neither Betsy's behavior on June 8 and June 10 nor her testimony at Ephraim's trial suggests

that her decision to confront her father's assaults was a carefully calculated strategy to destroy him. Her disclosures were halting, incomplete, suffused with shame. On June 8 she first hesitated for a couple
of hours before revealing anything to her mother, and then she told
Hannah only about that day's rape, keeping secret Ephraim's earlier
abuse. Later, when Esquire Walker appeared, she faltered and almost
brought the matter to an end when she broke down crying, unable to
repeat that day's disclosure until her mother came in to steady her.
From that day forward perhaps until September, when Attorney General Sullivan questioned her before the trial and then under oath,
Betsy clung to her old secret, fearful of telling her mother and hoping
to preserve some fraction of her honor. It was bad enough to tell the
world she had been raped; but to admit that she had been raped once
before and had concealed it might anger her mother and would be almost too humiliating to bear. Yet she did finally confess publicly that
she had been Ephraim's accomplice by hiding his previous crime.
The fact that she eventually made a public confession suggests that
she had by then resolved whatever anxieties she once felt about her
mother's response and so was confident of her mother's support during the trial. In court, under oath, when Sullivan asked the question
"Did he ever have any thing to do with you before?" she could not,
would not, conceal any longer. "Yes," she answered, "he attempted
twice before."[45]

The explanation Betsy gave for why she was now exposing these
facts was not straightforward like the rest of her testimony. It was
enigmatic, and its complexity helps us to understand how Betsy felt
in this crisis. When the judges asked her "How came you to tell of
this?"—that is, the prior assaults—she did not answer simply "because that is what happened" or "because I am sworn to answer." She
replied: "I thought I had as lieve [as soon] die one way as another."[46]
What did she mean? Which were the ways she imagined herself dying? She cannot have meant dying literally at Ephraim's hands as the

result of his death threats, because her disclosure of the June 8 rape had already given Wheeler sufficient motive to carry out his threat if the court set him free. If her testimony regarding the earlier assaults persuaded just one juror to believe the defense's claim of Betsy's consent, then it would undermine the case against her father. Only if her additional testimony strengthened the prosecution could it restrain Ephraim's vengeance.

What Betsy meant, we believe, was that she might as well die of shame for disclosing her complicity with her father, limited as it was, as die of guilt by continuing to hide the truth. Betsy's answer to the judge's question suggests that in the months following her thirteenth birthday she had reached a more mature consciousness of herself as a moral being—a consciousness that revivalists of the era often cultivated in young people. Whereas Betsy's concern with the way others viewed her had apparently earlier ruled her conduct, and feelings of shame and fear of rejection by her mother dominated her thoughts, now her own sense of herself—and perhaps of sin—seemed to guide her. How others would judge her remained important; but this was no longer as important as how she judged herself before God. She had placed her hand on the Bible and sworn to tell the truth, the whole truth; so she had no choice. Pushed to a turning point by the pretrial and courtroom interrogations, she was stricken by guilt for her own previous concealment. To the thirteen-year-old Betsy it was a crisis. Before the magistrates and gentlemen of the court, before her father in the prisoner's box, her brother on the witness bench, and her mother standing by, as well as the hundreds of men who strained to grasp her every word, she declared: "I had as lieve die one way as another."

Betsy Wheeler was, in the fullest sense, her father's victim. Growing up as an outsider at the margin of Berkshire society, she was wholly dependent on her family, her mother especially. From the beginning of her life Ephraim had been inconsistent as a father and absent for long periods during Betsy's early childhood.[47] He was an able-bodied man who did not stick to his work, a conniver who fell down on his promises. He also drank. Living under his rule from the ages of four to thirteen years, Betsy had learned to be close-mouthed and obedient, avoiding confrontation and surviving by concealment.

As she came closer to adulthood, Ephraim, for reasons of his own, sought to exert power over her sexually—through bribes if he could, through force if he must. And Betsy, not yet thirteen years old when he began, responded as she had learned was best for her own survival, by keeping quiet and hoping each of her father's advances would be his last. But by June 8, 1805, Betsy was almost thirteen and a half, and this third episode brought her to the realization that Ephraim would continue his assaults. When the little family group of father and two children stopped by the road in the lonely upland of Partridgefield she grew anxious, and when her father ordered her alone into the woods with him she resisted verbally. But he was her father, little Ephraim was watching, and she dared not defy him openly. He might, as fathers did, whip her. And she could not bring herself to explain openly before her little brother why she refused to accompany her father in search of avens-root, a medicine that could help her aunt's recovery from childbirth.[48] So, as she was used to doing, she obeyed, only to have him do his worst. When she emerged from the woods beaten and crying, she felt all was lost. Her father had defiled her; and, shaken by the attack, she felt helpless. She might as well go along with him, rather than go home to her mother with the shame and guilt that made the tears flow. Resignation and submission were, she had learned, women's virtues. They were the virtues that kept Abigail Abbot Bailey, a mature woman, silent for years.[49]

A present-day rape counselor might explain Betsy's behavior after the attack differently. Instead of resignation and submission, a modern clinician might see Betsy's responses as expressing "a sense of helplessness and loss of control, and even the threat of annihilation." These symptoms, together with Betsy's depressed, tearful demeanor, point to a diagnosis of posttraumatic stress disorder. Certainly Betsy displayed some of the signs of that condition, one that especially affects girls and women "who are psychologically vulnerable." For someone like Betsy, who "suffered physical injury (especially to the head) during the trauma," and who was the victim of "rape, incest, and domestic abuse," posttraumatic stress disorder provides a context for understanding her readiness to go with her father after the assault, as well as her reluctance to report it to her mother. This diagnosis emphasizes "the potential to 'victimize' a person" and so render her passive. Those suffering from the disorder also "tend to numb themselves to all thoughts, feelings, or actions that remind them of the traumatic event." So Betsy, who ultimately fought back publicly, does not completely fit the profile.[50]

Yet if on Saturday, June 8, Ephraim had persisted in his plan to take the children and separate them from their mother, perhaps Betsy would have deteriorated into a full-blown posttraumatic stress victim. Instead Ephraim changed the day's scenario from what he had impulsively announced. Perhaps because it was now raining harder and they would all be soaked, he decided this was not such a good day to set off on their own. Nor would he have been eager to return and face Hannah again after all that had transpired that day—their fight, Martin's putting him out of the house forcibly, and now his assault on Betsy. So he chose to send the children back home with orders to come to him the next dry day. For the moment he would go on to Isaac Odel's, where he had found shelter before and where no one would quiz him on Betsy's appearance or any of the day's other events.[51]

As a result, at her father's order Betsy went home with her brother, and as the distance between her and her father lengthened, her feelings of anger toward him and toward herself must have grown. She maintained her self-control so that she was able to hide the full story of what had happened from her brother and Hannah. But as she sat in the safety of Bill Martin's house with her mother nearby, and as she recovered from the immediate pain of her father's assault, she had the chance to reflect on what it would mean when the next dry day came and she must take Ephraim, Jr., and her baby sister and go to meet their father. Then she would once more be subject to his abuse, without any protectors, defeated, just as she had been a few hours before when she had emerged from the woods. It was this realization, most likely, that prompted Betsy to go into the other room and confess to her mother that Ephraim "had to do" with her.[52]

At first, telling her mother what Ephraim had done was an end in itself, a cry for help and a source of relief. But as Hannah took in the story she judged that Ephraim's crime was more than she and Bill Martin could manage. Ephraim was, moreover, still planning to take the children, and neither she nor Martin could stop him. So she called on Esquire Walker. From that moment onward the consequences of the accusation for Betsy and her immediate family took on a life of their own. Whether Betsy, Hannah, and Bill Martin knew it or not, what Ephraim had done might be considered a capital crime. Walker immediately took steps to arrest Ephraim and, after a hearing, had him locked up in Lenox jail.

Here Betsy found immediate relief. But it was only temporary. At the next session of the Berkshire County grand jury she would have to testify just as she had to Esquire Walker, and then repeat the story yet again before the Supreme Judicial Court. Otherwise her father would go free. This much Walker might have told her before he ordered Ephraim's arrest, or later, after the arraignment, when he sent Wheeler to jail.

We have no evidence of what doubts or questions ran through Betsy's mind in the summer of 1805. She apparently stayed on with her mother at William Martin's in June and July and then went to live at her uncle Isaac Odel's in August.[53] As the months passed Betsy and her family had plenty of time to reconsider whether to proceed with the accusation or to retract it. But Betsy stood fast. When she was put under oath at the trial she was more candid, more forthcoming than she had ever been before.

By the time Betsy gave evidence, she appears to have confronted the hard questions of what she should do and understood that she could control neither events nor the ways that others might judge her character. In coming to this realization she perhaps was influenced by the belief in natural depravity preached by pastors like the Reverend Gordon Dorrance of Windsor. Though 1805 was not a great revival year in Berkshire County, religious revivals occurred intermittently throughout Betsy's childhood. The repeated evangelical calls to all people, high and low—and especially youth—to open themselves to Jesus' message so that "the truth shall make you free" would have carried special meaning for Betsy as she prepared to face her father and all the world in open court.[54]

Once she came to Lenox, her mind appeared settled. She impressed Attorney General Sullivan as a girl of "understanding" who spoke in court with "great reserve and reluctance." She demonstrated her constancy when four times on four different days—twice before Justice Walker, and before the grand jury and the trial court—she repeated essentially the same account of events.[55] Though for rhetorical reasons both the prosecutor and the defense attorneys spoke of Betsy as a child, the composure she displayed in court marked her growing maturity. That she still felt wounded and remained troubled by the predicament of testifying against her own father was evident from her subdued manner. But now her concealment was over. She had told all, without tears, before a multitude of strangers.

Whether Betsy and Ephraim, Jr., stayed to the end of the trial was not recorded. They might have left just before nine P.M., when the court adjourned so that the jury could deliberate. But since they and their mother were boarding in Lenox for the trial, and since Betsy had come this far both emotionally and physically, it seems likely that she and Ephraim, Jr., stayed for the verdict. When it came, Betsy was vindicated, but for her there could have been no pleasure in the outcome.

On the night of Friday, September 13, sleep cannot have come easily to Betsy as she went to bed at William Whiting's house, just down the street from where her father lay in irons at the jail.[56] Thirteen days later she would put her mark on a petition to spare the life of Ephraim Wheeler. Though he had injured her, both her duty as a daughter and her feelings for her father, she affirmed, required her to "implore" mercy for the man who had so nearly destroyed her.[57]

CHAPTER FOUR

The Wife and Mother

I have ever lived most unhappily with my wife. I do not pretend that I am not passionate myself, or that I have not been many times to blame: but nobody knows, nor can know, the trials that I have had with her, encouraged as she has been, in her unkindness to me, by WILLIAM MARTIN and others. She has often told me, that if it were not wicked, she would poison me: or would bind me when I was asleep, and whip me to death. She was almost in the daily habit of wishing I was dead, so that she could put the children out, and be in as good a situation as she was before I saw her. She has now accomplished her purpose, by conspiring and procuring my death upon a false accusation.

[Ephraim Wheeler], *Narrative of the Life of Ephraim Wheeler. . . .* (1806)

Perhaps Hannah Wheeler leaned against the doorframe, holding her little child tightly in her arms as she watched the horse with its young riders, Betsy and Ephraim, Jr., disappear down the path behind Ephraim. It was not yet noon on June 8, that dreary Saturday that had been so stormy indoors. Earlier that morning Hannah's willingness to relocate the marital bed, moving it into a shared sleeping room, had led to a bitter fight with her husband. Now she faced the loss of her two older children.

Knowing Ephraim's violent nature, she worried. Months earlier, when the Wheeler family had moved into her sister Lucy Martin's household, she had hoped for better times. But conflict between Ephraim and her brother-in-law, Bill Martin, proved inescapable. That very morning, because of the dispute over the bed and the ensuing fracas, their neighbor, Justice Robert Walker, had fined the two men for fighting. When Hannah turned away from the doorway and back to caring for her sister Lucy, who lay in bed, Hannah had no way of knowing what her future as a wife and mother might be.

From the courtroom testimony we know what Hannah Wheeler did after Betsy and Ephraim, Jr., returned to the house later that afternoon. She called in Justice Walker and backed Betsy's charge against Ephraim. As a result, she gained legal supervision of their children and separated from her husband. Yet by choosing to call on the state in the person of Justice Walker, she brought Betsy's crisis and the Wheeler family's upheaval into the public arena, where the Berkshire community's standards of justice and the judgment of Massachusetts' highest officials, not her wishes, would rule.

According to Ephraim's courtroom defenders, John W. Hulbert and Daniel Dewey, Hannah invented Betsy's story deliberately, in order to put her husband out of the way and so gain control of their children. Wheeler himself made the same claim.[1] Such an assertion was not wholly far-fetched because according to Massachusetts law, so long as the children had a father, they belonged to him. Hannah Wheeler could of course run away from her husband—unhappy women fled abusive marriages with some frequency, especially in poor households, where they felt no material incentive to stay.[2] But to run from Ephraim meant leaving her children, especially Betsy, to their father's abuse. For Hannah this was unthinkable: she wanted to protect her children, not to flee her maternal responsibility. So, assuming Betsy's testimony was accurate and the child revealed the rape to her mother on the afternoon of June 8, 1805, what was Hannah to do? How, she must have wondered, should she respond?

One alternative was to seek some private, family means to curb her husband's violence. The scarcity of family violence cases in the courts and in other public records, as well as the uniqueness of the Wheeler rape-incest prosecution, demonstrates that most mothers kept such matters private. Few early American records of father-daughter rape survive in any form. But two late eighteenth-century New England examples enable us to grasp the complexity of such decisions and help us to understand why Hannah chose the exceptional route of going public.

In the 1770s a New Hampshire matron, Sarah Temple, discovered that her husband, Stephen, had repeatedly raped their twelve-year-old daughter. Unlike Hannah, she chose not to call in a justice of the peace. Instead, she tried to stop her husband's criminal abuse by threatening him with court and offering him a "second chance" if he would sign a written confession witnessed by two men, possibly her brothers. His statement, which described his incestuous rapes as a form of adultery injurious to his wife, with no mention of the harm to his daughter, gives a further reason why women so rarely confronted their husbands publicly. In his confession Stephen Temple explicitly gave his wife "full liberty if ever I behave myself unbecoming towards her or Susannah [the rape victim] or any of the rest [of the family] to carry a complaint to a justice of the Peace and have me punished according to law."[3] Inasmuch as all wives vowed obedience to their husbands in the marriage ceremony and were prohibited from testifying against them in court, it appears that many, like Sarah Temple, doubted the legitimacy of confronting their husbands publicly without first gaining permission.

Ten years later, however, after the Temple family had moved to Upton, in Worcester County, Massachusetts, Sarah sued her husband for divorce when she found him engaged in adultery. At that point she presented his earlier written confession to the Supreme Judicial Court. In addition, their now-married daughter swore that her father had assaulted her repeatedly and coerced her into keeping his crimes secret. Because she believed that Stephen Temple was incorrigible, Sarah Temple concluded that she could neither preserve family honor nor maintain her deference to patriarchy any longer. In the end, to curb her husband's criminal lust she went public, turning to the Supreme Judicial Court to obtain a measure of justice from the state—her freedom from such a marriage. No punishment was ever meted out against her husband.[4]

We do not know whether Hannah Wheeler knew anything of the Temple family's scandal, though its public exposure occurred when Hannah was nineteen years old and living only a few miles from the Temples and the courthouse where the Supreme Judicial Court heard the case. If Hannah had known of Sarah Temple's situation it would have given Hannah no encouragement to try to control her own husband privately. Sarah Temple, an enrolled church member, felt restrained by concern for her family's reputation and by the force of the patriarchal ethos. Yet not only did she fail to reform her husband; because of her readiness to conceal his misbehavior, she allowed it to continue. Though the preference for curbing a violent husband by private means was strong, achieving results was difficult. As was evident in the Temple family, the desire to maintain family reputation in a patriarchal society and to preserve the marriageability of daughters were powerful incentives to hide sexual abuse. In addition, religious scruples and concern for the property interests of wives and children could be further motives for concealment. Certainly these were among the primary reasons that Abigail Abbot Bailey of New Hampshire kept secret her husband's assaults on their fifteen-year-old daughter, Phebe, beginning in 1788.[5] As an intensely pious Christian, Abigail Bailey's immediate and sustained response to the crime was prayer and introspection. Even after her daughter was safe, having left her childhood home on her eighteenth birthday, as she was legally able to do, her mother still did not turn to the law. Bailey believed, "God's time seemed not yet to have arrived. I must still wait."[6]

Two years later, after further maltreatment and signs that Asa Bailey intended to cheat her of her share of the family property and transport away her younger children, God's time had come. She turned to her brothers and to the law and "swore the peace against my poor husband." The threat of legal procedures—possibly even a capital crime—was sufficient, and Asa capitulated. He made a property arrangement with his wife, leaving Abigail in control of the younger children. He departed for the West with several of his older sons. Only then did Abigail sue for divorce, charging Asa with having repeatedly violated the marriage covenant by his adulterous behavior and "cruelly injuring[,] abusing[,] and ill treating" her.[7]

The full extent of Asa Bailey's crimes became known publicly only after Abigail's death in 1815. At that point one of her sons arranged to publish her memoir, which traced the family ordeal and her largely private and religious response to it. Though Abigail's clergyman editor declared approvingly, "few lives of christians, in modern days, have afforded such rare material for instructive biography," he cautioned that Mrs. Bailey "did truly err in not having her husband brought to justice."[8]

Hannah could not have known of the Bailey family in 1805; but, like the Baileys, she had been steeped in a culture of keeping family matters private. She must also have known that the penalties for going public could be more direct and concrete than just the loss of reputation.[9] First, of course, she would excite the rage of a violent husband, perhaps in a losing cause at court. Moreover, if she and Betsy "won" and her husband was fined and/or imprisoned—the usual punishments—her family would be deprived of his assets and his earnings. For poor wives like Hannah these consequences usually kept them from resorting to the legal system.[10] Hannah's decision to support Betsy's accusation against Ephraim in the public arena cannot have been easy.

But without Hannah's support for Betsy's accusation the state could never have tried Ephraim Wheeler. On her own no thirteen-year-old girl could sustain a commitment to the prosecution over the three-month interval between her father's arrest and his trial. Indeed without the support of an adult, usually a middle-aged woman, so far as we know no child in early America ever pursued a sexual assault case.[11] One need not subscribe to the defense attorneys' argument that Ephraim's prosecution resulted from his wife's conspiracy to recognize that without Hannah Wheeler's decision to call in Justice Walker and to stand by Betsy, the case against Ephraim Wheeler could not have been initiated or maintained.

So in order to understand the Wheeler case we must consider it from the perspective of Hannah Wheeler—to our knowledge the only woman in all of early America who sustained her daughter's successful prosecution of her father for rape. But how are we to understand Hannah when, unlike her husband, she left no narrative of her life and, unlike her daughter, provided no testimony at the trial? The records are especially unfair to Hannah since the fullest account we have of her life comes from her estranged and embittered husband.

The problem of getting to know Hannah reveals the place of women, the poor, and people of color in early American public and private records. Hannah, like all wives in cases involving their husbands, was deliberately excluded from the court proceedings; as Attorney General Sullivan pointed out, "she cannot be a witness."[12]

In addition, since most public records were concerned with property, they concentrated on property holders and politics, areas where women were usually treated as accessories to men. So, like children and most people of color, women, especially poor women, were severely underrepresented in the documents.

Private records supply even less. In the exceptional cases where poor and common people wrote letters and diaries, those documents have rarely survived. Personal transiency, crowded quarters, and poverty seldom allowed succeeding generations to preserve papers that possessed no cash value. In the case of women's documents this was especially true because their papers dealt with domestic concerns that were not later seen as important, in comparison, for example, with the letters and diaries of Revolutionary War veterans. For the entire eighteenth century few women's diaries and journals survive, including only a handful of brief fragments written by women below the middle rank. Consequently it is no surprise that we have found no private documents in Hannah's hand.

Moreover, as far as we know—and we have searched widely in western Massachusetts sources—after the Wheeler case concluded, Hannah disappeared from public records in Berkshire and Hampshire Counties. She may have moved out of the region, remained propertyless, or died. Her name, Hannah Wheeler, was sufficiently common that linking her to an appearance of that name without further confirmation that it is the same person is unwise. And if she changed her name casually or by marriage, the difficulty of finding information becomes infinite. As a result, the largest single body of information we have on Hannah and her life comes from her husband's hostile narrative of his own life.

Nevertheless we were able to glean some additional facts about Hannah Wheeler from public records. Though too few and scattered to permit a detailed portrait, by using the facts we have, by making comparisons to other women, and by inference we can sketch Hannah's silhouette. We can imagine how Hannah came to back Betsy consistently, as few mothers would, during the summer of 1805. We do not know if Hannah was tall or short, slim or stout, but the record reveals a woman of conscience, determination, and strength—one who could make a hard decision and stand fast. To understand Hannah's determination to seek protection from the law we must understand her life history and that of her family. Only then can we appreciate the depth of Hannah Wheeler's quandary when she faced the crisis created by Ephraim's explosive behavior.

Hannah Wheeler was born in Sutton, Massachusetts, a farming town of about 2,100 people, on January 15, 1763, the fifth child, we believe, of Ichabod and Elizabeth Odel.[13] From the beginning Hannah's life was exceptional for the time and place in which the Odels lived (nearly forty miles west of Boston, in southern Worcester County) because her father was a man of color—identified as "negro" on the manuscript census of 1800 and listed in the "other persons" (that is, black, mulatto) category in the censuses of 1790 and 1800. Ichabod Odel was evidently firmly rooted in Sutton because he served with a local militia company in 1755 during the French and Indian War and again during the siege of Boston twenty years later.[14] Whether his wife, Elizabeth, was also a person of color we cannot say, since she died before the first U.S. census. The sole record in which her name appears, Sutton births, does not specify her or her husband's color or race. Because one of Sutton's neighboring towns was Grafton, a place where people of Nipmuc as well as mixed African-Indian-British descent dwelled during Ichabod and Elizabeth Odel's youth and middle years, both Ichabod and his wife Elizabeth may have been people of mixed-race descent.[15] The Odel surname, sometimes rendered as

Odle, Odell, or O'Dell, was Irish. That both parents shared mixed ancestry seems likely since in the decades after 1790 only some of their children were identified as "negro" or "colored" while others, including Hannah Wheeler, were not so labeled and so were evidently presumed to be white.

Not much is known of Hannah's childhood and youth in Sutton. The family was poor, certainly, since Ichabod Odel owned no land in Worcester County, a region of forests and small farms. Yet the Odels were apparently independent, for in the records of the town there is no entry "warning out" Ichabod Odel, and no sign that any in his family received town aid.[16] Hannah, it appears, worked at home and for other families, learning the womanly skills of preserving and preparing food, managing a kitchen garden, and spinning and sewing. She also learned the skill of writing, something neither her older brother Isaac nor her older sister Elizabeth ever mastered.[17]

That Hannah lived in crowded spaces with little privacy is certain. Even a generation after her youth, in a time of prosperity—1798—the average Worcester County dwelling had five or six people living in roughly 600-square-foot homes.[18] Among poor people in the 1760s and 1770s, space would have been more limited. In all likelihood Hannah shared a bed with some of her sisters, born between 1758 and 1766. This practice of brothers sharing beds with brothers, and sisters with sisters, was common even among more prosperous yeoman families on into the nineteenth century.[19]

What was Hannah's place in the family, and who were her siblings? So far as surviving records permit us to say, Hannah was one of eight children, six girls (the oldest, Releaf, then Molly, Elizabeth, Hannah, Lydia, and Lucy) and two boys (the elder, Isaac, and Ichabod, Jr.). She shared a common birthday with her three-years-younger sister Lucy, the girl who became William Martin's wife. In all probability the Odel family's minority status reinforced the interdependence that was characteristic of all families in the period. Emotional as well as practical reasons encouraged the Odels to be close-knit; they knew that their kinsmen provided their nearest, most reliable sources of help. Families of color were so few in Sutton, and in Worcester County generally (less than one percent), that the possibility of maintaining or creating distinct cultural practices was slim, and the Odels appear to have shared the values of the white Yankee majority that surrounded them.

Their naming pattern, for example, was indistinguishable from that of their white neighbors, a mixture of Bible and English names for their sons and daughters.[20] The fact that Betsy Wheeler was named for her grandmother, Elizabeth Odel, tells us that Hannah favored a traditional New England method of maintaining lineage. The Odel work ethic, too, and the fact that Hannah was literate—even to the point of signing her name—bespeak the family's assimilation of the common culture.[21] That Ichabod Odel twice joined in community military activity indicates Hannah's family was accepted among Sutton townspeople. We do not find their names in the records of the church, either as members or among church cases of discipline for fornication, drunkenness, or nonpayment of tithes, nor do they appear in the diary of the Reverend David Hall; so they were not among Sutton's converted Christians.[22] But in light of Massachusetts laws requiring church attendance, coupled with the fact that there is nothing to suggest that the Odels were nonconformists or at odds with community religious customs, they most likely attended church occasionally. Their acceptance of community custom was evident at the time of Hannah's betrothal to Ephraim Wheeler, when she sought a church wedding and had the banns duly published according to law.[23]

Certainly the Odels were like their neighbors in the difficult post-war period when, after a generation or longer in the same place, they pulled up stakes and departed Sutton and Worcester County for good. Since there is no record of a land sale by Ichabod Odel or his eldest son, Isaac, it is clear that the family did not have much in a material way to leave behind. In Berkshire and Hampshire Counties, where the Odels first appear in 1784, several Odels and their spouses would acquire small landholdings (they were among the bottom 5 percent of taxpayers), but this was not enough to prevent the men from being officially "warned out" of Cummington in the 1790s.[24]

Like most of the other poor people who moved into the region after the Revolution, they settled in the less desirable, more recently pioneered upland towns in the central and northern parts of the Berkshire-Hampshire highlands. The Odels in particular, who were marginal due to their color and their poverty, came to inhabit the most remote peripheries of the most remote townships—high forest lands in Worthington and Cummington in Hampshire County, and Windsor and Partridgefield (later renamed Peru) across the border in Berkshire County. Here the cohesiveness of the Odels as a family is striking. For when the sisters married—Elizabeth to Asa Dunbar in 1784, Lydia in 1788 to Joshua Dunbar, Hannah in 1791 to Ephraim Wheeler, Molly in 1793 to John Percip, Lucy in 1796 to William Martin, and Releaf in 1797 to Michael Pepper—they did not join their husbands' families—rather, they enrolled their husbands in the Odel network. This pattern of the Odel women's involving their husbands in their own family's interdependent web of relationships would apply to both Ephraim Wheeler as well as William Martin, and would provide the family matrix for the explosive events of June 8, 1805, which included Hannah's unusual decision to go beyond her own family to seek protection from the public authorities.[25]

The only account of Hannah's marriage that survives is Ephraim Wheeler's final reckoning, so we must tread cautiously. What appears certain is that Hannah must have weighed her prospects with care, because she entered the marriage deliberately, two years after her first acquaintance with Ephraim, and not, it appears, in response to any romantic impetuosity or in a hurried effort to legitimate a pregnancy. That she chose to marry Ephraim Wheeler, a poor drifter whom no one would have described as a "catch," is a measure of the lean marriage market for people of color in the Berkshire and Hampshire uplands, where over 99 percent of the people were white.

In contrast to their white female counterparts who often married according to their birth order before their twenty-fifth birthday, four of the six Odel sisters married late and out of birth order.[26] Only two, Lydia and Elizabeth, at twenty-four and twenty-five years respectively, married at close to the overall average age for women. Hannah's older sisters Releaf and Molly did not marry until they were at least thirty-five years old. And Lucy, who was younger, did not marry William Martin until the age of thirty.[27] Apparently, at age twenty-eight, when Hannah decided to marry Ephraim, she had concluded that he was as good a husband as she would find. On the positive side, Wheeler was a sturdy man who as a mariner had seen the world. Moreover, as demonstrated by his readiness to elope to New York State in order to secure a lawful marriage, he was committed to the union. As a light-skinned, seemingly white person herself, Hannah may also have sought the advantages of having a white husband and white children. Whether intentional or not, by marrying a white man, she set herself apart from her sisters, all of whom, regardless of their own physical appearance, married men of color. That Hannah Odel expressed her autonomy in this way was, perhaps, a mark of her independent temperament.

From the court proceedings and Ephraim's narrative it is obvious that Hannah's courtship and marriage were never the stuff of romance novels. Twice Hannah left her husband, and both times she proved capable of supporting herself and her babies with domestic work, though she may also have moved in for a time with her father, her older brother, or one of her sisters. Significantly, as hostile as Ephraim's account of Hannah was, he never claimed that she was dependent on him economically.[28] Nor did he assert the usual complaints of angry husbands, that his wife was lazy, intemperate, extravagant, or unfaithful.[29] The fact that Ephraim, even at his most bitter, found no fault with Hannah's housekeeping or motherly performance reinforces our sense that Hannah was a well-organized, competent person yoked to an unreliable husband.

Indeed, in light of what is known of Ephraim Wheeler and their marriage, one of the key questions is why Hannah continued to return to Ephraim, to bear his children, to pay his debts, and despite his many flaws to stay with him continuously from 1796 to 1805. As a frustrated wife in Vermont versified:

I'd rather live a single life,
Than pay his debts and be his wife;
For I am weak and full of fear
And debts grow heavier ev'ry year.[30]

It was not that Hannah felt contented. According to Ephraim's overheated account, she repeatedly complained that "if it were not wicked, she would poison me: or would bind me when I was asleep, and whip me to death." Moreover, he claimed, "she was almost in the daily habit of wishing I was dead, so that she could put the children out and be in as good a situation as she was before I saw her." Yet she stayed faithful to a husband who admitted to a "loose and irregular life . . . subject to violent and hasty passions." It is hard to believe that Hannah would have married Ephraim if she had known that he would later spend his "time and property," as he himself admitted, "in idleness, hard drinking and quarreling, neglecting industry, and the means of obtaining an honest livelihood for myself and family."[31]

Yet even after she had come to realize her husband's character she stayed with him, moving as he moved, each year to a different household.

Even today, when marriage counselors can be fully informed as to the facts of a relationship, it often remains a mystery why women stay in such conflicted, abusive, unhappy marriages. In Hannah's case we see four plausible reasons, though we cannot rank them in order of importance. First, there was the Odels' family culture and the matter of pride. Hannah's parents stayed together, as did her sisters and their husbands. She had sworn marriage vows, and it is reasonable to suppose that over the years Hannah came to feel she could manage the situation. As the one Odel sister who had married a white man she may have felt she had something to prove—she had made her bed, and she would lie in it.

A second possible reason Hannah stayed with Ephraim was her, and their, continuing aspiration to respectable husbandman or yeoman status. At least four of her sisters belonged to taxpaying, if modest, landowning households, as did her brother Isaac. With Ephraim she might achieve a similar status, whereas single or divorced she could only be a domestic worker in the houses of others. Third, one cannot dismiss the possibility that Hannah felt some continuing attraction and attachment to Ephraim. Something about him had drawn her to him initially, and there may have been moments when she felt touched by those facets of his personality. In addition, they had gone through a lot together, so they shared many experiences, many ties. And as she was faithful to Ephraim, so too was Ephraim faithful to her.

Finally—and this is what we believe to be the most important reason—since Ephraim never deserted them, Hannah could only sustain her attachment to her children and her hopes for them if she stayed in the marriage. Legally she had no right to abscond with the children, nor would such an attempt have much chance of success, since it would also require breaking her ties to her own family, her own network of support. It is in this context particularly that we need to consider Hannah's decision on June 8, and her perseverance in that decision through the succeeding days and weeks. By deciding to side with Betsy rather than her husband she was giving up any effort to vindicate her decision to marry him, giving up on her yeoman aspirations, and bidding farewell to all remaining attachment to Ephraim. By his actions on June 8, Ephraim forced her to choose between him and his patriarchal prerogatives on the one hand, and her loyalty to her blood relatives—including her younger sister Lucy Martin and her own child, Betsy—on the other.

On June 8, 1805, Hannah, Ephraim, and their three children had been living in the cramped Martin household for several weeks—an arrangement that cannot have been easy for either the Martins or the Wheelers. For although Hannah and Lucy Martin were close, Ephraim and Bill Martin shared a conflict-ridden history. Years before, Ephraim claimed, Martin and another man had attacked him in the road for no reason and, after Ephraim had successfully called on the law to punish them with fines, Martin and his companion had promised to get even.[32] So now, in the spring of 1805, for Ephraim to become a lodger in his black brother-in-law's household was humiliating. Over the years Wheeler had learned to accept, perhaps even to expect, assistance from his in-laws; but his relationship with Bill Martin was tense.

During the night when Lucy Martin went into labor, Ephraim had done the Martins a favor by going for the doctor. But when he returned early in the morning, Martin and Hannah had staged what he believed was a domestic revolt. They had moved the Wheelers' bed—the marriage bed that husbands were supposed to rule—out of the separate room the Wheelers had occupied and into a shared common bedroom. When Ephraim asked Hannah the reason, he said she answered, "it was Martin's orders, and that we must sleep there for the future." Her declaration angered Ephraim, and he immediately asserted his power as patriarch: "I told her it was my room, and my bed, and it should be brought back"—or else, he threatened, "she [Hannah] should not go into their [the Martins'] room to assist them."[33]

Over the years Hannah surely must have felt she had put up with a lot from her ne'er-do-well husband—frequent changes of household, paying out her own money to discharge his debts, finding the family shelter with her kinfolk when they had nowhere else to go—but this was too much. For Ephraim to forbid her to aid Lucy when her sister needed help was more than Hannah could bear. Contradicting Ephraim directly, she told him, as he reported, "that she would go, and that the bed should not be brought back." Hannah ignited her husband's rage, he claimed, by "adding an expression of contempt, too indecent to repeat."[34]

At this point Ephraim lost control. "Provoked," he said, "at her insolence," he snatched up an old bayonet and threatened Hannah.[35] Then, according to Bill Martin's trial testimony, the Wheelers' toddler, frightened by her parents' argument, ran into Martin's room and called for help.[36]

Martin's entrance into Ephraim and Hannah's fight did nothing to calm the conflict. Martin warned Ephraim: "I told him he had better not strike her." But Ephraim "swore he would," and admitted in his published account that he "struck her on the backside."[37] Martin responded by seizing Wheeler, and after a "severe scuffle" in which Martin acknowledged he had "struck" Wheeler, Martin forcibly put his brother-in-law out of the house. Still raging, Ephraim told Martin he would complain to Justice Walker, which he did, and Walker fined each of them a day's pay.[38]

After Martin threw Wheeler out of the house, Hannah may have imagined that her husband would cool off in time and, despite their hostilities, life would go on as before. They had often quarreled, and Ephraim's violence was nothing new.[39] So when Ephraim returned from making his complaint against Martin to Justice Walker, Hannah could not have anticipated that Ephraim would not only issue an entirely new threat, but would proceed immediately to act upon it. He decided, he said, "never to live with my wife anymore"; and he would take the children with him—Betsy to be put into domestic service, and Ephraim, Jr., to accompany him to sea.[40] In the distant past, when the children had been too young to work, it had been Hannah who took off with them, always leaving Ephraim behind. Now, for the first time, Hannah faced separation, forcible separation, from her children.

Hannah, who had lived in many households during her forty-two years, understood that as a wife she could do nothing legally to stop her husband. In Massachusetts, as elsewhere in the United States, free children were subject to their father's rule. The father was the guardian and could take them wherever he wished, or indenture them, without interference by their mother. In light of this widely understood reality, Wheeler and his defense lawyers claimed that Hannah invented the rape accusation and taught her children to testify falsely so as to keep them with her and dispose of her husband.

This argument, drawing on the stereotypes of a mother's fierce attachment to her offspring and her jealous rage against a deserting husband, possessed a certain logic. But as Attorney General Sullivan declared in court, there was no evidence to support such a claim. The facts as presented actually contradicted it, and the contrivance of the children's perjury would have been so remarkable that to manage it Hannah "must have had an uncommon share of ability, and incomparable degree of artifice, and more adroitness than the greatest lawyer."[41] In fact, instead of contriving how to bring Ephraim into court on a capital charge, Hannah must have hoped that her husband's passion would subside and, as had happened so often before, he would turn for assistance to the Odel family. Indeed when Ephraim did leave, taking Betsy and Ephraim, Jr., and his horse, his immediate destination was Hannah's brother Isaac Odel's house, several miles east over the hills in Cummington.

Hannah could only watch helplessly as Betsy and young Ephraim collected their few belongings and set out with their father on his horse. As the rain fell, and with no other plans in mind, she probably returned indoors to help her sister Lucy. As she worked, tending the fire, washing, preparing food, her anger toward Ephraim may have ripened, intensified by her sense of helplessness.

Several hours later, when Betsy and Ephraim, Jr., returned on the horse, Hannah was not necessarily surprised. She knew Ephraim was an impulsive, passionate man, and if he had changed his mind, it was not the first time. From Betsy's courtroom testimony it does not seem that Hannah interrupted her chores to make a fuss over their return. Nor did Betsy's bruised face and tear-reddened eyes lead Hannah to express sympathy immediately. She knew that her husband struck the children; that was part of their lives, and hers. But later, when they sat down to eat their midday meal, she must have seen something in Betsy's expression or manner that led Hannah to seek out a space in the crowded household where she could speak privately with Betsy.

That afternoon, when Betsy told of her father's attack, and that he "had to do" with her, Hannah was shocked. Almost immediately, without consulting anyone, neither her sister nor her brother-in-law who had defended her that morning, she decided to call on Squire Robert Walker, their neighbor. Perhaps she felt that Bill Martin's intervention that morning, though well-intended, had made matters worse. She may also have recognized that there was nothing she or her kinsmen could do within the law to stop Ephraim from taking the children, Betsy in particular. Over the years Hannah had learned to live with Ephraim's rages, his blows, his passions, his sexual demands. But what about her daughter Betsy, the child now on the edge of womanhood with whom she had bonded so closely when first she fled from Ephraim over a decade before? Hannah could not allow Betsy to be violated again.[42] Her heart compelled her to protect Betsy, and her duty as a mother before God demanded it. Ephraim the commandment-breaker could go to hell; but he must not take Betsy with him. Only the authority of the state, of the law, of Justice Walker, could block her husband's evil intentions. At the very least, Walker could advise a desperate mother what to do.

But right now Hannah must not leave her poor child alone. So she called Bill Martin and, he reported, "she wished I would go to Esq. Walker's—for something had happened," Hannah told Martin, "worse than his [Ephraim's] striking her." "What was it?" Martin asked, but Hannah preferred not to say. What Ephraim had done, Hannah said, "was almost too bad to tell." But Martin insisted: "I asked her to tell me." Finally, choosing the most indirect words to describe the unspeakable, she revealed that her husband "had had to do with Betsy."[43]

Half an hour later, when Martin returned with the justice of the peace, he had already explained "in part" the purpose of his call. While waiting for Squire Walker, Hannah must have told Betsy that the squire was coming to help them and that she must tell him what happened. But that was not easy. When Walker came into the Martin household he quite properly directed that he must interview Betsy alone so as to hear her statement free from external influences. Yet as we have seen, when he separated Betsy from her mother and began to question the child, Walker reported, "she immediately fell to crying." "I could get nothing from her," Walker testified, so he "called the mother in." Only then, under Hannah's reassuring gaze, could Betsy summon the courage to repeat her frightened account of her father's violence.[44]

Betsy was so shaken, and Walker himself was so affected by the emotional crisis he had stepped into, that he wanted to reassure Betsy and her mother, withdraw, and leave them to each other. Physical evidence of the assault he knew was necessary, so he asked Hannah if she had examined Betsy's body for proof of the violation. Hannah told him she had, and that Betsy had sustained private injury, so Walker, as he said, from "motives of delicacy" made no attempt to obtain independent confirmation.[45] Before returning home and to his own children Walker assured them that he would issue a warrant for Ephraim's arrest immediately and would hold a Justice's Court at his house to arraign Wheeler as soon as he could, probably Monday, June 10.

Between the time Walker left on the gloomy Saturday afternoon of June 8 and the following bright, cool, Monday morning, Hannah had plenty of time to reflect on the action she had led Betsy to initiate. During this interval she could not have known that Betsy's complaint was the capital charge of rape. This crime had never been charged in Berkshire County, although lesser sexual charges against fathers—lewd and lascivious conduct, and incest—had been tried. Justice Walker himself did not seem certain of the charge, since in the earliest document we have of the case, a "Bill of Costs" in Walker's hand dated June 10, 1805, he described Betsy's complaint as the crime of "having Carnol Knoledge [sic] of her Body," not rape.[46] At first Hannah may have supposed that her husband would be fined or whipped and sent to prison for several years. Such a punishment would protect Betsy until she was ready to leave home and make a life apart from her mother.

That Hannah was prepared to take the steps she did toward bringing Ephraim to justice demonstrates her confidence in Justice Walker and the authority he represented. In light of what had happened, Hannah surely believed it was right to bring her husband to trial. But if she was not also confident that the authorities would actually punish Ephraim she would have been foolish to involve them. After all, if Ephraim became so enraged and violent over the moving of his bed and his brother-in-law's intrusion into his family, then he might turn murderous if Massachusetts officials tried to restrain him and failed. Hannah's decision to call on the authorities expressed not only her own self-assurance, but also her belief that the state, the new Commonwealth of Massachusetts, could and would protect her and her children.

For the moment Hannah's life resumed a more ordinary rhythm. She could go back to helping in the delivery and aftercare of Lucy Martin's baby. And she would tend to her own three children. The day after the turmoil of June 8 was the Sabbath; but the women in a household with a newborn would not be idle. Sunday proved very rainy and even some of the most pious families in the neighborhood stayed home from church, so it is unlikely that Hannah brought her children to the Windsor meetinghouse to pray with the Reverend Dorrance, although she may have stopped her chores to pray privately at home.[47] In light of the shocks Hannah had so recently sustained—Ephraim's departure, his attack on Betsy, and Betsy's tearful recounting of the assault before Justice Walker—Hannah would want time to reflect. As a reader, she may have owned a small Bible, a prayer book, or a book of psalms. In their pages she may have found guidance and support. She could also have turned to her family. Her sister Lucy may have been some comfort and Bill Martin, who had come to her defense so forcefully, may have offered advice. Indeed, several of the Odel clan may have gathered with Hannah that Sunday.[48]

Monday dawned bright and cool, and Walker sent word that he was holding Ephraim in custody and that Hannah and her brother-in-law should come to his house with Betsy and Ephraim, Jr. There, either in Walker's "keeping room" (kitchen) or in his parlor and before her father's gaze, Betsy must report her complaint under oath, and Ephraim, Jr., must tell what he knew. While her children testified, Hannah stood by, listening, as she did when Ephraim denied the complaint and went on to ask Walker to have "the girl examined . . . by a Jury of Matrons and Physicians."[49]

Now Walker, having twice heard Betsy's account, and having been called in to his poor neighbors' household twice to deal with Wheeler's violence, may have lost patience with Ephraim. Walker may well have concluded that Wheeler had previously manipulated him and the law by convincing him to fine Bill Martin for violently ejecting Wheeler from Martin's own house. As a justice of the peace and as a father, Justice Walker found Betsy so much more believable than Ephraim that without any further physical examination of Betsy, he ordered Wheeler to be jailed for trial before the Supreme Judicial Court at its next session. Afterward, when he filled out the form requiring Betsy, Ephraim, Jr., Hannah, and William Martin to appear before the Supreme Judicial Court, he described Wheeler's crime as "Rape."[50] From June 10 onward, Hannah and Betsy knew that when Ephraim came to trial his life would be at risk.

When Squire Walker's court finished, Deputy Sheriff Francis Cooppers took Wheeler off to Lenox jail, a twenty-mile walk through the villages of Dalton and Pittsfield. Hannah, the two children, and Martin returned to the house. What Hannah was thinking we cannot know. Certainly she would have approved of Walker's having Ephraim locked up; otherwise she would not have encouraged Betsy to lodge her complaint. Yet we must not assume that she foresaw the capital charge against her husband. Now she knew that her decision to call on the state for protection had taken on an awesome seriousness. That night the stars shone brightly in the heavens above Windsor. If Hannah looked up at them she may have wondered whether she had counseled Betsy wisely. Though the day that was ending had brought them immediate safety, it had also seen the transformation of their private family crisis into a public matter. That night, though the growing season had been under way for weeks, a killing frost struck the region, foreshadowing perhaps the clear, cold justice of the state.[51]

During the next three months, as she awaited Ephraim's trial, Hannah had plenty of time to reconsider her judgment to support Betsy's complaint, and discuss it with her brother and sisters and their husbands. That the family did not simply and straightforwardly unite behind Ephraim's prosecution is suggested by the fact that Betsy did not remain with her mother at the Martin household throughout the summer. In August she went to live with her uncle Isaac Odel's family, probably because her labor was needed there, but possibly owing to tensions between Betsy and her mother, or because Isaac Odel wished to influence Betsy's resolve.[52] At the trial, remarkably, Ephraim called on his brothers-in-law, Isaac Odel and Michael Pepper, to challenge Betsy's veracity. Wheeler must have concluded that because Odel and Pepper did not support prosecuting him, they would help get him off by swearing that his daughter, their niece, was a liar. But as we have seen, their testimony that Betsy was "not believed so well as some" did not shake her credibility for the jurors.[53] Ironically, from the standpoint of Wheeler's defense, the evidence that Betsy did not live continuously under her mother's authority and that she was standing up for herself in a divided family reinforced both Betsy's character and that of her mother. Hannah had raised a respectable daughter who pursued justice despite enormous pressure.

During the trial Hannah was summoned to court and so witnessed the proceedings, though she was never called to testify.[54] It must have been grueling for her to sit in public view and be forced to relive the fight with Ephraim of June 8, and to hear again Betsy's, Bill Martin's, and Squire Walker's accounts of what happened. Moreover she had to accept silently the public abuse that the two urbane gentlemen— John Hulbert and Daniel Dewey, her husband's lawyers—condescendingly heaped on her before hundreds of spectators. In light of all that, the jury's verdict that evening must have come as a relief. To have come so far and suffered so much only to have Ephraim exonerated and, overflowing with rage, sent back to live with her, Betsy, and the younger children would have been a nightmare. The jury's verdict vindicated her judgment in seeking protection from Justice Walker and the state. Hannah's children—Betsy in particular—and Hannah herself would now be safe.

The next morning, when the court reconvened to pronounce her husband's sentence, whatever initial satisfaction Hannah felt was undercut. Judge Sewall's order that Ephraim Wheeler "be hanged by the neck untill he be Dead" was—as intended—awful. Perhaps Hannah's first reaction was a feeling of triumph. But within the next two weeks whatever sense of victory Hannah may have had was overtaken by other feelings. In her petition to save Ephraim's life Hannah's sentiments, though shaped and articulated by Ephraim's lawyers, the men who had attacked her in court, survive.[55]

Which words in the petition belong to Hannah and which to Hulbert and Dewey cannot be established with certainty. The overall tone and argument must have come from the lawyers, since Hannah's petition (marked also by Betsy and Ephraim, Jr.) complements their own plea for their client's life. We can, however, detect three themes consistent with our knowledge of Hannah. First, she claimed for herself and her children a special place in his punishment because "he hath greatly injured us" personally. Though properly deferential to the judicial process, she believed that as victims she and Betsy ought to be heard. Second, she asserted their claims of kinship as wife and children. Despite the injury Ephraim inflicted, their duty to a husband and father could not be erased. Though in angry moments Hannah herself had wished to kill Ephraim, she had always known that would be contrary to God—in short, "wicked."[56] Ephraim had wronged them grievously, but at the most elemental level she and the children still owed him some measure of loyalty. Third, although Hannah had no objection to the death penalty in general, and she certainly did not wish to see Ephraim freed from prison, she could not rest comfortably with the thought that her actions would send him to die.

On June 8 and June 10 Hannah and her daughter had sought protection only, not vengeance. Ephraim, she could not forget, was her husband of fourteen years with whom she had borne five children. Alone among those whose reactions are recorded, Hannah and her children expressed feelings of "awful anxiety," declaring themselves "most unhappy and distressed." This genteel language was very likely Daniel Dewey's, for he had used this vocabulary to describe Hannah's and the children's feelings in his and Hulbert's own petition. But such thoughts were never ascribed to anyone else; they were uniquely attributed to Hannah and the children. That her petition represented her views accurately Hannah attested by signing "Hannah Wheeler." That Hannah, alone among the Wheelers, could write her name was a rare achievement among poor Massachusetts women of color at that time and an emblem of her Sutton upbringing, her respectability in Yankee society, and her own self-respect.[57]

We do not imagine that the petition expressed all of Hannah's thoughts, or that having signed it she could escape struggling with the outcome of the trial. But this is the only record of her thoughts that survives. After September 26, 1805, Hannah vanishes from the public record. The Berkshire Court responsible for conferring guardianships shows no record of her being awarded legal guardianship of her children, a circumstance probably related to the family's poverty. Her disappearance from the records might also be the consequence of moving away, to New York State, the most common destination for Berkshire migrants, or to Vermont. Although most of the Odels stayed in Berkshire—two of Hannah's sisters died in Hinsdale (which abutted Windsor and Partridgefield) in the 1840s—and other kinsmen, the Martins, Dunbars, and Percips, also stayed on in the area, the lure of western New York had beckoned some of them. Where Hannah went, how long she lived, and when she died we cannot say. But we do know that on June 8 she resolved her quandary boldly, by calling on the state to make her family's crisis public business. When that business ended, so too did Hannah's historical visibility.

CHAPTER FIVE

The Condemned Man

I was born at *Rochester,* in the County of *Plymouth,* August 1st, 1762. My father, whose name was ISAAC WHEELER, was a sea-faring man, and sustained a decent reputation. My mother died of a pleurisy, when I was seven and an half years old; and about a year after, my father went to sea, and for grief at the loss of his wife, and other troubles of mind, flung himself overboard, and was drowned.

Being thus left an orphan, at the age of eight years and a half, I was, together with a brother and a sister, bound out to one JEDUTHAN HAMMOND, a shoemaker. He was a passionate and violent man, was extremely harsh and severe with us, and took no care for our instruction in learning or behaviour. After we had lived with him about four years, he in the year 1775, sold my brother to the owners of a privateer, for the remainder of his time.

[Ephraim Wheeler], *Narrative of the Life of Ephraim Wheeler.* . . . (1806)

Ephraim Wheeler was never a happy man or contented with his lot in life. But when he awakened on June 8, 1805, he had no reason to suppose that this particular Saturday would be any worse than other days, nor that within hours he would stand accused of a shocking crime. Yet before nightfall a warrant would be issued for his arrest, and two days later he would find himself locked into Lenox jail. Once more, he believed, he was the victim of malice and misfortune, but this time it was his own children who stood against him in a conflict that could put him to death. Though his life had been studded with disappointment—each gain that he made was snatched away, and every step forward seemed followed by a setback—now his name was ruined, and he stood on the verge of destruction.[1]

In jail Wheeler was angry and depressed, resistant to the ministrations of the clergymen who visited to pray with him. Shut off from the companionship of the Bible or secular books by his own illiteracy, he kept his own counsel. Usually close-mouthed about his past life, only when the gallows beckoned, on the very eve of the day he was slated to hang, did Wheeler consent to tell the story of his life to Heman Willard and a handful of witnesses. But the condemned man was hardly loquacious. Willard reported that "close and urgent interrogation" was required to extract Wheeler's account of himself; and even then Wheeler remained "anxious to conceal many important events of his life."[2] Wheeler's continuing anger at the authorities, at his wife and children, and at his fate made him anything but eager to review his life so as to "gratify the curiosity of the public."[3] Most likely it was the deep shadow of death, reinforced by the promise of payment, that led him to reveal as much as he did. If he was to die, he could at least tell his side of the story to defend himself, which he had been barred by law from doing in court. And Willard, the printer, would pay him for giving his life story for the press—a small sum that could buy Wheeler his final amenities, rum, tobacco, perhaps his favorite meal.

The men who interrogated Ephraim Wheeler wanted a chronological account of his life starting at the beginning because they believed that the origins of Wheeler's crime lay in his past experience. Criminal autobiographies, like the one they procured, were not only human interest stories enlivened by sensational acts, they were also didactic moral tales that helped readers to recognize and avoid the paths of evil. In earlier generations, when these accounts were written by clergymen, such criminal "lives" had stressed the Devil's power to exploit people's natural depravity. But now, in the early decades of the new republic, whether prepared by clergymen or journalists, these stories stressed childhood experience and parental moral guidance—in short, nurture and environment rather than inborn sinfulness. When Heman Willard and his collaborators extracted Wheeler's story for public consumption, they hoped readers would find it engrossing as well as instructive for the conduct of their own and their children's lives.[4]

Wheeler's *Narrative* is told in the first person and was "penned from his mouth"; but, like present-day celebrity autobiographies, it was not a verbatim text but an "as told to" account.[5] Drawn up by a journalist (probably Willard) in summary form, and with the participation of a clergyman (probably Samuel Shepard), the vocabulary, grammar, and organization were not the authentic product of the illiterate "author," although three witnesses swore that the content was his. We believe the *Narrative* to be reliable for the most part, because we can verify from other sources some of the "facts" Wheeler reports, and we see no reason why he would falsify other details that locals would readily know. That Wheeler's account, like other memoirs and autobiographies, is subjective and self-serving and may contain false and misleading statements is to be expected. Wheeler did not give this account under oath, it was never tested in court, and he was a convicted felon. So, like a jury, we have approached this evidence cautiously and critically. We have concluded that though Wheeler's narrative does not present "the whole truth and nothing but the truth," it does contain valuable information.

Wheeler began with his birth: "I was born at *Rochester,* in the County of *Plymouth,* August 1st, 1762."[6] At that time Rochester, a minor port and farming town founded in 1686 some fifty miles south of

Boston on Buzzard's Bay, was home to some 300 families, about 1,900 people. Like many coastal towns of the era, Rochester had both a community of farmers who dwelled inland and, on the Bay at Mattapoisett and Marion, small maritime settlements that engaged in deepwater trade and fishing. At the time of Wheeler's birth, during the waning months of the French and Indian War, the region was prospering. The prices of farm products had been pushed up by the demands of military forces and, with plenty of work both on land and on sea, the earnings of artisans and laborers had also increased. Although Ephraim was born into a poor family, general prospects in 1762 were favorable. By 1776 Rochester's population had grown by nearly one-third, to 2,450 people.[7]

Indeed the 1760s were the high point of Wheeler's childhood. His father, Isaac Wheeler, was a "sea-faring man" who, Ephraim said, "sustained a decent reputation." His mother, whose name is lost, bore Isaac Wheeler at least two other children, one boy older than Ephraim, and a younger girl. During Ephraim's earliest years it is unlikely that the little boy saw much of his father, since fishing and trading voyages usually kept men at sea for months at a time. Although a vigorous man in his twenties or thirties might earn as much as £30 a year (about half a country parson's stipend) fishing, and even more on a successful trading cruise, mariners rarely earned enough to accumulate property. Their families lived frugally, in cramped housing, usually on credit from one voyage to the next.[8] Ephraim had no complaints about his first seven years; however, the fact that neither his mother nor anyone else taught him to read or write was not only an indicator of family poverty, but also suggests that his mother too was illiterate. Indeed as a poor sailor's wife born in the 1720s or 1730s, it would have been somewhat unusual if Ephraim's mother had possessed these then predominantly masculine skills.[9]

"My mother died of a pleurisy, when I was seven and an half years old," Ephraim reported; and so in early 1770 he had to face a series of hard changes.[10] Since Isaac was seldom at home, he most likely paid to place the three children, aged between five and ten years, with a local relative or in the home of a neighbor. Too young to be productive, the children required a subsidy; and according to law their father, Isaac, was obligated to provide for them.[11] The next year, however, responsibility for Ephraim and his siblings fell to the town because Isaac Wheeler died—not heroically or by some tragic misfortune, but ignominiously. As Ephraim put it, "my father went to sea, and for grief at the loss of his wife, and other troubles of mind, flung himself overboard, and was drowned."[12]

Now the children were propertyless orphans, and the Rochester selectmen stepped in. Had there been relatives who were financially able, the usual policy would have been for the county court to grant guardianship to a relative and then to place the children in that family. But when no relatives were equipped to assume this legal and financial role, the town might face substantial expenses. The selectmen could, for example, choose to pay householders to board orphans, as they did for William Griffiths's children for more than ten years, starting in 1770. Over a decade the several Griffiths children lived in five different homes at a cost of over £60 to the taxpayers. This approach was disruptive to the children's continuity of relationships, especially among the siblings, and it was cumbersome to administer because every foster-care arrangement required the annual approval of the voters in a town meeting. In addition, Rochester voters were concerned with their tax burden. At a February 1771 meeting they were so troubled by inhabitants who "Live Idly & Mispend [sic] their Time" that they discussed building a workhouse "to set to work all Such Persons." But the workhouse proposal would have meant raising taxes to build, supply, and supervise it, so however worthy the idea, the town did nothing.[13] It was at this time that town officials had to confront the problem of the Wheeler orphans; the solution the selectmen chose, indenture to an artisan, was cheaper than boarding the children.

When a master could be found the indenture system provided one of the preferred ways of managing poor orphans. Depending on the children's ages, the town might not receive much money for the indentures; indeed, if the children were young it might have to pay a small sum. Indentures required that the children's physical needs be met and also that they would be educated and trained in a vocation. In some cases they could be kept together in a single household. Ideally, when the man who held the indenture was kind and had sufficient means to be generous, the indenture system could serve the needs of the orphans and the town as well as the master.

But according to Ephraim Wheeler, the man to whom the town fathers indentured the Wheeler orphans, the cordwainer (shoemaker) Jeduthan Hammond, was neither kind nor generous. Though Hammond came from a large and important Rochester family—his forbears had been among the first settlers and among his cousins were church and town leaders—he was poor. According to that year's tax valuation (1771) he owned only a small house with a shop either in it or adjoining, and a cow. Hammond, who was thirty-one years old, had seven years earlier married a fifteen-year-old orphan, Mary Jenney—most likely because he made her pregnant. Now, in 1771, when Hammond contracted to become master of the Wheeler children, he and his wife had only an infant daughter. Thus, by adding Ephraim and his siblings to the Hammond household, Jeduthan gained a head start toward possessing the child labor that was so vital to the New England economy.[14] In a few years Ephraim and his brother could be made into productive shoemakers, and their younger sister could help his wife, Mary, to maintain his home and raise his children. In the meantime the boys could do chores in the shop and around the house, thereby enabling him to produce more shoes. As servants indentured to the age of twenty-one, the Wheeler children's circumstances were much like slaves', except that unlike slave masters, their owner was poor and possessed only a ten-to-fifteen year interest in their well-being. But so long as Hammond did not abuse the children outrageously, they were his to do with as he wished.

For Ephraim, who had never spent much time with his own father, Jeduthan Hammond became his surrogate father from age eight until adulthood. Unlike the seafaring Isaac Wheeler, who was so often away, Hammond was a daily presence. For a dozen years Ephraim and Hammond worked side by side in the small shop, with the man teaching the boy how to make shoes. Years later, when asked to identify himself formally, Ephraim would use the same artisanal title as Hammond, "cordwainer."[15]

Hammond's conduct as master and as father figure made a deep impression on the boy, and in 1806 the forty-three-year-old Ephraim could scarcely remember anything good to say about him: "He was a passionate and violent man, was extremely harsh and severe with us, and took no care for our instruction in learning or behaviour."[16] Hammond did not head a pious household, and though he lived up to the letter of the indenture by training Ephraim as a shoemaker, he refrained from fulfilling the larger role of a master—supplying an education in literacy, morals, and religion. By Ephraim's own admission he too was a passionate, sometimes violent, man who failed to educate his own children.[17]

The similarities between indentured servitude and slavery were driven home to the thirteen-year-old Ephraim in 1775 when Hammond sold his older brother to the owners of a privateer to serve out his remaining time.[18] With Ephraim maturing as a tradesman, and with the demand for sailors rising in response to the Revolutionary crisis, Hammond's decision to sell the older Wheeler boy may have been a straightforward business decision. Alternatively, selling

Ephraim's brother could have been a disciplinary measure, either to punish misbehavior, or to head off an unruly combination between the two orphan boys. In any case, his brother's sale came at a critical time for Ephraim; it gave him a lesson in his own powerlessness just as he was beginning to form a mature masculine identity. For the present Ephraim had no choice but to submit to his master; but thirty years later his anger toward Hammond still burned.

What Ephraim remembered most vividly of his relation to Jeduthan Hammond was conflict and punishment. He continued to serve his master by making shoes until he was seventeen years old in 1779, at which time Hammond sold Ephraim's service to a privateer for a year. Thereafter, having tasted a measure of autonomy as a sailor, when Ephraim returned to Hammond's household in 1780, he was restive. With three years remaining on his indenture, Ephraim ran away from Hammond "on account of his cruelty" to the nearby port of New Bedford where, using the alias "Ephraim Barks," he signed on to another privateer for a year.[19] But when that service ended, Hammond found Ephraim on shore and brought him home. So angry was Hammond with his runaway bondsman, Ephraim recalled, that he "chained me to a shoe-bench, as a punishment."[20]

Later that year, believing that the shoe-bench manacles had taught Ephraim to be a faithful and obedient servant, Hammond left the youth at home while he seized the opportunity to earn some ready cash by enlisting as a three-month volunteer for the defense of nearby Rhode Island. Over twenty of his Hammond kinsmen had already served in Revolutionary armies. When the shoemaker-soldier took sick after only a month, however, he came home to Rochester and sent the nineteen-year-old Ephraim in his place. As on the privateering ships, Ephraim still had to take orders, but now he was once more beyond Jeduthan Hammond's immediate control. Ephraim was, moreover, in a world of young men where his own poverty and de-

pendent status hardly set him apart. As had been true of the privateering crews, the short-term enlisted men who served in defense of
Rhode Island were drawn from the poorest class of Yankees and immigrants, and included some men of mixed racial origins—white,
black, and Indian—characteristic of southern New England maritime
communities.[21] In the army, as on shipboard, they all shared the
rough equality of laboring men commanded by officers. For their
work, mostly the heavy labor of pick-and-shovel construction, Ephraim's illiteracy was no handicap. Instead, he found his strength and
vitality to be assets.[22] He had grown to be a man among men.

Yet when the twenty-year-old Ephraim returned to Hammond's
shop he was once more a bondsman, very much aware that in less
than a year, on August 1, 1783, he would become a free man. His frustration with his circumstances would evidently play a part in Ephraim's most critical confrontation with Hammond, a contest of anger
and willfulness in which Hammond defeated Ephraim. The drama
began probably in March 1783 with one of the ordinary setbacks of
late-winter agricultural life. Hammond had sent Ephraim with a team
of cattle to deliver some logs to a sawmill, and on the way the team
got mired in a mud hole. Whether Ephraim was angry at himself for
guiding the cattle into this slough and so took out his anger on the
animals or whether, as he said, he simply "whipped the cattle a little,
in order to get through," when Hammond saw Ephraim beating his
team, he became enraged. Picking up a wooden handspike that was
supporting the timber, Hammond hit the young man over the head
and, Ephraim said, "injured me much, and endangered my life."[23]

In principle, if the blow was as severe as he claimed, Ephraim
could have brought his master before a justice. Servants occasionally
won cases against their masters for cruelty, and Hammond might have
been fined or Ephraim might even have been released from his remaining months of service. But as a servant bringing his master to

court, the odds were against him; and in retaliation Hammond might punish him further.[24] So, deeply resentful, Ephraim "determined to live no more with him." Choosing his moment, early one morning Ephraim fled once more, this time to the north, in the direction of Boston.[25]

He walked quickly and made good time. By nightfall he had reached the village of Easton, about forty miles away from where he had started and less than a day's walk to Boston. But unbeknownst to Ephraim, Jeduthan Hammond was on horseback in hot pursuit; he caught up with the fugitive and seized him that very evening. Hammond was angry, and resolved to teach Ephraim obedience. So the next morning when they set out for Rochester Hammond "tied me [Ephraim] to his horses tail, with a rope about my neck, and in that manner led, or rather dragged me back to his house, forty miles in one day." So as to shame Ephraim further, "when we came to places where I was known, he would call the people out, and tell them that he had caught the runaway."[26] Being chained to his shoe bench had not taught Ephraim Wheeler to submit, nor had hitting him on the head with a club; Hammond hoped that public humiliation of the young man would finally break him.

But for the moment that, too, failed. Ephraim was indeed "mortified by this treatment," yet he would not give in. Angry and depressed, like Betsy many years later he was fatalistic. Using a phrase that is hauntingly familiar from Betsy's testimony, he admitted, "I thought it were as well to die one way as another." So no sooner was he untied from the horse's tail and allowed to enter his master's house than he took off once more—this time for Providence, some forty miles away. Considering all Ephraim had endured over the prior two days, his flight to the Rhode Island port was remarkable, even for a robust twenty-year-old. The older Hammond had no mind to pursue him again, but neither would he give up. So he sent his brother and another man to capture the wayward servant; and, Ephraim lamented, "I was pursued, caught, bound and carried back to my master" before he could board a ship. As he later explained: "now wore out with hardship, and cruel usage, and my spirits entirely depressed, I despaired of relief, and concluded to submit to my hard fortune . . . and do the best I could."[27] At last Hammond had broken Ephraim's spirit.

Finally, life was easier—master and servant made peace. Ephraim behaved "very steadily" and Hammond, Ephraim admitted, "treated me well."[28] By mastering his rage, toward both Hammond and his lot in life, Ephraim achieved an equilibrium that he would find hard to maintain as a free man. And in yielding to Hammond's authority he carried away two important lessons about patriarchy: that a master ruled his household as an act of will; and that when he was challenged, as Ephraim had challenged Hammond with disobedience, a patriarch could succeed only by combining force and intimidation.

Ironically, once Ephraim came of age and was free to leave, the young man who had thrice run away, recognizing that his master had "lately treated me well," contracted to stay on for a year as Hammond's hired man. And when that year was up in August 1784, Ephraim agreed to stay on still longer. Evidently now that Ephraim Wheeler was a free man, Jeduthan Hammond did not seem such a cruel master as before. It is worth noting that although Wheeler later characterized Hammond as "harsh and severe," Ephraim made no specific complaints of whipping, hunger, or inadequate clothing and shelter, hardships that indentured children sometimes endured. Indeed, now that Ephraim was regularly employed and saving money, his life seemed to be pointing toward the kind of modest independence that poor men in New England hoped to achieve.[29] At this time, he remembered, he was even courting a woman, Susanna Randal, and "expected to marry her."[30]

Whether this was all really so, or mostly the rose-colored nostalgia of a condemned man, cannot be established. What is clear, however, is that Ephraim's romance with Susanna Randal in 1783 and 1784 came to play a large role in his later understanding of himself and the world. Though he remained bitter about Jeduthan Hammond's rough treatment, it was his relationship with Susanna that he later believed was pivotal for his adult life. Ephraim's perception of himself as a victim seems to date less from his boyhood as an orphan than from his failure to win Susanna's hand.

No evidence survives to reveal Ephraim's earliest feelings about women and girls. Though he was at home with his mother during his first seven and a half years, apart from noting her death he said not a word about her in his narrative. Perhaps his memories from early childhood were made so painful by her sickness and death that he had learned to suppress all thoughts of her if he was to survive; and by the time he was in his forties he scarcely remembered her at all. Neither did he speak of his younger sister, though—except when he was away at sea or in the army—he lived in the same household with her until he was twenty-two or twenty-three years old.[31] The woman of his childhood whom he did recall was Mary Jenney Hammond. For just as Jeduthan Hammond was his father figure growing up, it appears that Mrs. Hammond was his surrogate mother. Though she would have four sons and four daughters of her own before Ephraim's departure, he believed she had treated him as if he, too, was her child. She was the only person in Ephraim's entire life whom he remembered in wholly positive terms: "Mrs. Hammond always used me well, and would frequently take my part, asking her husband how he could treat a poor orphan child so cruelly."[32] Though Ephraim's later career exposed his troubled relationship to women, both as husband and patriarch, Mrs. Hammond's kindness, and possibly love, gave him a lasting idea of the sympathy and comfort women could provide.

But according to Ephraim, after he suffered a serious setback in the fall of 1784, when he injured himself "by lifting a stone," Susanna Randal disappointed him. Because of the injury Ephraim was unable to work for a whole year. During that time the small property he had been able to accumulate working for Hammond was lost in payment to "Physicians and Nurses." When he recovered in 1785 he was penniless, but he still looked forward to marrying the woman he had courted. Susanna, however, was now unwilling. In telling the story Ephraim deflected blame away from Susanna by explaining that "her friends persuaded her to refuse me, because I was destitute of property."[33] Whatever the reality that lay behind Susanna's decision, Wheeler did not look into himself to explain her rejection, nor did he focus his frustration on her. Instead he blamed the misfortune on external circumstances: his lifting accident and the hostility of her friends.

Wheeler was not, to be sure, a reader of the sentimental, romantic novels that were so popular in his era; yet his response to being jilted was precisely that of a novel's man of feeling.[34] The disappointment of losing Susanna, Wheeler lamented, "was too great for me to bear; it lay with such weight on my mind, that I took no comfort day or night; I wandered about from place to place, in a very unsettled state of mind, and knew not what to do with myself."[35] With Susanna Randal he had hoped to become a husband and household head, a complete man. But now, with neither a master over him nor the comfort of a woman's kindness, Wheeler felt himself adrift. Because of a woman he had lost his way.

Some men in these circumstances would have turned to Jesus, finding a new hope in salvation. A few years earlier, when Ephraim was in his late teens, he had sought out Christian answers in Elder Asa Hunt's Baptist meeting in Middleborough, the town just north of Rochester. After the "remarkable dark day" in New England in 1780, many believed the daytime darkness was an immediate portent of the last judgment. Like many young common folk, Ephraim was caught up in the ensuing revival; and "for a long time," he reported, he "constantly attended" Elder Hunt's church.[36] But Ephraim never found Jesus, and by the time Randal jilted him in 1785, he was no longer attending church. He had tried religion, but turned away. Now, at a loss as to how to continue to live and work, he decided to return to sea: "to get rid of my troubles, I shipped myself on board the brig *James*, and sailed to Brazil."[37] Once more he would have a master over him, food and shelter would be provided, and he would have a regimen to follow, as well as the companionship of other poor, mostly unattached men with few prospects.

The yearlong voyage did not ease his mind. Like his father, who fifteen years earlier had gone to sea after losing his wife, Ephraim found the healing powers of ocean travel wanting. During this time, Ephraim remembered, "the distress and anxiety of my mind was so great, that I was many times tempted to plunge into the ocean, and drown myself and my troubles together."[38] Poor and untutored though he was, Ephraim described himself not as a tough, hard-bitten man of action, but as a vulnerable man of feeling. But unlike his father, Ephraim did not leap overboard and make the ultimate flight from his troubles, however much he was tempted. Instead he came ashore and headed inland, away from the familiar flatlands of southeastern New England, away from the scenes of past unhappiness.

He landed in western Massachusetts, in Hampshire County, a large upland agricultural region of some sixty townships, bisected by the wide, fertile Connecticut River valley. This home county of Judge Simeon Strong and his cousin Governor Caleb Strong was a land dominated by a standing order of orthodox clergymen and magistrates whose wealth was founded on trade and the ownership of land. In contrast to the region of Ephraim's birth, where religious dissent and the mixing of farming and maritime activities, as well as

blacks, Indians, and English people, made for a kind of popular plu-
ralism, Hampshire's stable, prosperous, farming townships encouraged county leaders to maintain the ideal of Calvinist uniformity. In
many of the long-settled farming communities and even in some of
the commercial centers, Baptists were few, Quakers unknown, and the
orthodox ruled without challenge. Only among the poorer towns at
the eastern and western rims of the valley were Baptists more numerous.[39]

In 1786, the year Ephraim came to the region, conflict over debt,
the law courts, and taxation was tearing Hampshire apart. Starting
that summer with peaceful protest meetings, and moving on to armed
crowds in the fall, farmers, many of whom owed debts they could not
pay, protested the legal system and then went on to block the operation of the courts. This uprising—known as Shays' Rebellion—also
led to fighting in Berkshire. The scale of the conflict was substantially
greater in the more populous Hampshire County than in its western neighbor; at its peak in January 1787, some 1,500 armed rebels
marched on the U.S. armory in Springfield. Among their number was
twenty-four-year-old Ephraim Wheeler who, having come to the area
prepared to find work as a shoemaker and farm worker, found himself
swept up in armed conflict. But the rebellion did not last long. At
Springfield Shays and his followers retreated after the officer defending the armory fired artillery into their midst, killing four insurgents
and wounding twenty others.[40] Ten days later, as Ephraim put it,
his service ended when "the insurrection was quelled by General
[Benjamin] Lincoln," whose troop of 3,000 men surprised the rebels
in the hill town of Petersham.[41]

Ephraim, like the others, scattered at the arrival of the government
forces; but he did not go far. Soon after, he landed a job just a few
miles away at Greenwich, a poor, upland farming town, where the
blacksmith, Jesse Hynes, hired Wheeler for a year to work the bellows

and pound iron.[42] This was hardly an opportunity, inasmuch as only Ephraim's strength and stamina were called into service, and none of his skills as shoemaker, sailor, or farm worker. But the work did provide a livelihood while the young drifter figured out what to do next.

It does not seem that Ephraim felt any certainty about where he should go or what he should do. Working for Hynes evidently did not suit Ephraim or his employer; when Wheeler had completed his year's labor with Hynes in 1788 he found work in the prosperous farming town of Hatfield, some fifteen miles to the west, in the Connecticut valley. Here he lighted only briefly. For when he learned that Susanna Randal, "the girl whom I had formerly courted," had left the Rochester area and had gone to work seventy-five miles away from Hatfield, at Saratoga, New York, Ephraim took off to see her. They had not seen each other for three years, and Ephraim hoped he could now persuade her to marry him. But when he met Susanna face-to-face, she told him that "she was soon to be married to another man." Once more Ephraim was heartbroken. "Foolishly," he admitted, he had pursued his impossible dream and as a result his "former wounds, which had been nearly healed, were all open again, and set a bleeding anew." Defeated in love, the young laborer pictured himself as a romantic victim, declaring that this rejection "compleated my misfortunes, and put the finishing stroke to my peace of mind."[43]

Because of Ephraim's elegant diction here, one wonders whether these were truly Wheeler's recollections of that sad time over fifteen years before. Perhaps the clergymen who visited him shaped his story so as to make the condemned man's narrative into a sermon exposing the misguided consciousness so common in romantic novels and poetry. It may also be that these were not Ephraim's precise sentiments at the time, but that in the course of reviewing his life he had come to take comfort from his legend of romantic loss as a way of justifying his failures to himself. Certainly the romantic outlook had been assimi-

lated in popular culture by 1806, finding expression in newspaper es-
says and verse as well as the love songs and tavern ballads of common
folk. If, as the illiterate Ephraim acknowledged, he drank too much
and did not live out the Yankee ideal of industry and thrift, it was not
he but his tragic disappointment that was to blame.[44]

Certainly Wheeler's life during the next few years was disordered.
In 1788, in "despair" at leaving Susanna, "the only object dear to me
on earth," Ephraim did not go to sea as he had three years before, nor
did he head farther west to seek out opportunities on the New York
frontier, a common Yankee destination. Instead he made his way east-
ward through Berkshire County until he landed at Windsor, in the
hills on the border with Hampshire. "Friendless and forsaken by all
the world," he stayed on for a year, getting stints of work at four
yeoman farms. The following year, 1789, when George Washington
took the oath to become the first president under the Constitution, Wheeler found work in the next town, Plainfield, in Hampshire
County.[45]

At this point he began to form a network of new relationships and
to think about the future. One of his new companions was Asa
Dunbar, a black yeoman and charcoal-maker. Together they agreed to
go to the Genesee country in far western New York to seek out the
prospects of working to own land. Wheeler, now twenty-seven years
old, hoped to become his own man rather than remaining an itiner-
ant laborer. But the Genesee plan faltered, and Wheeler stayed on
at Plainfield, where he worked for a farmer, Nathan Bealls. Later,
Wheeler believed, this period was fateful, because it was in Plainfield
that he met Hannah Odel, the woman of mixed racial ancestry who
would later become his wife.[46]

Although census and death records show that Wheeler's new cir-
cle of acquaintances included black and mixed-race people, both in
Wheeler's narrative and in the record of his trial race is never men-

tioned. It was not that people were color blind or indifferent to questions of race: newspapers regularly identified blacks, mulattoes, and Indians involved in crime; and Massachusetts had a long-standing statute, renewed in 1786, prohibiting marriage between whites "and any negro, Indian or mulatto."[47] This was the law that blocked Ephraim's marriage to Hannah in the town of Worthington. But until the early 1780s, when the Supreme Judicial Court ruled in several cases that the state constitution of 1780 had abolished slavery, virtually all blacks in Massachusetts had been slaves. Thus the categories for identifying people in law and public records had been those of freedom and slavery; social rank; occupation; and, in the case of women, marital status. In the legal records of the 1780s officials often used "Negro" or "Freeman" as surnames, a practice that faded once former slaves achieved an identity as free citizens. Although from 1790 onward racial identification was part of the U.S. census, the use of racial designations for people in Massachusetts legal records was irregular and incomplete. State legal procedures, which were largely wedded to past practices, seldom identified people by race.[48]

In society, however, during the early national era a rising color consciousness characterized all of New England, especially those commercially developed areas where most free blacks lived and where genteel, cosmopolitan social pretensions were advancing most rapidly. In these communities, the race hierarchy mattered; and unless blacks were clearly subordinate, whites felt demeaned by association with them. But on the upland Yankee frontier the old consciousness persisted, and color distinctions mattered less. In 1788, for example, a white congregation in Rutland, Vermont, ordained a mulatto, Lemuel Haynes, who had a white wife and who had served the region as a circuit rider. Only in a later generation would his parishioners come to view his color as a problem for the respectability of their congregation.[49] In the late 1780s and for some years thereafter in the Yankee uplands, among common folk color mattered less than property and such personal attributes as learning, piety, and industry.

Ephraim's relationship with Asa Dunbar and his subsequent connection to the Odels was thus merely unusual, not remarkable. Like them he was poor, a newcomer to the region, and struggling to find his footing in an economy that favored people with capital and kinship connections. With his past experience around the waterfront and at sea, he had most likely shared a bottle and bunked with men of color before. Coming into the Berkshire-Hampshire hill country alone, and depressed by Susanna Randal's renewed rejection, he may have counted himself lucky to find the fellowship of anyone who could offer a measure of support, however meager in material terms. Though he came to depend on these new companions, later he would complain of their influence on his decision to marry. "I never should have taken this foolish step," Wheeler declared, for it had caused his "ruin." Because his employer, Nathan Bealls, and others had urged the marriage at a time when he was vulnerable, he said that because of his "lonesome and despised condition" he had decided to marry Hannah Odel, the fair-skinned sister-in-law of his friend Asa Dunbar.[50] If Wheeler believed he had erred by marrying across the boundary of color, he never mentioned it in his narrative. Instead, when he thought back on his marriage in 1806, he regretted that he had married on the rebound from Susanna Randal's rebuff. Yet the chronology of Ephraim Wheeler's relationship with Hannah Odel suggests a somewhat different course of events, in which Ephraim had plenty of time to weigh a decision to which he was clearly committed.

Ephraim and Hannah met each other in 1789 when they were both working in Plainfield. He was about twenty-seven years old and she twenty-six. Though Wheeler may have been downcast at the time they met, two years passed before Ephraim and Hannah decided to marry, and there is no reason to suspect that they married in haste. They planned to get married from Hannah's father's house in the nearby town of Worthington. Hannah's father, Ichabod Odel, who had been identified as "negro" in the census a year earlier, evidently headed a churchgoing family, because instead of seeking marriage by a justice of the peace, the Odels went to the Worthington pastor, Josiah Spalding, who published the banns, the marriage notice, in the usual way so that Hannah and Ephraim could have a church wedding. Later, however, when Ephraim appeared before Spalding, the minister refused to marry the couple because he now realized that this would be an interracial union, and as such "contrary to the laws."[51] If Ephraim had any reservations about marrying Hannah, the Reverend Spalding's invocation of the state's marriage law gave him the perfect opportunity to back out.

But Ephraim, who admitted to evading other agreements, chose to move forward with his planned marriage to Hannah. To do so the couple skirted the law by traveling some thirty-five miles west, to New Lebanon, New York, where they found a justice of the peace, Eleazer Grant, to marry them. Unlike the Reverend Spalding, who knew the Odel family, Esquire Grant had no way of knowing that Hannah and Ephraim were not both white, and he joined the twenty-eight- and twenty-nine-year-old strangers without delay.[52] That Wheeler went to such lengths to marry Hannah suggests that however low he may have felt when he first met her, he now wholeheartedly embraced the idea of becoming her husband. As in the past, if Ephraim had felt trapped he would have taken off—back to the Massachusetts–Rhode Island coast that he knew or on to the New York frontier.

Legally married, the Wheelers returned to Ichabod Odel's house in Worthington. Although like many new couples they did not have the money to start their own household, by living frugally they hoped to move up into the ranks of property owners like Hannah's father and her sister Elizabeth's husband, Asa Dunbar.[53] In the hill towns at the Berkshire-Hampshire boundary, forest land was still available, and purchases on credit enabled men with few resources to get started. By living at Worthington for awhile, Ephraim and Hannah hoped to be able to launch their own household.

Yet by choosing to live under his father-in-law's roof Ephraim continued the subordinate and quasi-dependent status he had known since childhood. Lacking a family network of his own, Ephraim had found himself drawn into the Odel extended family from the time he linked up with Asa Dunbar. Since he was a poor, illiterate orphan far from home, he had to start at the bottom. Though Wheeler never admitted it, he may have chosen to marry Hannah partly because she could supply him membership in this larger group. Although theirs was a lowly black and mixed-race network of laborers, charcoal burners, and domestic servants, some of its members already were (and others would become) independent, though impoverished, husbandmen and yeomen. To the Odels, Wheeler's identity as a white man, as much as his able body, may have been an asset. During times of trouble over the next fifteen years Ephraim repeatedly fell back on this network—especially his brothers-in-law. They supplied the only safety net he had known since his hard tutelage under Jeduthan Hammond.

It was while Hannah and Ephraim were living at Worthington that Betsy, their first child, was born, in January 1792. But a few months later the new family came apart. Hannah, who was again pregnant, took Betsy and left Ephraim, evidently because he lacked the right combination of industry and thrift. As Wheeler explained, "my creditors crowding me for some debts which I owed, took from me my horse and cow, which was all the property I possessed, and my wife, in consequence of the straits to which I was reduced, then left me."[54] In a family economy where a husband's first duty was to provide for his wife and children, Ephraim began to look like a failure.

Earlier, when he went broke and so lost Susanna Randal, he could blame the lifting injury that had laid him up; but for this second loss of a woman he offered no explanation other than his general improvidence.[55] At this juncture if Ephraim felt no real commitment to marriage with Hannah he could have deserted his wife and baby and gone on to start a new life elsewhere. Had he done so, no police would have set out to find him; and, like many another deserting husband, he could have begun a new family all over again.[56] Instead, Wheeler stayed in the neighborhood, finding work here and there. After a year and a half, Ephraim had reformed himself sufficiently so that, as he put it, "my wife . . . agreed to live with me again." While they were separated Ephraim recalled that Hannah gave birth to their second child, an infant who survived only a few months.[57]

The Wheelers reunited late in 1794, when Betsy was almost three years old. Once more they would live under an Odel roof, this time at the recently purchased home of Hannah's older brother, Isaac, in Cummington. But the reunion was short-lived; Hannah once more took Betsy and left.[58] Though Ephraim never explained why Hannah left him, her departures coincided with his pursuit by creditors, and he admitted to problems with drinking and work discipline, so it seems likely that Hannah left him when instead of working he was spending their money on drink.

This time the separation lasted about a year. During that time, Wheeler claimed that his wife's groundless enmity toward him was acted out in the form of an unprovoked assault. Hannah, Wheeler complained, "laid a plot . . . to injure me" with William Martin, her younger sister Lucy's future husband, and another man, Samuel Peters, who may have been black.[59] Their plot unfolded during a "frolic" at Isaac Odel's house. Ephraim was "peaceably passing [in] the road," minding his own business, when the two men attacked him. "They dragged me from my horse, and beat me severely"—for what reason, Ephraim never explained, though it seems unlikely that they would have attacked him without cause. Perhaps he had failed to keep a bargain with one of the men, or perhaps they were paying him back for a wrong done to Hannah. It is significant that Wheeler did not call on friends of his own to settle the score—he may not have had any—but instead sought revenge by calling the law down on Martin and Peters by complaining to a justice of the peace. Ephraim was gratified that "they were both fined for the assault"; but that was not the end of it. Afterwards, Wheeler claimed, "they swore that if I did not pay the money [the fine] back to them, they would obtain satisfaction by abusing me; but in what way they never told me."[60] Though Wheeler had found a home within the Odel family network, now it was stained by bad blood.

To Ephraim's way of thinking, however, he was a blameless victim. And when, after several months passed, his wife once more returned to him at the end of 1795, he resumed his struggle to gain a foothold in society. Now for the first time the Wheelers would contract for a year's work as a couple, employed at Captain Absalom Blair's farm in Williamstown. With food and shelter included in their pay, Ephraim expected to save some of their earnings. The couple's resumption of marital relations is evident from the birth of another child, a son, in October 1796.[61] They had named Betsy for Hannah's mother, Elizabeth, a common practice in New England, but rather than name his new son Isaac after his own father, Wheeler expressed his patriarchal impulse by giving the baby his own name.[62] As Betsy was becoming her mother's daughter, he hoped that little Ephraim would be his father's son.

But Wheeler's capacity to move forward continued to falter. Even though he was living under Captain Blair's roof, with food and shelter found, he was once more "crowded with debts" and wearing out his welcome. This time, he said, "my wife assisted me to pay them, with eight pounds of her own money."[63] As angry as Ephraim was toward Hannah in 1806, as he awaited execution, he remembered that nine years earlier she had helped him with a substantial sum of her own earnings. Although as a man he could earn more than Hannah, lacking her work discipline and thrift he seemed unable to accumulate assets.

So at the beginning of 1797 Wheeler left Williamstown under a cloud and brought his family back again to Cummington, probably to his brother-in-law Isaac Odel's homestead. But they did not linger because Ephraim found the opportunity he had been seeking to rise into the ranks of landholders. In the neighboring Berkshire town of Partridgefield land was available on credit, and Wheeler, like scores of other poor men in the 1790s, "bought a piece."[64] That someone repeatedly pressed by creditors and as poor as Ephraim Wheeler could buy land seems astonishing until one considers the nature of the land and the terms of the purchase.

Partridgefield, the highest, most windswept township in the state, had been settled a generation earlier in the 1760s, so that by the 1790s virtually all its arable land had been cleared and cultivated. What remained was sloping forest land, and it was this hitherto valueless land that became the object of a small land rush in the 1790s, when the town's population soared by 32 percent, to 1,361 people, growing about three times as fast as the rest of Berkshire County.[65] The men who owned these forest lands were happy to sell on credit to poor but able-bodied men like Wheeler because by occupying the land and selling the timber, firewood, and charcoal they harvested, they improved it for future agricultural uses, chiefly grazing. If the purchasers could not make their payments, the improved land would revert to the original owner. Since the going rate for clearing timber was about $5 an acre, even if purchases failed the original owners could not lose.

When thirty-four-year-old Ephraim joined in this land rush he seems to have believed that at last he would succeed. All that was needed was hard work, and with his wife pitching in he believed he could make it. To help finance the first year, he contracted in May 1797 to log three acres of timber the following month for a Worthington farmer who would pay him $15.[66] Thereafter Ephraim could spend the rest of the year working on his own property, where, if he could earn at the rate of $15 a month, his household would be solvent.

But it was not that simple. Every month did not provide fifteen hours of light each day or a preponderance of dry, temperate weather. To create his own farmstead Wheeler had first to clear a patch of ground to plant foodstuffs. Then he must construct a dwelling. Even if he did all the labor himself, he still had to buy tools, nails, and some provisions. He could get the boards he needed by exchanging timber at the sawmill, but felling logs, stripping their branches, and hauling them to mill, like everything else, took time. And since Hannah was caring for Betsy, who was five years old, and nursing the infant Ephraim, Jr., she could share only some of the work or earn very little on her own.[67] By November 1797, when daylight lasted only nine hours, and Ephraim was sued for nonperformance by the farmer whose land he had agreed to log the previous spring, it is clear that Wheeler was falling behind his own expectations. Still he persevered. With the ground frozen, winter was the best time for logging if the snows were not too deep, and the 1797–98 winter was not especially severe. When the spring of 1798 began, there were grounds for hope: baby Ephraim had survived his second winter, Betsy had passed her sixth birthday, his wife stayed with him, and though a Hampshire court had rendered a judgment against Wheeler, so that he now owed $60 due to his failure to log the Worthington land, his creditors did not force him into prison for debt.[68] The coming year would be a crucial test for Ephraim's ambition to enter the class of landholding, voting, "independent" citizens of the republic. He would have to fell, strip, and haul a lot of logs in order to survive financially.

Ephraim makes no mention of illness or injury during this time in his life, nor does he blame his creditors, his wife, or the weather, so the fact that he did not clear as much timber as he needed in order to succeed must have mostly been caused by his inability to maintain a rigorous work discipline when he was his own boss. Looking back on his entire life he confessed: "I have spent my time and property in idleness, hard drinking and quarrelling, neglecting industry, and the means of obtaining an honest livelihood for myself and my family." The result of his failure in 1798 was that at the age of thirty-six Wheeler was forced to sell his house and his interest in the land and, with a wife and two children, move back into service as a farm laborer, this time for a Partridgefield farmer, George Pierce.[69]

From this time in late 1798 onward, Ephraim and his family never lived more than a year in one place. From Partridgefield they moved to Buckland, then back to Cummington, and on to Windsor, where they worked successively for two different farmers before moving back to Cummington again, and once more to Windsor. No farmer, it seems, was ready to keep Ephraim Wheeler on for two years in succession. So his family lived like nomads, going back and forth among a handful of hill towns that straddled the Hampshire-Berkshire boundary and repeatedly falling back on the Odel network in Cummington and Windsor for support.[70]

Throughout, Wheeler reported, "I have ever lived most unhappily with my wife"; yet several times he called on Hannah's relations for temporary shelter. Moreover, during these years Ephraim and Hannah had two more children, the one who was scalded to death in 1802, and another, a baby girl, born in 1804.[71] No doubt Ephraim and Hannah were unhappy as a couple, but their lives were bound together both by practical necessity and by their shared interest in their children and their belief in the common ideal of family.

Ephraim may have regarded his marriage to Hannah as a "foolish step," but, he said, "after I married her, I considered it my duty to live

View of Lenox, 1837. This view of a more developed Lenox village, looking northward toward the meetinghouse (on the hill to the left), shows the Berkshire County courthouse (at the far right) in which the Supreme Judicial Court sat to try Wheeler in 1805. (From John Warner Barber's *Historical Collections of Massachusetts.*)

Report

OF THE

Trial

OF

EPHRAIM WHEELER,

FOR A

Rape

COMMITTED ON THE BODY OF

BETSY WHEELER,

HIS DAUGHTER,
A GIRL THIRTEEN YEARS OF AGE.

---

*Before the Supreme Judicial Court, holden at LENOX,
within and for the County of BERKSHIRE, on
the second Tuesday of September, 1805.*

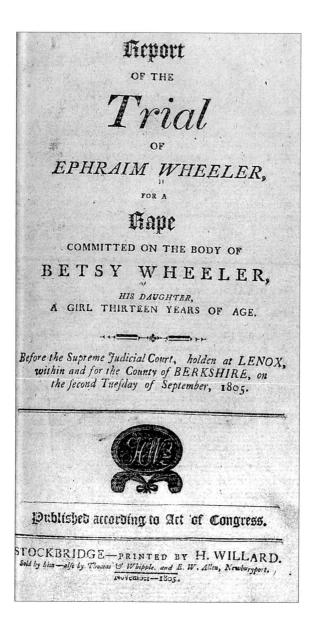

Published according to Act of Congress.

STOCKBRIDGE—PRINTED BY H. WILLARD.
Sold by him—also by *Thomas* & *Whipple.* and *E. W. Allen, Newburyport.*
November—1805.

Report of the Trial of Ephraim Wheeler, title page *(at left)* and James Sullivan's handwritten inscription *(above)*. The title page of the trial report displays the printer's emphasis on the fact that the victim was the daughter of the assailant. The crime was sensational because the rape was incestuous, a point the printer stressed in his newspaper coverage and in advertisements for the pamphlet. Yet the actual trial report was primarily didactic, not sensational or prurient. The copy shown here was a gift from the prosecutor, Attorney General James Sullivan, to his new pastor, the Reverend Joseph Stevens Buckminster, a star of scholarship and literature in Boston, and a founder of the Boston Athenæum. In the inscription (on the verso of the preface), taken from Quintilian's book on rhetoric, Sullivan seems to be describing the importance of the trial and his own courtroom oratory. It reads: "If the world is governed by Providence, it follows that good men must take part in managing public affairs: and if our souls have a divine origin, it follows that we have an obligation to strive for virtue and not be the slaves of the pleasures of our earthly body. Will not the orator often handle these themes?" Quintilian, *The Orator's Education,* ed. and trans. Donald A. Russell, Loeb Classical Library (Cambridge, Mass.: Harvard University Press, 2001), 5, 231. (Courtesy of the Boston Athenæum. Thanks to Daniel Caner for identifying Sullivan's passage in Quintilian.)

James Sullivan, 1807, by Gilbert Stuart. This portrait of James Sullivan was done two years after Wheeler's trial, when he was governor, and depicts him, book in hand, as the refined gentleman he had become. (Courtesy of the Massachusetts Historical Society.)

Daniel Dewey, ca. 1810. Dewey, who appears to be in his forties in this anonymous portrait, not long after he defended Ephraim Wheeler, went on to serve
in the U.S. Congress and as a justice of the Supreme Judicial Court. (Courtesy
of the Supreme Judicial Court of the Commonwealth of Massachusetts.)

Theodore Sedgwick, 1808, by Gilbert Stuart. Sedgwick's commanding presence comes through in this portrait of one of Wheeler's judges, who was also Berkshire County's leading Federalist and former Speaker of the U.S. House of Representatives. (Courtesy Museum of Fine Arts, Boston. Reproduced with permission. © 2002 Museum of Fine Arts, Boston. All rights reserved.)

Sedgwick homestead. The dwelling that Theodore Sedgwick built in 1786 is here seen from the rear, the east side of the Housatonic River. Though modest by the standards of the 1870s, when this romantic image was created, at the beginning of the century it had been seen as a great, eight-room mansion. (From Mary E. Dewey, ed., *Life and Letters of Catharine M. Sedgwick,* New York, 1872.)

To his Excellency Caleb Strong Esq.
Gov. of the Commonwealth of Massachusetts and
the Hon the Council of said Commonwealth.

　　　　　　Your unhappy petitioners, the
wife, and children of Ephraim Wheeler, now
under sentence of death for the crime Of
Rape committed on Betsey Wheeler one of your
petitioners, being his own daughter, approach
Your Excellency and Honors with Great anxiety,
in behalf of one who hath greatly injured us,
and implore your Excellency and Honors to
spare his life, by inflicting such other punishment
as to your Excellency and Honors may seem fit
and proper — No injury however great can obliterate
the remembrance, that Ephraim Wheeler is the
husband of one of your petitioners, and the father
of the other two — Duty must require it, and
our feelings strongly urge, that the crime which
he committed and of which we were the immediate
sufferers, might not affect his life — Your
Excellency and Honors will feel, that when
we ask, most earnestly ask for the life of our
Husband, and our Father, we perform a
duty which nature points out, and that
we must remain in awful anxiety, until

Until Your Honors determination shall be known — Hoping and trusting that Your Excellency will be disposed to exercise that most invaluable attribute; Mercy, we remain your most unhappy and distressed petitioners

Sept. 26. 1805°

Hannah Wheeler

Betsy her ✕ Wheeler
       mark

Ephraim his ✕ Wheeler Junr.
        mark

Wheeler family petition. This image of the family petition, dated September 26, 1805, is reproduced from the original in the Massachusetts Archives, Boston. Though the body of the text is written in an expert hand, we think that of Wheeler's attorney, Daniel Dewey, it is signed by Hannah Wheeler, whose labored signature suggests that although she had learned to write her name, she had few occasions for doing so. Beneath her signature are the marks of Betsy and Ephraim, Jr. The hierarchy of mother, older daughter, and younger son is represented in the placement of the signature and marks. The original documents are the size of foolscap, about 8.5 inches by 14 inches. So as to render it more legible, the image seen here has been electronically cleaned of staining and discolorations. (Courtesy of the Massachusetts Archives, Boston.)

Idle 'Prentice Executed at Tyburn, 1747, by William Hogarth. Hogarth's image of a London execution presents the reformers' belief that the execution ritual had descended into corrupt, vulgar spectacle.

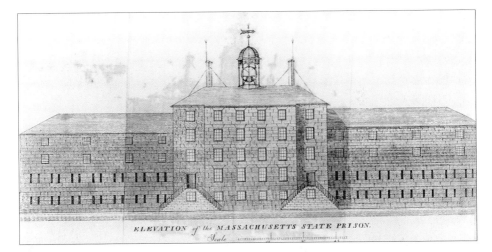

ELEVATION *of the* MASSACHUSETTS STATE PRISON.
Scale

Massachusetts State Prison, 1806. This simple drawing of the front of Charles Bulfinch's 1805 Massachusetts State Prison conveys the power, order, and permanence that the building was intended to express. Located at the water's edge in Charlestown, across the river from Boston, and constructed of cut granite, it was enclosed by high stone walls so that only the upper stories were visible from outside. (Courtesy of the American Antiquarian Society.)

Caleb Strong, 1807, by James Brown Marston. Unlike Theodore Sedgwick and James Sullivan, who chose as their portraitist Gilbert Stuart, painter of the new nation's great men, including George Washington and John Adams, former governor Caleb Strong turned to James Brown Marston, a thirty-two-year-old artisan listed as a "commercial painter" in the 1803 *Boston Directory*. Whether the choice of Marston was prompted by Strong's modesty or his frugality, we cannot say, but the portrait suggests why a colleague would refer to Strong's "honest face." (Courtesy of the Massachusetts Historical Society.)

The Reverend Samuel Shepard. The sitter's direct gaze was captured by an anonymous painter sometime in the 1830s. (Courtesy of the Williams College Museum of Art, gift of Miss Lucy A. Shepard, daughter of Samuel Shepard.)

Lenox Meetinghouse, ca. 1940. When it was opened in 1806, the meetinghouse had no clock; the front of the bell tower was decorated with a Palladian
window directly above the porch, with half-round windows on the sides. In
the graveyard at the far left can be seen the Reverend Shepard's memorial
stone, topped by an urn. (Photo from Olive A. Holton, *Lenox* [n.p., n.d.].)

Hanging at Castine, Maine, 1811, by Jonathan Fisher. This woodcut was made by the Reverend Jonathan Fisher after the execution of Ebenezer Ball at Castine, Maine, in 1811. It depicts a Massachusetts hanging that best matches the Wheeler execution as described in the *Pittsfield Sun* and *Western Star*. The Ball execution took place just five years after Wheeler's and, like Wheeler's, was held in an outlying part of the commonwealth. Note the officials in the foreground, the militiamen who encircle the scaffold, and the large crowd. (Courtesy of the American Antiquarian Society.)

Ing.d by P Halpin from a Painting by Ingham

Catharine Maria Sedgwick. Taken from an 1832 painting, this engraving of the genteel Catharine Sedgwick makes her appear younger than her forty-three years, suggesting how she may have looked when Betsy Wheeler faced her ordeal. (From Mary E. Dewey, ed., *Life and Letters of Catharine M. Sedgwick,* New York, 1872.)

with her, and treat her as a wife."[72] Twice Hannah had left Ephraim early in their marriage, but from the beginning of 1796 through early 1805 the two stayed together through ten moves. The tension between them boiled up repeatedly; as Ephraim complained, "she has often told me, that if it were not wicked, she would poison me: or would bind me when I was asleep, and whip me to death." So angry was she that "she was almost in the daily habit of wishing I was dead."[73] Though either Hannah or Ephraim could have abandoned the children and fled, as some impoverished people did to escape oppressive marriages, Ephraim and Hannah had yet another child and stayed together until the final illness of their employer, the Widow Converse, in early 1805 separated them. For the first time in a decade they lived and worked apart for three months before coming together once more at the home of one of Hannah's relatives, her sister Lucy Odel Martin and her husband, William Martin, the same man who had attacked Ephraim in the road outside Isaac Odel's ten years before.[74] That the months before their separation had been troubled is suggested by the likelihood that at least one of Ephraim's first two sexual attempts on Betsy dated from that time.

The reunion at the Martins' proved explosive. Ephraim detested being dependent on the favor of Hannah's younger sister and her husband, a man with whom he had old scores to settle. According to Wheeler's account of June 8, 1805, the pains of childbirth in the overstressed family set off a chain reaction of more or less repressed conflicts that blew up fatally. It began early that Saturday morning, when either Martin or Hannah asked Ephraim to call Dr. Asahel Wright because Lucy had gone into labor. When Ephraim returned from the errand he found that someone had rearranged the furniture on Bill Martin's orders. Hannah told him that "for the future" their bed had been moved out of the room they rented into another room, a bedroom where others slept, because Martin wanted the use of

Ephraim's and Hannah's room. Ephraim, assuming his role as household patriarch, laid down the law to his wife: "I told her it was my room, and my bed, and it should be brought back, or she should not go into their [the Martins'] room to assist them." But Hannah would not be bossed: "she replied that she would go, and that the bed should not be brought back," underlining her declaration with "an expression of contempt, too indecent to repeat." Now, "provoked at her insolence," Wheeler turned violent, grabbing "a bayonet, that happened to lie within reach, . . . I struck her on the back-side."[75]

Had the couple been living in their own quarters this particular fight would never have occurred, and if they had quarreled over something else, it might have burned itself out like others before it, leaving only lingering resentment. But now Bill Martin intervened to defend his sister-in-law, "attacking" Wheeler so that the two men engaged in what Ephraim called a "severe scuffle." When it was over Wheeler, believing himself the more injured party, went immediately to Justice Robert Walker's half a mile away to complain "of myself and Martin for the affray." Walker, who knew the Wheelers because they had recently lived with his old relative, the Widow Converse, during her final months, fined Ephraim and Bill $1 each and told them to behave.[76]

These humiliations at the hands of his wife and Bill Martin drove Ephraim over the line, a line he had not crossed since his battles with Jeduthan Hammond over twenty years before. Ephraim wanted out, only this time he would not be a runaway; he was the ruler of his family and he would leave on his own terms, taking the children. Ephraim Wheeler's account of events, including the alleged rape, warrants quotation in full:

> I now finally determined never to live with my wife anymore, but to take BETSY and EPHRAIM, my two oldest children, and go to the sea-side, and after putting BETSY out in some good place,

to take EPHRAIM with me to sea. Accordingly I told my children that they must go with me, and we all got ready and set out; but had not proceeded far, before the children cried and grieved so much, at the thoughts of parting with their mother forever, that I concluded to let them return; I also recollected some money due to me, which I wanted to collect before I went away: I told the boy to hold the horse, while BETSY went with me to get some avens-root, to send to their mother, and when we came back, they might both return home, and come to me again the next evening. I then went with BETSY a little way, not more than three or four rods [50–66 feet], and returned in as many minutes, and sent the children home. The odious crime, which is said to have been committed while I was alone with BETSY, and for which I must loose [*sic*] my life, I declare myself to be innocent of. The thoughts of such an act never entered my mind.

To Wheeler the gift of avens-root—a medicine believed to stop uterine bleeding—could have been a peace offering to dull the edge of his wife's and Bill Martin's hostility.[77] According to Ephraim the entire story of sexual assault was utterly false, fabricated so that Hannah and the children could stay together. Betsy was not the victim here, he was.[78]

When Ephraim Wheeler concluded his life story on the eve of his execution day, he seemed to be a changed man. During his eight months of incarceration he presented a surly, silent face to the world. Far from accepting his fate, Ephraim had twice attempted to escape from Lenox jail—and on February 7, less than two weeks earlier, with five others he had briefly succeeded.[79] But now, as had been true after his last escape from Jeduthan Hammond in 1783, he appeared to accept his fate. For the first time he spoke as if contrition and repentance had at last entered his mind. The cumulative efforts of the local clergymen who had visited and prayed with Wheeler during the five months since his conviction finally bore fruit.[80] In his changed demeanor there might be hope of the true repentance necessary for salvation.

Now Ephraim began to accept responsibility for at least some of his faults and failures. In a vocabulary supplied by the clergymen, Ephraim confessed "with shame, and the deepest sorrow, the loose and irregular life I have lived." Like his old master, Jeduthan Hammond, he admitted being "subject to violent and hasty passions, [and] I have indulged them without control," which resulted in injury to particular individuals and society as a whole. Nor had Ephraim dealt fairly and honorably with others: "I have often abused those who had done me favors, and were ready to repeat them, had they not been deterred by my ingratitude." Surely it was no wonder that Bill Martin, Asa Dunbar, and others in the Odel network had tired of assisting Ephraim. Nor was it surprising that farmers who had taken the Wheelers on for a year declined to renew their contracts in light of Ephraim's admission that "I have failed to fulfill my promises to the great injury of my neighbors and others, who were so friendly as to assist me, and trust to my word for payment." In towns where men and women routinely extended credit to each other from one year to the next, a reputation for fairness and honesty meant inclusion in the community. But Ephraim confessed that he had lived outside the boundary of Yankee ethics, defrauding people out of their property "by making what are called good bargains, by falshood [sic] and deception."[81]

In addition, Wheeler admitted to a deeper set of vicious habits: "idleness, hard drinking and quarreling, neglecting industry, and the means of obtaining an honest livelihood for my family." He went on to confess "I have ever kept the lowest and vilest company; neglected to attend the public worship of God, and shunned the society of discreet and honest people."[82] Here Wheeler presented himself, perhaps at clerical insistence, as an extreme example of the everyday sinner that every pastor addressed from the pulpit each Sunday. But that was as far as Ephraim would go in confessing sin. Contrary to the hopes of the magistrates and clergy, the man who could be impulsive and irresolute stood fast. Wheeler refused to confess to the crime for which he stood convicted.

More than that, Wheeler swore that he had not committed any capital crime, and demonstrated his new attitude of Christian forgiveness. Much as he abhorred the outcome of the trial, he acknowledged the "lenity and fairness" of it and warmly thanked his lawyers "for their efforts." Nor had he any complaints against the judges and jury, since "as the evidence was given" they were "bound to decide as they did." Ephraim was even more generous in thanking William Whelpley, the jailer, his family, and his employees for the "tenderness and humanity" of their treatment while he was in jail, "in sickness and in health." Similarly, "with pleasure" he thanked the clergymen who had visited him so many times while he was in chains.[83]

But Ephraim Wheeler's forgiveness also had an edge. In the list of officials he specifically acknowledged as fair and humane, he left out Justice Robert Walker because Walker "did not, agreeable to my earnest request, direct the girl to be examined, at the time I was before him [June 10], by a jury of Matrons and Physicians." If only Walker had ordered Betsy's examination, Ephraim was convinced he "should most certainly have escaped the dreadful fate" awaiting him.[84] A physical examination on June 8 or even June 10—an examination Judge Sedgwick agreed ought to have been done—would have blocked the whole proceeding against him. Because of Walker, Ephraim believed, he faced the gallows.

His final words to his family, to Hannah and Betsy particularly, reveal the ambivalence Ephraim felt about Christian forgiveness:

I freely and fully forgive my wife, my daughter, and all others concerned in my prosecution, for the destruction which they

185

have brought upon me, and I hope that God will also forgive them.

Though he followed the forgiveness formula prescribed by the clergy, the voice of the old Ephraim Wheeler, the victim who blamed others for his misfortunes, echoed in his words. "They" brought destruction "upon me," but Ephraim would forgive and so also might God forgive "them." Though Wheeler's was not precisely the voice of injured innocence—he was a sinner who asked "forgiveness of all I have offended or injured, and pray that God would pardon my numerous offenses" through Jesus—he still viewed himself as more sinned against than sinning. Nowhere in his entire admission of sins did he ever acknowledge any specific offense toward Hannah or Betsy or ask their forgiveness for his failures as husband, father, and patriarch. Ephraim was ready to apologize to God, the omnipotent source of all salvation, but not to his wife or children.[85]

Wheeler's narrative closes with an eloquent evangelical homily that makes no pretense to being Ephraim's words and that must have been composed by one of the clergymen, probably Samuel Shepard or Oliver Ayer, with Ephraim's consent. Like an execution sermon this coda exhorts its audience to consider "the dreadful evil of sin!" and to "prepare to meet your God, by a life of purity."[86] Including such a closing paragraph in Ephraim's "life" was part of the price a condemned criminal paid in order to bring his own story to the public. By accepting this exhortation in his name, Ephraim Wheeler ennobled his plight. Now, finally, he was seeking solidarity with all sinners, all the descendants of Adam and Eve who struggled to escape the clutches of sin and achieve salvation.

Ephraim Wheeler was not, he insisted, guilty of the crime of rape. Instead he professed to be a victim, not only of his wife and daughter's conspiracy to destroy him by their "false accusation," but also more generally.[87] Though he had begun life in an intact family, one calamity had followed another—his mother's death, his father's suicide, and his indenture to a cruel and violent man who cared only for Ephraim's labor, not his mind, his heart, or his soul. Overcoming all this, Ephraim had nevertheless begun to rise, placing his hopes on Susanna Randal, "the only object dear to me on earth."[88] But his hopes were twice dashed, first by her refusal to marry a penniless man, and then years later by her revealing to him that she would marry someone else. Ephraim thought of himself as the victim of a disappointed love, as a sensitive soul driven into a loveless marriage by his desperate loneliness.

Once he was married, the pattern of his victimization repeated itself. Though he never loved his wife, like a good patriarch he had fulfilled his "duty to live with her, and treat her as a wife."[89] Though Hannah had twice deserted him, in fourteen years he had never left her, and he had labored to maintain his family. Finally, when he threatened to leave with Betsy and Ephraim, Jr., as he had every right to do, this wife who had often wished him dead had accomplished her goal. By their perjured manipulation of justice, she and Betsy were sending him to the gallows.

That Ephraim Wheeler was also a sinful man, prone to the common vices of drinking, idleness, and passion—as well as dishonesty—he acknowledged. From the story he tells, Wheeler appears to have been a drifter and a drunkard who found security and purpose by linking himself to Hannah and her extended family. Evidently they were more disciplined than he, who appeared capable of hard work only in spurts except when he had a master ruling him. That he was no storybook hero ennobled by a galaxy of virtues is all too evident. But he was the hero of his own story, a common laborer who stayed with his family as he sought to realize the dream of patriarchy and landownership. That he could not achieve this Yankee and Jeffersonian ideal, that he failed even to measure up to his black in-laws, was more than a disappointment for him and his family; it fed the rage that drove Wheeler's fatal misbehavior of June 8, 1805, and the family tragedy. This was, to be sure, no tragedy of greatness on the classical model; it was a tragedy of the lowly, a tragedy of mediocrity.[90]

CHAPTER SIX

The Final Judgment

Your petitioners sensible of the high and agravated crime of which the said Wheeler has been convicted, never the less earnestly solicit your Excellency and Honors that his life may be spared, and that he may be confined in the Prison of the State during his life. Your Excellency and Honors will permit us to suggest that the object of punishment is to deter others from committing like Offences, and that in our opinion, confinement for life will have as great a tendency at least, to deter others, as even the punishment of death, for in the one case he will remain a monument of his own vicious conduct during his whole life, to be seen by thousands, who probably would never have heard that such a man or such a crime ever had existed. In the other case the punishment is inflicted in the presence of few. As our State prison is now nearly compleated; it will be in the power of Government effectually to prevent the said Wheeler from again injuring society. As we are assured it is the earnest wish of the wife of said Wheeler and his two children, who were more immediately injured, and by whose aid Government have been able to convict him, that his life might be spared, if consistent with the safety of society. As we are informed the revision of the said law against the crime of rape is now pending before the Legislature, and probably may be so modified at the next session, as to comport with our solicitation in this case. As we are informed your Excellency and Honors have seen fit and proper, in one case of rape to commute the punishment. . . .

Petition of Denison Robinson of Windsor and ninety-two others, "To his Excellency Caleb Strong. . . ." September 26, 1805

189

A fter Judge Sewall sentenced him on September 14, 1805, Ephraim Wheeler passed each day in chains, locked up in the Berkshire County jail. He had begun the ordeal of waiting for execution day. But on a bright, sunny Tuesday, September 24, John Hulbert and Daniel Dewey came to him with hope. They brought him the petition they had prepared on his behalf, seeking a pardon from the governor. Two days later Hannah, Betsy, and Ephraim, Jr., also petitioned Governor Caleb Strong, asking him to "exercise that most invaluable Attribute, Mercy," so as to spare "the life of our Husband, and our Father." On that same day reformers began to circulate a general petition in Berkshire County requesting the governor and the Governor's Council to spare Wheeler's life. Before the week was out, Ephraim himself had sent a petition to Boston entreating "his Excellency Caleb Strong" to grant "the greatest favor that it is possible for one human Being to grant to another . . . his life."[1] At least in some small way, Ephraim Wheeler began to hope.

When his attorneys drafted their pardon petition they were following a well-worn path in capital cases. Because the trial judgment was always rendered at the highest level in the Supreme Judicial Court, the state made no provision for any appeal process. But the governor and Governor's Council were vested with the authority to review all criminal sentences and the power to pardon convicts. Knowing this, when Hulbert and Dewey argued Wheeler's case on September 13 they were already laying the groundwork for his pardon claim. Although they lost Wheeler's case before the trial jury, they knew that since the adoption of the state's republican constitution in 1780, no man—whether black, Indian, or Irish—had been put to death for the crime of rape. Indeed, Massachusetts had not executed a white Yankee for rape since 1681.[2] These facts could not assure that the governor would spare Wheeler's life, but they must at least have been encouraging to Wheeler.

During the trial Attorney General James Sullivan had reviewed the pardoning process when he advised the jurors of their duties. Presenting a textbook analysis, he explained that the governor's power to pardon was not arbitrary. They must not grant pardons merely because they found the law "too severe" or because, though the judges and jury were satisfied with the trial, the court had erred. Nor was the governor supposed to grant a pardon due to "feelings of pity." He should employ this power only as a matter of public policy, as in the case of the Shays rebels, or where "an innocent person is in danger of suffering from error, or from surprize," and then only if his pardon would not contradict the authority of government or grant mercy to one person while denying it to others who were equally deserving.[3] According to this formal understanding of the pardon process, spelled out by the state's chief prosecutor, the pardoning power should be used rarely, so all efforts on Wheeler's behalf might well be fruitless.

But the actual record of gubernatorial pardons in the decade preceding Wheeler's sentencing shows that in practice the pardon process was not so cut and dried. Personal views, public sentiment, and political judgment all mingled in the minds of councilors and governors. Justice, they believed, must be tempered by mercy; and where life and death were at stake, executive officials did not necessarily go by the book. It is true that in cases where no one petitioned for a pardon the governor and council routinely accepted the decisions of juries and judges as final. But if judges raised doubts about the verdict, or if petitions for mercy were filed—whether it was the plaintive petition of a solitary convict or a group of petitions bearing dozens, or even hundreds, of signatures—the Governor's Council formed a subcommittee to weigh its recommendation deliberately; and when the governor received the council's advice he reflected before acting.[4] As a result, notwithstanding the strict limits Sullivan claimed on gubernatorial pardoning power, over the past decade Governors Samuel Adams and Caleb Strong had pardoned three of the four men sentenced to hang for crimes other than murder; and in the case of a single woman convicted of murdering her bastard daughter in 1803, Governor Strong would grant a full pardon in 1806.[5] Though Judges Sedgwick, Sewall, and Strong had adhered to the statute on rape by ordering Wheeler's death, there was certainly a possibility that the governor would commute his penalty, perhaps to life in state prison.

The judgment of the governor and council depended on a host of factors conditioned by social class and the legal and cultural climate of Massachusetts. In Europe and the Anglo-American world Enlightenment reformers had challenged traditional criminal codes even before the American Revolution. Then, in the era of the new republic, Americans everywhere questioned the use of capital punishment, and in every state they cut back on its use. As early as 1764, when Cesare di Beccaria, a young Italian nobleman, published his influential *Essay on Crimes and Punishments,* the English-speaking world took notice. From 1767 through the 1770s English translations, often including Voltaire's favorable commentary, appeared repeatedly. Sir William Blackstone, the lawyer whose *Commentaries on the Laws of England* so powerfully shaped Anglo-American practices, was arguing by the later 1760s that use of the death penalty, which then applied in over two hundred crimes, should be drastically cut back. Beccaria's argument for proportional punishments appealed to Enlightenment sensibilities, and Blackstone—who continued to support the selective use of the gallows—argued that to use death as the penalty for all sorts of property crimes was to cheapen it, and would alienate the populace from government and the ruling classes. Only by restricting its use to major crimes could the death penalty maintain its value as a deterrent.[6]

By the time of independence, American revolutionaries were acting on these new, more humane principles. In Maryland, for example, the 1776 Bill of Rights declared that "sanguinary laws ought to be avoided, as far as is consistent with the safety of the state"; and in the same year both Pennsylvania and New Hampshire made similar statements.[7] Enlightenment humanitarianism, reinforced by faith in the use of reason to address crime and its prevention, gave penal reform new vitality. During the 1780s and 1790s physician Benjamin Rush, a Pennsylvania signer of the Declaration of Independence, published repeated condemnations of capital punishment as being a monarchial, antirepublican practice.[8] Joel Barlow, the Connecticut Yankee *philosophe,* denounced the death penalty even more vigorously. "To plead that there is a necessity for that desperate remedy," Barlow declared, "proves a want of energy on the government, or of wisdom in the nation." Executing convicts was never justified because it substituted vengeance in place of correction. Ideally, he wrote, all constitutions would declare, *"the punishment of death should be abolished."*[9] A year later, William Bradford, the Federalist attorney general of Pennsylvania who later held the same office in the Washington administration, declared his opposition to capital punishment, even for such crimes as arson, rape, and murder.[10]

Yet in the early republic few reformers were prepared to follow Barlow's or Bradford's absolute prohibition against the death penalty. According to the Bible's first book, Genesis, the execution of murderers was almost a commandment: "whoso sheddeth man's blood, by man shall his blood be shed."[11] No state would set aside this ultimate punishment for murder. But for lesser crimes, such as sodomy and rape, burglary and robbery, counterfeiting and arson, some governments turned to incarceration. The new Northwest Territory, where no tradition was in place, moved the farthest, enacting a code in 1788 that restricted capital punishment to the crimes of murder and treason. Soon after, in 1790, the U.S. Congress, which also possessed no standing penal code, enacted one that recognized only five capital crimes—piracy, robbery, and counterfeiting in addition to murder and treason.[12]

A few years later the efforts of reformers showed results in the Chesapeake and Middle Atlantic states. In Pennsylvania, Rush's and Bradford's state, the legislature made first-degree murder the sole capital crime in 1794; and two years later Virginia, New York, and New Jersey also cut back on capital penalties.[13] During the Revolution Thomas Jefferson had proposed a model code that listed murder and treason as the only capital crimes, and that prescribed castration as the punishment for rape and sodomy. Decreasing executions and making the punishment fit the crime, Jefferson argued, were reforms that followed Beccaria's principles. Since juries refused to convict when they believed the penalties were too harsh, Jefferson claimed his reform would also enhance the enforcement of the laws. Although his proposal was never enacted, in 1796 Virginia made murder and treason the state's only capital crimes on the first offense; rape became the most severely punished lesser crime, carrying a term of ten to twenty-one years.[14]

In New York and New Jersey, where rape was also dropped from the capital list, the crime carried heavy penalties. New York's 1796 code specified life in prison, while in New Jersey incarceration was reinforced by the promise of hanging for a second offense.[15] Clearly, Americans were moving away from the British model that threatened death for a wide variety of offenders. Yet Beccaria and the other reformers did not triumph entirely. Too many voters believed in both the principle and the practice of capital punishment. In New England the old Puritan states of Connecticut and Massachusetts remained more strongly committed to hanging than a new state like Vermont or their neighbors to the south. Here the old rituals of execution day, complete with execution sermons, continued; and from the pulpit orthodox clergymen vigorously defended the death penalty.

At Lenox in Berkshire County, the Stockbridge pastor, Stephen West, proclaimed the necessity of capital punishment in his December 1787 sermon at the execution of two Shaysite burglars, John Bly and Charles Rose. "God," the fifty-two-year-old West declared, "has appointed civil rulers to bear his sword, to avenge the wrongs of society, and to execute wrath upon evil doers." West explained to his congregation, including Theodore Sedgwick, that "the good of society . . . absolutely requires . . . the death of the perpetrator . . . for a terror and warning to others." God might choose to extend forgiveness in heaven, but not "the civil magistrate . . . here in this world." Though others were moving to curb capital punishment, West harbored no doubts about using the gallows: "Men have a right to inflict capital punishments in every case wherein the good of society requires it." This judgment belonged to legislatures and magistrates.[16]

Three years later, when the state of Connecticut executed a black man, Joseph Mountain, for rape, the Reverend James Dana, a contemporary of West's, provided a more reform-minded, qualified defense of the death penalty, but a defense nonetheless. A just and humane government, Dana preached, would resort to executions only sparingly for such great crimes specified by God as murder, or where "the public safety clearly requires it." Leaning toward reform, Dana declared, "it doth honor to the wisdom as well as lenity of our legislators, that no more than six crimes are capital by law."[17] Rape was properly one of them. The fact that seven years earlier, with the legislature's approval, Connecticut's governor, Jonathan Trumbull, had commuted a white rapist's death sentence to castration—a Beccarian punishment—did not shake Dana's conviction that "*Ravishment* is such an outrage on humanity, an injury so great and irreparable, a crime so baneful and dangerous to society, that civilized nations have agreed to protect female honor from violence by making death the penalty for the crime."[18] Like other execution preachers of the era, Dana defended the religious and civic legitimacy of taking life.

That it was necessary always to make such a defense was partly a response to increasing opposition to hangings in New England. In 1791, for example, the Vermont legislature switched the penalty for rape from death to imprisonment.[19] Consequently when Massachusetts leaders such as Samuel Adams, John Hancock, and James Sullivan favored reforming the colonial criminal code in line with Enlightenment principles in the 1780s and 1790s, they were acknowledging the groundswell of popular reluctance to employ the death sentence.[20] At the 1794 burglary trial of two men in Salem a clergyman noted that because "the people suppose them to be capital offenders, it is hard to supply the jury, four have already paid their fines rather than serve." Later, after prosecutor James Sullivan rested his case, "the Jury sat all night, but could not be prevailed upon to bring in their verdict, guilty of death, so firm are the people against sanguinary Laws." Though Sullivan's indictment charged "burglary" and the jurors were supposed to either declare the defendants guilty of that crime or set them free, "they brought them in guilty of Thieft," whereupon the judges sentenced the convicts "to sit on the gallows, be whipped, & confined to labor 15 years."[21] Though the jurors believed the prisoners were guilty, they would not hang them.

During the 1790s and the first decade of the new century many people questioned the legitimacy of the death penalty, especially for crimes other than murder. At Dartmouth College in New Hampshire, a student orator in 1800 took on the question "Ought the punishment of Death to be abolished?"[22] In Berkshire County at Williams College, where Theodore Sedgwick, the Reverend Stephen West, and later Daniel Dewey and the Reverend Samuel Shepard served as trustees, the library owned a copy of "Beccaria on Crimes and Punishments," and a student society debated "Whether any crime but murder ought to be punished by death" almost annually (seven times) in the decade from 1795 to 1805. Usually the club of twenty or so students at this center of the orthodox Calvinist revival decided in favor of the broader use of capital punishment, but twice (1795 and 1801) they voted to restrict the penalty to murder.[23] Although, as the Williams College debates suggest, Federalists and orthodox Calvinists were more apt to support the death penalty than Republicans, dissenting Protestants, and Unitarians, the question was widely seen as a matter of personal conviction, not partisan allegiance.[24]

In Massachusetts as in other states the death penalty was part of the larger question of a suitable punishment regime for a republic. Most states had tackled this subject systematically in the 1780s or 1790s; but the Massachusetts legislature, having dealt with criminal laws briefly in the 1780s, postponed thorough consideration until after 1800. Then they acted to replace their ad hoc state prison in Boston harbor with a modern, five-story cut stone showpiece designed by the state's master architect, Charles Bulfinch.[25] Early in 1805, when this new state prison at Charlestown was nearing completion, the legislature called on Supreme Judicial Court justices Samuel Sewall and Nathan Dane to draft a plan for regulating the prison and for "an alteration of the Criminal Laws of the Commonwealth." Dane's and Sewall's proposals, which circulated inside the legislature and beyond in a sixty-four-page pamphlet, called for an end to the old corporal punishments of pillorying, whipping, branding, and cropping ears. Instead, the state would punish by "imprisonment and confinement to hard labour."[26]

As to the death penalty, in advising the legislators Dane and Sewall chose their words with care: "After an anxious revision of the Criminal Code," they were proposing "to retain the punishment of death." But in order to reduce the frequency of the death sentence, they urged changes in the definitions of robbery, burglary, and arson so that fewer offenders would fall under these capital headings. They left the death penalty in the 1784 reenactment of the colonial rape law intact. Sewall and Dane admitted that "feelings, seemingly compassionate and humane" might have led them to abolish the death penalty entirely. But since "there has been no experiment, of sufficient extent or continuance, to afford any decisive rule on this subject," they believed such a step would be hazardous to the "safety of this populous and wealthy community."[27] Let other states experiment; in Massachusetts the momentum of past practice remained powerful; change would be incremental.

The Sewall-Dane report was silent with respect to the crime of sodomy, so death penalty opponents seized the opportunity to vote that crime off the capital list by making it punishable by up to ten years in prison at hard labor. Having achieved that victory in early March 1805, the reformers proceeded to seek an end to the death penalty for rape.[28] On the afternoon of Thursday, March 7, their efforts reached a climax when the House of Representatives voted to amend the rape law. In place of hanging, the punishment would be "solitary imprisonment for four years & confinement afterward to hard labour for life." When the ballots were counted, 41 representatives supported the reform and 40 opposed it. By a single vote they had defeated the death penalty. The following day the reform bill was read again, and once more it passed. Now this reform measure went up to the Senate.[29]

But the Massachusetts Senate majority rejected the anti–death penalty amendment. So although the reform had passed one house, it ultimately failed. The following year, 1806, with the Wheeler case still fresh in some legislators' minds, the legislature enacted a new law on rape that retained the death penalty. In spite of the many supporters for bringing Massachusetts into line with other progressive states, in 1805 and 1806 these reformers failed to win their goal.

Because no record of the legislative debate survives, we are not sure how much the conflict over the extent of the death penalty was intertwined with partisan competition between Federalists and Republicans. Some Federalist judges, such as Samuel Sewall and Nathan Dane, favored some reforms to cut capital punishment, but their positions were more conservative than such Republicans as George Blake, Samuel Dana, and Thomas Allen, Jr., who proclaimed that murder and treason should be Massachusetts' only capital offenses.[30] But the division on capital punishment did not neatly follow party allegiances. The state's leading Republican, the party candidate for governor from 1804 until he died in 1808, was Attorney General Sullivan, who consistently defended the death penalty in courtroom oratory and who, as governor in 1807 and 1808, commuted no death sentences. In contrast, Sullivan's Federalist counterpart, Governor Strong, who took no public position on the death penalty, signed all of the new penal statutes—both the one that ended execution for sodomy and the one that retained it for rape. His several pardons suggest Strong's respect, even sympathy, for the reformers' position. Though capital punishment reform was more Republican than Federalist, it was often more a personal than a party question.

One scholar of Massachusetts public life at the beginning of the nineteenth century points out that in spite of sharp rhetorical combat, centrist politics, not partisan extremes, prevailed.[31] Certainly the approaches of Caleb Strong and his rival James Sullivan fit that pattern. Though each possessed a clear party identification, and Sullivan published repeatedly on state and national issues in the newspaper, both men sought to rise above partisanship and to present themselves as defenders of Massachusetts' Revolutionary heritage.

When it came to particular cases, deciding whether to hang or to pardon required state executive officers to consider justice not only according to the law, as the trial had done, but also more broadly. Their task was to consider justice in its fullest implications, for society as well as individuals. As in England, whose practices continued to influence American legal culture, officials viewed the pardoning process as crucial not only for reconciling justice and mercy, but also for maintaining public confidence in both the law and the state by softening some of the law's harshest consequences.

What were the ingredients of successful petitions? For colonial and early republican America very little is known. But eighteenth-century English experience supplies some background for assessing decisions in Massachusetts. A study of hundreds of English petitions from the years 1787 and 1790 reveals the factors that authorities weighed when they considered pardons: reputation for good character; motive; and whether the convicted person might be the victim of a malicious prosecution that created an injustice. In addition, English officials noted mitigating circumstances such as youth, prior military service, the need to support a family, and whether the convict was fully responsible at the time of the offense owing to drink, insanity, or some other mental handicap. English authorities, like their Massachusetts counterparts, were not eager to hang criminals.[32]

Still, many English pardon petitions failed. When the convict's bad character, aggravated violence, betrayal of trust, or prior criminal behavior would make his execution a powerful example to others, officials allowed public hangings to proceed. An eighteenth-century jurist expressed the prevailing belief that "the prisoners selected for capital punishment as an example to others should be chosen from the dangerous and incorrigible offenders."[33] Being convicted of a capital crime was not, by itself, sufficient for an execution.

The same considerations were evident in the Massachusetts pardoning process, although the death penalty was used sparingly compared to England, so most Massachusetts pardons concerned lesser crimes and only affected the extent of physical punishment or the length of prison terms, not life and death. Whereas English statutes identified over two hundred capital crimes, in Massachusetts the law called for hanging in only seven types of crime: arson or burglary at night; highway robbery; murder; rape; sodomy (reduced to a life prison term in 1805); and treason.[34] As a result Massachusetts officials considered pardons for only a small number of capital cases, and each of these involved a crime that society recognized as major.

During the decade before the governor and council evaluated Ephraim Wheeler's pardon, they had three times chosen to save the lives of men who were headed for the gallows. The first case, that of eighty-five-year-old physician John Farrell, suggests the power of petitions. In September 1796 the old man was indicted for "a venereal affair with a certain, female Brute Animal called a Bitch" and charged with "that detestable & abominable Crime of Sodomy (not to be named among christians) to the great displeasure of Almighty God, to the great scandal of all human kind . . . and against the Law, and Order of Nature."[35] At the Supreme Judicial Court sitting in Northampton, lawyer and soon-to-be Supreme Court justice Simeon Strong prosecuted Farrell in the absence of Attorney General Sullivan. The alleged sodomist was defended by the prosecutor's cousin, Northampton lawyer and soon-to-be-governor Caleb Strong, who had just returned from service in the U.S. Senate.[36] Farrell, who was a stranger in the area, could not offer character witnesses for his defense, and his accusers' testimony persuaded the jury to convict. Thereupon the judges, in accordance with the statute, sentenced Farrell to hang.[37]

That autumn Farrell three times petitioned Governor Samuel Adams and the council for a pardon. At first he claimed "innocence" asserting that "it was impossible for him to commit" the crime and that he was the victim of "a wicked combination."[38] Later Farrell retreated to the argument that he was "not guilty in the Manner which one

Witness against him testified," and he asked mercy for "a poor friend-less & distressed old Man" who was in "declining" health and "hastening to the Grave."[39] Farrell's appeals did not stop Governor Adams and the council from ordering Farrell's execution in February 1797.

But Farrell, whose court-appointed attorney, Caleb Strong, drafted two of his petitions and served as his advisor, did not give up.[40] First Strong pleaded for a delay so Farrell would have "further time to prepare for Death," and thus won a seven-week postponement.[41] During the reprieve Farrell's supporters from places he had lived before collected 446 signatures on four petitions to save the old man. In addition to repeating Farrell's own arguments, they claimed that two witnesses at the trial "were prompted to give Evidence against him from interested motives." Moreover, because Farrell was tried in a region where "he was a Stranger and friendless," he could not present character witnesses; this, they argued, gave the advantage to those who sought to convict him. Twenty-one of the petitioners swore they had known Farrell for four years and had never "known of his behaving himself in an Obscene manner but on the contrary he behaved himself as a peaceable member of Society." Not only that, according to thirty-eight signers Farrell had been "peculiarly successful in the cure of that hateful disease the Cancer."[42] If Farrell's life was spared, "he may be made the instrument of saving some other lives and possibly may communicate a knowledge of his art to some other physician and thereby render a service to the human race."[43]

Unlike the pleas of the condemned man, these citizens' petitions were not self-interested, and the 446 signatures weighed heavily against the judgment of the 12 trial jurors. Together these petitions supported three of the principles that in England could sustain a pardon: the convict possessed a reputation for good character; the evidence against him was tainted by self-interest; and if his life were spared he would serve the community as he had done before. Perhaps Governor Adams and the council also concluded that whatever might have transpired between the ancient physician and the dog, Farrell posed no threat of violence to the community. Accordingly, on March 8, 1797, in consideration of the humble supplications of "John Farrell & also a number of the good Citizens of this Commonwealth," Samuel Adams, the seventy-five-year-old Revolutionary patriot, freed the old physician with a full pardon.[44] Evidently, the governor and council decided that at a time when other states had reduced the penalty for sodomy, the interests of Massachusetts were best served by acceding to the reasonable pleas of so many citizens.

In another case, that of Lemuel Deming, a forty-seven-year-old Hartford native convicted of burglary, only a single petition signed by the condemned man led the council to recommend a pardon to Governor Strong. In court Attorney General Sullivan had persuaded the jury that on the night of February 11, 1803, Deming had broken into a home and stolen eight watches valued at $320, a sum equivalent to a working man's annual earnings. Following the statute against burglary at night, Sullivan called for Deming's life; and the court, which included Wheeler's judges Sedgwick, Sewall, and Simeon Strong among them, sentenced Deming to hang. A petition from his mother and his wife won him an eight-month delay. Thereafter Deming's lawyers, chiefly William Sullivan (son and law partner of the attorney general), gained several reprieves until finally, in January 1806, Deming won a conditional pardon. Deming's petition, which William Sullivan drafted and signed for his client, began by noting that the convict "is an american by birth, and was a soldier during the revolutionary war in the american army; & was in the service of the united states on board of the ships of war during the years 1798 and 1799." Deming's prior record was clean, and "his crime was the least atrocious that could be known under the name of burglary," a crime defined as breaking into a building or dwelling house at night with the intent to steal. Deming's conviction, moreover, was grounded on circumstantial evidence only, "the possession of goods stolen" on the night of the crime. To this petition Sullivan added his own postscript: "I believe the above statement to be true."[45] Because the governor and council considered Deming's and Wheeler's petitions at about the same time, and because the same councilors, Samuel Dexter and Artemas Ward, reviewed both Deming's and Wheeler's cases, the reasoning that governed the Deming case is especially pertinent to the thinking that shaped the council's decision on Wheeler. Neither man had been convicted of previous felonies or had committed murder or treason, so although the facts of the two cases were very different, neither prisoner could be executed as a matter of course.

Dexter and Ward were, like Deming and Wheeler, men in their forties, but unlike the two convicts, they were accomplished men of privilege. Both were Harvard graduates and Federalists who had been practicing law for over twenty years. Dexter was the more gifted, having won election to the Massachusetts legislature at the age of twenty-seven, to Congress at thirty-two, and to the U.S. Senate when he was just thirty-eight years old. By the time Dexter was weighing the fates of Lemuel Deming and Ephraim Wheeler, he had already served as Secretary of War and Secretary of the Treasury in the cabinets of Presidents John Adams and Thomas Jefferson. Dexter's distaste for partisanship and his talents as a conciliator, as well as his enthusiasm for temperance, made some Federalists uneasy. Nicknamed "Ambi" Dexter because of his bipartisan temperament, he would later allow Massachusetts Republicans to run him as their candidate against Governor Strong in 1814, 1815, and 1816.[46] By comparison Ward, the son and namesake of a Revolutionary War general, won election to the state legislature at the age of thirty-four years, and to Congress at age fifty-one. Never described as "brilliant," Ward's evenhanded temperament would suit him to service as chief justice of the Suffolk County Court of Common Pleas in Boston, a post he held from 1820 onward.[47]

Dexter and Ward's report to the council on Deming, written in Ward's hand, recommended a pardon based on mitigating circumstances and their explicitly political judgment regarding the wishes of the Massachusetts legislature and the public. Deming had indeed committed the "essence" of burglary at night, but since he made no attempt to resist arrest or to conceal his crime by setting fire to the burgled dwelling, his was not an aggravated example. Deming had neither threatened nor committed violence. They explained:

> It is not intended by the committee to express a disapprobation of the law which annexes the punishment of death to the crime for burglary when committed under circumstances of high aggravation, but considering the avowed purpose for which the state prison was created, and the present state of public opinion as to the application of capital punishment, it is presumed that if the Legislature were now to affix a punishment to a crime which had precisely the same shades of guilt which attended the commission of said crime by said Deming, that a milder punishment than death would, undoubtedly, be provided.

Putting themselves in the place of the legislature and the voters, the two Federalist lawyers recommended that Deming be excused from the gallows so long as he "submits to confinement at hard labor, in the State-prison in Charlestown during his life." The council and the governor accepted this reasoning, and on January 30, 1806, Strong commuted Deming's sentence by granting him this conditional pardon.[48] For Wheeler, the fact that Governor Strong and the council were willing to override the explicit language of the statute so as to accommodate anti–capital punishment opinion was surely encouraging.

Yet as promising as the Farrell and Deming pardons were for Wheeler's cause, those two crimes, involving no violence, set them apart from Wheeler's. It was Governor Strong's pardon for a rape convict that kindled the highest hopes for saving Ephraim's life. Jacob Azzett Lewis, a laborer, had been convicted for his June 1801 assault on Lydia Heald, the daughter of a Carlisle, Massachusetts, farmer. Indeed if it was still possible to execute anyone for rape in Massachusetts, Lewis, a dark-skinned foreigner also known as "Jacob Negross" and described in petitions as being "of the Hindoo race," was a likely candidate. The four men who had been executed for rape in the neighboring jurisdictions of Connecticut, New Hampshire, and New York since 1790 had all been black.[49]

According to a Boston newspaper, Lewis had raped the "innocent, modest, & well educated" daughter of Captain John Heald on her tenth birthday as the child was walking home from school. Lewis, who was returning from bringing his master's two sons to their academy in a carriage, overtook Lydia on the road near the home of her "respectable family." He persuaded her to ride with him and, when the girl stepped into the carriage, Lewis forcibly "violated" her. According to Lydia's testimony "he threatened her, that if she cried or resisted he would kill her with a knife, which he said he had in his pocket." When Lewis released her, the child "ran home to her mother . . . and complained." Later "marks of extreme violence on her were proved," and when Lewis was seized "he had a knife in his pocket, which he attempted to conceal."[50] Attorney General Sullivan convinced the jury he was guilty.[51]

But initial defeat in the courtroom did not discourage the convict's lawyers, both Jeffersonian Republicans—one of whom, George Blake, was a 1789 Harvard graduate who had studied law under James Sullivan and held appointment by President Jefferson as United States Attorney for the Massachusetts district.[52] Blake, who had spoken out in court to defend freedom of the press against the Sedition Act two years earlier, saw in the Jacob Azzett Lewis case an opportunity to strike a blow against capital punishment.[53] The strategy to save Lewis's life, however, was not merely political. Blake and his colleague, Samuel Dana, plotted a petitioning campaign that argued for mercy on traditional grounds, in addition to challenging the use of capital punishment. And they proposed a cost-free alternative to hanging their client: deportation.

The plea for mercy on which Jacob Azzett Lewis put his mark was a closely written 1,300-word essay that, except for the challenge to capital punishment, previewed the arguments in the additional citizens' petitions. Clearly Blake and Dana judged that it would be unwise for an ignorant young foreigner to challenge the legitimacy of the Massachusetts penal code, so they confined their challenge to some of the citizens' petitions.[54] If the council and governor chose to tally the signatures, they would find that 107 of Lewis's 121 petitioners supported ending capital punishment for rape.

The arguments that Blake, Dana, and their allies presented are especially significant compared to the pleas made on Wheeler's behalf to the same governor less than four years later. Though Wheeler's lawyers may not have seen these petitions, the Jacob Azzett Lewis pardon was public knowledge in Berkshire in 1805, and Wheeler's politically connected attorneys were familiar with the kinds of appeals petitioners generally used. To be sure, the specific arguments employed in the Lewis petitions were tailored to the circumstances of his case, but they were drawn from the standard repertoire of pardon justifications.

Lewis's first argument, and that of all on his behalf, portrayed the convict as peaceful and penitent, and with an otherwise faultless record. Because of his youth (claimed at around sixteen years, though the newspaper reported him "over twenty"), his ignorance, and his alien status, Lewis, it was argued, was not fully responsible for his actions.[55] He went on to challenge the jury's judgment of the case. Though convicted of rape, Lewis's petition claimed that the intercourse was consensual; similarly, all of the public petitions cast doubt on the reliability of Lydia's testimony.[56] Being ten years old, she had reached the legal age of sexual consent, but petitioners argued she was a mere "infant" and not fully cognizant of the meaning of an oath. Lewis claimed that Lydia, overcome by shame at her own actions, later decided to uphold her own and her family's reputation by denying consent and swearing to rape.[57] In reality, if Lydia felt shame about having sex voluntarily with the East Indian servant, she and her family would have kept their silence, a rebuttal James Sullivan doubtless would have made in court. But petitions were one-sided, and Blake wanted to cast doubt on the verdict so as to attract signers for his client. He also neglected to mention that if Lydia had been only one day younger, Lewis's crime would have been statutory rape, making the question of consent irrelevant.

Lewis even contested the evidence of the crime. Lydia was not seriously injured: "no other mark of violence appeared on her body except such as would have been the result of an intercourse, whether voluntary or involuntary."[58] Though the Lewis petition spoke the rhetoric of contrition and deference, it challenged the verdict directly. When they were up against James Sullivan, George Blake and Samuel Dana had failed to convince the jury; but if their petition arguments could attract enough signers, they would advance their campaign for both Lewis and the cause of capital punishment reform.

All seven public petitions echoed Lewis's own petition, but six also stressed further restriction of the death penalty. Four identical petitions, signed by a total of 107 men, declared that "many Citizens entertain doubts of the expediency of Capital punishment, and of the right of civil society to inflict it, except in the cases of Treason and Murder for which there seems to be a warrant in the Holy Scriptures."[59] Despite the statutory penalty for Lewis's crime, he should not be put to death.

To reinforce this point George Blake and Samuel Dana proposed an alternative that was not covered in the penal code. They wrote into all the petitions that they would give their bond for $2,000 to assure that, if pardoned, Lewis would "depart to his native Country of the East Indies and never more return to this or any of the United States."[60] The convict would thus pose no threat to American society and there would be no public cost, either for execution or incarceration. Though no record of the council's deliberations on Lewis's case survives, their judgment and that of the governor was merciful. On March 12, 1802, Caleb Strong issued a pardon for Lewis, commuting the sentence, provided that he depart immediately for India. Unlike the four "black" men convicted for rape in Massachusetts between 1711 and 1769, "Jacob Negross . . . labourer, otherwise called Jacob Azett Lewis," escaped the gallows.[61]

For Ephraim Wheeler and his counselors John W. Hulbert and Daniel Dewey, the Lewis pardon, set alongside those granted to Deming and Farrell, gave solid reason for hope. Governor Strong himself had pardoned two of the condemned men, and he had argued vigorously on behalf of the third. Moreover, though a decision concerning Deborah Stevens, who had been convicted of the murder of her three-year-old daughter in 1803, remained pending as of January 1806, she had not been executed; and in May Governor Strong, with the advice of the council, would grant her a pardon as well.[62] To Wheeler, locked up in chains awaiting execution, Caleb Strong could be a godsend. It seemed that if Wheeler's petitions could display his submissive attitude, throw doubt on the evidence, and question the legitimacy of capital punishment for his crime, and if numbers of men supported his cause, he might win commutation of his sentence.

Yet there were no assurances. Since Governor Strong had taken office in the spring of 1800, he had signed three death warrants: in 1801 for Jason Fairbanks, a respectable young man who used a knife to murder the woman who spurned him; in 1802 for Ebenezer Mason, a Yankee farmer who, in anger over an inheritance, killed his brother-in-law with a shovel while they were at work manuring a field; and in 1804 for Jack Battus, a nineteen-year-old mulatto laborer who raped and then murdered a thirteen-year-old white girl. Except for Fairbanks, who pleaded innocence due to temporary insanity and became the subject of a romantic pamphlet biography, these convictions went unchallenged, and there were no petitions for Governor Strong to consider.[63]

But the pardon arguments for two cases that would later come before Governor James Sullivan and the council in 1808 were rejected. The first, a noncapital case, concerned a young white man, Nathan Coye, whom James Sullivan as attorney general had successfully prosecuted for Coye's assault with intent to rape a black girl in December 1805, just three months after the Durwin and Wheeler trials. Sentenced to three years in the Hampshire County jail, after Coye had served more than two years his lawyer prepared a petition, which the prisoner signed, pleading to be excused from the last nine months. Though Coye asserted that he humbly accepted the decisions of jury and judges, his petition restated the standard defense against rape: the ease of making the charge "and the extreme difficulty of defending against it." In addition, after "the sufferings he has endured," Coye claimed that he had "made some atonement for the immorality and indecency" of his past, and he asked that his "unhappy case" be reviewed. Attached to Coye's petition was his prison-keeper's testimonial to Coye's "orderly regular & submissive conduct" in jail. In addition, a prominent Northampton gentleman attested that he had known Coye since infancy, that Coye came from a respectable Connecticut family, and that he believed Coye's record was clean apart from the present conviction. Buttressing these arguments was a personal letter to one of the councilors from another Northampton gentleman, who asserted that he had "heard one or two of the Grand Jurors say" that from the beginning they "were much divided whether they should even find a bill" against Coye; and that the trial jury, too, was "long in deliberation." If clemency were denied, this gentleman warned, "I am really apprehensive it will produce a delirium" in Coye.[64] These arguments, voiced in March 1808, convinced neither the council nor the governor, and they let Coye's sentence stand.

Four months later the authorities weighed the capital case of Joseph Drew, a twenty-four-year-old blacksmith from Falmouth, Maine. In January, Drew had swung a four-foot wooden club into the head of a Cumberland County sheriff, Ebenezer Parker. A week later, when Parker died of the injury, the state charged Drew and his friend, Levi Quimby, with murder. At the trial Quimby, who had supplied the weapon, was acquitted, but Drew, who had wielded it, was convicted and accordingly sentenced to hang. Late in June, Drew's friends sent three petitions to Governor Sullivan and the council.[65]

One was a simple plea signed by twenty-three men, including several elite community leaders, asking to commute Drew's sentence to "hard labor" for life on the grounds that such clemency would not prejudice "the interests of Society."[66] A second petition, from Isaac Ingalls, one of the trial jurors, reported that he never believed Drew's assault to be murder because "Drew had no melless a fore thought" and "there was not time for the hueman pashens to cool." Ingalls claimed Drew to be "gilty of manslater ondley," although as a juror he had submitted to the majority who had argued that one man should not override the judgment of "Eleven men."[67]

The third petition came from Joseph Drew himself. Drafted, no doubt, by his lawyer, it recapitulated the courtroom defense and added a sentimental appeal. Drew emphasized his youth, mentioned the pain his death would cause his brothers and sisters, and stated that it would "bring down the gray hairs of an aged Father & Mother with sorrow to the grave." He attributed his crime to "rashness" and "unjustifiable zeal" on behalf of his friend Quimby. Drew claimed he had only intended to drive Parker out of their workshop, which, he asserted, the victim had "unlawfully forced open" and entered. Because all agreed that the whole event "lasted but a minute," he could not have acted with malice aforethought, and he referred to Juror Ingalls' petition, in which the latter admitted yielding to the majority. Drew closed with a declaration of repentance and vowed to be useful to society and "settle his peace with a gracious and merciful God" if the governor and council would spare his life and send him to prison.[68]

Sullivan had not prosecuted this case, but he and the councilors knew that Drew's statement was less than complete. Deputy Sheriff Parker had come to arrest Quimby, and the two men had resisted. The jurors had decided that the deadly assault was not the spontaneous act of passion that Drew claimed; and if the council and governor were to reverse every case where one juror yielded to his peers and later recanted, they would make chaos of Massachusetts justice. Accordingly, the council "Unanimously advised that a pardon or commutation be not granted," and Governor Sullivan allowed Drew's execution to proceed.[69] The denial of clemency here, as in the Coye case, where only nine months in prison were at stake, shows that the executive branch would not readily set a jury decision aside. Indeed, apart from Wheeler's case, between 1795 and 1808 pardons were granted for capital sentences only when, as in the Farrell case, there was danger of creating a grave injustice, or when, as in the Farrell, Lewis, Deming, and Stevens cases, concern about the legitimate use of capital punishment could be invoked.

The governor who would hear the council's recommendation on Wheeler and join them in deciding his fate was Caleb Strong, a tall man of medium build, with a long face, dark complexion, and blue eyes.[70] Temperamentally he was the essence of a Yankee gentleman. Born in 1745 and descended from a well-established Northampton family, he prepared for Harvard College with a parson in York, Maine. After graduation from college in 1764, Strong returned to Northampton. Like Sullivan, who made his way despite epilepsy and a limp, Strong, too, suffered a handicap—poor eyesight, the result of smallpox he contracted after college. During the several years when Strong was virtually blind, his father and sisters read to the young graduate, including law texts, and he became a careful listener. When his sight recovered partially, he trained with patriot lawyer Joseph Hawley, winning admission to the bar in 1772, the same year he was first elected a Northampton selectman. His election at the age of twenty-seven marked both the stature of his family and his promise for public service.[71]

From then on, like Sullivan, Strong mixed public service and his law practice. Chosen to his town's committee of correspondence in 1774, he went on to serve in the House of Representatives and the state's constitutional convention where, with Sullivan, he was one of a handful of men who helped draft the new Massachusetts constitution. Under this new government he would win election to the state senate repeatedly during the 1780s, the decade when he successfully defended the freedom of ex-slave Quok Walker and so won the constitutional decision in the Supreme Judicial Court that abolished slavery in Massachusetts in 1783.[72] His selection as a delegate to the United States Constitutional Convention in 1787 was a mark of the esteem that the then forty-two-year-old Strong commanded among his colleagues, as well as a recognition of his popularity and eminence in western Massachusetts.

A supporter of the new federal government and the Washington administration, Strong served as a U.S. senator from 1789 through

1796, when he resigned so as to return to Northampton and the practice of law. He arrived just in time to defend John Farrell and to gain the old man's pardon from hanging. Strong remained in Northampton until a divided Federalist party, seeking to defeat Elbridge Gerry, a popular Republican, nominated him for governor in 1800. Because Strong was well known among the farmers of central and western Massachusetts he defeated Gerry, but only by 100 votes. Recognizing the importance of reconciliation after the partisan battle, during Strong's inaugural procession he stopped his carriage at the house of Samuel Adams, alighted, and uncovered his head as he stepped forward to shake hands with the aged Republican patriot, who stood in the doorway. This gesture to a prominent Gerry supporter was not merely good theater; it was also characteristic of Strong's pragmatic, conciliatory brand of Federalism, which drew on shared Revolutionary ideals. In succeeding years Strong won reelection, usually by much larger margins, until James Sullivan nearly won the office in 1806, and did win it in 1807. Never one to promote controversy or to advance extreme or unpopular opinions, Strong returned to the governorship in 1812 and held it through 1816, when he retired to care for his wife, Sarah, in her last illness. By the time of his own death in 1819, Strong was recognized as the leading figure in Massachusetts politics of his generation.[73]

By all accounts it was Strong's steadiness and moderation that propelled him in front of men who were more articulate, imaginative, and intellectually adept. During the struggle over ratification of the U.S. Constitution in 1788 the brilliant Essex County lawyer Theophilus Parsons was reported to have told Strong, "you can do more with that honest face of yours than I can with all my legal knowledge."[74] After his death a friend and political associate described Strong as possessing "little of boldness or novelty" but "much of sound judgment, of foresight and decision."[75] A household patriarch,

Strong married his pastor's daughter, Sarah Hooker, in 1777; their marriage lasted until her death forty years later. At that time, of their nine children, only four survived. Tested repeatedly by such private trials of mortality, as well as by questions of life and death in public affairs, Strong was remembered as a man who possessed "a happy control of his affections . . . he was never known to be discomposed by violent passion."[76] This was the man who would in the end give the order either to save Ephraim Wheeler's life or to take it.

Strong would not, of course, decide Wheeler's fate on his own. As in every other case the Governor's Council would first study the convict's petitions and then recommend action. For Ephraim Wheeler four petitions were filed, each of which made distinct arguments and pleas. Together they questioned whether Ephraim's execution would serve the cause of justice.[77]

One of the petitions was from Ephraim himself, and it was brief. In a single paragraph drafted by his lawyers, Wheeler expressed contrition, just as Farrell, Deming, and Lewis had done before him; but unlike them he offered no exculpatory arguments. Ephraim's petition simply read, "Your unhappy petitioner . . . asks for his life— Conscious of the enormity of the Offence of which he stands convicted." Volunteering for a life in prison, Ephraim swore that "Confinement under any circumstances and for any period of time, would be deemed a great favor." Appealing to the governor's "known humanity," Ephraim declared he would try to make "his future life . . . in some measure Attone for the errors of the past." Consistent with his plea at the trial—and like Farrell and Lewis—Wheeler did not admit guilt for the crime, but in other respects his petition followed the penitence formula. The illiterate Wheeler signed with a cross.[78]

The petition of Ephraim's wife and older children, again drawn by the lawyers, was also only a single paragraph in length, and it too appealed for mercy. If the councilors and the governor could be reached emotionally, then Hannah's, Betsy's, and Ephraim, Jr.'s, plea might help save the convicted man. They approached "your Excellency and Honors with Great anxiety," as victims begging mercy for "one who hath greatly injured us." Drawing on Strong's and the other magistrates' belief in the sanctity of family and the institution of patriarchy, they affirmed that "no injury however great can obliterate the remembrance, that Ephraim Wheeler is the husband of one of your petitioners and the father of the other two." Though they were personally the "immediate Sufferers" of the crime, they pledged that not only their duty to a husband and father but also their "Feelings strongly urge" that some other punishment be imposed, and Ephraim's life spared. The petition closed by reminding the magistrates that until they pardoned Wheeler, his family would remain "most unhappy and distressed," living each day "in awful anxiety." Unlike her husband, who could not sign his name, Hannah Wheeler placed her unpracticed signature at the foot of the text. Betsy made her mark directly below her mother, and Ephraim, Jr., put his smaller mark below Betsy's. Neither the governor nor the councilors had ever seen a family document quite like this one, and it must have reinforced their sense of the gravity of their decision.[79]

Daniel Dewey and John W. Hulbert prepared the most complex and tightly argued of the petitions supporting Ephraim. In contrast to the lawyer-drawn petitions for Farrell, Deming, and Lewis—in which the attorneys did not explicitly petition on their clients' behalf—both of Wheeler's attorneys presented this petition in their own names and signed it. They began by expressing deference to the proceedings of the Supreme Judicial Court and the decision of the jury. Then Dewey and Hulbert repeated two arguments they had offered in court: first, the evidence came from two children, aged thirteen and eight years; and second, "the wife of the prisoner was also principally concerned in originating the prosecution." While the judges had set these arguments aside at the trial, these were significant points in making the case for a pardon. If the youth of the witnesses tainted their testimony and the prosecution could reasonably be seen as a wife's challenge to her husband by proxy, then the larger purposes of justice would be better served by commutation of the sentence rather than execution.[80]

They followed their legal challenge with a plea that reinforced the family's emotional appeal by focusing on the unnatural circumstances of the case:

> Since the conviction and sentence of the prisoner both his children and his wife perceiving the awful event which awaits him, and considering the part which they have taken in the prosecution, however just and proper it may have been are filled with anxiety and distress—although the crime with which the prisoner was charged be a heinous and detestable offence, yet it seems strange and unnatural that a man should be convicted of a capital offense, and suffer the pains of death on the testimony of his own children—as the wife and children of the prisoner deeply lament his present unhappy condition, and earnestly pray his life may be spared.

The implication of Dewey and Hulbert's reasoning was that the children's testimony had given the prosecution its victory, and if the state were to execute Ephraim Wheeler it would be repaying the children's "just and proper" conduct by making them and their mother victims again. After all, Betsy and Ephraim, Jr., had been willing to overcome their properly ingrained subordination to their father so as to testify in court. Surely the governor and council ought to reckon with "the anxiety and distress" of the prisoner's family. "Confinement to hard labor for life or years," they believed, "would sufficiently maintain the dignity of the law and Government."

If the magistrates followed this path a penitent Wheeler might at some distant day be pardoned and restored to his family or enabled to be of "service to his Country." Dewey and Hulbert were not, they wrote, sufficiently informed to comment on Wheeler's "former character," but as far as they knew he had a clean record until the present conviction. As the head of a household with a wife and three children, this "healthy, robust man, of between thirty and forty years of age; capable of enduring labor and fatigue," might by his earnings support his family—but only "if his life is spared." Though their petition could not express the clear character endorsement and promise of future service that the cancer doctor Farrell mustered, their statement was comparable to the petitions on behalf of Deming and Lewis.

Dewey, in whose hand the petition was drafted, dated it September 24, 1805, and signed first. Hulbert signed beneath him, with a flourish. To these signatures the statement "I most humbly join in the prayer of the above petition" was added at the foot of the page, with a tiny *x,* the mark of Ephraim Wheeler, symbolizing the convict's melancholy self-pity. On an additional page, six other Berkshire men, who claimed to be "acquainted with the circumstances" of the case, joined in the petition. One was Elijah Northrup, the Lenox farmer whose widowed brother Job had been prosecuted for incest eight years before and convicted of lewd and lascivious conduct with his daughter (Job had since moved to New York state). Another was Wheeler's jailer for the past three months, William A. Whelpley.[81] Most significant politically was the signature of Woodbridge Little, a leading Pittsfield Federalist, trustee of Williams College, and longtime opponent of Thomas Allen, his outspoken, anti–capital punishment Republican pastor.[82] By combining legal argument with an appeal for recognition of the victims' wishes, Dewey and Hulbert's petition picked up support and commanded serious consideration.

Like the Jacob Azzett Lewis pardon campaign of 1801, which may have been Dewey and Hulbert's model, the effort to save Wheeler included an overtly political, but not partisan, petition. It was signed by a cross-section of the county's voters—93 men, mostly residents of Windsor, where the Wheelers lived, and drawn from the supporters of both parties. Land and probate records have enabled us to determine the occupation and social status of three-quarters (70) of these signers. Over half (40) were farmers, mostly (30) from the middling yeoman class. Another third (20) were landowners and merchants, styled "Gentleman" in the records. The remainder included blacksmiths, shoemakers, traders, and a nail-maker. In addition, two Congregational clergymen signed: the Reverend Thomas Allen, the aged Pittsfield Jeffersonian; and the Reverend Gordon Dorrance, the evangelical pastor in Windsor. Those who could not be found in the records did not own Berkshire County land in 1806, and so were mostly husbandmen or artisans.[83] This community petition was a 580-word statement that began in the usual way, with an acknowledgment of respect for the process that led to Wheeler's conviction. But unlike the Dewey and Hulbert, Farrell, or Lewis petitions, Wheeler's public supporters made no attempt to challenge the evidence or to excuse or exonerate the convict. Instead, they acknowledged Wheeler's guilt for his "high and aggravated" offense and took their stand on how best to deter the crime of rape. Incarceration in the state's showcase prison would display Wheeler as "a monument of his own vicious conduct during his whole life, to be seen by thousands who probably would never have heard that such a man or such a crime had ever existed." In contrast, they claimed his public execution would be carried out "in the presence of few." Since the new state prison was available, the government could "prevent the said Wheeler from again injuring society."[84] This petition sought first to deter crime, not to extend mercy.

The second argument, however, repeated one of Dewey and Hulbert's themes: justice for Wheeler's family. The authorities should commute Wheeler's sentence because that was "the earnest wish" of his wife and children, "by whose aid Government have been able to convict him," and because the state has the ability to lock him away so that he cannot injure "society." Returning to the principle of capital punishment, the petition pointed out that the law for the punishment and prevention of rape "is now pending before the Legislature, and may probably be so modified at the next session" as to agree with their request. By commuting Ephraim's sentence to life in prison, the governor and council would only be anticipating the legislature by a few weeks or months—whereas to hang a man on the eve of a change in the law seemed unfair and unreasonable.[85]

This petition of 93 Berkshire voters closed with a pointed reference to the Jacob Azzett Lewis pardon: "we are informed your Excellency and Honors have seen fit and proper, in one case of rape to commute the punishment." Appealing directly to Governor Strong's "known humanity," and to the governor and council's power to exercise mercy, the petitioners closed by declaring that "the commutation we have solicited, would be highly grateful to the feelings of a large proportion of the inhabitants of this county." Their statement invited the state's magistrates to consider the electoral consequences of their judgment on Wheeler's life in a year when the contest between Federalist Caleb Strong and Republican James Sullivan was so close that ultimately it would be decided by fewer than fifty votes.[86]

During the autumn of 1805 these four petitions—Ephraim's, Hannah and the children's, Dewey and Hulbert's with the addendum of six men, and that of the 93 Berkshire voters—totaling 102 signatures plus three signing marks—arrived at the grand, golden-domed state capitol in Boston. For weeks the small packet of folded papers awaited action behind the white colonnades and red brick walls of Bulfinch's masterpiece. At its regular meeting on October 16 the governor and council set a date for Wheeler's execution, February 20, 1806, but then they turned to other business, dealing with a wide range of administrative matters and a handful of pardon cases. Three and a half months passed before they took up Wheeler's case again, considering his petitions on Tuesday, February 4, only sixteen days before the execution date.

On that Tuesday, just after ten in the morning, nine councilors, all Federalists, attended in addition to Governor Strong and the lieutenant governor, Edward H. Robbins.[87] Among these eleven gentlemen only two, Strong and Councilor Nathan Cushing, had taken part in the pardoning of Jacob Azzett Lewis. But at the council's last meeting only five days earlier, all had joined in commuting Lemuel Deming's death penalty to life in prison.[88] Moreover they had unanimously accepted the reasoning of two fellow-councilors, lawyers Samuel Dexter and Artemas Ward, that "if the Legislature were now to affix a punishment to a crime which had precisely the same shades of guilt" as Deming's, "a milder punishment than death would, undoubtedly, be provided."[89] Such a governor and council surely would be inclined to seize the opportunities for pardon that the Wheeler petitions offered.

As in the Deming case and the Lewis case before it, Wheeler presented himself as humble and contrite, ready to accept any alternative to hanging. Like Lewis, Wheeler had over a hundred men calling for mercy on much the same grounds that the council had just affirmed to justify Deming's pardon. Moreover, among Wheeler's petitioners there were seventy-four men from the town where he lived, Windsor, men who had at least a passing acquaintance with him and his family. Windsor's Calvinist pastor, Gordon Dorrance, was among Wheeler's petitioners, as was his neighbor, Robert Walker, the arresting justice of the peace who had first taken Betsy's testimony. In addition, important Federalists, such as Woodbridge Little, and Republicans, including the Reverend Thomas Allen and his son Thomas, Jr.—both death penalty reform advocates—were signers. So too were Simon Larned, the county sheriff, and Joshua Danforth, Berkshire's postmaster.[90]

But the council's committee report on the Wheeler petitions was very different from the Deming report it had considered five days earlier. Instead of concentrating on the issue of capital punishment, Dexter and Ward found only one question that might justify a pardon: "the credibility of the principal witness in the trial." Dewey and Hulbert had argued this point in court and in their petition, and now the two-man committee considered it in their report to their fellow councilors and Governor Strong:

> on enquiry into the circumstances of the case they do not find anything peculiar as the ground for granting the prayer of the petitioner unless questions as to the credibility of the principal witness in the trial should be considered such. It does not appear that the Court were dissatisfied with the verdict; but the Committee have reason to presume the contrary; yet from the different effect that the same evidence often has on different minds, perhaps, if the evidence had on the trial were submitted to Committee for a decision, they might doubt whether it would be perfectly safe to convict of so high an offense on such evidence.[91]

Without explanation the committee that had urged clemency for Deming rejected the mercy arguments of the injured Wheeler family and the appeal of ninety-three men who wanted to reform the penalty for rape.

The justification for embracing penal reform for Deming but rejecting it five days later for Wheeler probably lay in the councilors' interpretation of Massachusetts' recent legislative history, in which both the pardoning power and the penalty for rape had been considered with some care. Two years earlier, in January 1804, Governor Strong had asked the legislature for the authority to commute the death penalty to life in prison because, he argued, "the degrees of guilt in persons convicted of the same crime may be so different as to render it fit and necessary to make a difference in the punishment, and to soften the rigour of the law." He had illustrated his reasoning with an example: "the man who enters unarmed into a dwelling-house in the night time and steals to satisfy his hunger, is obviously less criminal than he, who breaks in for the purpose of rifling the house, and arms himself with design to destroy the life of the owner if he obstructs him." The first case was little more than larceny, Strong asserted, whereas the second "offender displays a most depraved and malignant spirit, and his life would be thought dangerous to society."[92] Both the House and the Senate agreed with the governor, and in March 1804 passed a law that gave the executive the authority to grant conditional pardons by commuting the death penalty to life in prison for burglary convicts like Deming.[93]

But the legislature's action on the penalty for rape was different. When the House of Representatives passed the law reducing the punishment for rape nearly a year before, in March 1805, it was only by a single vote, and the Senate then rejected the reform. The councilors likely saw the legislature's action in March 1805 as a narrow but explicit affirmation of the status quo. Though the governor and the councilors could not know on February 4, 1806, that in just five weeks the legislature would enact a new rape law that retained capital punishment, they could, however, assess the sentiments of the legislators and so may have anticipated this outcome.[94] Wheeler's 93 anti–death-penalty petitioners admitted both his guilt and the aggravated nature of his crime. Under these circumstances, and in contrast to the Deming case, if the council and governor were to pardon Wheeler on reform grounds, they might be violating the terms of their pardoning power, usurping the duties of the legislature, and insulting it.

Instead the committee dwelt on Betsy's testimony. It was, beyond question, exceptional to hang a man based on a child's uncorroborated testimony; and the jury's decision to believe Betsy's testimony could not be regarded as infallible. Moreover, although on the record the judges seemed satisfied with the verdict, Dexter and Ward must have possessed opposing information, because they reported that they had "reason to presume the contrary." Though the committee made no definite recommendation on Wheeler's cause, they concluded that Wheeler's guilt was open to reasonable doubt. As jurymen Dexter and Ward implied that they would have voted to acquit.

In coming to this judgment the committee pointed the council's discussion to the trial, not the death penalty. Presumably they reported orally on the reason they believed the judges were not satisfied with the verdict; perhaps it was the government's failure to produce physical evidence of the rape. The councilors could also have read and discussed the evidence presented in the only full record of the case, the *Report of the Trial of Ephraim Wheeler,* which had been available since November.[95] Moreover, since they called Attorney General Sullivan into their chamber "to advise" with them, they might have questioned him on Betsy's credibility as well as other facts and circumstances of the case.[96] When the councilors themselves considered the case, doubtless comparing it to Deming's, Lewis's, and others, they disagreed. Samuel Dexter, the former cabinet secretary under Presidents Adams and Jefferson, evidently strongly believed that Wheeler's life should be spared. The independent-minded Dexter, the most distinguished lawyer in the room, tried to persuade his colleagues that Betsy's testimony was not sufficient to hang a man; but he failed. The other councilors, including President Washington's Secretary of War, Henry Knox, concluded that the judgment of the trial jury and the Supreme Judicial Court must be maintained.

According to standard practice, Secretary of State John Avery entered the committee report into the council's official record. But contrary to usual practice he inserted six words into the record that were not part of the committee report, not part of the indictment, and not part of the judgment before the Supreme Judicial Court. Those six words echo the title page of the printed trial report (and we have placed them in italics here): "Ephraim Wheeler, convicted before the Supreme J. Court at Lenox in the County of Berkshire in September 1805 of a rape *on the body of his daughter*."[97] Though court records nowhere acknowledged the fact of incest directly because, as James Sullivan, Daniel Dewey, and John W. Hulbert agreed at the trial, it was legally irrelevant, the council judged that Wheeler's crime could not be pardoned because he had raped his own child. Worse, from the trial evidence it appeared that his rape was not a single, impulsive act, but part of an escalating pattern. The statute did not recognize these shades of aggravation, but the councilors did. Though there was some public support for a pardon and some councilors harbored doubts about Wheeler's trial, all except Dexter recommended that the governor maintain the death sentence for the man who raped his daughter.

The record does not show whether Caleb Strong participated in their discussion. Most likely the near-blind sixty-one-year-old listened as his colleagues teased out the implications of the arguments and weighed the consequences of the available paths. One path, which had served Lemuel Deming's cause and John Farrell's, as well as New Yorker Stephen Arnold's, was a delay of execution. A plea that Wheeler needed more time to prepare his soul for eternity could scarcely have been denied, inasmuch as governors granted such delays routinely. But this was not available for Ephraim Wheeler because none of his petitioners asked for it.

Years before, when Caleb Strong sought to save the life of John Farrell, Strong had sought a delay, which he then used to collect testimonials and hundreds of signatures for his client. But this strategy did not, evidently, appeal to Hulbert and Dewey, the likely planners of Wheeler's petitioning effort. Wheeler, unlike Farrell, did not have scores of men who would testify to his character and usefulness, so the best time to seek signatures was right away, while interest in the trial and in capital punishment was high in Berkshire County. Since their client was probably impatient for a pardon as he awaited execution, and since they had the precedent of the humane Strong pardoning Jacob Azzett Lewis, acting immediately seemed wise. But with hindsight we can see that if Wheeler's execution had been delayed beyond March 1806, and if the legislature had then ended capital punishment for rape, Wheeler's sentence would probably have been commuted. Alternatively, one or more delays might have enabled Wheeler to develop a record as a contrite model prisoner, and as time passed public outrage over Wheeler's crime and memory of it would likely have faded. Indeed if Wheeler professed his penitence and gave his hard-luck life story to a printer he might even, like Stephen Arnold, attract a certain public sympathy as an unhappy sufferer languishing in jail.[98] When the political season had passed, the executive might have quietly commuted his sentence to life in prison. But in the fall of 1805 Dewey and Hulbert did not follow this line of reasoning. As a result, Governor Strong had to choose between life and death.

Caleb Strong did not linger over his decision. If service in the high councils of Massachusetts and the United States had not made him familiar with the messy lives of all kinds of people, then his long experience as a selectman, justice of the peace, and attorney in Northampton had given him a feeling for the tests and troubles his neighbors faced. He knew too well that contracts turned sour, investments failed, and farms were foreclosed routinely. Too often he had witnessed life-changing injuries and illnesses and the deaths of children, parents, spouses. In his official capacity Strong had repeatedly dealt with people high as well as low who went out of control and misbehaved; and he had often attended the needs of poor people, some of

whom deserved aid, comfort, and perhaps pity rather than punishment. He had never before dealt with someone just like Ephraim
Wheeler, but he knew that regardless of the newspaper publicity
Ephraim was no more a monster than his elderly client John Farrell
had been. He also knew that Betsy Wheeler's "awful anxiety" was the
honest truth. She, of all people, must feel "unhappy and distressed."
How could she not?

While Strong listened to the councilors discussing the Wheeler
petitions and the issues they raised, he was no doubt weighing the
merits of the arguments in the context of precedents reaching back
ten or even twenty years. As a lawyer trained to strip away extraneous
issues so as to simplify decision-making, Strong's fondness for reason
and the calculation of future consequences may have led him to make
a mental ledger, with the reasons to pardon Wheeler on one side and
the reasons to let the law take its course on the other. In Wheeler's favor, certainly, was the fact that the evidence in his trial, however plausible and probable, was less than conclusive. Though the judges did
not officially challenge the jury's decision, they had not been fully
satisfied with the trial. Councilors Dexter and Ward had concluded
that they would have acquitted Wheeler. It was also in Wheeler's favor that Berkshire voters of both parties and so many men from
Wheeler's own town took up his cause so as to advance capital punishment reform. Strong, like the councilors, saw reform as important;
indeed, in the last week the governor and council had embraced it by
pardoning Deming. The Lewis pardon was also a reason for pardoning Wheeler. Strong could have thought back to 1802 and asked himself, as the petitioners did, if it was just to save Lewis's neck, why not
save Wheeler's? After all, the state now had an advanced and secure
prison where Wheeler could safely be locked up for good. Finally,
there were the facts that Wheeler had no prior convictions and that
his victim, Betsy, appealed for mercy.

On the other side of the ledger stood the statute: death was the penalty for rape. Moreover, though Betsy pleaded mercy for her father, the state prosecuted Ephraim on its own behalf, not Betsy's, and his punishment was a public matter. Whatever doubts existed regarding the evidence in the trial, according to the jury Wheeler was guilty, a verdict the judges endorsed publicly with their death sentence. Strong, like his councilors, recognized that because the legislature had affirmed the death penalty for rape within the past year, it would not be prudent politically or constitutionally to set the law aside in anticipation that the legislature might possibly change its mind. Strong also knew that by advocating the commutation policy in 1804, by signing the new sodomy law in 1805, and now by pardoning Deming, he had already signaled his moderate support for reform. It was not necessary to pardon Wheeler too.

The precedent of his own pardon for Jacob Azzett Lewis was pertinent, of course, but Strong knew that anyone who compared the cases closely would see important differences. In the first place, when he had pardoned Lewis it had been eighteen years since the legislature had prescribed the penalty for rape by merely renewing the colonial statute in 1784.[99] He knew that between 1784 and 1802 the movement to curtail the use of the gallows was growing. Consequently in 1802 he and the council had not needed to worry about contradicting the legislature, as now they did. In addition, the particulars of the two cases differed. Lewis was a young foreigner who, being unfamiliar with Massachusetts law and custom, could be seen as not fully responsible. Wheeler, by contrast, was a middle-aged Yankee husband and father. In addition, Lewis's crime was less aggravated—it was a sudden, impulsive act. But the testimony in Wheeler's case showed that his assault was part of a repeated pattern of abuse. Finally, Lewis had opportunistically raped a stranger for whom he bore no responsibility. But Ephraim Wheeler's assault was on his own daughter, a child who by the laws of God and man he was bound to protect.

Though the law did not take note of Wheeler's relation to his victim, the council did by stating that relation in its record. So, finally, did Caleb Strong, who united with their judgment.[100]

Ultimately Wheeler's crime was not only an assault on Betsy, it was also an attack on patriarchy—a perversion of the ruling ideal of fathers as masters of their families. Just as Strong and his generation had revolted against a monarch who transgressed the laws of God and man to make war on his subjects, Strong and the council revolted against a father's assault on his daughter. In contrast to most abuse cases, the issue of a father's authority to discipline his child could not extenuate Wheeler's crime. He had raped his own daughter. To commute Wheeler's sentence, Strong and the councilors concluded, would proclaim that the death penalty no longer applied to the worst possible rape in Massachusetts. This they would not do.

As the winter dusk settled over Boston that Tuesday afternoon, John Avery, the Secretary of State, writing for the governor and council, penned a letter to the sheriff of Berkshire County, Simon Larned:

> His Excellency the Governor has laid before the Council for their Consideration the petition of Ephraim Wheeler and several other petitions on behalf of that unhappy prisoner now in your Custody; and after maturely considering every Circumstance relative to the said Convict: The Council have advised that the prayer of the said Ephraim's petition be not granted: You will therefore conform to the direction of the Warrant heretofore transmitted to you for the Execution of the said Ephraim Wheeler.[101]

In a few days Larned would hold this letter in his hands and know that he must organize an execution in Lenox. Contrary to his own humane principles, his duty directed him to carry out the hanging of Ephraim Wheeler.

The Execution

He was taken from the Gaol at 11 o'clock, and, accompanied by the Sheriff and his Deputies, with the customary guard of Cavalry and Infantry, moved with the greatest solemnity to the Meeting-House, where a Sermon, well adapted to the occasion, was delivered by the Rev. Mr. Shepard. The concourse of People assembled was conjectured to be not less than 5000; not 100 of which, it is believed, but would have greatly rejoiced had his punishment been commuted, and he been confined to hard labor in the States' Prison for life. The Sheriff, Col. Larned, executed the sentence of the law on the unhappy criminal at 3 o'clock, with marks of great sensibility, tenderness, and compassion. He made no confession of the crime for which he suffered; but just before he was turned off declared his innocence of it, that he had been accused wrongfully, and that he forgave his accusers and all the world, and desired the Rev. Mr. Ayre, who was with him on the scaffold, to make proclamation of the same, which he did in a very pathetic manner. Not the least disorder took place among this large collection of people, nor any injury happened to any ones person, but an awful, attentive solemnity appeared on the face of the whole assembly.

Pittsfield Sun, or Republican Monitor, February 24, 1806

Ephraim Wheeler stayed up on Wednesday night, February 19, 1806, as thunder rolled across Berkshire County.[1] Most likely he fortified himself against his fears with the sailor's friend, rum, or with brandy purchased from the jailer. By selling his story he could ease his last day on earth with a few comforts, and at the same time tell his tale of victimization and injustice. So at long last, and still reluctantly, Ephraim had agreed to an interview with Heman Willard, the printer. By the dim light of a candle or two, he haltingly revealed his life history to a handful of witnesses in Lenox jail. Afterward, though he may have felt a measure of relief, he probably slept only fitfully until the gray dawn of his execution day.[2] Though each of us must spend a last day on earth, we normally depart at an unplanned moment, whenever illness or accident takes us. In contrast, Ephraim Wheeler's last hours were carefully planned, scheduled by the authorities according to rituals established to reinforce the truths of religion, the principles of social order, and the power of the state.

At 11:00 A.M. Sheriff Simon Larned was to lead Ephraim in a mile-and-a-half procession northward, past the courthouse where back in September Betsy's testimony had convicted him, then on up the hill to the just-completed meetinghouse overlooking the village. Accompanied not only by the sheriff and his thirteen deputies, but also by the cavalry and infantry troops of Berkshire County, the authorities intended Ephraim to be the center of attention for a crowd of thousands during the next four hours. First the Reverend Samuel Shepard would preach, using Ephraim Wheeler's life and death to dramatize the Christian message of hope for salvation.[3] Next, the sheriff would lead Wheeler and the crowd back through the village and down to the gallows, the site of the climax of the day's drama. There, Wheeler would speak his last words of repentance, a clergyman would lead a prayer for his soul, and Sheriff Larned would perform his duties as hangman.[4] By the time dusk fell that evening, no one among the thousands who witnessed the day's pageant of justice would doubt the commitment of Berkshire leaders and their community to preserving a peaceable, orderly, and just society.

This was the scenario planned for Ephraim Wheeler's execution day, and it was essentially the same as executions that had preceded his for over a century in Massachusetts. Always the governor and council allowed an interval of weeks or months between sentencing and execution so that the convict had time to repent in preparation for death; always they set the time of execution in the afternoon; and normally the execution was preceded by a sermon to teach the lessons of sin, repentance, and salvation. The scaffold performance, too, allowed for the criminal to make a speech of warning and repentance before a clergyman led the multitude in a prayer for the convict's soul. Only then did the sheriff "turn off" the convict by hanging. For seven generations Massachusetts Puritans had made their highest criminal punishment, hanging, into a sacred community ritual. At the opening of the new century of a republican age, however, their tradition was beginning to unravel.[5]

No one had been executed in Berkshire County for almost twenty years, and since that time principled and articulate opposition to capital punishment had been growing. Moreover, common folk in eastern Massachusetts had begun to shrug off the high seriousness that authorities invested in this theater of righteous power. When day dawned on a rainy February 20 in Lenox, while Ephraim was worrying about the noose that would be placed around his neck, Sheriff Larned, the county clergy, and the militia officers might well have wondered whether the old script would still play in the orderly, dignified way that they intended.

Ironically, the official charged with managing the awful ceremony was Sheriff Simon Larned, a county leader and father of seven children who a few months earlier had signed the anti–capital punishment petition to save Wheeler's life. The fifty-two-year-old war veteran from Connecticut had risen to the rank of captain during the Revolution, and afterwards had married the "adorable Miss Ruthy Bull, of Hartford," before coming to Pittsfield to make his way as a merchant and operator of an iron forge.[6]

Larned's public career began with election to the state legislature in 1791, and thereafter he moved up to become county treasurer and then sheriff.[7] In 1804 he was suddenly elevated to the U.S. Congress when he soundly defeated Daniel Dewey—having won every single Pittsfield vote and even Dewey's home town by a wide margin.[8] But evidently Larned did not like the life of a congressman. He never again ran for office, although he did accept election as major-general of the county militia. With his large family and various business dealings rooted in Berkshire County, Larned preferred to stay home.[9] Now, however, on February 20, 1806, he was paying the price of his decision to remain a county leader. Against his own best judgment he would have to do something terrible—hang a man. Although Larned could be sure he would have many friends in the crowd that day, the thousands who were expected to watch the hanging might still be unruly. The crowd might not try to save Wheeler from the noose, but they could still make a mockery of the official plan to use this execution to teach the basic principles of the established social order.

By 1800 the traditional execution ritual in both its Puritan and Anglican formats had long been questioned. Critics on both sides of the Atlantic argued that public hangings encouraged precisely the kind of brutal and vicious sensibility that executions were supposed to deter.

Genteel observers of such spectacles reported that instead of promoting Christian virtue and respect for law, hangings encouraged a cynical contempt toward religious and civil authorities. Indeed as far back as 1725 English social critic Bernard Mandeville had described London hangings as "one continual Fair, for Whores and Rogues of the meaner Sort" and "void of that decent Solemnity that would be required to make them awful." Later, in 1741, that great popularizer of the new, humane sensibility, novelist Samuel Richardson, published a critique of London's hanging ritual.[10] In Richardson's account, an earnest country gentleman witnesses a "prodigious" mob that gathers for the monthly exercise. By following the "melancholy cavalcade" on horseback from the Newgate prison to "the fatal tree" at Tyburn, the site of London's gallows, he can observe the whole ritual as it unfolds. Some of the prisoners in the cart showed their "horror and despair" while others "swore, laugh'd, and talked obscenely" as they were greeted by acquaintances bidding them goodbye. As the prisoners' cart passed a church, the bell ringer cried out a prayer; "but the noise of the officers, and the mob, was so great, and . . . made such a confused noise, that I could not hear the words." Indeed the crowd was so numerous and the procession so disorderly that it came to a halt at thirty-yard intervals, and at each stop friends of the criminals brought them wine, which they "greedily" drank.[11]

Finally, when the cart reached Tyburn, "the scene grew still more shocking." The clergyman who preached to the criminals and the crowd "was more the subject of ridicule, than of their serious attention," and "the psalm was sung amidst the curses and quarrelling of hundreds of the most abandon'd and profligate." The sight of the prisoners should have produced a silent awe, but instead it led to "a barbarous kind of mirth, altogether inconsistent with humanity." Then, as soon as the "poor creatures were half-dead," some in the crowd fought over possession of the corpses, either to provide burial, or to sell them to surgeons: "the contests between these were fierce and bloody, and frightful to look at." As Richardson's gentleman departed this appalling scene, instead of the sorrowful solemnity appropriate to the "untimely deaths of . . . members of the community" he witnessed "a kind of mirth, as if the spectacle they had beheld had afforded pleasure instead of pain." For Richardson the execution ritual was all "hurry and confusion, racket and noise, praying and oaths, swearing and singing psalms." It was shameful.[12]

At about the same time that Richardson, the literary moralist, was pointing at the English execution ritual in dismay, his contemporary, the great visual satirist William Hogarth, graphically depicted a scene to match Richardson's verbal sketch. Hogarth's 1747 *Idle 'Prentice Executed at Tyburn* portrays a raucous multitude, said to number in the tens of thousands, mostly in a vast crowd at the site of London's gallows, but with others standing on a hillside or in galleries constructed so as to supply a better view of the spectacle. Here worldly and vicious amusement mock moral and religious sentiment. The real action is not so much the hanging—the gallows stand waiting in the distance—as the crowd. Hogarth's foreground vignettes show a boy picking the pocket of a cake-seller; a woman smashing the face of a boy who is dumping her wheelbarrow; a drunken man cruelly swinging a dog by its tail; a ragged woman with babe in arms selling copies of the prisoner's yet-to-be-delivered "Last dying Speech & Confession"; a child being trampled by the throng; a soldier, emblem of the British state, stuck knee-deep in mud—and two boys making fun of him. The largest foreground figure is a scathing reminder of British justice, personified by a sturdy butcher whose knife hangs from his belt while he holds his judicial wig aloft on a pole.

Hogarth elaborates on the corruption of the execution scene in the middle ground. Here mounted soldiers, pikes in hand, escort the prisoner's cart, while a preacher harangues the doomed man as, propped against his coffin, he reads from a Wesleyan prayer book. England's established churchman rides aloof in a carriage, and the hangman, smoking his pipe, lounges atop the scaffold. The utter absence of religious authenticity is represented by the image of a large, buxom old bawd, who drains a glass of gin while hypocritically casting her eyes and her free hand toward heaven.[13] For Hogarth, like Richardson, the reality of the execution ritual nourished only brutality and alienation, utterly contradicting its high purposes.

But the callous cynicism of executions as they were carried out by the dozen each year at Tyburn did not represent the whole of England or its American colonies. In London a community of vice flourished amidst the anonymity of the great metropolis; but in English provinces or across the Atlantic in Massachusetts, community elites still sought to maintain the moral order. Clergymen and magistrates made the occasional hanging into a solemn event where they could teach piety and order. At midcentury, while the doings at Tyburn were shocking cosmopolitan Londoners like Richardson and Hogarth, in the midlands Job Wells—a man who, like Wheeler, was convicted for raping his daughter—went to his execution according to the old script. Brought first from the jail to church for a sermon, and then carted atop his coffin to the gallows, Wells accepted his guilt and repented publicly. Accompanied on the scaffold by a churchman who prayed loudly for his soul, Job Wells's last words, "Lord, have Mercy upon me," properly completed the day's message.[14]

But two generations later, at the end of the eighteenth century, the brutal, irreverent, Tyburn-style spectacle was gaining ground all over Britain and in America. The large crowds that gathered predictably for executions offered commercial opportunities, and in an era when commerce and its ethos reached ever more widely into the British and American countrysides, the momentum that was pushing this once-solemn spectacle into becoming a vicious and vulgar carnival seemed irresistible. This transformation was one of the reasons that Enlightenment elites were drawn to Beccarian reform. As Blackstone and American defenders of the death penalty pointed out, a few well-chosen executions could serve the interests of public order and the state, whereas indiscriminate resort to hanging made a mockery of justice, the state, and religion.[15]

In Massachusetts in the aftermath of Shays' Rebellion in 1787, James Sullivan, an active supporter of capital punishment, urged just such restraint in connection with the leaders of the recent armed uprising. Even though a number of men had been tried and convicted for the high crime of treason, Sullivan argued that Massachusetts must not follow Britain's "sanguinary disposition [which] daily gluts the grave." The people in the countryside, he said, already displayed "a gloomy silence and a solemn awe at the power of the government," and to carry out executions would only serve to provoke disaffection, since "it was the wish of many thousands of the people that these unhappy commotions should be settled without further loss of life."[16] It was in response to such feelings that Governor John Hancock pardoned the convicted leaders of the rebellion. Though the Shays uprising had killed several men, put thousands of armed men in the field, and shut down state courts and county government for months, the state executed no one for strictly political or military offenses. John Bly and Charles Rose, the two Shaysites who were put to death at Lenox in December 1787, six months after the round of pardons, had gone on a crime spree, and a Berkshire jury had convicted them of burglary, not treason.[17]

Reform-minded arguments and popular doubts put the death penalty on the defensive in Massachusetts, but the use of the gallows continued. Even so, there were problems. In 1795 when the state executed a former slave, Pomp, for the subversive crime of murdering his master, a Salem clergyman remarked that the text of the condemned man's last words, which were sold on a printed sheet, "has a tendency to make Dying Speeches ridiculous."[18] Commercial exploitation of sentiment was overtaking the execution's official religious, political, and social messages. Five months later the same cleric attended an execution when the solemn dignity of the event was shattered because "the Rope broke" and it was necessary that the "senseless" body be "hoisted again."[19] Here, careless preparation by officials made the state look inept, if not ridiculous.

A few years later, the corrupt, carnivalesque tendencies of the ceremony became manifest at the execution of a burglar, Samuel Smith, who stood in the cart loudly and piteously pleading for his life as he was brought to the gallows at Concord. Moreover, contrary to the official script, though he acknowledged his criminal acts, he disclaimed responsibility for them. Standing before a crowd of men, women, and children, he blamed his brutal father for first driving him to steal, then his first love, who had stolen his cash, and finally his vicious, disloyal wife. Instead of prayerful repentance, Smith died denying his own guilt.[20]

Smith's misbehavior was matched by the noisy, emotional crowd. The sheriff, who turned the execution over to a deputy because he himself was overcome by emotion, failed to cover the dying man's head with the traditional long white cap. So when Smith was "turned off" the agonies of strangulation on his face were visible to the spectators. As the criminal hung *"suspended by the aid of Hemp from the Gallows, dancing a Spanish Fandango in the air—and screwing up the muscles of his phiz, into the most ghastly distortions,"* women fell to the ground fainting, with their skirts thrown up so far as to destroy all "modesty and decorum."[21] Instead of the "gloomy silence and solemn awe" Sullivan had witnessed twelve years earlier in 1787, the execution of Samuel Smith in the country town of Concord in 1799 was a chaotic monstrosity that subverted the lessons of Christian redemption and state power.[22]

Gradually Massachusetts leaders came to recognize that such travesties of the execution ritual had become the rule, not the exception. In 1822 Josiah Quincy, one of Boston's most prominent citizens and a defender of capital punishment, would castigate the state's execution ritual as an utter failure—one that promoted vice more than virtue. Quincy's characterization of Massachusetts executions recalled Richardson and Hogarth. The vast audience that engulfed the scaffold was deaf to all moral and religious instruction, Quincy complained; it was a "vacant, gaping, thoughtless, jesting crowd . . . perverted to base excitement and vulgar curiosity, in witnessing each other's sufferings." Moreover, because printers had replaced execution sermons and "dying warnings and last confessions" with accounts of criminal "hardihood," "escapes," and exploits, they had now transformed the gallows villain into a "hero and saint."[23] Quincy's pronouncements vividly reinforced the judgment of the state prison warden, Gamaliel Bradford, who had recently declared against capital punishment entirely. "Not one in a thousand in the community sees the tragedy performed," Bradford argued, "and those who do . . . have a variety of other sentiments to attend to, besides the idea of its being an example."[24]

In Berkshire County, physician Asa Greene expressed similar views in the press, declaring that public hangings tend "to harden the heart and render the spectator himself more likely to commit murder." Although clergymen had always contributed to the execution ritual, now Greene asserted it was "a vile taste that leads people to such shocking sights." Those who participated displayed "a lamentable want of feeling."[25] Indeed by the 1820s some of Berkshire's clergymen agreed. Though the Reverend David Dudley Field, successor to death penalty defender Samuel West at Stockbridge, had himself delivered an execution sermon in Connecticut in 1816, by 1829 he "questioned whether such publicity in putting criminals to death, subserves the cause of justice and public virtue."[26] Though capital punishment still had broad support all over New England and much of the North, many had come to believe that this public ritual was so cruel and degenerate that it debased, rather than expressed, community values.[27]

Twenty years earlier, in 1806, though the execution ritual was losing its prescribed character and communal legitimacy in eastern Massachusetts, it might still be serviceable in a county like Berkshire, where population growth and commercial development proceeded slowly and where the Calvinism of the religious revival flourished. Yet the men who expected to play major roles in the ritual, Sheriff Simon Larned, the Reverend Samuel Shepard, and, at the scaffold, the Reverend Oliver Ayer of West Stockbridge, could not be certain that all would go smoothly. Reverend West, who had preached the execution sermon of Rose and Bly in 1787, could have assured his official colleagues that in spite of Berkshire's mobbish record, on that December afternoon eighteen years before, the two executions had gone quietly enough. And West knew that in 1806 the people, though divided among several religious denominations (not to mention the unchurched) and separated by competing party allegiances, were still more united than they had been at the end of 1787.

Indeed from the perspective of leaders like Simon Larned, part of the threat of disorder lay in the fact that many were united in opposing Wheeler's execution. He himself had joined a hundred other men in petitioning for commutation; and as a militia general, longtime Republican leader, and former congressman, Larned knew that for each man who took the trouble to proclaim his beliefs by signing Wheeler's petition there were more, perhaps many more, who privately felt the same way. Larned and the others may also have known that just seven months before, eighty-five miles to the west at Cooperstown, New York, there had been a near riot when, moments before he was to hang, child murderer Stephen Arnold gained a reprieve. In a scene much like Samuel Smith's hanging at Concord, "women shrieked; some of them wept aloud; some fainted; men raged and swore." Passion overwhelmed reason, and because the state did not that day hang the murderer, "some rough fellows captured a dog, named him 'Arnold,' and hung him on the gallows."[28] Larned, the militia officers, and the clergymen recognized that when a vast crowd gathered for an execution, almost anything could provoke an emotional outburst and undermine the moral intentions that guided, as Richardson delicately put it, the "untimely deaths . . . of members of the community."[29]

On the unseasonably warm, cloudy day of February 20, 1806, as the mist rising from the melting snow hung like smoke in the air, the Congregational meetinghouse loomed above the village and grew larger as Ephraim approached. The chains that still held Wheeler's wrists and ankles rattled as his two-wheeled farm cart pulled by a common horse bumped its way northward, past the courthouse where 159 days before Judge Strong had sentenced him to hang. Up the hill he went, surrounded by hundreds of men and women and their children, all, like the horse, breathing hard as they mounted the hill—thousands of feet tramping along the thawing, muddy road that ran with water. No matter how much people had greased their shoes and boots with tallow the night before, by the time they reached the church they would have wet feet.

Inside the elegant, freshly painted structure every box pew was filled; and in the aisles, around the three-sided balcony, and jammed into the vestibule men and women who had come early stood, anticipating the experience that lay ahead. Though many people seated in the high-walled box pews could not see the prisoner, there must have been a murmur among the parishioners when Ephraim entered through the pedimented main door. With his escort of deputies he clanked his way forward to his seat before the pulpit on the rough pine coffin he was scheduled to occupy. To Ephraim, who in his forty-three years had seldom seen the inside of a meetinghouse, the consciousness of people gazing intently at him must have been disconcerting, leading him to turn inward and, as he had through much of his trial, to try to mask his feelings. Gazing vacantly ahead, he had only to hold out for a few more hours before his suffering would end. As Ephraim composed himself, abruptly from behind him sounded the purposeful thump of dry, well-shod feet on the wooden treads of the long, curving stairway that led up to the circular pulpit on a fluted column high above the congregation.[30] The Reverend Samuel Shepard was about to preach Ephraim Wheeler's execution sermon.

The contrast between the cleric above and the convict below was dramatic: Wheeler, ragged and disconsolate, sitting on his coffin; and the Yale graduate, self-assured and immaculate in his black gown, looking down on the man whose death would be his text. Shepard, who was born in Chatham (now Portland), Connecticut, in 1772, had been an outstanding student, ranking second in his graduating class in 1793. Soon after, the orthodox deacons at Lenox invited the vivacious Calvinist to preach for them; and in 1795, at the age of twenty-three, he was ordained in an outdoor ceremony beside Lenox's small, run-down original meetinghouse. In the same years that Ephraim Wheeler was trying and failing to enter the ranks of the yeomanry, the orderly, punctual, decisive Shepard was building up his congregation. In 1799, the year the defeated Ephraim gave up on his farm in Partridgefield, Shepard achieved his greatest revival, when in a single year his urgent call to embrace Jesus won sixty converts for the Lenox church.[31] Praised both for his piety and for his cheerful temperament, the swarthy, thickset, thirty-three-year-old family man who mounted the pulpit on February 20, 1806, was a rising star of orthodox Congregationalism.[32] Just one week earlier, the Massachusetts House of Representatives had elected Shepard over the Unitarian William Bentley of Salem, a Republican, to deliver the state election sermon at Boston that coming May.[33]

But as Shepard looked out over the packed meetinghouse, inhaling the air ripe with the smell of hundreds of bodies crammed together in wet woolens, neither pride nor self-importance entered his mind. Never before had the young minister preached the sermon before an execution; and the throng who waited eagerly to hear him speak, as well as the sight of Wheeler in chains, charged up his emotions. Here was a moment, the very best moment, to preach the word of God. Though Shepard had surely read his colleague Stephen West's execution sermon of 1787 for Bly and Rose, in contrast to his older neighbor he would supply no justification for the death penalty, no discussion of the legitimacy of the state, no mention of Wheeler's crime—indeed no secular discourse at all. Shepard planned to speak with the single purpose of bringing everyone within the reach of his voice to Jesus.

"Probationers," he began, linking everyone together, including Ephraim and himself, in the moral trial of earthly life that determines our eternal future, "we are all bound to another state of existence—to a world of light and joy, or to the regions of darkness and woe."[34] Calling on his "loud, mellow, and flexible voice," and speaking "with great animation," Shepard effortlessly filled the meetinghouse with his message.[35] Everyone, whether the "unhappy man, under sentence of death," the dignitaries, the common men and women, or the preacher himself, must recognize that "in our hearts we carry our title either to eternal glory, or infinite wretchedness."[36]

We are "called," the preacher explained, "to attend the execution of an unhappy man" both as a civic and a sacred duty. At this very moment "our minds should be filled with awe" as we look at a man who is "standing on the borders of the eternal world" and who is in "imminent danger" of damnation. Regardless of the prisoner's outward appearance, Shepard imagined that Wheeler must be crying inwardly, "Lord, save me," the passage from the book of Matthew that Shepard had chosen as his text. Shepard's words, the preacher hoped, might still help to save Wheeler's soul, just as Wheeler's approaching death could bring others to recognize that Jesus Christ is "the *only Saviour* of perishing sinners."[37]

Shepard continued with an exposition, familiar to churchgoers, of the basic Christian doctrine of original sin and salvation according to the orthodox belief that none of us can be saved by good works or by a simple act of divine mercy. Salvation came only through Christ, who gave his blood to pardon our sins. God did not, Shepard explained, forgive sins randomly or promiscuously, because that would send us the wrong message. But when sinners truly believed in Jesus and genuinely repented, God generously granted them forgiveness. Christ was both *"able"* and *"willing"* to save sinners.[38]

Looking out at the people who packed his meetinghouse, and down at Ephraim, Shepard carefully explained the nature of "Gospel repentance." This was not, he said, the regret we feel when we have injured others or ourselves, or when we have acted so as to make us liable to punishment. True repentance demanded the realization of our own "sin and guilt, a sorrow for sin, as being against God." Recognizing our own sinful natures, Shepard explained that we must actively turn to holiness and to God. Moreover, just as some people embraced a shallow, earth-centered repentance, so they could also feel a hollow faith. If we professed belief in God's promise of salvation but then lived comfortably in sin, that was not true belief. Those who truly love God, Shepard exhorted the crowd, "will admire, adore and serve him—will be just, peaceable and benevolent—will be sober, chaste and temperate."[39] Though the pastor did not single out the sinner who sat beneath him on the coffin, Ephraim Wheeler had been none of these. As he had admitted just the night before, Ephraim's "violent and hasty passions . . . hard drinking and quarrelling" had ruled his behavior.[40] If he was listening as the Reverend Shepard spoke, Ephraim would have found no comfort in the preacher's words.

Nor would Shepard's lesson have been soothing for many others in the packed meetinghouse. For although the minister extolled Jesus as a friend who never failed, he reminded everyone that those who had no faith could have no hopes for eternity. They would be judged with their "accomplices in wickedness" by the very God whose precious love they had "despised." Vividly evoking the sinner at the Day of Judgment, Shepard cried out, "Hark! His sentence is pronounced, and his doom irrevocably fixed. . . . He beholds heaven lost—forever lost, and knows he is sinking into sorrows which will never have an end! See him, friendless, disconsolate, and despairing! See the unmixed misery." "Language," Shepard said, his words trailing off, "fails in the description."[41]

Having evoked the sinner's terrible moment of damnation, the young evangelist invited the congregation to turn with him to contemplate "the unhappy man before you, who is this day to suffer an ignominious death." Addressing Ephraim explicitly for the first time, Shepard looked down to the sturdy, middle-aged man seated in shackles on his coffin and tried to awaken him from his spiritual slumber:

> I speak to you, emphatically, as to a dying man. For, what mean the removal of bolts and bars, the rattling of chains, and the grating of the prison doors on their rusty hinges, which we have heard this day? What mean these guards, and this crowded assembly with which you are surrounded in the house of God? What mean those instruments of execution, prepared near the

place, where the sighs and the groans of the prisoner often assail the ears of the compassionate visitor or the passing traveler? What means this coffin upon which you are placed in our view? What means the grave already opened in yonder vale? These— all these announce your fate. Ah! How few, the remaining moments of your life![42]

Seeking to bring everyone in the sanctuary to the keenest realization that a death was imminent, Shepard publicly reproved Ephraim, not for his grievous sins but for failing to embrace Jesus. This was a message that many listeners might apply to themselves. Repeatedly, Shepard reminded Ephraim, "I have attempted . . . to instruct you in the things which relate to your future well being," but only God could know "what improvement you have made of such instructions and of all the solemn counsels, warnings, and admonitions you have received from others."[43] In the end, responsibility for Ephraim's eternal soul belonged solely to the sinner.

But in this, Shepard emphasized, Wheeler was not alone—he belonged to the human community. "Mere curiosity" did not bring these hundreds to the meetinghouse: "No. *We* feel for *you,* in your present awful condition—standing, as you do, on the borders of two worlds, just ready to launch into an untried—an eternal state!"[44] In truth, Ephraim's condition was everyone's. We are all praying for you, Shepard assured him; our prayers for you are this minute going before God. The hundreds who had gathered were, like Ephraim Wheeler, probationers, and their prayers for his salvation were emblems of this common bond.

Shepard then began to animate his "loud, mellow, and flexible voice" so as to create the emotional crescendo that could bring Ephraim and many others to soul-saving repentance on this dreary February day. Setting an example to the whole assembly, Shepard dramatically pleaded with Ephraim:

Why—O why will you forsake your own mercies? Will you not bestow, on eternity, one serious thought? Will you not shed a tear for your own soul? . . . Fall, then, instantly at [Christ's] feet, crying "Lord save me, or I perish"—"God be merciful to me, a sinner!" Consider that you have no time to loose [*sic*]. Your heaven or hell may hang suspended on the present moment.[45]

The one true path was clear: "Fly, then, fly without delay, to the ark of safety."[46] Jesus would save.

For the guilty Ephraim who sat before Shepard, the pastor's catalog of his sins must have seemed especially pointed, but the evangelist so generalized Ephraim's sinfulness that the convict's case would touch many others as well:

Look into your heart, how vile! Look back on a life, all covered with pollution! In a few moments, you will, by the light of eternity, see your moral state just as it is. Your sins will all be set in order before your eyes. All your sins of childhood, of youth, and of riper years—all your sins of thought, speech and behaviour—your sins resulting from every relation, every condition of life—your neglected opportunities—abused privileges—yea all your wickedness of heart, and your whole life of guilt will rise up to view!

Commiserating while he admonished the star sinner in the congregation, Shepard concluded, "How dreadful, to go into eternity, with your sins unpardoned, your nature unsanctified, and, your heart, in no degree right before God." While addressing Ephraim specifically, the preacher's words applied equally to all the unconverted mothers, fathers, sons, and daughters in the meetinghouse. As if to reinforce this connection, Shepard looked down from the pulpit to say to Wheeler, "this day will end your probation."[47] Because he had addressed the entire assembly as "probationers" at the outset, his use of the term now implied that Ephraim's dire straits were only the most extreme version of the human condition.

Though directing his words at Ephraim, Shepard continued speaking to the whole group. "While you hesitate, you perish," he warned, reminding the throng of the truths he had earlier proclaimed. Jesus died "on the tree" to save "the 'chief' of sinners"—and he was both "*able* and *willing* to save all" who came to him. As we consider the impending execution, Shepard reflected, we must all "be impressed with the solemnity of eternal scenes." The man seated before them was not some alien monster, but "a fellow-mortal, destined by his crimes to an untimely death." This example of untimely death should awaken everyone present—married couples, parents, youth— all should recognize their duties to God and to each other, remembering that if they differed from Ephraim Wheeler, they must not feel proud, but only "thankful for any restraints which are laid upon the evil propensities of the human heart."[48]

The Reverend Shepard closed his sermon with a prayer, fervently calling on the entire gathering to join in seeking salvation for the man whose lifeless corpse they would soon witness swinging from the gallows crossbar:

> Let all who have an heart to pray, behold the man! and carry him, this moment, in the arms of their faith and prayer to the throne of grace—lay him down at the feet of divine sovereignty—and, ask that his sins may be done away by divine mercy, and his pardon be sealed in Heaven before he goes hence to be here no more!

Then the powerfully built clergyman's composure broke—and with it, we may imagine, that of many among those crowded together in the meetinghouse. Shepard concluded in broken fragments, speaking of "the painful scene before us," ending finally with the thought that "silent tears and that anguish of soul" inspired by the "multiplied miseries" which our sinning has brought upon us "must speak the rest."[49] In this, the only execution sermon he would ever give, Reverend Shepard had moved himself and probably many others to weep over Ephraim Wheeler, the father who had raped his daughter and who had now become the emblem of fallen man.

Having finished, Shepard climbed down from the pulpit. Whether the tearful clergyman took Ephraim's hand and met the doomed man's eye, wet or dry, is nowhere recorded. But Ephraim "was much affected and apparently penitent."[50] In the next hour the two would see each other once more at the gallows. Now, before Wheeler left the meetinghouse, he spoke with the man who had written down his life story the night before, claiming that many years before, in France, "he [Wheeler] should have lost his life, had it not been for the interposition of friends."[51] Maybe Ephraim clung to the hope that once more friends would appear to save him, despite all the doom and gloom of the crowded church, Shepard's sermon, and the coffin. One hundred men, he knew, had asked the governor to save his life, including Sheriff Larned, the man who was holding either his pardon or his death warrant until the last moment. Governor Strong had saved others before him, so perhaps Ephraim imagined that the whole day's rituals would be merely a fearsome charade.

But there was no time to reflect on this hope. The grim-faced deputies hoisted Ephraim and his coffin and carried him out of the meetinghouse and into the rain. When they set him down in the cart for the ride back down the hill to the gallows and to his freshly dug grave, it would have been hard for Ephraim Wheeler to maintain any flicker of hope amid the ominous, monotone drumbeat of the marching militiamen. All around him, as far as he could see, people were flocking by the hundreds, even thousands, down the road toward the scaffold. Unlike the scene that Richardson and Hogarth depicted at Tyburn,

Berkshire farm families did not stop the procession to bring the condemned man drink or to say good-bye. Their hats and bonnets drip-
ping rain, they neither jeered nor cheered but watched Ephraim in
the solemn, awestruck silence that the magistrates had hoped to see.
If there was to be disorder at the execution, it would not be the work
of a lighthearted, scoffing crowd.[52]

When the procession arrived at the plateau on the hillside below
the village, where the newly constructed pine scaffold stood waiting,
it was about two in the afternoon. Despite the size of the crowd, estimated at 5,000 people (over four times the number who dwelled in
Lenox), Sheriff Larned and the other officials brought Wheeler to his
place on the scaffold punctually and arranged themselves nearby
without incident. The master of this deadly ceremony was the sheriff,
Simon Larned, and though the merchant-soldier-politician from
Pittsfield had never before supervised a hanging, he guided the traditional proceedings in a businesslike manner. Perhaps, as he reflected
on the scene before him, he thought back to where he had been just
one year before—sitting in the Capitol in Washington, D.C., as Berkshire's representative in the U.S. Congress. That seemed long ago
and far away; now, contrary to his personal sense of right and wrong,
he must hang a man.

But not quite yet. First came the final effort to save the sinner's
soul. Shepard's neighbor and colleague, the Reverend Oliver Ayer of
West Stockbridge, went to Ephraim to pray with him before the
crowd. Though Ayer's prayer was not recorded, in substance it must
have been much like those delivered at other New England executions of the period: a last call for true repentance, for God's mercy,
and for salvation through Jesus. To the majority of spectators, who
believed in the power of prayer, the sight of thousands of their neighbors uniting with the clergyman to pray must have been a soul-stir-
ring experience. Ever since the Great Awakening in the 1740s great

evangelists, such as George Whitefield, had moved the spirits of thousands of men, women, and children crowded together for open-air prayers. Though Oliver Ayer was not George Whitefield, the scene of the two men standing by the gallows, one calling up to the heavens, the other listening with his head bowed, lent the moment unusual power. Ephraim was about to be sent off to heaven or to hell.

After the prayer was over, Sheriff Larned approached Ephraim and, as was customary, invited him to speak. This was the moment when, if all went according to plan, the whole ritual would be validated by the convict's own endorsement of the proceedings. Like Job Wells fifty years before in Hertfordshire, Ephraim would confess his guilt for the crime and ask the forgiveness of all those whom he had injured in his life. Further, he would publicly acknowledge the fairness and justice of both his trial and his penalty. He might also go on to urge others to avoid the vices that had brought him to the gallows—his drinking, his violent anger, his cheating, and his refusal to live among godly people as a pious, hardworking churchgoer. Such statements had formed the substance of criminals' last words and dying confessions since the Puritan era. They were supposed to demonstrate the sinner's contrition and reinforce the official messages of both the church and the state on that day.

But Ephraim Wheeler chose not to speak; instead he beckoned to the Reverend Ayer and asked the pastor to proclaim Ephraim's last thoughts. Quickly and quietly, Wheeler told Ayer what he wanted him to say. Though Ephraim seemed "much affected and apparently penitent" as he stood on the scaffold facing his coffin and his grave, he still refused to confess to the crime of rape because he believed he was innocent. And rather than apologize to Betsy and Hannah, he repeated the claim that he was a victim of his "accusers" and their wrongful testimony. Instead of asking forgiveness for his offenses against his family, his neighbors, and society, he did the opposite;

through Reverend Ayer he took the martyr's stance, publicly forgiving "his accusers and all the world."[53]

Ephraim's having absolutely denied his guilt, as well as the fact that he said nothing at all to defend the fairness of his trial and the justice of his punishment, reinforced the rebellious connotations of the speech he directed Ayer to give. An address such as Wheeler's, delivered "in a very pathetic manner" by the practiced clergyman with whom the thousands had just joined in prayer, could provoke unrest. Lenox, after all, was the capital of a county where partisan politics were closely contested, a county where even after Shays' Rebellion the standing order of church and state only barely held the reins of authority. Back in September the Baptists had won a test against the orthodox in *Smith v. Dalton,* and now Ephraim Wheeler was publicly proclaiming himself to be the victim of a miscarriage of justice. With scores, maybe hundreds, of men opposed to his execution, officials had cause for concern that the silent crowd might turn into a rowdy mob. When Ayer finished delivering Ephraim's defiant speech, officials knew that their plan for the day had just been knocked off course and that disorder was a real possibility.

Such thoughts, however, did not deter Sheriff Larned from the duties of his office. Perhaps because of his own personal popularity in Berkshire County—only recently 2,084 men, 61 percent, had voted to elect him to Congress over Daniel Dewey—and the fact that he was the highest civil officer publicly known to oppose Wheeler's hanging, no one raised their voice to challenge him.[54] Now, with prayers and speeches finished, Larned must get on with his repellent task.

Larned ordered Ephraim's fetters to be broken and removed so that the condemned man could move freely. For Ephraim it was a fateful, desperate moment—one that he had dared hope would spare his life. As a justice of the Supreme Judicial Court explained, "a reprieve or pardon is usually deferred until the hour of execution has arrived."

This was the time when "government may interpose its clemency, and rescue the miserable offender from anticipated punishment."[55] Opponents of the death penalty who had petitioned for Wheeler stood gathered at the gallows and they, too, felt expectant as Sheriff Larned took out the death warrant that Governor Strong had sent in October and that had just recently been confirmed. Shielding it as best he could from the light rain that was falling, Larned read aloud to Ephraim Wheeler and the crowd:

> We therefore, by and with the advice of Our Council pursuant to the statute in such case made and provided, command you that on Thursday the twentieth day of February next between the hours of twelve and three of the Clock in the day time at the usual place of execution you cause execution on the person of the said Ephraim Wheeler to be done & performed in all things according to the form and efect [*sic*] of the said Judgment and sentence for which this shall be your sufficient Warrant. Hereof fail not at your peril.[56]

Stilted and formal as the warrant sounded, its meaning was unmistakable: there would be no reprieve; Ephraim Wheeler must hang.

As this realization swept through the crowd there was an unhappy stir of discontent, even anger. Hundreds of people, thousands according to Pittsfield's Reverend Thomas Allen, had expected the governor to pardon Wheeler and had supposed that when Sheriff Larned pulled out a paper and began to read, their sheriff would be proclaiming Wheeler's reprieve. But as Simon Larned spoke, their hope, and Ephraim's, collapsed. No matter the pleas from Hannah and the children, especially Betsy, to save a father's life. No matter that 103 Berkshire voters had asked in the name of justice and humanity to spare the criminal from the rope. No matter that capital punishment reform had almost overtaken the crime of rape in Massachusetts. As Larned read the death warrant line by line, the crowd realized that although Massachusetts had pardoned the Shaysites at the gallows in 1787 and had not executed anyone for the crime of rape in twenty-seven years, the state was about to hang Ephraim Wheeler. Disappointment and disgust showed on many faces, including, no doubt, that of the Reverend Allen, who long ago had led the region to resist Boston rule; but the crowd behaved.[57]

Larned refolded the warrant and returned it to his pocket. Now, according to the law that he had sworn to uphold, it was his duty to kill a fellow man. Unlike Joseph Hosmer, the Middlesex County sheriff who had backed out of his responsibilities at Samuel Smith's execution in 1799, Larned had steeled himself for the work.[58] First, he slowly guided Ephraim to the edge of the platform beside the hinged plank that extended beyond it and beneath the crossbar that carried the rope. Then Larned set a white stocking cap on Ephraim's head and carefully lowered the noose over it, gently pulling the hemp rope snug around the condemned man's throat. At the last moment the sheriff would pull the cap down over Wheeler's face to cover it and bind his arms so they would not flail wildly or clutch at the noose. Hangings were grim enough, officials reasoned, without seeing the dying agonies and disfigurement of the person's face for several minutes as the rope tightened and strangled him.[59]

Larned must then guide Wheeler out onto the plank beneath the crossbar. If the condemned man refused, the deputies would have to carry him bodily out onto the fatal plank. But Wheeler, responsive perhaps to the "sensibility, tenderness, and compassion" that Simon Larned expressed as he went about his awful work, cooperated, stepping out onto the plank. Since he was, he believed, not guilty, he could hope for God's pardon. Now Larned drew the rope taut over the crossbeam, tied it to the post, and descended the scaffold stairs. The dreaded moment had finally arrived, both for Ephraim Wheeler

and for Simon Larned: briskly the sheriff released the plank supporting Wheeler so that it folded down flat against the platform. So
Ephraim fell—not fast enough to break his neck, but enough to
tighten the noose around his windpipe. For several minutes the
doomed man struggled, kicking, and then his corpse hung still above
the heads of Larned and the clergymen. The show was almost over,
and "an awful, attentive solemnity appeared on the face of the whole
assembly."[60]

One more chore remained. According to custom Ephraim's body,
befouled by urine and excrement during his death agony, must be laid
to rest beneath the gallows. This task belonged not to Larned, but to
his deputies; and with the crowd still watching, they carried the
coffin, on which Ephraim had so recently sat, to where his body now
hung. They pulled off the lid, and one man climbed to the platform to
cut the body down so that they could lower Ephraim's lifeless corpse
into the pine box. Then out came hammer and nails, and with two
dozen sharp blows they spiked the coffin shut. Retrieving the gallows
rope from the crossbar, the deputies formed a U with it on the soggy
ground and laid the coffin across the U so that four men, two on each
side of the heavy box, could lift it by the rope and lower it slowly into
the grave. By three o'clock, right on schedule, the body of the man
the state had killed was lying in the ground and a deputy was shovel-
ing muddy clods of earth to cover it.[61] Where Ephraim Wheeler's
soul had gone, no one knew.

Then the thousands who had gathered began to move away. Some
crowded into Lenox's taverns to warm themselves with drink before
they walked home. Others left quickly so as to take advantage of the
two and a half hours of remaining daylight for their journey. Those
who had left horses tied in different corners of the village hastened to
them, perhaps with a handful or two of oats to fuel their trip along
muddy roads and paths. That day's events had given 5,000 witnesses,

children and adults, much to ponder—their own mortality, the condition of their souls, the power of the community embodied by the state. Whether justice had truly been done was a question for some, wholly apart from the issue of capital punishment. For if Wheeler was guilty, why did he not confess, as most convicts did? Denial gained him nothing, and his eternal soul was at stake. Maybe Betsy really had lied to get rid of her tyrant father. Maybe the jurors, horrified by Wheeler's supposed crime and overawed by Attorney General Sullivan's masterful performance, had rendered the wrong verdict.

As they made their way home the spectators could also reflect on the leaders whom they had witnessed in action. The Reverend Shepard, moved to tears by Wheeler's fate, had made a convincing case that God, who was ready to pardon even that hideous sinner, would pardon every sinner who came to him in Jesus' name. The Reverend Ayer had stood with the prisoner, prayed with him, and at the end spoken for him. Ayer, too, had shown a forgiving heart, and had put aside his own opinions so as to give the condemned man a voice. And then there was Sheriff Larned, whom many knew as Simon Larned the merchant in Pittsfield, their militia officer, and the man for whom they cast their ballots. Larned had endured the most dreadful test—the duty of killing a man in cold blood whose life he believed should be spared. Yet Simon Larned had done his duty, and with dignity.

Some, especially husbands and wives who fought bitterly, and those who knew Hannah Wheeler and the children personally, must have wondered what Wheeler's widow and the orphans whose testimony had convicted him were feeling. We doubt that Wheeler's nearest kin were part of the great throng that day, though Bill Martin and some of the Odels may have come to witness their brother-in-law's end. Hannah, Betsy, and Ephraim, Jr., could not feel triumphant no matter where justice lay. The price was too high. Ephraim's violence had cost him his life, and would shadow theirs forever.

People and Memory

There have been six executions in the County for capital offenses. It is not known that either of the criminals was born in the County, though one or two of them had lived in it for some time.

John Bly and Charles Rose, one a foreigner and the other an American, were executed Dec. 6, 1787, for burglary committed in Lanesborough, under pretense of getting supplies for men engaged in the Shays' Insurrection.

Ephraim Wheeler, of Windsor, was executed Feb. 20, 1806, for a rape, committed upon his own daughter.

Ezra Hutchinson of Stockbridge, was executed for the same offence, Nov. 18, 1813.

Peter Johnson, a black man, from Sheffield, but a native of the State of New York, was executed for the same crime also, Nov. 25, 1819.

Samuel P. Charles, an Oneida Indian, who had lived some time in West Stockbridge, and been distinguished for base morals, was executed Nov. 22, 1826, for murdering a man of colour in Richmond.

These executions were all performed in Lenox, and drew together an immense multitude of spectators. It is much to be questioned whether such publicity in putting criminals to death, subserves the cause of justice and public virtue.

[David Dudley Field and Chester Dewey],
A History of the County of Berkshire, Massachusetts. . . . (1829)

H uman tribunals see but imperfectly," one of Wheeler's judges later observed.[1] And in Berkshire just after Sheriff Larned "turned off" Ephraim Wheeler, no one could be absolutely certain that his execution had served the cause of justice. Because Ephraim persisted in denying his guilt when concealment and lying could serve no practical purpose, the people of Berkshire were left to wonder whether his punishment was just. Two days after the hanging, printer Heman Willard used his *Western Star* to confirm that "different opinions . . . will be entertained." The problem was how to reconcile Betsy's sworn accusations with Wheeler's consistent denials. When Willard published Wheeler's *Narrative* about two weeks after the execution, he reinforced doubts about "this awful and mysterious affair" by noting that after Wheeler's conviction the prisoner had "told a Gentleman . . . that whatever he had done to his daughter, it was with her consent." To further tantalize readers, Willard darkly asserted that whether Wheeler "was guilty or innocent of the crime . . . , of this we are sure, that wickedness of the blackest nature has been practiced, either by him or his family."[2]

Into Wheeler's *Narrative* Willard injected his own interpretation of events. Seeking to reconcile Wheeler's claim of consent with Betsy's testimony to the contrary, he concluded that Wheeler must have misjudged Betsy's response, supposing she "did not make so violent and persevering resistance to the outrage" to meet Wheeler's understanding of the crime of rape. Willard suggested that "the awe and respect, which a child naturally feels toward a parent" must have muted Betsy's resistance, even though she was "wholly averse to his design." This "supposition" was "reasonable" because it cleared Hannah Wheeler of the charge of conspiracy and Betsy from that of perjury while also freeing Wheeler from "the awful guilt of leaving the world with a known and premeditated lie in his mouth." Wheeler, he claimed, had all but admitted to incest.[3]

The printer further reported that the men "most conversant with Wheeler during his confinement"—clergymen, county officials, and lawyers—"are all convinced beyond a doubt, that he was actually guilty of the fact charged"; but Willard preferred to leave the question open, perhaps to bolster sales of the *Narrative*. As he summarized in the *Western Star:* "as he [Wheeler] was convicted, after a fair and candid trial, upon the clearest and most positive testimony, he must have been guilty, or the prosecutors and witnesses must be atrocious *perjurers, conspirators,* and *murderers;* to the Searcher of all hearts we must leave him and them."[4] On February 22, 1806, it was too soon to admit the possibility of error, though Willard recognized that Wheeler's life had turned on the meaning of the single word "consent."

The manipulative printer closed his comments by taking his cue from the Reverend Shepard, urging readers to leave the matter to God's judgment, "instead of disputing and wrangling about that which is now unalterable":

Friend! Ask not what persons doom'd to die
To what abode they go;
When knowledge would but sorrow spy
'T were better not to know.
To live uprightly then is surely best;
To save ourselves, and not condemn the rest.[5]

Owing to the partisan division in the county and the approaching election for governor, however, any doubts about Ephraim Wheeler's guilt were immediately overshadowed by a debate over the legitimacy of his punishment. As a result, the moral, ethical, and familial dimensions of the execution quickly faded. The Reverend Thomas Allen, the Pittsfield Jeffersonian who with his son and namesake, the attorney and state representative, advocated imprisonment instead of the death penalty for the crime of rape, initiated the controversy. Two days after Willard had tacitly endorsed Wheeler's execution, the Reverend Allen used his nephew's *Pittsfield Sun* to attack Governor Strong for rejecting Wheeler's pardon petitions. In contrast to the account of Wheeler's hanging in Willard's Federalist *Western Star,* Parson Allen's anonymous report on the same event challenged both the execution and the motives of the Federalist rulers who had ordered it. Outraged by the failure of the petitioning effort, Allen attacked Governor Strong and his party as defenders of "the sanguinary principle of a monarchial system." In contrast to Governor John Hancock, who years before had pardoned an assortment of convicted Shaysite leaders, Allen wrote, Governor Strong *"rejected"* a petition "signed by a large number of respectable citizens, praying that the criminals [sic] life might be spared, and his punishment commuted to that of perpetual imprisonment to hard labor." Ignoring all such pleas, the Federalist Strong had "ordered [Wheeler] for execution!"[6]

This, Allen declared, was typical of "our political opponents," the Federalists, many of whom "are peculiarly sanguinary in their temper and dispositions." Referring to the efforts of his son and others to replace the death penalty for rape with life at hard labor, Allen implied that Strong not only had rejected the intentions of the legislature, but also had acted arbitrarily, since he had earlier "commuted the punishment of a similar criminal." Strong and the Federalists would pay, however. The governor's conduct, Allen claimed, would teach "the people" that "our sanguinary code, which grew out of monarchy," was wrong. Now is the time, Allen proclaimed, to ameliorate that code so that "no crime will be punishable with death, except murder." The aged, forty-year incumbent at Pittsfield's first church closed by paraphrasing Beccaria's core principle: "punishments should be proportional to the nature of crimes against society." Calling for Governor Strong's defeat at the polls, Allen hoped that this execution would be the final act of his administration.[7]

Wheeler himself, of course, was only incidental to the Reverend Allen's and the *Pittsfield Sun's* arguments. The Jeffersonians wanted to have the argument both ways, and though Heman Willard admonished others against "disputing and wrangling," he devoted nearly half of his pamphlet *A Narrative of the Life of Ephraim Wheeler* to reprinting the whole partisan controversy. Willard complained that the Jeffersonian *Sun* had referred to Ephraim as "that HARDENED VILLAIN" before his execution, but that afterwards he became "the unhappy criminal" and "wretched convict," sympathetic identities better suited to his new role as the victim of the bloodthirsty Federalists.[8] Because Willard and other Berkshire Federalists took up the partisan challenge of the Reverend Allen's and the *Sun's* treatment of Wheeler's execution, both parties shifted attention away from Wheeler's case, away even from the question of capital punishment. Instead, newspaper readers would be led to compare the character of Governor Strong and the Federalists with that of the Reverend Allen and the Jeffersonians.

In his pamphlet *A Narrative of the Life of Ephraim Wheeler,* Willard noted that "this is the commencement of Electioneering for the Spring campaign."[9] Indeed Wheeler's life became largely a political tract because so much of it was given over to reprinting the newspapers' partisan debate. By reissuing material from the *Sun* of February 24 and three pieces from the March 1, 1806, *Western Star,* Willard evidently hoped to increase the pamphlet's sales among his Federalist clientele while also unmasking Allen's demagogy. In doing so, Willard made Wheeler's case into little more than an occasion for a Federalist attack on the Jeffersonians that was almost as preposterous and misleading as Allen's opening sally.

Several of the Federalists' points against Allen were right on target.

First, they noted, Governor Strong, like Governor Hancock and every other governor, did not act alone, but with the advice and consent of the council. That was why all of the petitions for Wheeler had been addressed to the governor and the council, never the governor alone. In addition, in the Wheeler case, Strong and the council were upholding both the law and the constitution. And since the Reverend Allen found nothing bloodthirsty in Hancock's 1787 decision to let burglars Bly and Rose hang, his contrast between Hancock and Strong was a sham. Moreover, Federalists pointed out, the Jeffersonian favorite, James Sullivan, had argued publicly that Wheeler's sentence should be carried out; and, just like Strong, he would have signed Wheeler's death warrant. That Allen would attack Strong as "sanguinary" but then "pass over the Sheriff, who executed the criminal, and many others that had an agency in the prosecution" displayed his "party" purposes. Indeed the Jeffersonian parson's entire effort to use this episode to label Federalists as "sanguinary monarchists" was "hypocritical" and "libellous" because Federalist legislators had also played leading roles in the movement to shift the punishment for rape away from the gallows to imprisonment.[10] This much of the Federalist rebuttal was well taken.

But the Federalist rejoinder to Allen also included specious arguments. Most important, they argued that the *Pittsfield Sun* had set up Governor Strong so that Jeffersonians would be able to vilify him no matter what he did. By first characterizing Wheeler as a "hardened villain," Willard's pamphlet argued, Jeffersonians had positioned themselves to berate Strong if he showed leniency toward Wheeler, just as New York Jeffersonians had recently attacked the Federalist governor of New York when he yielded to petition pressure and granted a reprieve to child murderer Stephen Arnold.[11] Now, Federalists claimed, Jeffersonians switched their stance so as to depict Wheeler as an "unhappy," "wretched" object of pity who "must suffer death" not because of his heinous crime, but because a Federalist held office. These assertions overlooked the fact that the Reverend Allen had long been on record as an opponent of the death penalty for rape and as a petitioner for Wheeler's life. Nor was there any merit in the Federalist claim that Allen "by his writings and declarations approbates and encourages" the crime of rape, or that Allen had sought to use Wheeler's execution to "promote sedition and rebellion, and . . . to light the torch of civil war."[12] But Parson Allen had thrown down the partisan gauntlet with his self-righteous imprecations against "sanguinary monarchists," as he called the Federalists.

Indeed the exaggerated Federalist language that blended vilification and vituperation was a reminder of the intensity of the contest between the two camps. Willard claimed that the rival *Sun* was produced by a "reptile Editor" whose "wickedness" was well known. Two other Federalist contributors to Willard's pamphlet referred to the "malignity and wickedness," the "malevolence," the "diabolical wickedness," the "villany [*sic*]," and the "base and scandalous" character of Allen's execution report, which, they declared, marked Allen and his Jacobin friends as enemies "of decency and good order."[13]

This rhetorical battle shows how some of Berkshire's newspaper-reading elite could swiftly incorporate any public event into the existing matrix of partisan competition. Evidently Thomas Allen hoped that the feelings of distress aroused by Wheeler's execution might propel James Sullivan into the governor's chair, while Heman Willard and other Federalists were determined to uphold their governor so as to assure his reelection. Yet their controversy over the execution was local and did not reach beyond Berkshire County. Even in the Housatonic valley it had little staying power. Phinehas Allen did answer the *Western Star's* March 1 attacks on his uncle, but only in a single editorial. After first mocking the Federalists' overheated and "slanderous" rhetoric, he restated the Reverend Allen's assertion that

Governor Strong could and should have commuted Wheeler's sentence to life in prison. "This," he declared, "was the wish of the citizens of Berkshire, a few *monarchists* excepted." With that repetition of its own partisan assertions, the *Pittsfield Sun* closed the debate over Wheeler's execution, confidently declaring victory.[14]

In less than a month partisan interest, caught up with Strong's and Sullivan's April gubernatorial contest, moved on to other issues. Elsewhere, in Massachusetts, Connecticut, and New York, if any report of Wheeler's execution was reprinted at all, it was usually taken from the noncontroversial and approving *Western Star* account.[15] When a Jeffersonian paper like the *National Aegis* in Worcester did reprint the Allen report from the *Sun,* Worcester County Federalists ignored its partisan claims. In Boston, the Jeffersonian paper did not even mention Wheeler's execution.[16] As far as politics were concerned, Wheeler's execution generated controversy only in Berkshire, and even there it faded quickly from view. Its only echo came three years later when, to justify their separation from the Reverend Allen's congregation in 1809, his former Federalist parishioners complained of their pastor's partisan conduct, including the Wheeler execution episode.[17]

From the standpoint of electoral politics, then, Ephraim Wheeler's execution was merely incidental. But from the perspective of public policy, Wheeler's crime and punishment cast a longer, darker shadow. For in the generation leading up to 1806 in Massachusetts, and throughout the United States, it had become almost unthinkable to hang a man for the crime of rape, so powerful was the movement toward Beccarian reform. But now in Massachusetts, following the reformers' failure to remove rape from the state's capital list in 1805 and 1806, execution was deemed not only lawful but also acceptable. As in the eighteenth century, prosecutors seldom brought and won a rape case, but when a jury did convict a man of this crime, after 1806 he was likely to hang. Indeed, though Berkshire County remained sparsely populated, with never as much as 8 percent of the state's inhabitants, there were two more executions for rape at Lenox in the fifteen years after Wheeler's demise, and in neighboring Hampshire County there was another. Evidently the ideology and ethos of capital punishment and the execution ritual persisted, especially in these staunchly Calvinist western counties, where commercial culture developed more gradually than in the eastern half of the state.[18]

One cannot be sure that Wheeler's conviction and execution smoothed the way for Ezra Hutchinson's demise at Lenox seven years later. But when one considers that the nineteen-year-old Hutchinson's rape of fifteen-year-old Lucy Bates was an impulsive act, and that nothing in the surviving record indicates that the young farmer was a hardened offender, the state's readiness to hang him suggests that the Wheeler case had set a severe precedent for punishment. Since Hutchinson owned thirty-one acres of land in Stockbridge valued at $300 and headed a household that included his mother and two younger sisters, Governor Strong and the council might have reasoned that the youth could repent and reform so as to live a productive life after serving a term of years in the state prison.[19]

But no one petitioned on Ezra's behalf in 1813—not his mother and sisters, not his Stockbridge neighbors, and not his attorneys, Eli P. Ashmun and Wheeler's own onetime counselor, John W. Hulbert. Perhaps Hulbert, having tried and failed in Wheeler's pardoning campaign of 1805 when the anti–capital punishment movement was at its height, advised that petitioning for Hutchinson would be a waste of time. Hutchinson's own viewpoint, expressed in his *Solemn Address and Dying Advice,* published by Heman Willard, suggests that although Hutchinson, like Wheeler, did not admit guilt and viewed his sentence as unjust, his attorneys convinced him he had no hope of a pardon. Their advice echoes in Hutchinson's conclusion that though he believed his victim consented, "nothing appears in the case that palliates the enormity of my crime or renders me a subject of mercy, and there is no way for me to escape punishment."[20] Ephraim Wheeler had been hanged, and so must Ezra Hutchinson.

In the fall and winter of 1805–1806 many Berkshire citizens had hoped for a pardon in the form of a commutation of Wheeler's sentence, and Daniel Dewey and John Hulbert, as well as Ephraim Wheeler, believed there was a chance his life would be spared. But on November 18, 1813, though Ezra Hutchinson's crime had not been aggravated as Wheeler's had been, and though he, like Jacob Azzett Lewis, was a young man who protested that his victim had yielded voluntarily, the state put the nineteen-year-old Yankee to death without debate or discussion. Indeed, though Phinehas Allen's *Pittsfield Sun* printed an announcement of Hutchinson's execution beforehand, his paper did not report further on the event.[21] Though Caleb Strong was again the governor, this time there was no condemnation of "sanguinary" Federalist punishments; there was no mention of the hanging at all.

The change in the climate of public opinion is apparent in another western Massachusetts rape case, from Hampshire County, also from the fall of 1813. Henry Pyner, a Northampton black man who had previously served three years in the state prison for grand larceny, was convicted of the rape of an unmarried white woman and, like Hutchinson, was sentenced to die. In contrast to Jacob Azzett Lewis and Ephraim Wheeler, and like Ezra Hutchinson, Pyner inspired no pardoning effort, no petitions, and no protest against his execution.[22] Just seven years earlier the execution of a man for rape had excited controversy that reached from Berkshire County to the state legislature, but in 1813 the hangings of Pyner and Hutchinson were seen as unexceptional. Six years later, at Lenox, the state would execute yet another rapist, Peter Johnson, "a black man." A vast crowd, estimated at 10,000, gathered to view this spectacle, which followed the traditional script even more closely than did Wheeler's. There was a sermon at the meetinghouse by a young Dartmouth graduate, the Reverend James Bradford of Sheffield, and a further address at the gallows by the Reverend Robert Chapman.[23] There was a penitent convict who "acknowledged his guilt and the justice of his sentence." And there was a well-behaved crowd, whose prayers "ascended to heaven" on Johnson's behalf. All testified to the continuing legitimacy of the old execution ritual in predominantly Calvinist Berkshire County.[24]

But the old ways would not last much longer. The December 1819 newspaper report of the Johnson execution stressed that the magnet for the vast crowd was "that curiosity which impels to scenes of agony," and in the next decade the voices of a Pittsfield physician and a Stockbridge pastor would join the chorus of Massachusetts leaders who condemned public executions.[25] Massachusetts carried out its last execution for rape in 1825 at Worcester, when it put to death a twenty-six-year-old white man, Horace Carter, for attacking a seventy-eight-year-old poorhouse resident.[26] By 1830 reformers in the Massachusetts legislature were beginning a concerted movement to end, or at least curtail, the state's capital punishment laws. Significantly, two of the prominent reformers were sons of James Sullivan and Theodore Sedgwick, men who bore much of the responsibility for hanging Ephraim Wheeler.[27]

During the next two decades anti–capital punishment reformers in Massachusetts and much of the northern United States launched campaigns that demonstrated the growing American aversion to capital punishment and to public executions especially. What had been reluctance among jurors to send fellow humans to the gallows in the 1790s became outright refusal in the 1830s and 1840s. Between 1835 and 1849 the state tried more than twenty men for murder, but juries convicted most of them of the noncapital crime of manslaughter only, or else acquitted them. Only three men—a white Yankee, a black mariner, and an Irish immigrant—were hanged.[28] In 1839 Massachusetts dropped armed burglary and robbery from the list of capital crimes, and in 1852 the state finally ended hanging for rape, treason, and arson. This left murder as Massachusetts' sole capital crime—still buttressed by the passage from Genesis, "whoso sheddeth man's blood, by man shall his blood be shed."[29]

It is unlikely that Hannah Wheeler, born in 1763, lived to see enactment of the law that would have spared her husband's life. Indeed, when and where she died, whether in a distant farming town, a city, or in Berkshire County, remain a mystery, since after Ephraim's trial she vanishes from the records.[30] But if after Ephraim's death she continued to make her way doing domestic work, it is likely that she found places near her kinfolk in central Berkshire County. Her brother Isaac stayed on for a few more years at his twenty-four-acre farm that straddled the Peru-Cummington boundary, and then sold it to his and Hannah's brother-in-law, a man of color named John Percip.[31] Other sisters and their husbands owned small amounts of property in the neighboring towns of Windsor, Hinsdale, and Dalton.[32] In March 1806 Heman Willard had reported that Hannah Wheeler's "deportment . . . has been, in the general estimation, decent and irreprehensible"; with such an upright and hardworking reputation, there was no need for her to move on.[33] As in the past, Hannah most likely continued to live near her family.

Two of Hannah's sisters did live on into the 1840s in Hinsdale, a town just west of Windsor. One, Lucy Martin, whose "lying in" brought about the displacement of Ephraim Wheeler's bed that so enraged him on June 8, 1805, was described as "colored" by the clergyman who noted her passing in 1843; when her sister, Molly

Percip, died in 1846, however, the church records made no mention of race.[34] Presumably church authorities did not realize that these two elderly women bearing different surnames were sisters. It had been this way throughout the Odels' lives; record-keeping was inconsistent, and some in the family carried visible signs of their mixed-race identity while others—like Hannah and Molly Percip—were taken to be white.

Betsy too must have been regarded as white, since no one ever commented on her complexion or race, either at the time of the trial or afterward.[35] As with Hannah, we have no record of where Betsy may have lived after the trial. Following a father's death county authorities usually named the mother as guardian to the children, but though guardianship records of the period survive, there is no evidence that such a formal provision was made for the Wheeler children, perhaps because their father had died without any property. But whether or not Hannah was Betsy's legal guardian, Betsy probably stayed near her mother, perhaps even working in the same household. Like her brother, Ephraim, Jr., Betsy was old enough to be placed separately, but owing to the traumatic events leading up to the elder Ephraim's execution, it seems likely that Hannah and the children would have drawn together—though not necessarily all under the same roof.

What happened to Betsy and to Ephraim, Jr., remains a mystery. Since Wheeler was a common surname in western Massachusetts, and Ephraim a common forename, and Ephraim, Jr., was not identified in a guardianship decree or connected to a piece of real estate, the boy is impossible to trace.[36] The U.S. Census identified only household heads, so women's names were recorded much less frequently than men's; and it is not remarkable that searches of public and church records have not turned up Betsy's movements either. People like Betsy, who had no property, did not enter the land records or have estates that went through probate, nor were they listed on the tax rolls. As a propertyless single woman Betsy Wheeler was unlikely to be drawn into court for defaulting on a contract; nor was she likely to have been tried for a criminal offense. "Warning out" lists, on which some poor people (such as Ephraim Wheeler and the Odel men) were recorded through the 1790s, were discontinued after 1800 owing to changes in the state's poor laws.[37] As a result, finding a particular poor person in early nineteenth-century records is much like looking for a needle that may never even have been placed in a haystack.

Betsy Wheeler may not even have kept the name she was born with; indeed, given her experience she may have shed her Wheeler identity as soon as she could. From her and her mother's petition to save Ephraim's life it is evident that she was troubled by the outcome of her testimony against her father. His assault, the trial, and his execution were memories that she could not escape, and they were bound up with her name, a name that had been linked with his in newspapers throughout the region and on the title pages of a trial report and an execution sermon. As the best-known thirteen-year-old in a fifty-mile radius, one who had testified against her father before hundreds of spectators in open court, Betsy must have recalled painful memories every time she gave her name to a stranger. Whether in seeking work or in a casual encounter, the moment she uttered the words "Betsy Wheeler" her vulnerability came to the fore, and she could not have helped imagining what others must be thinking.

In order to assume a new identity Betsy had two possibilities: she could either call herself by a different name and invent a fresh personal history or marry and take her husband's name. For Betsy, both courses of action must have seemed perilous. So long as she stayed near her relatives, and perhaps as long as she stayed in Berkshire County where people might recognize her, she could only be "Betsy

Wheeler." But if she traveled to Hampshire County or New York or Vermont, Betsy could take on a new name and a new life story. In an era before identification cards and bureaucratic record-keeping, women as well as men possessed the power to invent new identities. Where there were no family connections or property records to reveal the fraud, it was easily done. One entered a new place, told a plausible story, and lived the lie. Ephraim Wheeler himself admitted that he had used an alias as a young man during one of his escapes from Jeduthan Hammond. Stephen Burroughs, another Yankee who was the early republic's most famous impostor, even wrote a best-selling book about how he had repeatedly changed his identity.[38] Betsy Wheeler may not have had the guile to carry out such a transformation, but surely such a strategy would have been possible by the time she turned twenty-one years of age in 1813—the same year that Ezra Hutchinson's trial and execution vividly reminded Berkshire County people of her father's fate just seven years before.

Betsy might also have chosen to join the celibate Shaker community at Hancock, near Pittsfield, though no record of her joining survives. Betsy's other alternative, marriage, may have been distasteful to her in light of her own and her mother's personal experiences; it cannot ever have been easy for her to trust a man after what she had been through. Still, her uncles appear to have been decent enough, and her uncle Bill Martin had stood up for Betsy and her mother at the time of the trial. At the beginning of the nineteenth century the economic, social, and cultural pull of marriage for young women was so powerful and pervasive that it surely would have influenced Betsy, whether or not she chose to marry. We cannot say with what frequency girls who were victims of sexual abuse went on to marry in the early republic, but anecdotal evidence suggests that these girls, like others, did commonly marry. Hannah Northrup, the fifteen-year-old daughter of the Lenox farmer who was convicted in 1798 of lewd and lascivious conduct with her, went on to marry after the family moved to New York state, as did Susanna Temple of Upton, a victim of paternal incest in the 1770s. Decades later Vermont pauper Sarah Avery, the fourteen-year-old victim of forty-four-year-old Joseph Burnham in 1826, also went on to marry.[39] Betsy's suffering must have resembled that of the other girls, and their trauma did not stop them from pursuing a conventional life. Like her mother, Betsy could not have brought many assets to the marriage market. But if, like Hannah, she was hardworking and competent, some poor man—maybe white, maybe black, maybe of mixed race—might have set aside her troubled past and offered her a new name and a new identity as his wife.[40]

Whether Betsy married or stayed single, whether she lived only briefly after her father's execution or lived on to be a centenarian in the 1890s, we do not know. But we can be sure that for however long Betsy lived she bore the scars of the events of 1805 and 1806 when, while still a child, she had been forced to make a terrible choice between herself and her father. As long as she lived that choice was part of her.[41]

Ephraim's lawyers, John W. Hulbert and Daniel Dewey, whose defense of their client had slandered Hannah and the children as conspirators and Betsy as a perjurer, bore no such scars from the episode. Though the trial and especially the pardon campaign were defeats for them, no lawyer was expected to win every case; and they did win favorable recognition for their efforts on Wheeler's behalf. Hulbert, who had been a leader in the state legislature in 1805, continued to be one of Berkshire's leading Federalist activists. With other county notables—including the Jeffersonian sheriff Simon Larned—he went on to become a director and investor in Pittsfield's short-lived Berkshire Bank. Later, though he would fail in defending Ezra Hutchinson in

1813, he would twice win election to the U.S. Congress, serving from 1814 to 1817. In the latter year, however, the deeply indebted Hulbert borrowed money and, with his wife and two teenage daughters, moved west to start over at Auburn, New York. He would remain in Auburn until his death in 1831 at the age of sixty-one.[42]

Daniel Dewey, Hulbert's fellow Federalist, was even more successful than his sometime colleague. A longtime pillar of Williams College, holding the office of treasurer from 1798 to 1814, like Hulbert he served in the state legislature, including three terms (1809–1812) on the Governor's Council. Later he, too, won election to the U.S. Congress. But just as he began his first and only term in the U.S. House of Representatives in March 1813, his wife of over twenty years, Maria Noble Dewey, died at the age of forty-two. Dewey, who had for his client's sake been quick to brand Hannah Wheeler as an attacker of the patriarchal order, suggesting that she formed "the abominable design of prosecuting her husband for a capital offense, and taught her children . . . the story they should tell," now idealized his own wife's submissive femininity. With three surviving sons aged eight, thirteen, and twenty years, Daniel Dewey had many reasons to mourn her loss.[43]

It was partly owing to parental considerations that Dewey resigned his post in Congress to take a seat on the state Supreme Judicial Court when Governor Caleb Strong offered it in 1814. But Dewey served only briefly on the bench; he died the following year at the age of forty-nine. Daniel Dewey's legacy was a distinguished succession of Massachusetts lawyers and jurists extending, so far, through seven generations.[44] For Dewey, like the other legal professionals drawn into the case, the story of Ephraim, Hannah, and Betsy Wheeler did not loom large in their busy lives for long.

For the prosecutor, James Sullivan, any thoughts of the Wheeler case were swiftly set aside by a far more controversial criminal case in the next county, Hampshire. Here he won a murder conviction against two Roman Catholic Irish laborers just two months after Ephraim's execution—and only two weeks after Sullivan had again lost the gubernatorial election to Caleb Strong, this time by a handful of votes. As in Wheeler's trial, Sullivan's prosecution of Dominic Daley and James Halligan rested on circumstantial evidence and the testimony of a child, in this case a thirteen-year-old boy. Though Sullivan, himself sensitive to anti-Irish slurs, kept appeals to prejudice out of the prosecution, public opinion ran so high against the Catholic immigrants that weeks later when Father Jean Cheverus, a French priest (later bishop, then cardinal), came from Boston to pray with the prisoners in the jail, he could scarcely find anyone to give him lodging.[45]

Sullivan knew Cheverus, but he may have been disturbed by the French priest's attack on the New England execution ritual. After insisting that as the condemned men's coreligionist he, Cheverus, should preach the execution sermon, the priest upbraided the crowd who had come to witness the execution. The cosmopolitan and enlightened veteran of the horrors of the French Revolution declared that the spectators were not civic-minded Christians, but corrupt sinners who took pleasure in "the sufferings of others." Taking particular aim at the women in the crowd, the priest castigated them for treating the execution as "an inviting entertainment for your curiosity."[46] James Sullivan, who had twice battled in the courts to secure full equality for Catholics (and lost), could not have been pleased with the priest's critique of a ritual he defended.[47]

But as 1806 wore on, Sullivan's concerns about religious freedom and anti-Irish bias were overshadowed by the fierce partisan battle between the Federalists and the Republican party he headed. His Federalist adversaries, concerned that they would lose the governorship in 1807, mounted a venomous, underhanded attack on the attorney general. Having held onto the governorship in 1806 only by disqualifying some 357 ballots from the town of Lynn, where shoe-makers had misspelled the candidate's name as "Sulvan," and by voiding others from Maine due to similar errors, Federalists now filled their press with insulting half-truths and innuendos aimed at destroying Sullivan's support. The attorney general had, they said, no Revolutionary War record; he had supported the Shaysites and op-posed the Constitution; and he was hostile to both George Washing-ton and John Adams. On top of all that, the Federalists claimed that James Sullivan was a dishonest, money-grubbing opportunist.[48]

The old revolutionary's long public record and wide popularity immunized him to some degree; but in a close competition he felt he must defend himself—which he did in a widely distributed, eight-page *Address to the Electors of Massachusetts*.[49] The outcome of the election in early April 1807 was a James Sullivan victory over Caleb Strong, largely provided by majorities in Maine and in Berkshire County. When Sullivan took office in the spring of 1807, foreign pol-icy issues and especially Jefferson's trade embargo dominated politi-cal debate. In that year and the next, when Sullivan was reelected, reform of the criminal code and the question of capital punishment had passed out of Massachusetts public discourse. Governor Sullivan may have given a thought to Wheeler's case and that of Daley and Halligan in July 1808 when he and the council denied a petition to save a young Yankee murder convict, Joseph Drew, from the gallows; but if so, there is no evidence of it. Later that year the sixty-four-year-old Sullivan, his health declining due to congestive heart failure, would himself die, peacefully, in an upstairs chamber of his Boston mansion.[50]

James Sullivan, Wheeler's prosecutor, outlived Ephraim by less than three years; the judge who pronounced the fatal sentence did not live even as long as the condemned man. Simeon Strong, the sixty-nine-year-old jurist who was known for his wisdom, piety, learning, and judgment, died "after a very distressing illness" on December 14, 1805, three months to the day after he had for the only time in his life ordered publicly that a man "be hanged by the neck until he be Dead."[51]

Simeon Strong's death at the end of 1805 was soon followed by a falling-out between Wheeler's two remaining judges, Theodore Sedgwick and Samuel Sewall. Chief Justice Dana having recently retired, Governor Caleb Strong would appoint a new chief justice for the Supreme Judicial Court. Sedgwick believed that, as the oldest and most prominent of the sitting judges, he should be elevated to the chief's position. In addition, Sewall had told Sedgwick that if, as in the past, one of the present judges were promoted, he presumed it would be Sedgwick. So Sedgwick was disappointed when Governor Strong appointed Theophilus Parsons, a brilliant Boston attorney, Chief Justice; and he was stunned to learn that Strong had appointed Parsons to the post at the urging of Sewall. In April 1806 Sedgwick would sit with Sewall on the bench while they tried Daley and Halligan for murder; but he was seething. With his wife in deep depression and with his last public ambition thwarted, the proud Federalist felt insulted by his colleagues and by the party's leaders. He threatened to resign. Only if leading members of the bar would publicly express their confidence by urging him to stay on would Sedgwick consent to remain on the bench.[52]

This fracture in the Federalist leadership at a time when Republicans were poised to win the state led the Federalist elite to make an urgent effort to soothe Sedgwick's vanity. Lawyers across much of Massachusetts, from the counties of Essex and Middlesex in the east to Worcester and Hampshire in the west, rushed to endorse Sedgwick; and in Boston the Federalist leaders of the Suffolk County bar signed an address praising his abilities and accomplishments. Ironically, the leading Boston organizer on behalf of the old Federalist was William Sullivan, James's son, and among the signers were Samuel Dexter and Artemas Ward, the two councilors who had so carefully considered Wheeler's pardon petitions.[53] By that time, May 1806, three months had passed since Wheeler's execution; with so many urgent concerns crowding the minds of Sedgwick, the governor, and the councilors, it would be surprising if they still gave a thought to Ephraim Wheeler, a man whose life had been briefly but decisively in their hands.

A year or so later Theodore Sedgwick entered once more the ranks of widowers when Pamela Dwight Sedgwick's miseries at last came to an end. He would marry again in November 1808, but his young wife proved "delicate" as well as irritable, and the relationship was troubled from the beginning. Late in 1812, while on court duty in Boston, the sixty-seven-year-old Sedgwick fell ill—probably with bronchial pneumonia—and never recovered. Before his death in January 1813, Judge Sedgwick called clergyman William Ellery Channing to his bedside and revealed that though he had been a faithful parishioner of Calvinist Stephen West in Stockbridge for over twenty-five years, at heart he was a religious liberal, a Unitarian.[54] In so doing, the baron of the Berkshire Federalists revealed that his devotion to Congregational orthodoxy was less a matter of theology than a commitment to the social order. No doubt the same commitment to order—perhaps especially when the truth was cloudy and justice doubtful—had ruled his judgments on the bench as well.

The surviving judge in the Wheeler affair, Samuel Sewall, though eleven years younger than Sedgwick, did not last much longer. He, too, spent the years after the Wheeler case on the bench. Governor Strong appointed Sewall as Chief Justice in 1813 following the death of Sedgwick's rival, Theophilus Parsons, but Sewall's chief justiceship was brief. While traveling the circuit, the short, stout Sewall was cut down by a heart attack in June 1814 at Wiscasset in Maine. By odd coincidence this death of the last of Wheeler's judges created the vacancy that enabled Governor Strong to bring Wheeler's defender, Daniel Dewey, to the bench of the court that had tried Ephraim nine years before.

Sewall, perhaps more than any of the high state officials associated with Wheeler's trial and punishment, had appreciated the complexity of securing justice for the forty-three-year-old laborer. Because Sewall had drawn up a comprehensive revision of Massachusetts' criminal code, he knew better than most that the Massachusetts punishment for rape would seem unjust in much of the nation. Possessing his own copy of Beccaria's *Essay on Crimes and Punishments* with Voltaire's commentary, this former U.S. senator well knew that the enlightened world would view Wheeler's punishment as barbaric.[55] And as a scion and namesake of the great-grandfather who in 1692 had acted to hang the witches at Salem but who had publicly recanted in 1697, Sewall understood the danger of misplaced zeal. Those hangings at Salem, enlightened men believed, formed the greatest blot on Massachusetts' proud history.

Yet Judge Sewall also recognized and shared in the political and legal culture of his native state. For these reasons he had resisted Thomas Allen, Jr., and the anti–capital punishment reformers in early 1805 and had found himself later that year having to enforce the death sentence on Ephraim Wheeler for rape.[56] Yet Sewall, unlike Sedgwick, was not self-righteous on the bench. He was ready to express publicly "sentiments of pity" towards a murderer or a rapist, and ready also to admit that "human tribunals see but imperfectly." Even after juries convicted defendants, Sewall spoke of their guilt conditionally, believing that God alone knew the whole truth. For him, delivering the sentence of death was a "painful duty."[57]

Indeed we believe that it was Samuel Sewall who communicated the judges' doubts about the evidence in Wheeler's trial to councilors

Samuel Dexter and Artemas Ward, who then referred to these doubts in their report on Wheeler's pardon. Sewall, alone among Wheeler's judges, had worked closely with the legislature in 1805, and only he lived close enough to Boston to be in the thick of the state's politics. Moreover he was not only cautious about inflicting the death penalty, he was also ready to act covertly, particularly on an issue where his headstrong colleague, Theodore Sedgwick, felt strongly.[58] In February 1806 only Sewall was positioned in proximity to councilors Dexter and Ward when they reviewed the Wheeler petitions, so only he could have spoken with them informally. Sewall, the sole Episcopalian sitting in judgment on Wheeler, possessed a more cosmopolitan perspective on Massachusetts' ancient execution ritual than his colleagues, as well as a family legacy of concern over its abuse. Indeed Sewall may have tried to save Wheeler's life via the council on the technical legal grounds of children's testimony and the lack of physical evidence. This would save his state from the disgrace of hanging a man for rape. If so, then Sewall would not have forgotten either the poor man who stood before him weeping in the Lenox courtroom, nor that man's grisly fate. By 1814, when Sewall died, he had participated in a half-dozen more death sentences, including Ezra Hutchinson's, and he personally had at least twice ordered men to be hanged. If he reflected back on the Wheeler case, he must have remembered it as a turning point, one that marked the end of the movement to reform capital punishment in his lifetime.

Simon Larned, too, would have remembered Ephraim Wheeler; and, because he resigned his post as county sheriff in 1812—before Ezra Hutchinson's execution—he would have given thanks that he never again would have to hang anyone. But the fifty-nine-year-old Larned, though wealthy, did not retire to a life of ease in his two-story, center-hallway house.[59] The aging Jeffersonian volunteered to serve the United States in President Madison's war against Britain in 1812.

Once more he led Yankee infantrymen against the British, as he had done over thirty years before. At the war's end Larned enjoyed the satisfaction of having twice fought for American independence; but he would enjoy retirement for only a few years. He died unexpectedly in 1817—like Sullivan, at the age of sixty-four.[60]

One man who carried Wheeler's memory with him across generations was the Reverend Samuel Shepard. Although there is no evidence to suggest that the longtime Lenox clergyman was preoccupied by Wheeler's fate, we believe it is significant that although the state executed at least three more men at Lenox during his pastorate, Shepard never again chose to preach an execution sermon. His theology did not change—he remained a Calvinist in the mold of Jonathan Edwards to the end—but as public sentiment toward hangings changed, and as he grew older, Shepard evidently lost the evangelical zeal for those occasions that he so feelingly expressed as a young man in 1806. Many years later, when Shepard came to preach his fiftieth anniversary sermon in 1845, he stressed once more the universality of death; but now when the seventy-three-year-old pastor looked down from the high pulpit in the Lenox meeting house, he did not point to the imminent death of a criminal, but to his own. Just as Ephraim Wheeler's mortality expressed the common fate, so too did his own: "The throbbing heart will be stilled, and we shall be at rest. Our funeral will wind its way; its sacred rites will be performed; the grave clods will be thrown in; our friends will then return, and we shall be left behind to darkness and to worms."[61]

Shepard knew very well the afflictions that death visited upon the living. He had prayed with bereaved families hundreds of times, and he himself had already buried a young son who "was with the summer flowers cut off," as well as the boy's mother, "the companion of my youth, who bore with me the heat and burden of the day." But when the old preacher looked out from the pulpit he reminded his listeners that grief, too, was transitory. There would be laughter and song again in the very bedchambers where we die, and "the heavens shall be as bright over our *graves,* as they are now over *our path.*"[62] On earth life was ephemeral. Only in heaven could it be everlasting.

Samuel Shepard's sermon implicitly denied all memory of Ephraim Wheeler. His theme was that "all things earthly, [are] changing and transitory," and according to this line of belief he needed to stress that "we become forgotten and clean out of mind."[63] But as Shepard stood in the pulpit thinking back over the thousands of sermons he had delivered from that very spot, he must have remembered his singular experience of preaching over a man seated before him on a coffin, a man in chains, bound for the gallows. Publicly, however, Shepard chose to forget the man whom he had visited in jail and over whom he had shed tears in the packed meetinghouse. For to hold in remembrance that sinner convicted of a hideous crime while declaring thousands of good Christians forgotten would be to contradict his own message. From the perspective of Berkshire County's keepers of memory, Ephraim Wheeler and his crime and punishment were best forgotten. Though his assault had unexpectedly thrown Wheeler up out of obscurity, by the death of the Reverend Shepard on January 5, 1846, it seemed that the case of the man who once committed a rape upon the body of his daughter was forgotten.

To a large extent it was. When the Reverend David Dudley Field, the Stockbridge pastor, joined with the Reverend Chester Dewey, the principal of Pittsfield's Berkshire Gymnasium, to assemble their *History of the County of Berkshire* in the 1820s, they preserved the annals of towns and churches and public officials extensively, but they limited their remembrance of crime to a half-page listing of six executions, including "Ephraim Wheeler, of Windsor," who "was executed

Feb. 20, 1806, for a rape, committed upon his own daughter."[64] No elaboration was suitable, in their judgment.

This indeed seems to have been a general view, at least among most of the producers and patrons of print in the county. Yet there was one person, a member of the Reverend Field's own parish, who chose to remember and to reimagine Ephraim Wheeler's crime, his victim, his trial, and his punishment. That person was Judge Sedgwick's youngest daughter, Catharine Maria, a girl just two years older than Betsy Wheeler. She would grow up to become one of the foremost writers of didactic fiction of her generation. To her the story of Ephraim Wheeler and of Betsy and Ephraim, Jr., was unforgettable, and worthy to be told.

That Catharine Maria Sedgwick knew the Wheeler case can hardly be doubted. Everyone in Lenox and the neighboring town of Stockbridge during the trial in 1805 would have heard or read something about Ephraim Wheeler and his daughter Betsy. Fifteen-year-old Catharine, who was serving as deputy housekeeper in Judge Sedgwick's home while her mother was ill, cannot have been ignorant of the case. Moreover, at home the judge often discussed court cases with his children. The fact that Catharine was a girl would not have excluded her from such serious, worldly conversation, because Theodore Sedgwick routinely invited her along as his companion when he traveled the court circuit; and when he was away, she reported on politics in her letters to him.[65] It is possible that Judge Sedgwick brought Catharine to the Lenox courthouse to witness the trial.

When she grew up to become an author, Catharine Sedgwick's stories often involved themes of crime and punishment, and she became an advocate for prison reform. Frequently her stories used thinly disguised Berkshire people and settings; one, "Berkley Jail," was set in the Berkshire County jail where Ephraim Wheeler was incarcerated. In addition, Sedgwick asserts the authenticity of some of her stories, even referring directly to trial reports. With these facts in mind we can only read her 1837 story "Daniel Prime" as a fictionalized representation of the horrifying tale of Ephraim Wheeler and his family.[66]

Sedgwick begins by setting the story in the past, when she was a little girl and too young to be told about Daniel Prime. Later, when she did learn the story from a "dear old servant and friend . . . substantiated by an examination of judicial records," she told her readers it was the story of a father's murder of his daughter.[67] For her often youthful audience the less salacious, but more horrific, crime of filicide was more acceptable than that of incest-rape. Instead of presenting Wheeler's ruling motive—probably patriarchal rage toward his disobedient wife and the children who preferred their mother to him—the fictional villain Daniel Prime (a surname that was found in Wheeler's town of Windsor) was driven by greed, a central concern of Sedgwick's middle-class readers.[68] To enhance her readers' ability to identify with the characters, and in keeping with their tastes, the author elevated the social status of her protagonists, who were not the poorest laborers, but members of Berkshire's yeoman class.

In other ways the story of Daniel Prime followed that of Ephraim Wheeler. Prime, too, twice assaulted his daughter, "Sybil," a name that, with the syllables reversed (Bilsy) closely resembles "Betsy." Like Betsy, Sybil concealed the first attack from her mother. For Sybil as for Betsy, her father's second assault took place in a patch of woods at a moment when she was temporarily separated from her younger brother, a boy about the same age as Ephraim, Jr. He had gone to look not for the little-known avens-root, but for the widely familiar sassafras. As with Ephraim Wheeler, Daniel Prime was brought down by the testimony of his child—not the daughter he had killed, but the son who witnessed his crime.

The actual crime of course was different. Prime, who was driven by greed, not anger or lust, killed his daughter with a blow to the head. For these details Sedgwick closely followed the testimony from a different case, the trial of Daley and Halligan for the 1805 murder of Marcus Lyon. As with the Wheeler trial, her father had officiated, she may have attended, and a printed trial report preserved details of the courtroom testimony. In her story, Sedgwick had Prime drag the body to a nearby stream and conceal it underwater by weighing it down with stones, just as Daley and Halligan had done. And, like Daley and Halligan, she had the greedy Prime steal the cash that his victim carried, money that when found on his person helped seal his conviction.[69]

To soften the impact of the Wheeler family drama and give it a more hopeful ending, Sedgwick has the pardon petition of Prime's son, whose testimony had convicted the father, granted. The governor, who felt compassion for Prime's family, chose to regard the criminal's avarice as a form of insanity and so decided "to commute the sentence of death to banishment."[70] Catharine Maria Sedgwick no doubt felt great sympathy for Betsy Wheeler, so in her retelling the child's plea to save a father's life was granted, and instead of the gallows Daniel Prime/Ephraim Wheeler was punished by exile in the manner of Jacob Azzett Lewis.

In this disguised version Sedgwick preserved the story of Ephraim Wheeler's crime and punishment. Refashioned as a middle-class morality tale, in a gift book of stories, *The Magnolia for 1837*, she retold the story as fiction. But except for the rare historical compilation of hangings in Berkshire County, the actual story faded from view. The *Report of the Trial of Ephraim Wheeler, for a rape committed on the body of Betsy Wheeler, his daughter, a girl thirteen years of age*, and *A Narrative of the Life of Ephraim Wheeler; who was executed at Lenox (Massachusetts), February 20th, 1806* were ephemeral works. Poor people of small accomplishments, like the Wheelers and the Odels, were best forgotten.[71] As the Reverend Shepard had pointed out in his fiftieth-anniversary sermon, succeeding generations could not recall those who came before, or they remembered very selectively. When children grew into adulthood and made lives for themselves, the world seemed fresh and new.

Why, then, have we chosen to reconstruct the Wheelers' family crisis and public responses to it? One reason is that old taboos concerning discussion of sexual abuse and family violence have fallen away, and this two-hundred-year-old story seems important and perhaps instructive for our own time.[72] Like the inhabitants of early republican Berkshire County, we in the twenty-first century are horrified when men batter their wives and abuse their children; and we, too, intervene to provide protection and to mete out justice. Legislators, courts and police, social service agencies, family relations therapists, schoolteachers, and private citizens confront the same kinds of issues that are embedded in the Wheelers' conflicts; and the tension between therapeutic and punitive responses continues. The story of Hannah and Ephraim Wheeler and their children cannot, of course, tell us how we should respond to rape or incest. But if we recognize that there were no easy remedies long ago in a community that was both smaller and more homogeneous than ours, we can better appreciate the complexity of addressing these crimes in our own time.

Another reason for considering the Wheeler case is that it led to the gallows. Capital punishment was—and is—a complex and controversial exercise of state power. Though we are separated from the early republic by two centuries, the controversies over the use of the death penalty—involving Biblical prescription, deterrence, and vengeance on the one hand and social utility and sanctity of life on the other—are familiar. So, too, is the question of whether justice can be truly even-handed, capable of treating people of different rank, color, and reputation equally. Examining the Wheeler case enables us to recognize that, as with family violence, the difficulties we face in making life-and-death judgments have been with us for generations.

In reconstructing this long-ago drama, we can contemplate what happened with some detachment. We can try to understand the villain as well as his victim, the defense as well as the prosecution, and the people who debated and then executed the death penalty, confident as they were that religious precepts should be entwined with the workings of the state.

What was the meaning of the Wheelers' tragedy? For Betsy the attack of June 8, 1805, was devastating. Her father was forcing her to choose between entering into a state of sexual bondage under his direct control, which would send her to hell, and turning to the law for protection. If the law failed she could expect Ephraim's revenge; if the law succeeded, it might take her father's life. Her decision to turn to Justice Walker and Attorney General Sullivan would not have been possible without her mother's backing. But it was Betsy, not Hannah Wheeler, who had to stand up in court and testify. It was Betsy alone who had to live the rest of her life knowing that by defending herself she had brought down her parent.

Hannah's burden was less. Betsy's courage freed Hannah from an abusive, irresponsible husband, a man she may once have loved but had grown to fear and despise. Betsy's brave decision saved the family for Hannah, who became its new head. The guilt that she, like Betsy, experienced was the price she paid for seeking family protection from a legal system that operated to serve the public and the community at large, not to resolve family problems.

For Ephraim Wheeler the assault on Betsy and its consequences was the climax of a hard life, one in which he had never learned to accept responsibility for his actions. His rage—triggered by his wife's accepting the orders of her black brother-in-law, not his, and by his own ejection from the house by the same man—fed on his sense of failure as a husband, father, breadwinner, and patriarch. Still seething, he asserted his mastery over his wife and family by once more assaulting his seemingly defenseless daughter. That he had committed rape he denied to himself even as he stood at the gallows, because as a boy raised under Jeduthan Hammond's rough tutelage he had never learned the difference between consent and submission. In Ephraim's mind, when Betsy, overpowered and frightened, submitted to her father on June 8, he reckoned that was consent.

When the Berkshire agents of Massachusetts government, in collaboration with high state officials, decided to bring Ephraim Wheeler to trial, they acted so as to defend and affirm the most fundamental principles of their culture and of the social order that sustained it. Repeatedly they had demonstrated that they saw paternal sexual abuse as a perversion of patriarchal authority and would not tolerate it—not by Job Northrup, not by Abner Durwin, and certainly not by the accused rapist, Ephraim Wheeler. God's covenant with fathers, embodied in state law, directed that they both command obedience and supply protection, nurture, and instruction. A father who violated that covenant flouted the law and must be brought to justice. The family patriarchs who tried Ephraim Wheeler, from the judges on the bench to the jurors in their box and the prosecutor who argued before them, all saw in Betsy's testimony against Ephraim a violation so shocking and egregious that, despite their reluctance to send a man to the gallows for rape, they would do exactly that.

Much the same was true for the council and Governor Strong. They sought to be discriminating in their use of the death penalty and frugal in their resort to the gallows. They had spared Jacob Azzett Lewis, Lemuel Deming, and Deborah Stevens, convicted of rape, burglary, and murder. But even as they recognized the flaws in the evidence against Ephraim Wheeler, they refused to commute his sentence. The legislature, they knew, had just recently reviewed the penalty for rape, and the lawmakers had narrowly affirmed capital punishment. If the governor and council now pardoned the perpetrator of this most aggravated version of the crime, they would—in a year of the keenest political competition—be seen as violating their constitutional duty.

To the Berkshire County community that managed Wheeler's execution ritual, though his death was clearly a powerful and, for some, excessive assertion of state authority, it was also freighted with larger meanings. For many, no doubt, the taking of Wheeler's life expressed vengeance against a vile man. To self-righteous spectators, such a concrete illustration of the motto "The wages of sin is death" gave reassurance of the preservation of the moral and social order. But for Christians of the Reverend Shepard's stamp, the hanging of Ephraim Wheeler recalled the scene on Calvary, where two thieves were crucified alongside of Jesus. Wheeler's punishment, insofar as it brought others in Berkshire to a sense of sin and salvation in Christ, was an act of atonement—a kind of community sacrifice that transcended the brutal scene before their eyes. When these Christians listened under a gray sky to the prayers of the Reverend Ayer and then watched Ephraim's once vital body go limp, they were reminded of mortality, judgment, and divine mercy. They were "thankful" to God for themselves, their loved ones, and their neighbors "for any restraints which are laid upon the evil propensities of the human heart."[73]

Did Ephraim Wheeler receive justice at the hands of the authorities? In some ways he did. As James Sullivan and Theodore Sedgwick argued, the truth of Betsy's testimony convicted him. To claim that she or her mother made up the story out of whole cloth was as preposterous as the idea that Betsy, having first consented to sexual relations, later decided to reveal herself and her father in this shocking way.

Although the evidence was flawed because of the absence of both physical evidence and corroborating testimony, the twelve jurors who watched and listened to Betsy and Ephraim, Jr., reached their unanimous verdict quickly. They believed the children told the truth. Afterward Wheeler's advocates, who never challenged his guilt, mounted a well-crafted legal, personal, and political appeal for a pardon—an appeal that very nearly led the governor and council to save Wheeler for the state prison. In the end, however, like the jury, the executives sustained the idea of justice that was written into law.

But whether hanging Ephraim or any man for rape in 1806 could be called just was certainly doubtful from the perspective of those who looked northward to Vermont or southward to the middle Atlantic and Chesapeake states. When one considers the pardon granted by Caleb Strong and the council to Jacob Azzett Lewis in 1802, their decision to execute Wheeler for exactly the same crime in 1806 looks arbitrary. At the trial James Sullivan had argued that Ephraim Wheeler's relation to his victim had no bearing on the question of his guilt or innocence and that the jury should focus only on the crime charged in the indictment. But the governor and council were not so narrowly bound. They were not deciding whether Wheeler was guilty, but how he should be punished; and in their rejection of the Wheeler pardon petitions they made a point of mentioning the convict's relation to his victim. Had they been willing to focus on the crime only, or even ready to give weight to Betsy's appeal for her father's life, they could have chosen to send Ephraim Wheeler to the state prison for life. In light of the broad movement to curtail the use of capital punishment in the early republic, we believe such a punishment would have been just.

We authors belong to a different generation, hold different religious beliefs, and share a sensibility removed from that of 1805–1806. Like Catharine Maria Sedgwick, who was prepared to save Daniel

Prime's life for the sake of Prime's son, we believe that saving Ephraim's life for Betsy's sake would have been just. Life in prison was still a harsher penalty than some states inflicted for rape. In short, we do not share the governor and council's belief that the full measure of the statutory penalty was here required.

Many years after Wheeler's execution, in 1849, Herman Melville, a longtime Pittsfield resident and a reader who annotated Field and Dewey's list of Berkshire County hangings, personally attended a hanging in London. "A most wonderful scene," Melville noted, "a most wonderful, horrible, & unspeakable scene." So too, we think, was Ephraim Wheeler's final scene for those who witnessed it. Victimizer and victim all at once, the despicable Ephraim Wheeler died a hideous death. Yet as horrific as we find Wheeler's execution, it was the outcome of a careful and conscientious effort to achieve justice. And in witnessing Ephraim's killing, the people who judged him acknowledged that they, like the convict, must prepare to face divine judgment, where mercy and punishment would be in perfect balance. Ephraim Wheeler was a vicious man, but still a man; and with Melville we believe that "whenever we recognize the image of God let us reverence it; though it swing from the gallows."[74]

NOTES

ACKNOWLEDGMENTS

INDEX

ABBREVIATIONS

AAS	American Antiquarian Society, Worcester, Massachusetts
GCMin	Governor's Council Minutes, Massachusetts Archives, Boston
GCP	Governor's Council Pardon File, Massachusetts Archives, Boston
GCPNG	Governor's Council Pardons Not Granted File, Box 1 (1785–1810), Massachusetts Archives, Boston
GCRec	Governor's Council Records, Massachusetts Archives, Boston
Hearn	Daniel Allen Hearn, *Legal Executions in New England: A Comprehensive Reference, 1623–1960* (Jefferson, N.C.: McFarland, 1999)
MA	Massachusetts Archives, Boston
MHS	Massachusetts Historical Society, Boston
Narrative	[Ephraim Wheeler], *A Narrative of the Life of Ephraim Wheeler; who was executed at Lenox (Massachusetts) February 20th, 1806; for a rape on the body of his daughter: penned from his mouth, and signed by him, the evening before his Execution* (Stockbridge: Printed by H. Willard, March 1806)
PS	*Pittsfield Sun, or Republican Monitor*
Shepard, *Execution*	Samuel Shepard, *A Sermon, delivered at Lenox, (Massachusetts) February 20th, 1806: being the day of the Execution of Ephraim Wheeler, pursuant to his sentence, for a rape committed on his daughter, Betsy Wheeler* (Stockbridge: Printed by H. Willard, March 1806)
Sibley	Clifford K. Shipton, *Sibley's Harvard Graduates* (Boston: Massachusetts Historical Society, [various dates])
SJC	Massachusetts Supreme Judicial Court

Trial Report
[Ephraim Wheeler], *Report of the Trial of Ephraim Wheeler, for a rape committed on the body of Betsy Wheeler, his daughter, a girl thirteen years of age. Before the Supreme Judicial Court, holden at Lenox, within and for the County of Berkshire, on the second Tuesday of September, 1805* (Stockbridge: Printed by H. Willard, November 1805)

INTRODUCTION

1. Shepard, *Execution,* pp. 13–14.

2. The description of the execution scene is from *PS,* Feb. 24, 1806, p. 3. All information on the weather comes from Caleb Hyde, Jr.'s "Thermometrical Diary," 1798–1820, Lenox Library Association, Lenox, Mass.

3. Record of the SJC, Lenox, Book 2, 344, MA.

4. *Narrative,* p. 7.

5. See GCPNG.

6. *Narrative,* pp. 3–12.

7. The last previous execution for rape in Massachusetts was at Worcester in 1779 (Robert Young, b. Ireland, was executed). Hearn, pp. 161–162.

8. Information on Wheeler's life comes from his *Narrative,* as does information that the accusation took him by surprise. The indictment is in the Trial Report, pp. 5–6. The tabulation of convictions and executions comes from records of the Massachusetts Supreme Judicial Court in Boston and Berkshire. Most information on Sullivan comes from Thomas Coffin Amory, *Life of James Sullivan with Selections from His Writings,* 2 vols. (Boston, 1859).

9. Information on Massachusetts rape trials comes from Barbara S. Lindemann, "'To Ravish and Carnally Know': Rape in Eighteenth-Century Massachusetts," *Signs: Journal of Women in Culture and Society* 10 (1984): 63–82. Also on eighteenth-century rape trials, see Cornelia Hughes Dayton, "Rape, the Problematics of a Woman's Word," in *Women before the Bar: Gender, Law, and Society in Connecticut, 1639–1789* (Chapel Hill: University of North Carolina Press for the Institute of Early American History and Culture, 1995), pp. 231–284. The Wheeler case is described in a letter from Heman Willard, the Stockbridge printer, to newspapers such as *Boston*

Weekly Magazine, Sept. 21, 1805, no. 43, p. 191, and the *Richmond (Virginia) Enquirer,* Oct. 8, 1805, p. 3.

10. Information on the race of Hannah Odel Wheeler's family comes from the United States censuses of 1790 and 1800, and the vital records of Hinsdale, Massachusetts. See pp. 309, n. 66; 316, n. 16; 358, n. 34.

11. Family Petition, Sept. 26, 1805, GCPNG.

12. Wheeler's thoughts are from his *Narrative.* Information on the petitions is from GCPNG. Identification of the petitioners comes partly from the petitions themselves, partly from land records at the Berkshire County Register of Deeds in Pittsfield and Adams, and from other sources. Information on Strong's pardon of the East Indian, Jacob Azzett Lewis, is from GCRec and GCPNG.

13. The execution ritual of the Shays era is described in Gregory H. Nobles, "The Politics of Patriarchy in Shays's Rebellion: The Case of Henry McCulloch," in Peter Benes, ed., *Families and Children,* Dublin Seminar for New England Folklife Annual Proceedings, 1985 (Boston: Boston University, 1987), pp. 37–47. For Stephen Arnold see Alan Taylor, "'The Unhappy Stephen Arnold': An Episode of Murder and Penitence in the Early Republic," in Ronald Hoffman, Mechal Sobel, and Frederika J. Teute, eds., *Through a Glass Darkly: Reflections on Personal Identity in Early America* (Chapel Hill: University of North Carolina Press for the Omohundro Institute of Early American History and Culture, 1997), pp. 96–121.

14. Natalie Zemon Davis, *The Return of Martin Guerre* (Cambridge, Mass.: Harvard University Press, 1983); Edward Muir and Guido Ruggiero, eds., *History from Crime* (Baltimore: Johns Hopkins University Press, 1994).

15. For penal reform in Massachusetts we have relied on Adam Jay Hirsch, *The Rise of the Penitentiary: Prisons and Punishment in Early America* (New Haven: Yale University Press, 1992). The change in the sodomy law is in the legislative records in the Massachusetts Archives, Boston. For the Berkshire newspaper controversy over Wheeler and capital punishment see *Narrative,* pp. 13–23.

16. Theodore Sedgwick and Caleb Strong were on opposite sides of the antislavery case *Exeter v. Hanchett,* with Strong arguing for freedom. Yet in 1781, notes Emily Blank, "Theodore Sedgwick, Hanchett's lawyer, had suc-

cessfully defended Mum Bett (Elizabeth Freeman) in her quest for freedom." Emily Blank, "Seventeen Eighty-Three: The Turning Point in the Law of Slavery and Freedom in Massachusetts," *New England Quarterly* 71 (March 2002): 39–40. The Catharine M. Sedgwick story, which presents an altered version of the Wheeler episode, is "Daniel Prime," in *The Magnolia for 1837* (New York, 1836), pp. 281–311.

17. *PS,* Feb. 24, 1806, p. 3.

18. Ibid.

1. THE SETTING

1. [David Dudley Field and Chester Dewey], *A History of the County of Berkshire, Massachusetts; in Two Parts* (Pittsfield, 1829), pp. 7–11, 14. The mountain chains are identified on pp. 16–17. Later the mountains in both ranges came to be called "the Berkshires."

2. Description of Berkshire and its fauna and flora is based on [Field and Dewey], *History of the County.*

3. Ibid., pp. 243, 247.

4. Richard D. Brown, "'Not Only Extreme Poverty, but the Worst Kind of Orphanage': Lemuel Haynes and the Boundaries of Racial Tolerance on the Yankee Frontier, 1770–1820," *New England Quarterly* 61 (1988): 513; Joseph Carvalho, *Black Families in Hampden County, Massachusetts, 1650–1855* ([Boston, Mass.]: New England Historic Genealogical Society; [Westfield, Mass.]: Institute for Massachusetts Studies, Westfield State College, 1984).

5. U.S. Census, *Heads of Families at the First Census of the United States Taken in the Year 1790: Massachusetts* (Washington, D.C.: U.S. Government Printing Office, 1908), p. 39. In the town of Windsor, reference to Ichabod Odill [*sic*], family of seven in the category for nonwhites who were not Indians. We thank Arvilla L. Dyer of Plainfield, Massachusetts, for identifying black inhabitants of Berkshire in her letter of July 1996.

6. [Field and Dewey], *History of the County,* p. 12, population of Berkshire towns, 1790–1820.

7. Richard D. Birdsall, *Berkshire County: A Cultural History* (New Haven: Yale University Press, 1959), pp. 221–222.

notes

8. Richard E. Welch, Jr., *Theodore Sedgwick, Federalist: A Political Portrait* (Middletown, Conn.: Wesleyan University Press, 1965), pp. 51, 52.

9. Hearn, pp. 172–173, 412, cites SJC case no. 160576; *Hampshire Gazette,* Oct. 17, 1787, p. 3, col. 1, Dec. 19, 1787, p. 3, col. 3; Leonard L. Richards, *Shays's Rebellion: The American Revolution's Final Battle* (Philadelphia: University of Pennsylvania Press, 2002).

10. Louis P. Masur, *Rites of Execution: Capital Punishment and the Transformation of American Culture, 1776–1865* (New York: Oxford University Press, 1989), pp. 29–33; John L. Brooke, "'To the Quiet of the People': The Revolutionary Settlement and Civil Unrest in Western Massachusetts, 1774–1789," *William and Mary Quarterly,* 3d ser., 44 (1989): 441.

11. Bidwell to David Daggett, Tyringham, June 16, 1787, *Proceedings of the American Antiquarian Society,* new ser., 4 (1885–87): 368–369.

12. Welch, *Theodore Sedgwick;* Thomas Lawrence Davis, "Aristocrats and Jacobins in Country Towns: Party Formation in Berkshire County, Massachusetts (1775–1816)" (Ph.D. diss., Boston University, 1975); James H. Robbins, "Voting Behavior in Massachusetts, 1800–1820: A Case Study" (Ph.D. diss., Northwestern University, 1970).

13. *PS,* May 27, 1805, p. 3, col. 2 (hereafter, e.g., 3:2).

14. Birdsall, *Berkshire,* p. 184; David W. Conroy, *In Public Houses: Drink and the Revolution of Authority in Colonial Massachusetts* (Chapel Hill: University of North Carolina Press for the Institute of Early American History and Culture, 1995).

15. Richard D. Brown, *Knowledge Is Power: The Diffusion of Information in Early America, 1700–1865* (New York: Oxford University Press, 1989), chaps. 6, 7.

16. Based on authors' inspection of Sedgwick house, and on general works on Berkshire history and New England architectural history.

17. David Jaffee, "The Village Enlightenment in New England," *William and Mary Quarterly,* 3d ser. (1990): 327–346. See also Richard L. Bushman, *The Refinement of America: Persons, Houses, Cities* (New York: Knopf, 1992).

18. Joseph A. Conforti, *Samuel Hopkins and the New Divinity Movement:*

Calvinism, the Congregational Ministry, and Reform in New England between the Great Awakenings (Grand Rapids: Christian University Press, 1981).

19. Henry F. May, *The Enlightenment in America* (New York: Oxford University Press, 1976); Irene Q. Brown, "Death, Friendship, and Female Identity during New England's Second Great Awakening," *Journal of Family History* 12 (1987): 367–387, and "Friendship and Spiritual Time in the Didactic Enlightenment," in Elise Marienstras and Barbara Karsky, eds., *Autre temps, autre espace: Etudes sur l'Amérique préindustrielle* (Nancy: Presses Universitaires de Nancy, 1986), pp. 111–127.

20. *PS,* Aug. 4, 1804, 2:2, reprinted from *Richmond Examiner.*

21. *PS,* March 26, 1804, 4:1, reprinted from *Danbury Republican Farmer.*

22. Jaffee, "Village Enlightenment"; Richard D. Brown, "The Emergence of Urban Society in Rural Massachusetts, 1760–1820," *Journal of American History* 59 (1974): 29–51, and "The Emergence of Voluntary Associations in Massachusetts, 1760–1830," *Journal of Voluntary Action Research* 2 (April 1973): 64–73; William Allen, *Sermon Preached before the Auxiliary Society for Promoting Good Morals, and the Female Charitable Society of Williamstown, June 7, 1815* (Pittsfield, Mass.: Phinehas Allen, 1815), cited in Nancy F. Cott, *The Bonds of Womanhood: Woman's Sphere in New England, 1780–1835* (New Haven: Yale University Press, 1977), p. 215.

23. Birdsall, *Berkshire,* p. 67n.

24. Ibid., p. 67. Concern over Universalism is evident in two advertisements that appeared in the *Western Star,* Oct. 25, 1806, 3:3–4. Lemuel Haynes, *Universal Salvation a very Ancient Doctrine, and the Devil the Preacher* (Brattleboro, Vt., 1806); Josiah Spalding, *Universalism Confounds and Destroys Itself; or, Letters to a Friend: In Four Parts* (Northampton, 1805). As a Worthington, Massachusetts, clergyman in 1791 Spalding refused to join Ephraim Wheeler and Hannah Odel in marriage.

25. [Field and Dewey], *History of the County,* p. 163.

26. Birdsall, *Berkshire,* pp. 153, 154, 183n; Henry Miller Lydenberg, "The Berkshire Republican Library at Stockbridge, 1794–1818," *Proceedings of the American Antiquarian Society,* new ser., 50 (1940): 111–162.

27. Sermons compiled from Ralph R. Shaw and Richard H. Shoemaker, comp., *American Bibliography: A Preliminary Checklist for 1801–1819* (New York: Scarecrow Press, 1958–1983).

28. [Field and Dewey], *History of the County,* pp. 86–89; Birdsall, *Berkshire,* pp. 28–29.

29. Laurel Thatcher Ulrich, "Wheels, Looms, and the Gender Division of Labor in Eighteenth-Century New England," *William and Mary Quarterly,* 3d ser., 55 (1998): 3–38. Christopher Clark, *The Roots of Rural Capitalism: Western Massachusetts, 1780–1860* (Ithaca, N.Y.: Cornell University Press, 1990).

30. John Warner Barber, *Historical Collections, Being a Collection of Interesting Facts, Traditions, Biographical Sketches, Anecdotes, &c., Relating to the History and Antiquities of Every Town in Massachusetts* (Worcester, 1841), p. 67.

31. Ibid., pp. 79–80.

32. Birdsall, *Berkshire,* pp. 227–228.

33. For the contract of the Lenox courthouse, which provides a detailed description of the building, see David Oliver Merrill, "Isaac Damon and the Architecture of the Federal Period in New England" (Ph.D. diss., Yale University, 1965), appendix, pp. 495–496. George H. Tucker, *Berkshire County: Its Shire Towns and Its Courthouses* (Pittsfield, Mass.: n.p., 1918), pp. 4–5.

34. Olive H. Colton, *Lenox* (n.p., 194-?), p. 7.

35. Merrill, "Isaac Damon and the Architecture," p. 499.

36. For details on the "Goal [*sic*] and Goal [*sic*] House," see ibid.; for the jailer, see ibid., pp. 496–499.

37. Ibid.; [Field and Dewey], *History of the County,* p. 103. The cost of the new meetinghouse was $4,833.33. Willard A. Hanna, *The Berkshire-Litchfield Legacy: Litchfield, Ancram, Salisbury, Stockbridge, Lenox* (Rutland, Vt.: C. E. Tuttle Co., 1984), p. 102; Martha J. McNamara, "Disciplining Justice: Massachusetts Courthouses and the Legal Profession, 1750–1850" (Ph.D. diss., Boston University, 1995).

38. Henry Taft, *Massachusetts Eagle,* Sept. 25, 1834, quoted in Birdsall, *Berkshire,* p. 243.

39. Peter T. Mallary, *New England Churches and Meetinghouses, 1630–1830,* photographs by Tim Imrie (New York: Vendome Press, 1985), pp. 126, 127. Barber, *Historical Collections,* p. 89, reports construction of the Richmond meetinghouse in 1794 at a cost of $4,000.

40. Quoted in Mallary, *New England Churches,* p. 127.

41. [Lenox], *The Centennial Anniversary of the Dedication of the Old Church on the Hill, Lenox, Mass., June 12, 1906* (Pittsfield, Mass.: Sun Printing Co., 1908), pp. 15–17.

42. Barber, *Historical Collections,* p. 93; see also Douglas L. Winiarski, "'Pale Blewish Lights' and a Dead Man's Groan: Tales of the Supernatural from Eighteenth-Century Plymouth, Massachusetts," *William and Mary Quarterly,* 3rd ser., 55 (1998): 497–530.

43. Sarah Snell Bryant diary, 1795, Houghton Library, Harvard University, Cambridge, Mass.: Wednesday, June 10: "PM a thunder shower[.] Mr. Fish set out for Gilsom Wilbers hous [*sic*] bewitched"; Sunday, June 14: "clear went to church Mr. Leland preached. Went to Mr. Wilbers to lay the devil at night."

44. [Field and Dewey], *History of the County,* p. 174.

45. *PS,* Aug. 31, 1805, 3:4.

46. Both the *Western Star* (Stockbridge) and the *Pittsfield Sun* included crime stories from time to time. The citations that follow come from the complete run of the *Pittsfield Sun* because for the year 1805 few issues of the *Western Star* survive. Our assessment of the *Western Star* is based on an incomplete run from Jan. 12, 1801, through July 7, 1804, and scattered issues from 1805 and 1806.

47. By the end of the century, Massachusetts had half as many slaves per capita as did Connecticut, and it had abolished slavery earlier. Evidently Massachusetts also had a different history of prosecution for rape. Especially in frontier communities such as Berkshire, that difference may in part have come from a view of patriarchy that included the more active role of the state. Cornelia Hughes Dayton concluded in her chapter "Rape, the Problematics of a Woman's Word": "By the end of the eighteenth century, a consensus had been reached in Connecticut that only black men deserved to die

on the gallows for sexual assault. The few white men convicted of raping children or adult women succeeded in obtaining commuted sentences. . . . After 1700, the only coercive sexual act for which white men were universally punished was father-daughter incest, and such cases occurred too infrequently to offer women much assurance that excessive male violence would be detected and stopped." *Women before the Bar: Gender, Law, and Society in Connecticut, 1639–1789* (Chapel Hill: University of North Carolina Press for the Institute of Early American History and Culture, 1995), pp. 282–283. If Berkshire was unlike Connecticut in that it still brought forward capital rape cases at the turn of the century and beyond, so was Upper Canada, which was also rural and newly settled. There, such cases occurred until the middle of the nineteenth century. As Dayton had noticed in eighteenth-century Connecticut, Patrick O'Connor found in Upper Canada that a preponderance of cases involved young girls. But adult women also sued their assailants, and courts believed them. Moreover, state authorities recognized that women's role in the economy required their protection both within and beyond the household. In 1820, a pardon effort for a convicted rapist failed on the ground that "to protect from similar outrage the Persons and habitations of that numerous class of females whose Occupations retain them alone in their houses the greatest part of their Time, in absence of their Husbands, fathers, and Brothers." In Patrick J. Connor, "'The Law Should Be Her Protector': The Criminal Prosecution of Rape in Upper Canada, 1791–1850," in Merril D. Smith, ed., *Sex Without Consent: Rape and Sexual Coercion in America* (New York: New York University Press, 2001), pp. 103–135, esp. pp. 111, 123–124.

48. *PS*, March 4, 1805, p. 3.

49. Ibid., June 22, 1805, 3:3.

50. Alan Taylor, "'The Unhappy Stephen Arnold': An Episode of Murder and Penitence in the Early Republic," in Ronald Hoffman, Mechal Sobel, and Fredrika Teute, eds., *Through a Glass Darkly: Reflections on Personal Identity in Early America* (Chapel Hill, N.C.: University of North Carolina Press for the Omohundro Institute of Early American History and Culture, 1997), pp. 96–121; *PS*, Aug. 10, 1805, p. 3.

51. *PS,* Apr. 1, 1805, pp. 2–3; Apr. 15, 1805, p. 1.

52. Ibid., May 13, 1805, 2:4.

53. Ibid., May 20, 1805, 1:2–4.

54. Ibid., Aug. 31, 1805, 2:4.

55. Ibid., Aug. 31, 1805, 3:1.

56. Daniel A. Cohen, *Pillars of Salt, Monuments of Grace: New England Crime Literature and the Origins of American Popular Culture* (New York: Oxford University Press, 1993); Karen Halttunen, *Murder Most Foul: The Killer and the American Gothic Imagination* (Cambridge, Mass.: Harvard University Press, 1998); Daniel E. Williams, ed., *Pillars of Salt: An Anthology of Early American Criminal Narratives* (Madison, Wis.: Madison House, 1993).

57. Frederick Calvert, Baron of Baltimore (1731–1771), *The Trial of Frederick Calvert, Esq.; Baron of Baltimore, in the Kingdom of Ireland, for a Rape on the Body of Sarah Woodcock; and of El. Griffinburg, and A. Harvey, otherwise Darby, as Accessaries before the Fact . . . on Saturday, the 26th of March, 1768 . . .* (London [i.e., Boston]: [Mein and Fleeming], 1768).

58. *Cuckold's Chronicle: Being Select Trials for Adultery, Imbecility, Incest, Ravishment, &c,* vol. 1 (Boston: Printed for Those who Choose to Purchase, 1798), pp. iv, v (reprint of Lemoin's London edition of 1793).

59. Nathaniel Price, *The Trial of Nathaniel Price: for Committing a Rape on the Body of Unice Williamson, a Child between 10 and 11 Years of Age, at Brooklyn in King's County, in May 1797 . . .* (New-York: Printed for Elijah Weedg [1797]).

60. *Western Star,* Oct. 31, 1801, 4:2, advertisement for printing by subscription.

61. *Hampshire Gazette* (Northampton), Dec. 4, 1805, 3:3, to Jan. 1, 1806, 4:2; *Richmond Enquirer,* Oct. 8, 1805, 2:2–3.

62. *Newburyport Herald,* Oct. 1, 1805, 3:2, Oct. 11, 1805, 1:1, Oct. 25, 1805, 3:2, Dec. 17, 1805, 3:3, and *passim* to Feb. 4, 1806, 1:2.

63. See Trial Report.

64. Thomas Coffin Amory, *Life of James Sullivan with Selections from His Writings* (Boston, 1859), vol. 2, p. 46. The pastor was Joseph Stevens

Buckminster, the Unitarian pastor of the Brattle Street Church. The pamphlet is in the collection of the Boston Athenæum.

2. THE TRIAL

1. This and all other references to the weather come from Caleb Hyde, Jr.'s "Thermometrical Diary," 1798–1820, Lenox Library Association Collection, Lenox, Mass. The quotation that opens this chapter is from a Sept. 14, 1805, letter of Willard's that was also published in the *Boston Weekly Magazine* (no. 43, p. 191). Female as well as male readers would have been attracted to this page, which also contained foreign and domestic news reports, including a notice of the fifth anniversary of the "Boston Female Assylum [*sic*]" society and two paragraphs, entitled "Celibacy and Marriage" and "The Common Process of Marriage," by "Ollapod," marriage and death announcements, and the city's official list of weekly burials. Though we have consulted over twenty newspapers, we have not conducted a systematic search for copies of this Willard letter. In both cases where it appeared, Willard was identified only by his initials.

2. Ours is a generic description of "court culture" ca. 1790–1830 based on a variety of sources, chiefly Thomas Coffin Amory, *The Life of James Sullivan with Selections from His Writings* (Boston, 1859), vol. 1, pp. 260–262; Henry Taft, *Massachusetts Eagle*, Sept. 25, 1834, quoted in Richard D. Birdsall, *Berkshire County: A Cultural History* (New Haven: Yale University Press, 1959), p. 243.

3. Biographical information on Strong comes from Franklin Bowditch Dexter, *Biographical Sketches of the Graduates of Yale College with Annals of the College History* (New York, 1896), vol. 2 (May 1745–May 1763), pp. 437–439; Clifford K. Shipton, "Simeon Strong," in *Sibley*, vol. 14 (1756–1760) (1968), pp. 93–95; Timothy Dwight, *Travels in New England and New York*, ed. Barbara Miller Solomon (Cambridge, Mass.: Harvard University Press, 1969), vol. 2, pp. 250–252.

4. Richard E. Welch, *Theodore Sedgwick, Federalist: A Political Portrait* (Middletown, Conn.: Wesleyan University Press, 1965), p. 32.

5. The chief biographical source for Sedgwick is Welch, *Theodore Sedg-*

wick, and Welch's two-volume typescript "Theodore Sedgwick (1746–1813): Federalist," at the Stockbridge Library Association, Stockbridge, Mass. Sedgwick's public career is summarized in U.S. Congress, *Biographical Directory of the United States Congress, 1774–1989,* Kathryn Allamong Jacob and Bruce A. Ragsdale, editors-in-chief (Washington, D.C.: U.S. Government Printing Office, 1989), p. 1787. Many of Sedgwick's papers are at the Massachusetts Historical Society, though not his judicial notes. Reminiscences of Sedgwick by his daughter, Catharine, are in *Life and Letters of Catharine M. Sedgwick,* ed. Mary E. Dewey (New York, 1872).

6. Biographical information on Sewall comes from the online *Biographical Directory of the United States Congress, 1774–Present* (1998), *http://bio guide.congress.gov/scripts/biodisplay.pl?index=S000259; Appleton's Cyclopedia of American Biography* (New York, 1888), vol. 5, p. 469; Alden Bradford, *Biographical Notices of Distinguished Men in New England: Statesmen, Patriots, Physicians, Lawyers, Clergymen, and Mechanics* (Boston, 1842), pp. 367–368; Samuel Roads, *The History and Traditions of Marblehead* (Boston, 1880), pp. 135, 206; L. J. Bigelow, *Bench and Bar: A Complete Digest of the Wit, Humor, Asperities, and Amenities of the Law* (New York, 1871), pp. 141–142. See also *Catalogue of the Library of the late Chief Justice Sewall: to be sold at auction Sep. 2, 1814, at the store of Whitwell & Bond* (Cambridge, Mass., 1814); Samuel Sewall and Nathan Dane, *Communication from the Hon. Samuel Sewall, Esq. and the Hon. Nathan Dane, Esq.: accompanied with several bills for the regulation of the State Prison, and an alteration of the criminal laws of the Commonwealth* (Boston, 1805).

7. Shipton, "Simeon Strong," *Sibley,* vol. 14 (1756–1760) (1968), pp. 93–95.

8. Welch, *Theodore Sedgwick,* p. 249n.

9. Catharine Maria Sedgwick, n.p., May 25, 1853, in Dewey, ed., *Catharine Maria Sedgwick,* pp. 25, 26.

10. Ibid., p. 80 (Catharine Sedgwick to Theodore Sedgwick, Stockbridge, April 1, 1804); Samuel Sewall to Theodore Sedgwick, Marblehead, May 4, 1806, Sedgwick Papers I, Theodore Sedgwick, MHS.

11. Bradford, *Biographical Notices,* pp. 367–368; Bigelow, *Bench and Bar,*

pp. 141–142; Roads, *History and Traditions of Marblehead,* pp. 52, 135, 206, 210, 212, 213, 214, 217–218n, 218; Richard E. Welch, Jr., "The Parsons-Sedgwick Feud and the Reform of the Massachusetts Judiciary," *Essex Institute Historical Collections* 92 (April 1956): 172–174; whole article, pp. 171–187.

12. Amory, *Life of James Sullivan,* vol. 1, p. 261n.

13. Ibid., vol. 1, pp. 201–203, vol. 2, pp. 70–80. Sullivan believed that Sedgwick played politics with the execution question, switching from a position of leniency during Governor Bowdoin's tenure to a position of severity after Hancock became governor, so that Hancock would have to bear the odium of executioner.

14. James Sullivan to Theodore Sedgwick, Boston, Sept. 22, 1787, Sedgwick Papers I, Theodore Sedgwick, MHS.

15. Amory, *James Sullivan,* vol. 1, p. 20.

16. Ibid., p. 31.

17. Ibid., p. 26.

18. Ibid., pp. 21–28, 30.

19. Ibid., pp. 33n–34n (letter from John Adams to Abigail Adams, York, Me., June 29, 1774).

20. Ibid., p. 32; Shipton, "James Sullivan," in *Sibley,* vol. 15 (1761–1763) (1970), p. 300.

21. Amory, *James Sullivan,* vol. 1, p. 31.

22. Ibid., p. 381.

23. Ibid., pp. 50–51, 56–58, 78–79, 107–109, 380–381.

24. "Bills Drawn by James Sullivan 1782," Robert Treat Paine Papers, reel 118, MHS.

25. Amory, *James Sullivan,* vol. 1, chaps. 7, 9, 12; vol. 2, p. 323 (judgment of John Quincy Adams on Sullivan's legal practice in his 1809 obituary of Sullivan).

26. Ibid., vol. 1, pp. 267–269, 339, 350, 347.

27. Ibid., vol. 2, p. 62; Shipton, "James Sullivan," *Sibley,* vol. 15 (1761–1763) (1970), p. 317.

28. Amory, *James Sullivan,* vol. 1, pp. 356–360.

29. Ibid., pp. 356–367, 375–376.

30. Ibid., pp. 178–179.

31. Ibid., p. 253.

32. *Independent Chronicle* (Boston), Oct. 19, 1801, p. 3.

33. Amory, *James Sullivan*, vol. 1, pp. 294–295 (we have inverted the last two phrases); SJC, August 1795–February 1797, p. 110, MA.

34. Amory, *James Sullivan*, vol. 1, p. 349; vol. 2, pp. 398–399 (letter to Mehitable Sullivan Cutler, Boston, Mar. 30, 1800).

35. Karen Halttunen, "Humanitarianism and the Pornography of Pain in Anglo-American Culture," *American Historical Review* 100 (April 1995): 303–334; Thomas L. Haskell, "Capitalism and the Origins of Humanitarian Sensibility," *American Historical Review* 90 (April 1985): 339–361.

36. SJC, Berkshire County, Book 2, September Term 1805, MA.

37. William C. McLoughlin, *New England Dissent, 1630–1833: The Baptists and the Separation of Church and State* (Cambridge, Mass.: Harvard University Press, 1971), vol. 1, pp. 657–658; vol. 2, p. 1077.

38. *PS*, Sept. 21, 1805, 3:3; the same encomiums appeared in other Jeffersonian papers, such as the *Independent Chronicle* of Boston, the *National Aegis* (Worcester), the *Eastern Argus* (Portland, Maine), and the *Salem Register.*

39. SJC, Berkshire County, Book 2, September Term 1805, pp. 342–343, MA.

40. Ibid., pp. 312–313.

41. Nancy F. Cott, "Eighteenth-Century Family and Social Life Revealed in Massachusetts Divorce Records," *Journal of Social History* 10 (1976): 20–43.

42. SJC, Berkshire County, Book 2, September Term 1805, pp. 341–342.

43. Ibid.

44. Philip Doddridge (1702–1751), *A Plain and Serious Address to the Master of a Family, on the important subject of Family Religion* (Stockbridge: H. Willard, 1804), p. 15. On distribution of this sermon, see [Congregational Missionary Society], *An Address of the Congregational Missionary Society, in the counties of Berkshire, Columbia, and their vicinities, to the Churches & Congregations. Also a Report of the Trustees. . . .* [September 1804–September 1805] (Stockbridge: H. Willard, 1805), p. 14.

45. Heman Willard, letter, Sept. 14, 1805, in *Boston Weekly Magazine,* Sept. 21, 1805, no. 43, 191:2, and *Richmond (Virginia) Enquirer,* Oct. 8, 1805, 2:2–3.

46. Trial Report, pp. 5–6. The language of the 1753 indictment of Job Wells was almost identical: see *The Trial of Job Wells of Redburn in the County of Hertford, for a Rape committed on the Body of his own Daughter, Maria Wells,. . . .* (London, 1753), pp. 3–4. In October 1804 the Supreme Judicial Court had taken these same actions before accepting the guilty plea of John Battis: Ephraim Williams, *Reports of Cases Argued and Determined in the Supreme Judicial Court, of the State of Massachusetts from September 1804 to June 1805—both inclusive* (Northampton, 1805), pp. 95–96.

47. Trial Report, p. 6; J. M. Beattie, *Crime and the Courts in England, 1660–1800* (Princeton: Princeton University Press, 1986), p. 336; William E. Nelson, *The Americanization of the Common Law: The Impact of Legal Change on Massachusetts Society, 1760–1830* (Cambridge, Mass.: Harvard University Press, 1975), p. 100.

48. Trial Report, p. 6.

49. Alan Rogers, "Murder and Due Process in Colonial Massachusetts," *Supreme Judicial Court Historical Society Journal* 2 (1996): 3; Beattie, *Crime and the Courts,* pp. 356–362; and J. M. Beattie, "Scales of Justice: Defense Counsel and the English Criminal Trial in the Eighteenth and Nineteenth Centuries," *Law and History Review* 9 (1991): 221–267.

50. Trial Report, p. 6.

51. *The Massachusetts Register and United States Calendar, for the year of our Lord 1805 . . . : containing civil, ecclesiastical, judicial, and military lists in Massachusetts. . . .* (Boston, [1804]), p. 108.

52. Biographical information on Hulbert from U.S. Congress, *Biographical Directory of the United States Congress,* p. 1229, and from Hulbert genealogical materials in the Berkshire Atheneum collection in the Pittsfield Public Library. Hulbert was a member of all three "secret" literary societies while at Harvard as a student in the 1790s: Phi Beta Kappa; the Porcellian Club; and the Hasty Pudding, where he served as president. *Catalogue of the Harvard Chapter of Phi Beta Kappa, Alpha of Massachusetts* (Cambridge, Mass.:

Riverside Press, 1896), p. 195; *Porcellian Club Centennial, 1791–1891* (Cambridge, Mass.: Riverside Press, 1912), p. 55; *First Catalogue of the Hasty Pudding Institute of 1770* (n.p., n.d.), p. 28. We are grateful to Leon Jackson for this reference.

53. *History of Berkshire County, Massachusetts, with Biographical Sketches of Its Prominent Men* (New York, 1885), vol. 1, p. 338.

54. SJC, Berkshire County, Book 2, May Term 1802, pp. 66–67, MA.

55. Biographical information on Dewey from U.S. Congress, *Biographical Directory of the United States Congress,* p. 903, and Dewey-Bliss Family Papers, AAS. Dewey's appointment to act as state prosecutor is in SJC, Berkshire County, Book 2, p. 283 (April 1805), MA.

56. *History of Berkshire County,* vol. 1, pp. 335–336.

57. The Trial Report lists the jurors on p. 7. Information on their origins and occupations comes from Berkshire County land, probate, and vital records.

58. The information summarized here was culled from the land and probate registries of Berkshire County in Pittsfield, from the National Archives microfilm edition of the United States Direct Tax of 1798 (Massachusetts and Maine), vital records (both printed and manuscript), as well as the *Massachusetts Register . . . 1805* (Boston, 1804); [David Field and Chester Dewey], *A History of the County of Berkshire, Massachusetts; In Two Parts* (Pittsfield, Mass., 1829); and various local histories.

59. Courtroom description based on "Report of the Committee on the Public Buildings to be Erected in Lenox, Massachusetts in 1787," Records of the Court of General Sessions of the Peace of Berkshire County, New Record, vol. 2, pp. 315ff, 329ff; Old Record, pp. 447ff, 497ff, MA, transcribed in David Oliver Merrill, "Isaac Damon and the Architecture of the Federal Period" (Ph.D. diss., Yale University, 1965), pp. 495–496; Committee Report on alterations to the Berkshire County Courthouse, 1812, Berkshire County Court of General Sessions, file papers, 1812, Massachusetts Archives, Boston (courtesy of Martha J. McNamara); Martha J. McNamara, "Disciplining Justice: Massachusetts Courthouses and the Legal Profession, 1750–1850" (Ph.D. diss., Boston University, 1995); and George H. Tucker, *Berk-*

shire County, Its Shire Towns and Its Court Houses (Pittsfield, Mass., 1918), pp. 4–5.

60. Edward Livingston, "Introductory Report to the Code of Procedure," *Complete Works of Edward Livingston on Criminal Jurisprudence* (New York, 1873), vol. 1, p. 387. First published in 1820 for Louisiana, and quoted in Nelson, *Americanization of the Common Law*, p. 98.

61. The image of Sullivan is from his 1807 portrait by Gilbert Stuart at the MHS. The characterization of his style is based on Amory, *James Sullivan*, vol. 2, pp. 9–12, and on a reading of Sullivan's arguments in the trials of Jason Fairbanks (1801), Dominic Daley and James Halligan (1806), and Thomas O. Selfridge (1806), as well as Wheeler.

62. Trial Report, p. 7.

63. Ibid., pp. 7, 8. The execution of aristocrats as well as common men for sexual crimes had a long history, and Sullivan may well have read of the seventeenth-century Castlehaven case. See Cynthia B. Herrup, *A House in Great Disorder: Sex, Law, and the Second Earl of Castlehaven* (New York: Oxford University Press, 1999). Sullivan erred in stating that eight crimes were punishable by death. Six months earlier the legislature had reduced the penalty for sodomy to life in prison. Sullivan employed a rhetorical formula he had used before, and so overlooked the statutory change.

64. Trial Report, pp. 8–9.

65. Ibid., pp. 10, 11.

66. The *Vital Records of Hinsdale, Massachusetts, to the Year 1850* . . . (Boston: n.p., 1902) records the deaths of two of Hannah Odel Wheeler's married sisters. Only Lucy Odel Martin (p. 86) is listed as "colored": "Martin, Lucy, wid., colored, Jan. 5, 1843, a 75 y. 355 d. Church Rec., [wid. William, Jan. 5, 1842, a 76 Grave Stone]." Her sister Molly, who is *not* identified racially, appears on p. 89: "bo. Sutten, wid. John old age, April 24 [1846], age 88." Hannah Odel's father, Ichabod Odel, was listed in the nonwhite, non-Indian category in the 1790 U.S. census for Windsor and in the same category in the 1800 U.S. census for Cummington, where the word "Negro" was entered next to his name in the manuscript census. We suspect that Isaac Odel, like his father, was recognizably black and that he was probably

counted as black in the 1790 census as part of Ichabod's household. But we cannot be certain because Isaac, who turns up in the land records as a "husbandman," and also in tax and warning-out records, cannot be found as the head of a household in a U.S. census, the chief source of racial identifications in Massachusetts ca. 1790–1810.

67. Trial Report, p. 12.

68. Although there were exceptions, wives were defined as their husbands' subordinates and as having no independent legal existence; hence the prohibition against calling a wife to testify against her husband. According to the widely used authority, the English legal scholar Joseph Chitty, "the only natural relation . . . which the law regards as destroying [a witness's] competency, is that of husband and wife. . . . This relation, from its peculiar nature, as absorbing the legal existence of the woman, is an absolute bar to the admission of any evidence either for or against each other. . . . And parties, thus connected, are not allowed to give any evidence which may even tend to criminate the other." Such testimony was seen to be partial, or likely to cause dissention between spouses. Only a few exceptions to this rule were allowed: when a woman was forcibly married she could testify against her husband, when she was subjected to "violent injuries to her person," or when she made "dying declarations" and her husband was suspected of her murder. Even in cases of high treason a wife's duty to the crown did not supercede her obligation to her husband. Joseph Chitty, *A Practical Treatise on the Criminal Law. . . . With additional notes . . . by Richard Peters, Jr.* [Philadelphia, 1819], vol. 1, pp. 484–485. See also Mary Beth Norton, "The Law of Marital Submission," in *Founding Mothers and Fathers: Gendered Power and the Forming of American Society* (New York: A. A. Knopf, 1996), pp. 83–95.

69. Trial Report, p. 12.

70. Ibid., p. 13.

71. Barbara S. Lindemann, "'To Ravish and Carnally Know': Rape in Eighteenth-Century Massachusetts," *Signs: Journal of Women in Culture and Society* 10 (1984): 63–82; Beattie, *Crime and the Courts,* pp. 125–127. See also note 92 below. Men feared "malicious prosecutions" for rape and accordingly treated rape charges with skepticism.

72. Trial Report, p. 13.

73. Ibid., pp. 13–14.

74. Ibid., p. 14.

75. Ibid. This was precisely the position taken by Chitty, *A Practical Treatise on the Criminal Law,* vol. 2, p. 575.

76. Trial Report, pp. 14–15.

77. Ibid., p. 15.

78. Ibid.

79. Ibid., pp. 15–16.

80. Ibid., p. 16.

81. Ibid.

82. Ibid.

83. Ibid., pp. 16–17.

84. Ibid., p. 17.

85. Ibid.

86. Ibid., p. 18; *PS,* Jan. 18, 1802, 4:2.

87. Trial Report, p. 18.

88. Lindemann, "To Ravish and Carnally Know"; Cornelia Hughes Dayton, "Rape, the Problematics of a Woman's Word," in *Women before the Bar: Gender, Law, and Society in Connecticut, 1639–1789* (Chapel Hill: University of North Carolina Press for the Institute of Early American History and Culture, 1995), pp. 231–284; Beattie, *Crime and the Courts,* pp. 440–449; V. A. C. Gatrell, *The Hanging Tree: Execution and the English People, 1770–1868* (Oxford: Oxford University Press, 1996), pp. 472–491.

89. Trial Report, p. 19.

90. Ibid., p. 20.

91. Ibid.

92. Sir Matthew Hale (1606–1676), *History of Pleas of the Crown, or a Methodical Summary of the Principal Matters Relating to that Subject* (London, 1736 [first pub. 1678]), quoted in Blackstone, *Commentaries,* vol. 4, p. 215, cited in Beattie, *Crime and the Courts,* p. 125.

93. Trial Report, pp. 22, 37–38, 41.

94. Ibid., pp. 23, 24, 27.

95. Ibid., pp. 20–31.

96. Ibid., p. 40.

97. Michael Pepper had married Releaf Odel Dec. 1, 1797, in Cummington. See *Vital Records of Cummington, Massachusetts, 1762–1900,* compiled by William W. Streeter and Daphne H. Morris (Cummington, Mass.: Streeter and Morris, 1979), p. 143. Pepper also appears in the United States Direct Tax of 1798 as better off than Isaac Odel. See National Archives microfilm edition of the 1798 Massachusetts Tax Valuation: "C" list, vol. 20, p. 557, and New England Historic Genealogical Society, *An Index and Guide to the Microfilm Edition of the Massachusetts and Maine Direct Tax Census of 1798,* Michael H. Gorn, ed. (Boston: New England Historic and Genealogical Society, 1979). Pepper, who was from Partridgefield, owned thirty-two acres valued at $87.50, revalued at $78.75. Isaac Odel was cited as the occupant and owner of twenty acres in the same town, valued at $50, readjusted to $45 (ibid., p. 555). Odel is not identified as "Negro," though two Pittsfield men on the same tax list for that town were. Wheeler, who also lived in Partridgefield at the time, did not appear on the tax list. Isaac Odel's rank is from the Hampshire County Land Registry, land records, where he is identified as a husbandman and also as a yeoman. His small tax payments make "husbandman" seem apt: on Jan. 29, 1794, Isaac Odel is listed as paying 1 shilling 9 pence poll tax (William Streeter copy of Tax Record of Cummington).

98. Trial Report, p. 38.

99. Ibid.

100. Ibid., p. 36.

101. Ibid., pp. 36–37, 43, 22.

102. Ibid., p. 43.

103. Ibid., p. 44.

104. Ibid.

105. Henry Campbell Black, *Black's Law Dictionary,* 4th ed. (St. Paul, Minn.: West Publishing Co., 1951), p. 1731, describes a partial verdict: "In criminal law, a verdict by which the jury acquit the defendant as to a part of the accusation and find him guilty as to the residue." See also Joseph Chitty

on criminal procedures. J. S. Cockburn, "Twelve Silly Men? The Trial Jury at Assizes, 1560–1670," in J. S. Cockburn and Thomas A. Green, eds., *Twelve Good Men and True: The Criminal Trial Jury in England, 1200–1800* (Princeton: Princeton University Press, 1988), pp. 171–176, explores the autonomy of juries and their readiness to choose outcomes other than guilty or not guilty of the charge(s) in the indictment.

106. Trial Report, pp. 45, 46, 47.

107. Ibid., pp. 48–50.

108. Ibid., p. 50.

109. Ibid., pp. 50, 37, 38, 52, 53.

110. Ibid., p. 55.

111. Ibid., pp. 55, 56.

112. Ibid., pp. 23, 56, 57.

113. Ibid., pp. 58, 59.

114. Ibid., pp. 60, 61.

115. Ibid., pp. 62, 63.

116. Ibid., p. 64.

117. Ibid., p. 65.

118. Ibid.

119. Ibid., pp. 65, 66.

120. Ibid., pp. 67, 68.

121. Ibid., p. 70.

122. Ibid., p. 71. "Voluntary" and "intercourse" reversed by us.

123. Ibid., p. 73.

124. Ibid., p. 75. We have reversed the order of Sedgwick's phrases.

125. Ibid., p. 76, on Massachusetts law regarding jury proceedings. The restriction regarding food and drink had English origins: see Chitty, *A Practical Treatise on the Criminal Law,* vol. 1, p. 516; Heman Willard, letter, Sept. 14, 1805, in *Boston Weekly Magazine,* Sept. 21, 1805, no. 43, 191:2, and *Richmond (Virginia) Enquirer,* Oct. 8, 1805, 3:2–3.

126. Details of the verdict ceremony are not recorded in the Trial Report; the prescription is given in Chitty, *A Practical Treatise on the Criminal Law,* vol. 1, pp. 518–519, and reported in *The Trial of Stephen Arnold for the*

Murder of Betsy Van Amburgh . . . June 4th, 1805 (Cooperstown, [1805]), pp. 21–22.

127. *Narrative,* p. 5. For the court procedures and language used in Connecticut capital cases, which parallel those of Massachusetts, see Superior Court Records, "Reasons of the Court," Box 47, Connecticut State Library, Hartford, Conn., pp. 2–5. We are grateful to our colleague, Cornelia Hughes Dayton, who supplied us with a copy of this document.

128. Heman Willard, letter, Sept. 14, 1805, in *Boston Weekly Magazine,* Sept. 21, 1805, no. 43, 191:2. Six months prior to sentencing Wheeler, Sewall had coauthored a report reaffirming the death penalty for rape: *Communication from the Hon. Samuel Sewall, Esq.,* pp. 5–7, 36–39.

129. *Connecticut Journal and Advertiser* (New Haven), Oct. 3, 1805.

130. Trial Report, p. 76.

131. Nathaniel Ames, diary entry, Dedham, Aug. 7, 1801, *Diary of Dr. Nathaniel Ames of Dedham, Massachusetts, 1758–1822,* ed. Robert Brand Hanson (Rockport, Me.: Picton Press, 1998), vol. 2, p. 748.

3. THE DAUGHTER

1. All information on local weather is taken from Caleb Hyde, Jr.'s "Thermometrical Diary," 1798–1820, Lenox Library Association Collection, Lenox, Mass.

2. Betsy's inability to write is evident from her "x" mark on the petition of September 26, 1805, GCPNG.

3. *Narrative,* p. 5; *Vital Records of Sutton, Massachusetts, to the end of the year 1849* (Worcester, Mass.: Franklin P. Rice, 1907), p. 124.

4. "Names of persons warned to depart the town by Asa Gurney Constable," 1793, Town of Cummington Records, electrostatic copies owned by William Streeter, Northampton, Mass.; Douglas L. Jones, "The Strolling Poor: Transiency in Eighteenth-Century Massachusetts," *Journal of Social History* 8 (1975): 28–54, and his "Poverty and Vagabondage: The Process of Survival in Eighteenth-Century Massachusetts," *New England Historical and Genealogical Register* 133 (1979): 243–254; Ruth Wallis Herndon, *Unwelcome Americans: Living on the Margin in Early New England* (Philadelphia: University of Pennsylvania Press, 2001).

5. Larned in Rollin H. Cooke, "Pittsfield Families," Berkshire Atheneum, Pittsfield, Mass., vol. 6, pp. 115–117; Hulbert in Berkshire Genealogy, Berkshire Atheneum, Pittsfield, Mass., from Sheffield cemetery inscription.

6. *Narrative,* p. 5, reports the death of the child, but not its name or sex.

7. Laurel Thatcher Ulrich, "Martha Ballard's Girls: Women's Work in Eighteenth-Century Maine," in Stephen Innes, ed., *Work and Labor in Early America* (Chapel Hill: University of North Carolina Press, 1988), pp. 83–86, and her "Housewife and Gadder: Themes of Self-Sufficiency and Community in Eighteenth-Century New England," in Carol Groneman and Mary Beth Norton, eds., *"To Toil the Livelong Day": America's Women at Work, 1780–1980* (Ithaca: Cornell University Press, 1987), pp. 21–34, also her *A Midwife's Tale: The Life of Martha Ballard Based on Her Diary, 1785–1812* (New York: Vintage, 1991).

8. Records in Hampshire County Registry of Deeds, Northampton, Mass., and Berkshire County Registry of Deeds, Pittsfield, Mass. Odel owned this property from 1793 to 1808, when he sold it to his brother-in-law, Robert Percip. Tax record from William Streeter, Cummington Records.

9. *Narrative,* pp. 6, 8.

10. Ibid., p. 6. [U.S. Census], "Population Schedules of the Second Census of the United States, 1800," Microcopy no. 32 (Washington, D.C., 1959), Roll 13 (Massachusetts: Berkshire County), Williamstown, n.p., for Absalom Blair; Probate File 2815, Probate Clerk's Office, Berkshire County Court House, Pittsfield, Mass.; Gloria L. Main, "Naming Children in Early New England," *Journal of Interdisciplinary History* 27 (1996): 1–27.

11. See Gloria L. Main, "An Inquiry into When and Why Women Learned to Write in Colonial New England," *Journal of Social History* 24 (1991): 579–589; E. Jennifer Monaghan, "Literacy Instruction and Gender in Colonial New England," *American Quarterly* 40 (1988): 18–41; William J. Gilmore, "Elementary Literacy on the Eve of the Industrial Revolution: Trends in Rural New England, 1760–1830," *Proceedings of the American Antiquarian Society* 92, pt. 1 (1982): 87–178.

12. *Narrative,* p. 6. There is no record of a deed in Wheeler's name in the Berkshire County Registry of Deeds; hence it is likely that he entered into an unofficial arrangement with a landowner. On May 15, 1797, Wheeler agreed

to clear three acres of timber in June for Adrian Fitch in Worthington in exchange for $15. Wheeler never did the work, and a judgment was entered against him on Nov. 17, 1797, in the Court of Common Pleas for Hampshire County, which met at Northampton, Mass., vol. 24 (1797–98), p. 191. In 1798 Michael Pepper paid tax on a property in Partridgefield (1798 Massachusetts Tax Valuation, vol. 20, p. 557, C list).

13. The population of Partridgefield (Peru) grew 31 percent in the 1790s to peak in 1800 at 1,361 people. It declined by 33 percent between 1800 and 1810, and was down a full 45 percent by 1820, when the township counted only 748 people [David Dudley Field and Chester Dewey], *A History of the County of Berkshire, Massachusetts; in Two Parts* (Pittsfield, 1829), p. 12.

14. *Narrative,* p. 6; George Pierce family in [U.S. Census], "Population Schedules of 1800," Roll 13 (Massachusetts: Berkshire County), Partridgefield, facing p. 189.

15. [Field and Dewey], *History of the County;* Richard D. Birdsall, *Berkshire County: A Cultural History* (New Haven: Yale University Press, 1959), chaps. 1 and 2 (pp. 1–32).

16. [U.S. Census], "Population Schedules of 1800," Roll 15 (Massachusetts: Hampshire County), Cummington, p. 511, reports "Ichabod Odell Negro" and a five-person household in the category for nonwhites and non-Indians. *Vital Records of Hinsdale, Massachusetts, to the Year 1850* (Boston: n.p., 1902), p. 86, "Martin, Lucy, wid., colored, Jan. 5, 1843, a 75 y. 355 d. (Church Rec.)," p. 89 (for Molly Percip). See also "Aftermath," note 34. None of the Wheelers (including Hannah Odel Wheeler) was identified in any record as black, Negro, or colored. Hannah's marriage to Ephraim Wheeler was planned for Worthington, until the local clergyman discovered the racial impediment; Hannah and Ephraim were then married in New Lebanon, New York, by justice Eleazar Grant, who probably assumed they were both white. *Narrative,* p. 5.

17. *Narrative,* p. 6; the death is recorded in *Vital Records of Windsor, Massachusetts, to 1850* (Boston: New England Historic Genealogical Society, 1917), p. 151 (unnamed Wheeler child, 15 months, 1803).

18. The date of birth and the sex of child are pieced together from information in *Narrative,* p. 7, and Trial Report, pp. 16, 17.

19. Joan Jacobs Brumberg, *The Body Project: An Intimate History of American Girls* (New York: Random House, 1997), p. 3 (and p. 218, n. 1), notes that when Susanna Adams, the eleven-year-old granddaughter of Abigail Adams, reached menarche in 1808, her grandmother was shocked. Brumberg goes on to assert (without any clear authority) that "in the early nineteenth century, menarche—first menstruation—typically occurred at fifteen or sixteen." She also reports (pp. 218–219, n. 4) that earlier menstruation linked to improved nutrition in infancy and childhood, and the decline of infectious diseases produced larger, healthier young women who menstruate earlier." We are grateful to Charlotte G. Borst and Robert A. Wells for this reference.

20. Characterization of Wheeler from Trial Report, pp. 15–17, and *Narrative,* p. 8.

21. Trial Report, pp. 13–14.

22. All the towns Betsy lived in were located within ten miles from where she was born, except for Williamstown, about twenty miles distant.

23. [Abigail Abbot Bailey], *Religion and Domestic Violence in Early New England: The Memoirs of Abigail Abbot Bailey,* edited with an introduction by Ann Taves (Bloomington: Indiana University Press, 1989 [first pub. 1815]), pp. 1, 7, 12, 16.

24. Ulrich, *Midwife's Tale,* pp. 117, 115–116.

25. Quoted in: J. M. Beattie, *Crime and the Courts in England, 1660–1800* (Princeton: Princeton University Press, 1986), p. 125.

26. V. A. C. Gatrell, *The Hanging Tree: Execution and the English People, 1770–1868* (Oxford: Oxford University Press, 1996), chap. 7, "The Rape of Elizabeth Cureton: A Microhistory."

27. *Diary of Martha Ballard, 1785–1812,* ed. Robert R. McCausland and Cynthia MacAlman McCausland (Rockport, Me.: Picton Press, 1992), p. 573 (entry for Mar. 29, 1802). Lincoln County Records of the Supreme Judicial Court, vol. 2, Lincoln County Courthouse, Registry of Deeds, Wiscasset, Me.

28. *Boston Weekly Magazine,* Sept. 21, 1805, no. 43, 191:2.

29. Conclusion based on digital searches in Early American Imprints, the American Antiquarian Society online catalog, and the Early English Short

Title Catalogue; *The Trial of Job Wells of Redburn in the County of Hertford, for a Rape committed on the Body of his own Daughter, Maria Wells, . . . August, 1753. . . .* (London, 1753).

30. Records of the SJC, Berkshire County, 1797, 1805, MA. From 1695 onward incest was not a capital crime in Massachusetts because, grouped with blasphemy and witchcraft in a 1692 statute, the Privy Council disallowed it in 1695. The legislature never reinstated capital punishment for incest. Rape, however, was a capital crime in Britain and the colonies.

31. Trial Report, p. 74.

32. Governor Morgan Lewis's argument is discussed in Alan Taylor, "'The Unhappy Stephen Arnold': An Episode of Murder and Penitence in the Early Republic," in Ronald Hoffman, Mechal Sobel, and Fredrika Teute, eds., *Through a Glass Darkly: Reflections on Personal Identity in Early America* (Chapel Hill: University of North Carolina Press for the Omohundro Institute of Early American History and Culture, 1997), p. 116. James Sullivan to Mrs. Cutler (Mehitable Sullivan Cutler), Boston, Mar. 30, 1800, in Thomas Coffin Amory, *The Life of James Sullivan: with Selections from his Writings* (Boston, 1859), vol. 2, pp. 398–399.

33. Philip Greven, *The Protestant Temperament: Patterns of Child-Rearing, Religious Experience, and the Self in Early America* (New York: Knopf, 1977), and his *Spare the Child: The Religious Roots of Punishment and the Psychological Impact of Physical Abuse* (New York: Vintage, 1992).

34. Taylor, "'The Unhappy Stephen Arnold,'" pp. 101–102.

35. Trial Report, p. 13.

36. Ibid., p. 17.

37. Ibid.

38. *Windsor Vital Records,* p. 62 for birthdates of Walker's nine surviving girls and two surviving boys, p. 111 for his marriage to Esther Chaffe on Oct. 30, 1783, and p. 149 for his death, Jan. 4, 1834, at the age of nearly eighty-one years. The widow Esther W[alker?] Convers died May 30, 1805, at age eighty-four. Based on family naming and marriage patterns we believe that Robert Walker was related to her. His daughter, Esther Walker, became the second wife of Amasa Convers, Jr., in 1812. *Windsor Vital Records,* pp. 126–127.

39. Trial Report, pp. 17, 18.

40. Ibid., p. 18.

41. Robert Walker, Justice of the Peace, Bill of Costs, June 10, 1805, *Commonwealth v. Wheeler,* SJC Records, MA.

42. Ibid. and Robert Walker, Justice of the Peace, Recognizance of Betsey Wheelor [*sic*], Ephraim Wheelor [*sic*] Junr Hannah Wheelor [*sic*], June 10, 1805, *Commonwealth v. Wheeler,* SJC Records, MA.

43. For characteristic responses of posttraumatic rape victims, see Karen J. Carlson, Stephanie A. Eisenstadt, and Terra Ziporyn, *The Harvard Guide to Women's Health* (Cambridge, Mass.: Harvard University Press, 1996), pp. 43–55, 495–497; and Judith Lewis Herman and Lisa Hirschman, *Father-Daughter Incest,* rev. ed. (Cambridge, Mass.: Harvard University Press, 2000).

44. [Bailey], *Religion and Domestic Violence,* pp. 175–177.

45. Trial Report, p. 12. For an analysis of modern rape trials and their effect on survivors who testify, see Laura Hengehold, "Remapping the Event: Institutional Discourses and the Trauma of Rape," *Signs: Journal of Women in Culture and Society* 26 (2000): 189–214. Her quote from the work of Linda Alcoff and Laura Gray (p. 194) is germane for understanding Betsy's initial refusal to speak about her father's first assault. While Alcoff and Gray's findings support the notion that a survivor's testimony can be part of the rape victim's recovery from the ordeal, they argue that it can also become coercive. They note, "it may be that survival itself sometimes necessitates a refusal to recount or even a refusal to disclose and deal with the assault or abuse, given the emotional, financial, and physical difficulties that such disclosures can create." Linda Alcoff and Laura Gray, "Survivor Discourse: Transgression or Recuperation?" *Signs: Journal of Women in Culture and Society* 18 (1993): 281.

46. Trial Report, p. 13.

47. According to Edward Westermarck (1862–1939), violation of the incest taboo may be explained by the interruption of the normally close living experiences of siblings as well as parents and children, particularly during "the first two to three years of life," when "sexual aversions" normally develop: Arthur P. Wolf, "Westermarck Redivivus," *Annual Review of Anthro-*

pology 22 (1993): 160, whole article on pp. 157–175. We are grateful to our colleague, Ronald P. Rohner, for this reference.

48. Samuel Stearns, *The American Herbal, or Materia Medica, Wherein, the Virtues of the Mineral, vegetable, and animal productions of North and South America are laid open, so far as they are Known.* . . . (Walpole, N.H., 1801), pp. 52–53, on avens *(Geum urbanum):* "the root is a gentle stypile, corroborant and stomachic. It grows in New England. It strengthens the tone of the viscera, and helps debilities of the system in general." Avens, water *(Geum Rivale),* used by South Americans and Canadians also: "The root is a powerful astringent." According to the compact edition of the *Oxford English Dictionary* (Oxford: Oxford University Press, 1971), vol. 2, p. 1210, stypile, or stypsis, "has a binding effect on the stomach or bowels and arrests hemorrhage." [Field and Dewey], *History of the County,* p. 76, lists *geum rivale,* avens-root, as growing in May in wet marshy areas.

49. [Bailey], *Religion and Domestic Violence,* p. 7.

50. Carlson et al., *Harvard Guide to Women's Health,* pp. 495–496.

51. Reconstructed from Trial Report and *Narrative.*

52. Trial Report, p. 17.

53. Ibid., p. 53.

54. Field and Dewey, *History of the County,* pp. 160–162, 339–340, 454–455, and passim. "The truth shall make you free," John 8:32. On Dorrance, see John L. T. Phillips, "Sketches of the Early Ministers of Windsor," *Berkshire Book: by its Historical and Scientific Society,* vol. 1 (Pittsfield, Mass., 1892), pp. 55–59.

55. Trial Report, pp. 56, 57.

56. Ibid., p. 14. Whiting's property is in Land Registry, Berkshire County Courthouse, Pittsfield, Mass.

57. Petition of Hannah Wheeler, Betsy Wheeler, and Ephraim Wheeler, Jr., Sept. 26, 1805, in GCPNG.

4. THE WIFE AND MOTHER

1. Trial Report, pp. 30, 31, 41; *Narrative,* p. 6.

2. Mary Beth Sievens, "'The Wicked Agency of Others': Community,

Law, and Marital Conflict in Vermont, 1790–1830," *Journal of the Early Republic* 21 (2001): 19–39.

3. Stephen Temple, housewright, and Sarah, divorce case, 1783, SJC Suffolk Files, Case no. 129821, Stephen Temple document dated Winchester [N.H.], June 24, 1772, vol. 795, p. 150, MA; Nancy Cott, "Eighteenth-Century Family and Social Life Revealed in Massachusetts Divorce Records," *Journal of Social History* 10 (1976): 29; Rosemary O'Day, *The Family and Family Relationships, 1500–1900: England, France, and the United States of America* (New York: St. Martin's Press, 1994), p. 164.

4. Temple Divorce Case, 1783, in SJC Suffolk Files, vol. 795, p. 150 for Susannah Wood's deposition of June 23, 1783. Susannah's marriage to John Wood and that of her brother to his sister is in *Vital Records of Upton, Massachusetts, to the end of the year 1849* (Worcester, Mass.: F. P. Rice, 1904), pp. 65, 66, 67, 69; 136, 151. For the adulterous life of Stephen Temple, see Lois or Louisel Bingham [Binaham] and birth of Pliny Bingham, February 1778. *Vital Records of Westborough, Massachusetts, to the end of the year 1849* (Worcester, Mass.: F. P. Rice, 1903), p. 19; Temple's remarriage in 1784 is on p. 136.

5. [Abigail Abbot Bailey], *Religion and Domestic Violence in Early New England: The Memoirs of Abigail Abbot Bailey,* ed. with an intro. by Ann Taves (Bloomington: Indiana University Press, 1989), pp. 36–37. The original edition was published in Boston in 1815 and was edited by Ethan Smith. The title page featured Bailey's connection to New Hampshire and her husband's name and status prominently: *Memoirs of Mrs. Abigail Bailey, who had been the wife of Major Asa Bailey, formerly of Landaff, (N.H.) written by herself.* In 1816 a widely read evangelical periodical recommended this work as "one of the most interesting pieces of religious biography, we ever read. . . . [of an] artful, overbearing, cruel, brutal husband." *Panoplist and Missionary Herald for the Year 1815,* 12 (1816): 125.

6. [Bailey], *Religion and Domestic Violence,* pp. 82–83.

7. Ibid., pp. 171–172, 186, 197n.

8. Ibid., pp. 52, 72n. The hazards of accusing a respectable man of incest are treated in Louise Barnett, *Ungentlemanly Acts: The Army's Notorious In-*

cest Trial (New York: Hill and Wang, 2000), pp. 16–18. In 1879 Captain Andrew Geddes accused fellow officer Louis Henry Orleman of committing incest with his daughter; as a result Geddes, not Orleman, was court-martialed.

9. Laurel Thatcher Ulrich, *A Midwife's Tale: The Life of Martha Ballard, Based on Her Diary, 1785–1812* (New York: Vintage, 1991), on the case of Rebecca Foster, the wife of a clergyman, pp. 115–126.

10. Sharon Block, "Lines of Color, Sex, and Service: Comparative Sexual Coercion in Early America," in Martha Elizabeth Hodes, ed., *Sex, Love, Race: Crossing Boundaries in North American History* (New York: New York University Press, 1999), pp. 141–163; James D. Rice, "Laying Claim to Elizabeth Shoemaker: Family Violence on Baltimore's Waterfront, 1808–1812," in Christine Daniels and Michael Kennedy, eds., *Over the Threshold: Intimate Violence in Early America* (New York: Routledge, 1999), pp. 185–201; and Sean Moore, "Justifiable Provocation: Violence against Women in Essex County, New York, 1799–1860," *Journal of Social History* 35 (2001–2002): 889–918.

11. A fourteen-year-old, Sarah Avery, pursued the case against Joseph Burnham only after she gained the support of an older matron: *Trial of Joseph Burnham* [for Rape], *before the County Court held at Woodstock, in the County of Windsor, June, 1826* (Woodstock, Vt., 1826). The same had been true for Maria Wells in 1753; see *The Trial of Job Wells, of Redburn, in the County of Hertford, for a Rape committed on the Body of his own Daughter, Maria Wells.* . . . (London, 1753), pp. 5–6. See also Sharon Block, "Coerced Sex in British North America" (Ph.D. diss., Princeton University, 1995).

12. Trial Report, p. 61.

13. *Vital Records of Sutton, Massachusetts, to the end of the year 1849* (Worcester, Mass.: Franklin P. Rice, 1907), p. 124. It appears that before 1758 the Odels' two oldest children, Isaac and Releaf, were born, though both births went unrecorded. Starting in 1758 the other Odel births were registered in the town. Population figures from Evarts B. Greene and Virginia D. Harrington, *American Population before the Federal Census of 1790* (Gloucester, Mass.: P. Smith, 1966 [first pub. 1932]), p. 25.

14. William A. Benedict and Hiram A. Tracy, *History of the Town of Sutton, Mass., from 1704 to 1876* (Worcester, 1887), pp. 779, 782; Ichabod Odel, private in John Fry's company, Willard Regiment, Crown Point campaign, July 21, 1755–Dec. 12, 1755, and other campaigns: K. David Goss and David Zarowin, eds., *Massachusetts Officers and Soldiers in the French and Indian Wars, 1755–1756* ([Boston, Mass.]: Society of Colonial Wars in the Commonwealth of Massachusetts, New England Historic Genealogical Society, 1985), p. 66. Ichabod Odel of Sutton was a private in Captain Isaac Bolster's company, in Colonel Ebenezer Larned's regiment. He enlisted June 1, 1775, and appears on a muster roll Aug. 1, 1775, and on the company return, Roxbury, Oct. 1, 1775, serving altogether two months and five days. Massachusetts, Secretary of the Commonwealth, *Massachusetts Soldiers and Sailors of the Revolutionary War* (Boston: Wright and Potter Printing Co., 1896–1908), vol. 11, p. 621.

15. Daniel R. Mandell, "The Saga of Sarah Muckamugg: Indian and African American Intermarriage in Colonial New England," in Hodes, ed., *Sex, Love, Race*, pp. 72–73; also Mandell, "Shifting Boundaries of Race and Ethnicity: Indian-Black Intermarriage in Southern New England, 1760–1880," *Journal of American History* 85 (1998): 472–473. Mandell points out (472) that Irish servant women sometimes became the mates of black men, Indians, or mixed-race men. (Sutton and surrounding area had some Irish migration in the middle of the century.) *Worcester County, Massachusetts, Warnings, 1737–1788*, with an introduction by Francis E. Blake (Camden, Me.: Picton Press, 1992 [first ed. 1899]), pp. 35, 91; Ann Marie Plane, *Colonial Intimacies: Indian Marriage in Early New England* (Ithaca, N.Y.: Cornell University Press, 2000).

16. Sutton town and church records, Sutton, Mass. Admittedly these records are not so complete as to make our assertions conclusive. Analysis of data in Benedict and Tracy, *History of . . . Sutton,* and in *Worcester County, Massachusetts, Warnings* suggests a pattern of economic stress. Sutton people were being warned out in other towns, while Sutton also warned out people often identified as poor. Those from Sutton ordered to leave other communities in the 1750s included 3 individuals plus a family; in the 1760s,

58 individuals plus 2 families with unspecified numbers of children; in the 1770s, 23 individuals and 1 family; and in the 1780s, 8 individuals. An additional sign of pressure is the high number of warnings-out in Sutton itself between 1744 and 1767, the years that figures are available. In the 1740s 8 individuals, including 3 children, were on the list. In the 1750s at least 83 persons were warned out, including 15 families and 34 children. Between 1760 and 1767 138 persons (98 adults, 42 children) were warned out, including 29 family groups. We conclude that the 1760s, the decade when Hannah was born, was a period of significant mobility in and out of Sutton; but the Odel family persisted and so was probably not at the bottom of the social order.

17. Isaac Odel made his mark on the sale of his property, April 16, 1808. Hampshire County Land Registry, Northampton, Mass., Book of Deeds, p. 311. For Elizabeth (Odel) Dunbar's mark on a property transaction dated March 3, 1791, see Hampshire County Land Registry, Northampton, Mass., Record Book no. 2, p. 701.

18. Jack Larkin, *The Reshaping of Everyday Life, 1790–1840* (New York: Harper and Row, 1988), pp. 109–115, 121–130.

19. Ibid., pp. 124–125; on the persistence of sharing beds see Christopher Clark, ed., "The Diary of an Apprentice Cabinetmaker: Edward Jenner Carpenter's 'Journal,' 1844–45," *Proceedings of the American Antiquarian Society* 98, pt. 2 (1989): 303–394.

20. See Gloria L. Main, "Naming Children in Early New England," *Journal of Interdisciplinary History* 27 (1996): 1–27.

21. Although Hannah could sign her name in 1805, her older sister Elizabeth could not. On a deed recording the sale of property in 1791, Elizabeth made her mark, whereas her husband, Asa Dunbar, signed. Record Book no. 2, p. 701 (February 22, 1791).

22. Sutton church records: 1718–1857, 1743–1845, 1743–1767, 1744–1784, 1746–1815, microfilm at AAS; and David Hall, diaries, 1740–1789, MHS.

23. *Narrative*, p. 5.

24. "Names of persons warned to depart the town by Asa Gurney Constable," 1793 [Town of Cummington], William Streeter, Northampton, Mass., copy. Other property holders were also warned out at this time.

25. For births of six of the eight Odel children, see *Vital Records of Sutton*, p. 124. For the marriage of Elizabeth (b. 1759) to Asa Dunbar in 1784, see p. 322; also listed in William W. Streeter and Daphne H. Morris, *Vital Records of Cummington, Massachusetts, 1762–1900* (Cummington, Mass.: Streeter, 1979), p. 113. Four other marriages of Odel sisters were recorded in Cummington: Lydia (b. 1764) to Joshua Dunbar in 1788 (p. 113); Molly (b. 1758) to John Persip in 1793 (p. 143); Lucy (b. 1766) to William Martin in 1796 (p. 133); and Releaf Archaelis (b. ?) to Michael Pepper (p. 143). For Releaf's birth, see note 13 above. In 1791 Hannah (b. 1763) was the third to marry, but she and Ephraim went to New Lebanon, New York. *Narrative*, p. 15.

26. For typical marriage age in their era, and the diminishing importance of birth order for sisters marrying, see Daniel Scott Smith, "Parental Power and Marriage Patterns: An Analysis of Historical Trends in Hingham, Mass.," in Michael Gordon, ed., *The American Family in Social-Historical Perspective*, 3rd ed. (New York: St. Martin's Press, 1983), pp. 260–264. Robert A. Wells, *Population of the British Colonies in America before 1776: A Survey of Census Data* (Princeton: Princeton University Press, 1975).

27. See note 25.

28. Hannah and Ephraim separated briefly in February 1805, seemingly owing to the last illness of their employer, the Widow Converse. Randolph Roth suggests that male dependence on wives may have moderated male violence in northern New England after the Revolution. See Randolph A. Roth, "Spousal Murder in Northern New England, 1776–1865," in Daniels and Kennedy, eds., *Over the Threshold*, p. 78.

29. Sievens, "'The Wicked Agency of Others.'"

30. Ibid., p. 30, quoting *Vermont Journal*, July 17, 1798.

31. *Narrative*, pp. 6, 8.

32. Ibid., p. 6.

33. Ibid., p. 7.

34. Ibid.

35. Ibid.

36. Trial Report, p. 17.

37. Ibid.; *Narrative*, p. 7.

38. Trial Report, p. 17; *Narrative,* p. 7. A day's pay was roughly $1.00.

39. Trial Report, p. 17.

40. *Narrative,* p. 7.

41. Trial Report, pp. 59, 62.

42. Responses of wives married to violent husbands and mothers of incest victims are treated in Christine A. Dietz and John L. Craft, "Family Dynamics of Incest: A New Perspective," *Social Casework: the Journal of Contemporary Social Work* 61 (1980): 602–609; Jarris Tyler Johnson, *Mothers of Incest Survivors: Another Side of the Story* (Bloomington: Indiana University Press, 1992), esp. chap. 5, "The Mothers Respond," pp. 50–75. See also E. Sue Blume, *Secret Survivors: Uncovering Incest and Its Aftereffects in Women* (New York: John Wiley, 1990); Karin C. Meiselman, *Incest: A Psychological Study of Causes and Effects with Treatment Recommendations* (San Franscisco: Jossey-Bass, 1979), and her *Resolving the Trauma of Incest: Reintegration Therapy with Survivors* (San Francisco: Jossey-Bass, 1990). For other works on family violence, incest, and family therapy, see pp. 47–48, nn128–131, 138–139, in Ann Taves's commentary on [Bailey], *Religion and Domestic Violence.* The last twenty years of research and treatments on incest are reviewed in the afterword to the most recent edition of Judith Lewis Herman with Lisa Hirschman, *Father-Daughter Incest* (Cambridge, Mass.: Harvard University Press, 2000). We thank Stephen A. Anderson, Preston Britner, James O'Neil, and Ronald Rohner in the School of Family Studies at the University of Connecticut for their helpful suggestions on these topics. See also note 57 below.

43. Trial Report, p. 17.

44. Ibid.

45. Ibid., p. 18.

46. Bill of Costs, June 10, 1805, *Commonwealth v. Wheeler,* SJC, Berkshire County, MA.

47. Sarah Snell Bryant diary, Cummington, June 9, 1805, Houghton Library, Harvard University.

48. The next day, Monday, June 10, 1805, Martin collaborated in the prosecution by accepting bond for the appearance of Hannah, Betsy, and

Ephraim, Jr., to testify. Recognizance, June 10, 1805, *Commonwealth v. Wheeler*, SJC, Berkshire County, MA.

49. Bill of Costs, June 10, 1805, *Commonwealth v. Wheeler*, SJC, Berkshire County, MA; *Narrative*, p. 7.

50. Recognizance, June 10, 1805, SJC, Berkshire County, MA. In an 1829 English rape case the adult victim was given a physical examination two days after the assault, and the defendant was convicted. See V. A. C. Gatrell, *The Hanging Tree: Execution and the English People, 1770–1868* (Oxford: Oxford University Press, 1996), p. 468.

51. Sarah Snell Bryant diary, June 8–11, 1805, Houghton Library, Harvard University.

52. James Sullivan in Trial Report, p. 57.

53. Ibid., p. 38.

54. Ibid.

55. Petition of Hannah Wheeler, Betsy Wheeler, and Ephraim Wheeler, Jr., Sept. 26, 1805, in GCPNG.

56. *Narrative*, p. 6.

57. It is noteworthy that Hannah could sign her name while her white husband could not. One factor contributing to conflict in a violent marriage appears to be a wife who is more educated than her husband: Stephen A. Anderson and Margaret C. Schlossberg, "Systems Perspectives on Battering," in Michèle Harway and James M. O'Neil, eds., *What Causes Men's Violence against Women* (Thousand Oaks, Calif.: Sage Publications, 1999), p. 145; and G. T. Hotaling and D. B. Sugarman, "A Risk Marker Analysis of Assaulted Wives," *Journal of Family Violence* 5 (1990): 1–13. Hannah's ability to write her name was rare among women of color. Ruth Herndon's work on surviving warning-out records in Rhode Island, 1750–1800, identified over 500 heads of transient households, including 79 women of color. Of those, only 6.3 percent could sign their name, in contrast to the 28.5 percent of the white women and 77 percent of the white men. Male household heads of color were more than three times as likely (20.8 percent) to be able to sign than were the women of color. Ruth Wallis Herndon, *Unwelcome Americans: Living on the Margin in Early New England* (Philadelphia: University of

Pennsylvania Press, 2001), Appendix A1, p. 206. Since Herndon estimates that half of the individuals warned out in Rhode Island in the period 1750–1800 were born in either Massachusetts or Connecticut, her study has significance for all of New England.

5. THE CONDEMNED MAN

1. *Narrative*, pp. 3–12.

2. Ibid., p. 10.

3. Ibid., p. 3.

4. Daniel A. Cohen, *Pillars of Salt, Monuments of Grace: New England Crime Literature and the Origins of American Popular Culture, 1674–1860* (New York: Oxford University Press, 1993), chaps. 1, 4; Karen Halttunen, *Murder Most Foul: The Killer and the American Gothic Imagination* (Cambridge, Mass.: Harvard University Press, 1998), chap. 1; Lincoln B. Faller, *Turned to Account: The Forms and Functions of Criminal Biography in Late Seventeenth- and Early Eighteenth-Century England* (Cambridge: Cambridge University Press, 1987); *Narrative*, p. 12.

5. *Narrative*, p. 1 (title page).

6. Ibid., p. 3.

7. *Vital Records of Rochester, Massachusetts to the Year 1850*, vol. 1 (Births) (Boston: New England Historic Genealogical Society, 1914), p. 3 (on population for 1765, 1776, 1790, 1800: no boundary changes during these decades). *Vital Records of Mattapoisett and Old Rochester, Massachusetts, Being a History of These Towns and also a part of Marion and a portion of Wareham* ([Mattapoisett, Mass.:] Mattapoisett Improvement Assoc., 1932); Daniel Vickers, *Farmers and Fishermen: Two Centuries of Work in Essex County, Massachusetts, 1630–1850* (Chapel Hill: University of North Carolina Press for the Institute of Early American History and Culture, 1994), chaps. 4 and 5.

8. *Narrative*, p. 3; Vickers, *Farmers and Fishermen*, pp. 171–186; Evarts B. Greene and Virginia D. Harrington, *American Population before the Federal Census of 1790* (Gloucester, Mass.: P. Smith, 1966 [first pub. 1932]), p. 28, shows 1.2 families per house in Rochester in 1765.

9. E. Jennifer Monaghan, "Literacy Instruction and Gender in Colonial New England," *American Quarterly* 40 (1988): 18–41; Gloria L. Main, "An Inquiry into When and Why Women Learned to Write in Colonial New England," *Journal of Social History* 24 (1991): 579–589; Kenneth Lockridge, *Literacy in Colonial New England: An Inquiry into the Social Context of Literacy in the Early Modern West* (New York: Norton, 1974).

10. *Narrative*, p. 3.

11. Barry Levy, "Girls and Boys: Poor Children and the Labor Market in Colonial Massachusetts," *Pennsylvania History* 64 (1997): 287–307.

12. *Narrative*, p. 3.

13. Rochester Town Records, Rochester, Mass., Record Book no. 3, pp. 101–104. In 1773 the town meeting voted to use part of the old meeting-house as a workhouse; however, the town did not supply provisions, tools, and a master so as to make the workhouse operable until 1781. It lasted until 1792 (*Vital Records of Mattapoisett and Old Rochester*, p. 144).

14. *Vital Records of Mattapoisett and Old Rochester*, pp. 363 (Mary, wife of Jeduthan), 368–369 (member of Second Church in Rochester); Levy, "Girls and Boys."

15. *Adrian Fitch v. Ephraim Wheeler*, Nov. 17, 1797, Hampshire County Court of Common Pleas, Hampshire County Courthouse, Northampton, Mass., vol. 24 (1797–98), p. 191.

16. *Narrative*, p. 3.

17. Ibid.; Trial Report, pp. 17, 42, 64, 72–73, 75.

18. *Narrative*, p. 3.

19. Ibid. Why he chose this unusual surname we can only conjecture. He may have selected it to avoid questions about relatives and connections. He may also have intended a private joke involving canine speech.

20. *Narrative*, p. 3. Contemporaries would have viewed Wheeler's story of childhood and youth as sad, but commonplace, as suggested by the biographical sketch of Orrin Webber, an 1802 Brimfield, Massachusetts, native who landed in the state prison in the 1820s. Like Wheeler, Webber was bound out at an early age, abused by his master, ran away repeatedly, and remained uneducated. Jared Curtis, *Buried from the World: Inside the Massa-*

chusetts State Prison, 1829–1831, the Memorandum Books of the Rev. Jared Curtis, ed. and with an intro. by Philip Gura (Boston: Massachusetts Historical Society, 2001), pp. 33–34.

21. W. Jeffrey Bolster, *Black Jacks: African American Seamen in the Age of Sail* (Cambridge, Mass.: Harvard University Press, 1997), pp. 26–38, 188, 235, table 1; Elaine Forman Crane, *Ebb Tide in New England: Women, Seaports, and Social Change, 1639–1800* (Boston: Northeastern University Press, 1998); James Oliver Horton and Lois E. Horton, *In Hope of Liberty: Culture, Community, and Protest among Northern Free Blacks, 1700–1860* (New York: Oxford University Press, 1997), pp. 38–39, 70–72; Daniel R. Mandell, *Behind the Frontier: Indians in Eighteenth-Century Eastern Massachusetts* (Lincoln: University of Nebraska Press, 1996), pp. 172–190.

22. In September 1805 Wheeler's lawyers, John W. Hulbert and Daniel Dewey, described the forty-three-year-old Wheeler as "a healthy robust man, of between thirty and forty years of age." Petition of Sept. 24, 1805, in GCPNG.

23. *Narrative*, p. 4.

24. [Venture Smith], *A Narrative of the Life and Adventures of Venture, a Native of Africa, but resident above sixty years in the United States of America* (New London, 1798), p. 9, describes a slave successfully complaining to a justice of the peace in mid-eighteenth-century Connecticut.

25. *Narrative*, p. 4.

26. Ibid.

27. Ibid.

28. Ibid.

29. Ibid., p. 3; Vickers, *Farmers and Fishermen*, pp. 258–259, and his "Competency and Competition: Economic Culture in Early America," *William and Mary Quarterly*, 3d ser., 47 (1990): 3–29.

30. *Narrative*, p. 4.

31. Ibid., pp. 3, 10–11. At the time of Wheeler's incarceration he reportedly said that his sister was living in Fabius, New York. He also claimed an aunt and uncle (Haskin) in Cambridge, New York, to whom he tried to flee when he briefly escaped from Lenox jail.

32. Ibid., p. 4.

33. Ibid. A search of the vital records of the towns of Bristol and Plymouth counties revealed no one named "Susanna Randal" or variant spellings; the Randal (or Randall, or Randol) name appears in *Vital Records of Rochester*, vol. 2, pp. 183–184; also Rochester Town Records, Record Book 3, pp. 101, 104, 198, 200v, 201, 205v.

34. British and American writers developed the "man of feeling" idea ca. 1750–1830. Samuel Richardson and Laurence Sterne popularized the ideal of a man who combined reason and emotion, moral courage and refined sensibility. Henry Mackenzie's *The Man of Feeling* (London, 1770), like the works of Sterne and Richardson, was widely read on both sides of the Atlantic and helped create a literary cliché of emotional masculine sensibility that became the subject of satire by the 1820s. Because the "man of feeling" had originally been a gentleman, it is striking that in 1806 the lowly Ephraim Wheeler would express this identity in his *Narrative*. G. J. Barker-Benfield, *The Culture of Sensibility: Sex and Society in Eighteenth-Century Britain* (Chicago: University of Chicago Press, 1992); Andrew Burstein, *Sentimental Democracy: The Evolution of America's Self-Image* (New York: Hill and Wang, 1999); John Mullan, *Sentiment and Sociability: The Language of Feeling in the Eighteenth Century* (Oxford: Oxford University Press, 1988).

35. *Narrative*, p. 4. On courtship ideals and the novels of the era, see Ellen Rothman, *Hands and Hearts: A History of Courtship in America* (New York: Basic Books, 1984); Karen Lystra, *Searching the Heart: Women, Men, and Romantic Love in Nineteenth-Century America* (New York: Oxford University Press, 1989); Hanna W. Foster, *The Coquette*, edited and with an introduction by Cathy N. Davidson (New York: Oxford University Press, 1986); Susanna Rowson, *Charlotte Temple*, edited and with an introduction by Cathy N. Davidson (New York: Oxford University Press, 1986).

36. *Narrative*, p. 4. The dark day was May 19, 1780, and the darkness was actually caused by smoke from a distant forest fire; see David Ludlum, *The Country Journal New England Weather Book* (Boston: Houghton Mifflin, 1976), p. 21. On Elder Hunt and Wheeler's religion, see William G. McLoughlin, *New England Dissent, 1630–1833: The Baptists and the Separa-*

tion of Church and State (Cambridge, Mass.: Harvard University Press, 1971), vol. 1, p. 595; vol. 2, pp. 761–762, 764; *Narrative,* p. 8.

37. *Narrative,* pp. 4–5.

38. Ibid., p. 5.

39. Richard D. Brown, "Regional Culture in a Revolutionary Era: The Connecticut Valley, 1760–1820," in Gerald W. R. Ward and William N. Hosley, Jr., eds., *The Great River: Art and Society of the Connecticut Valley, 1635–1820* (Hartford, Conn.: Wadsworth Atheneum, 1985), pp. 41–48.

40. David P. Szatmary, *Shays' Rebellion: The Making of an Agrarian Insurrection* (Amherst: University of Massachusetts Press, 1980), pp. 101–102; Leonard L. Richards, *Shays's Rebellion: The American Revolution's Final Battle* (Philadelphia: University of Pennsylvania Press, 2002).

41. *Narrative,* p. 5; Szatmary, *Shays' Rebellion,* pp. 104–105.

42. *Narrative,* p. 5.

43. Ibid. The Rochester town records include Randals, and they are connected to Saratoga Springs, New York.

44. Ibid., pp. 5, 8.

45. Ibid., p. 5.

46. Ibid. For Odel genealogy and race see chap. 4, notes 13, 14, 24, 25.

47. Samuel Freeman, *The Massachusetts Justice: Being a Collection of the Laws of the Commonwealth of Massachusetts, relative to the Power and Duty of Justices of the Peace* (Boston, 1802), pp. 239–242, provision on race, p. 242.

48. Quasi-official records kept, often irregularly, by clergymen did refer to race, as did some town records.

49. Timothy Mather Cooley, *Sketches of the Life and Character of the Rev. Lemuel Haynes, A.M.* (New York, 1837), chaps. 5, 14; Richard D. Brown, "'Not Only Extreme Poverty, but the Worst Kind of Orphanage': Lemuel Haynes and the Boundaries of Racial Tolerance on the Yankee Frontier, 1770–1820," *New England Quarterly* 61 (1988): 502–518; Joanne Pope Melish, *Disowning Slavery: Gradual Emancipation and "Race" in New England, 1780–1860* (Ithaca: Cornell University Press, 1998), pp. 1–3, 38–40, and passim; Daniel R. Mandell, "Shifting Boundaries of Race and Ethnicity:

Indian-Black Intermarriage in Southern New England, 1760–1850," *Journal of American History* 85 (1998): 466–501.

50. *Narrative*, p. 5.

51. Ibid.

52. Ibid.; Franklin Ellis, *History of Columbia County, New York* (Philadelphia, 1878), p. 321.

53. Record Book no. 2, Hampshire County Registry of Deeds, Northampton, Mass., p. 655, describes Asa Dunbar of Plainfield as a yeoman on Sept. 7, 1790, when he sold ninety acres of land in Plainfield to Ebenezer Parsons of Goshen for £29 (copy of deed registered Nov. 19, 1790). On Feb. 22, 1791, he is identified as a "husbandman" when he sold a "certain Farm or Track of Land in Plainfield" to Edmund Lazell of Cummington for £260 (p. 701). The registrar recorded: "Asa Dunbar & Seal Elisabeth Dunbar & Seal her Mark," on March 3, 1791; Hannah's sister could not sign her name. Evidence that Elizabeth and Hannah's father, Ichabod, had a house in Worthington is from *Narrative*, p. 5, when Wheeler wrote that around the time of his marriage Hannah's "goods were moved to her Father's house in Worthington."

54. *Narrative*, p. 5. Separations were not so unusual: see Hendrik Hartog, *Man and Wife in America: A History* (Cambridge, Mass.: Harvard University Press, 2000), pp. 30–39, 83.

55. *Narrative*, pp. 5, 8.

56. See, for example, the divorce granted to Martha Molloy of Hallowell, Maine, in 1801, on grounds of desertion and adultery. Laurel Thatcher Ulrich, *A Midwife's Tale: The Life of Martha Ballard, Based on Her Diary, 1785–1812* (New York: Vintage Books, 1991), pp. 200–201. The three Books for the Supreme Judicial Court, meeting at Lenox, 1797–1814, include seventeen divorce petitions by women that resulted in divorce, and a total of twenty-four petitions, nearly two-thirds initiated by women. One case was not settled and involved countersuits between a husband and wife. Five husbands initiated the remaining cases. Adultery was usually the ground of divorce, often also involving desertion and sometimes a subsequent marriage. The divorce for Bethea Nelson of Stockbridge against her husband, a

butcher, was granted on the grounds of extreme cruelty; their marriage began in 1789—two years before Hannah married Ephraim—and ended in 1812. Both short and long marriages ended in divorce. See Mary Beth Sievens, "'The Wicked Agency of Others': Community, Law, and Marital Conflict in Vermont, 1790–1830," *Journal of the Early Republic* 21 (2001): 19–39.

57. *Narrative*, pp. 5, 6.

58. Ibid., p. 6; Hampshire County Land Registry, Book of Deeds, vol. 10, p. 242, Aug. 6, 1794, purchase of four acres in the southwest corner of Cummington by Isaac Odel, "yeoman," for £20. Odel sold this piece, which included a "dwelling house," on Apr. 16, 1808, for $200. Odel certified the contract with his mark, not a signature (Book of Deeds, vol. 36, p. 311).

59. *Narrative*, p. 6. The records of Cummington are full of the Odels and their various marriages to blacks, including Asa Dunbar, Joshua Dunbar, William Martin, Michael Pepper, John Persip, and James Smith. The same records also mention a Sally Peters, possibly a relative of Samuel Peters. This information courtesy of Arvilla L. Dyer, taken from William W. Streeter and Daphne H. Morris, *The Vital Records of Cummington* (Cummington, Mass.: Streeter, 1979).

60. *Narrative*, p. 6; Court of General Sessions of the Peace, County of Berkshire, Lenox, vol. 1, p. 253. As for the approximate amount of the fine, it may have been similar to that of Peter Tufts of Windsor, who, at the court session of Sept. 11, 1797, was fined $3 for each of several assaults.

61. Ephraim, Jr., born Oct. 3, 1796. Trial Report, p. 14.

62. *Narrative*, p. 6.

63. Ibid.

64. Ibid.

65. [David Dudley Field and Chester Dewey], *A History of the County of Berkshire, Massachusetts; in Two Parts* (Pittsfield, 1829), pp. 12 (population statistics), 443–445 (description of Partridgefield, whose name was changed to Peru in 1806).

66. *Adrian Fitch v. Ephraim Wheeler*, Nov. 17, 1797, Hampshire County Court of Common Pleas, vol. 24 (1797–1798), p. 191, located in Northampton, Mass.

67. Beulah Prince, like Hannah a mother of color, did domestic work for Ballard. Ulrich, *Midwife's Tale,* pp. 165, 206, 218, 222, 225, 393.

68. *Adrian Fitch v. Ephraim Wheeler,* Nov. 17, 1797, Hampshire County Court of Common Pleas, vol. 24 (1797–1798), p. 191, located in Northampton, Mass.

69. *Narrative,* pp. 6, 8.

70. Ibid., p. 6.

71. Ibid.

72. Ibid., p. 5.

73. Ibid., p. 6.

74. Ibid.

75. Ibid., p. 7.

76. Ibid. Such an admonition for good behavior was standard, although there is no record of it in this and many other cases. Robert Walker's records as justice of the peace do not survive so far as we know. For his kinship to the Converse family, see chap. 3, note 38.

77. Avens-root, or purple avens *(geum rivale)* is common in the Northeast. Also called "Indian chocolate," because a drink was made from the boiled root, sugar, and milk. James Sullivan, early in the trial, described it as "a vegetable substance, used by some people there, in the place of chocolate" (Trial Report, p. 11). The root was used medicinally to treat dysentery, upset stomach, and uterine bleeding. John E. Klimas and James A. Cunningham, *Wildflowers of Eastern America* (New York: Alfred A. Knopf, 1974), p. 126 and no. 270. See also chap. 3, note 48. Medicinal qualities of this plant discussed in Samuel Stearns, *The American Herbal, or Materia Medica, Wherein, the Virtues of the Mineral, vegetable, and animal productions of North and South America are laid open, so far as they are Known.* . . . (Walpole, N.H., 1801).

78. *Narrative,* p. 7.

79. *Connecticut Gazette* (New London), Feb. 26, 1806, 3:3.

80. *Narrative,* p. 8; the likely clergy were Samuel Shepard (Lenox), Oliver Ayer (West Stockbridge), Stephen West (Stockbridge), Alvan Hyde (Lee), and possibly Gordon Dorrance of Windsor, who was among those who had petitioned to spare Ephraim's life.

81. Ibid.

82. Ibid.

83. Ibid., pp. 7–8.

84. Ibid., p. 7.

85. Ibid., pp. 7–8.

86. Ibid., pp. 8–9.

87. Ibid., p. 6.

88. Ibid., p. 5.

89. Ibid.

90. Daniel A. Cohen, "Homicidal Compulsion and the Conditions of Freedom: The Social and Psychological Origins of Familicide in America's Early Republic," *Journal of Social History* 28 (1995): 725–764.

6. THE FINAL JUDGMENT

1. GCPNG.

2. William Cheney, executed at Boston in 1681 for rape. Cotton Mather reported that the authorities approved a reprieve for Cheney, but withheld it because the unrepentant convict refused to listen to his execution sermon (Hearn, p. 54). Barbara S. Lindemann, "'To Ravish and Carnally Know': Rape in Eighteenth-Century Massachusetts," *Signs: Journal of Women in Culture and Society* 10 (1984): 77, reports five rape cases in the years 1780–1799, with no convictions. Examination of the Records of the Governor's Council, the body that set the dates for execution, indicates no executions for rape in the years 1800 through 1805. Jack Battus, a black youth who murdered his rape victim, was executed for murder in 1804.

3. Trial Report, pp. 49, 50.

4. Joshua Corlis was convicted May 16, 1798, for the murder of his wife; but the judges continued the case for sentencing and recommended a pardon to the governor because "they had strong doubts of the sanity" of Corlis. GCP, July 3, 1798.

5. The cases of John Farrell, Jacob Azzett Lewis, Lemuel Deming, and Deborah Stevens are discussed later in this chapter. Samuel Smith, a repeat

offender, was executed. *Last Words and Dying Speech of Samuel Smith, Who was Executed at Concord, in the County of Middlesex, and Commonwealth of Massachusetts, the 26th of December, A.D. 1799, for the Crime of Burglary* (Boston, 1799), broadside, AAS.

6. J. M. Beattie, *Crime and the Courts in England, 1660–1800* (Princeton: Princeton University Press, 1986), pp. 556–557. See also Stuart Banner, *The Death Penalty: An American History* (Cambridge, Mass.: Harvard University Press, 2002), chap. 3. The first edition of Beccaria in the United States appeared in South Carolina in 1777, followed in Philadelphia in 1778 and 1793.

7. Bradley Chapin, "Felony Law Reform in the Early Republic," *Pennsylvania Magazine of History and Biography* 113 (1989): 167.

8. Louis P. Masur, *Rites of Execution: Capital Punishment and the Transformation of American Culture, 1776–1865* (New York: Oxford University Press, 1989), pp. 62–63, 65.

9. Joel Barlow, *A Letter to the National Convention of France on the Defects in the Constitution of 1791* (New York, 1792), in Charles S. Hyneman and Donald S. Lutz, eds., *American Political Writing during the Founding Era, 1760–1815* (Indianapolis: Liberty Press, 1983), vol. 2, pp. 833–834.

10. William Bradford, *An Enquiry How Far the Punishment of Death is Necessary in Pennsylvania* (Philadelphia, 1793), pp. 29, 31, 35, 65; Masur, *Rites of Execution,* pp. 61–62.

11. Gen. 9:6, King James version.

12. Chapin, "Felony Law Reform," p. 182.

13. Ibid., p. 180.

14. Kathryn Preyer, "Crime, the Criminal Law and Reform in Post-Revolutionary Virginia," *Law and History Review* 1 (1983): 58, 60, 62, 68–70, 76–77.

15. Marybeth Hamilton Arnold, "'The Life of a Citizen in the Hands of a Woman': Sexual Assault in New York City, 1790–1820," in Kathy Peiss and Christina Simmons, eds., *Passion and Power: Sexuality in History* (Philadelphia: University of Pennsylvania Press, 1989), p. 48; John E. O'Connor, "Le-

gal Reform in the Early Republic: The New Jersey Experience," *American Journal of Legal History* 22 (1978): 99–100.

16. Stephen West, *A Sermon Preached in Lenox, in the County of Berkshire, and Commonwealth of Massachusetts; December 6th, 1787: At the Execution of John Bly, and Charles Rose, for Crimes of Burglary* (Pittsfield, 1787), pp. 4–5, 6.

17. James Dana, *The Intent of Capital Punishment: A Discourse delivered in the city of New-Haven, October 20, 1790, Being the day of the execution of Joseph Mountain, for a rape* (New Haven, 1790), pp. 6–7. Cornelia Hughes Dayton, *Women before the Bar: Gender, Law, and Society in Connecticut, 1639–1789* (Chapel Hill: University of North Carolina Press for the Institute of Early American History and Culture, 1995), pp. 270–271, provides analysis of Dana's essay.

18. Richard Gaskins, "Changes in the Criminal Law in Eighteenth-Century Connecticut," *American Journal of Legal History* 25 (1981): 337; Dayton, *Women before the Bar,* pp. 248–249; Dana, *Intent of Capital Punishment,* p. 9. The continuing legitimacy of the death penalty is suggested by publication in 1791 of a manual for clergymen by the rector of Newport, Rhode Island's Episcopal Trinity Church: William Smith, *The Convict's Visitor; or Penitential Offices Consisting of Prayers, Lessons, and Meditations, with Suitable Devotions before, and at the Time of Execution* (Newport: Peter Edes [1791]).

19. Bradford, *An Enquiry into How Far the Punishment of Death,* p. 30.

20. Linda Kealey, "Patterns of Punishment: Massachusetts in the Eighteenth Century," *American Journal of Legal History* 30 (1986): 365.

21. [William Bentley], *The Diary of William Bentley, D.D., Pastor of the East Church, Salem, Massachusetts* (Gloucester, Mass.: P. Smith, 1962), vol. 2, p. 112, Nov. 11, 14, 1794.

22. Unidentified manuscript, 11.5 folio pages, possibly by Daniel Webster, Dartmouth College Archives. At Harvard College the Phi Beta Kappa Society debated the question "Whether society have a right to inflict capital punishment for any crime but murder," April 15, 1796, when John W. Hulbert, who was a member of Phi Beta Kappa, may have been in residence (Phi Beta

Kappa Records, vol. 1, Harvard College Archives). We thank Leon Jackson for this reference in an e-mail message of Jan. 28, 2000. For college debates on capital punishment see Masur, *Rites of Execution,* pp. 52, 174n6.

23. Records of Philotechnian Society Debates, 1795–1819, Williams College Archives; *Catalogue of the Books in the Library of Williams College* (Stockbridge: H. Willard, 1812), p. 33. "Beccaria on Crimes and Punishments" was part of the Adelphic Union Library at Williams College in 1812 (Williams College Archives).

24. Chapin, "Felony Law Reform," p. 165.

25. Adam Jay Hirsch, *The Rise of the Penitentiary: Prisons and Punishment in Early America* (New Haven: Yale University Press, 1992), pp. 47–56.

26. Samuel Sewall and Nathan Dane, *Communication from the Hon. Samuel Sewall, Esq. and the Hon. Nathan Dane, Esq. accompanied with Several Bills for the Regulation of the State Prison and the alteration of the Criminal Laws of the Commonwealth* (Boston, 1805), p. 4. Four hundred copies were printed by order of the legislature.

27. Ibid., pp. 5, 6.

28. Journal of the Senate, vol. 25 (May 1804–March 1805), pp. 423, 432, MA. Provisions in the law are in William Charles White, *A Compendium and Digest of the Laws of Massachusetts* (Boston, 1810), vol. 3, p. 1202.

29. Journal of the House of Representatives, vol. 25 (May 1804–March 1805), pp. 312, 318; vol. 26 (May 1805–March 1806), pp. 150, 266, 292, 302, 208, MA.

30. "George Blake," in James Spear Loring, *The Hundred Boston Orators* (Boston, 1852), pp. 253–255; "Samuel Dana," in Samuel A. Greene, *The Lawyers of Groton* (Groton, Mass., 1892), p. 33; for Thomas Allen, Jr., see Thomas Lawrence Davis, "Aristocrats and Jacobins in Country Towns: Party Formation in Berkshire County, Massachusetts (1775–1816)" (Ph.D. diss., Boston University, 1975), pp. 233, 369; *Sibley,* vol. 15 (1761–1763) (1970), pp. 161, 163.

31. Ronald Paul Formisano, *The Transformation of Political Culture: Massachusetts Parties, 1790s–1840s* (New York: Oxford University Press, 1983), pp. 57–83.

32. Peter King, "Decision-Makers and Decision-Making in the English Criminal Law, 1750–1800," *Historical Journal* 27 (1984): 43–46. Pardoning in America is discussed in James D. Rice, "The Criminal Trial before and after the Lawyers: Authority, Law, and Culture in Maryland Jury Trials, 1681–1860," *American Journal of Legal History* 40 (1996): 455–475.

33. Sir John Fielding quoted in Beattie, *Crime and the Courts in England,* p. 448.

34. "Legislative History of Capital Punishment in Massachusetts," Appendix C, *Report and Recommendations of the Special Commission Established for the Purpose of Investigating and Studying the Abolition of the Death Penalty in Capital Cases . . . December 30, 1958,* House Document no. 2575 (Boston: Wright and Potter, 1959), pp. 98–99.

35. Conviction Record, John Farrell, fourth Tuesday, September 1796, SJC, Northampton; GCP.

36. Ibid. supplies record of Simeon Strong as prosecutor, and Caleb Strong and his wife's brother, John Hooker (Yale, class of 1782) of Springfield, as defense counsel.

37. Ibid. Beattie, *Crime and the Courts in England,* p. 448, reports that "to have no [character] witnesses at all was almost certain to be disastrous, especially if the crime charged was particularly serious. . . . [T]he odds were heavily against a stranger who brought no support of any kind."

38. John Farrell Petition beginning "May it please your Excellency," n.d. [1796], GCP.

39. John Farrell Petition, Nov. 30, 1796, GCP.

40. Comparison of handwriting of John Farrell petition of Nov. 30, 1796, and undated petition beginning "Most humbly shews" with Caleb Strong letters to Timothy Pickering, Northampton, Aug. 22, 1795, Pickering Papers, MHS, and to Theodore Sedgwick, Northampton, Jan. 4, 1797, and Feb. 26, 1798, Sedgwick Papers I, Theodore Sedgwick, MHS. We thank Nicholas Graham and Carrie Foley at the Massachusetts Historical Society for locating handwriting samples.

41. Feb. 2, 1797, GCP.

42. John Farrell Petitions [n.d.; 1796?], the first beginning "We the sub-

scribers Inhabitants of the County of Worcester" and the other beginning "Most humbly shews," GCP.

43. Petition of David Thomas and 16 others on behalf of John Farrell [n.d.; 1796?], GCP.

44. GCP.

45. Papers docketed as "Lemuel Deming's petition for commutation of sentence of death—& report of Comtee of Council—Accepted. Rd. January 30th 1806," GCP.

46. "Samuel Dexter," in Alan Johnson and Dumas Malone, eds., *Dictionary of American Biography,* vol. 5 (New York: Scribner's, 1930), pp. 280–281; [Lucius Manlius Sargent], *Reminiscences of Samuel Dexter* (Boston, 1857), pp. 15–17, 22, 24, 39–43; Thomas Coffin Amory, *The Life of James Sullivan with Selections from his Writings* (Boston, 1859), vol. 2, p. 6; David Hackett Fischer, *The Revolution of American Conservatism: The Federalist Party in the Era of Jeffersonian Democracy* (New York: Harper and Row, 1965), p. 259.

47. "Artemas Ward," in *Biographical Directory of the United States Congress, 1774–1789* (Washington, D.C.: Government Printing Office, 1989), pp. 2005–2006; Fischer, *Revolution of American Conservatism,* pp. 276–277.

48. Ibid. The committee report is dated Jan. 29, 1806, and the council action Jan. 30, 1806.

49. Docketed "Copy of a Record of the Conviction of Jacob A. Lewis for a Rape" and petitions on behalf of Jacob Azzett Lewis, including convict's petition dated "Concord Gaol, Nov. 24th, 1801," GCP. Statistics on neighboring jurisdictions compiled from Hearn, and Daniel Allen Hearn, *Legal Executions in New York State: A Comprehensive Reference, 1639–1963* (Jefferson, N.C.: McFarland, 1997).

50. *Independent Chronicle* (Boston), Nov. 9, 1801, pp. 2–3. Virtually the same story was reprinted in the *Salem Gazette,* Nov. 11, 1801.

51. Sullivan is identified as prosecutor in Supreme Judicial Court records of the J. A. Lewis case, GCP.

52. "George Blake," in Loring, *Hundred Boston Orators,* pp. 253–255;

Amory, *Life of James Sullivan,* vol. 2, p. 88. The court assigned Samuel Dana to serve as Blake's co-counsel for Lewis.

53. Amory, *Life of James Sullivan,* vol. 2, p. 67.

54. Attribution of drafts to Blake and Dana based on internal evidence and comparisons of their handwriting: George Blake to Samuel M. Hopkins, Esq., Boston, Mar. 22, 1806, C. E. French Collection, MHS; Samuel Dana to Thomas Richardson, Groton, June 28, 1798, Charles Pelham Greenough Papers, 1669–1963, MHS. The writing on the convict's petition of Nov. 24, 1801, appears to match Blake's handwriting; and three petitions, dated November 1801, December 1801, and Dec. 11, 1801, appear to be in Samuel Dana's hand.

55. *Salem Gazette,* Nov. 10, 1801.

56. See the following works by Sharon Block: "Defining Rape in Early America: A Sexual Continuum and Created Consent," paper delivered at Omohundro Institute of Early American History and Culture, Williamsburg, Va., 1996; "Coerced Sex in British North America, 1700–1820" (Ph.D. diss., Princeton University, 1995); and "Lines of Color, Sex, and Service: Comparative Sexual Coercion in Early America," in Martha Elizabeth Hodes, ed., *Sex, Love, Race: Crossing Boundaries in North American History* (New York: New York University Press, 1999), pp. 141–163.

57. Jacob Azzett Lewis Petition, Nov. 24, 1801, GCP.

58. Ibid.

59. Conclusions drawn from Jacob Azzett Lewis petitions nos. 5, 6, 7, 8. Nos. 2, 3, and 4 appear to be in the hand of Samuel Dana. The quotation is from number 5, whose first signer is William Winthrop.

60. Pardon copy in the hand of Samuel Dana, March 29, 1802, GCP.

61. Pardon, March 12, 1802, GCP; Hearn, pp. 111–112 (Mingo), 123–124 (Jack), 126 (London), 149–150 (Arthur).

62. May 29, 1806, GCRec, vol. 34 (1803–1807), p. 365, MA.

63. The Fairbanks murder case generated sensational press coverage. The failed courtship of genteel young people offered a narrative resembling a romantic novel. See Daniel A. Cohen, *Pillars of Salt, Monuments of Grace: New England Crime Literature and the Origins of American Popular Culture, 1674–1860* (New York: Oxford University Press, 1993), pp. 184–192.

64. Nathan Coye Pardon Petition and letters, March 1808, GCPNG. The letter on possible delirium is from Elijah H. Mills to Samuel Fowler, dated Northampton, March 2, 1808; the note on Coye's family origins is from Edward Ruggles, also dated Northampton, March 2, 1808.

65. Copy of SJC Record in case of Joseph Drew, June 10, 1808, in GCPNG. See also [Joseph Drew], *The Life and Confession of Joseph Drew who was Executed at Portland, Maine, July 21, 1808, for the murder of Ebenezer Parker, a deputy sheriff of Cape Elizabeth* (Northampton, 1808).

66. Petition on behalf of Joseph Drew signed by Henry Abraham L. Dearborn, Stephen Longfellow, et al., Portland, Maine, June 24, 1808, GCPNG.

67. Isaac Ingalls, n.p., June 24, 1808, "This may certify whome it may Concern," GCPNG.

68. Petition of Joseph Drew, Portland Gaol, June 24, 1808, GCPNG.

69. Docketed on verso of Petition of Joseph Drew addressed to His Excellency James Sullivan, Esq., by Henry Abraham L. Dearborn, Stephen Longfellow, et al. of June 24, 1808.

70. "Caleb Strong," in *Sibley*, vol. 16 (1764–1767) (1972), p. 103; whole sketch, pp. 94–110.

71. Ibid., pp. 94–100.

72. Ibid., p. 96.

73. Ibid., p. 99–110.

74. Ibid., p. 97.

75. Alden Bradford, *Biography of the Hon. Caleb Strong, several years the Governor of the State of Massachusetts* (Boston, 1820), p. 26.

76. Ibid., p. 28. Strong's father-in-law, the Reverend John Hooker, was the successor to Jonathan Edwards in Northampton.

77. All of the petitions for Wheeler and the Governor's Council committee report are in GCPNG.

78. The petition in Wheeler's name is dated Sept. 28, 1805.

79. The petition of Hannah, Betsy, and Ephraim Wheeler, Jr., is dated Sept. 26, 1805.

80. The petition of Daniel Dewey and John W. Hulbert is dated Sept. 24, 1805.

81. Attached to the petition of Daniel Dewey and John W. Hulbert, dated Sept. 24, 1805. The Northrup connection is from Ansel Judd Northrup, *The Northrup-Northrop Genealogy: A Record of the Known Descendants of Joseph Northrup, who came from England in 1637, and Was One of the Original Settlers of Milford, Conn., in 1639; with Lists of Northrups and Northrops in the Revolution* (New York: Grafton Press, 1908), pp. 44–46.

82. Richard Birdsall, *Berkshire County: A Cultural History* (New Haven: Yale University Press, 1959), pp. 89–91.

83. Compiled from the Berkshire County land registry and probate records located in Pittsfield and Adams, Mass.

84. Petition of Denison Robinson et al. on behalf of Ephraim Wheeler, Sept. 26, 1805, GCPNG.

85. Ibid.

86. Ibid. Shipton, "Caleb Strong," *Sibley*, vol. 16 (1764–1767) (1972), p. 101, reports a margin of 40 or 176 votes, depending on how the vote was figured. Many Sullivan ballots were disqualified because his name was misspelled: in Lynn, 357 ballots marked for "James Sulvan" were disqualified. Amory, *Life of James Sullivan*, vol. 2, p. 158.

87. GCRec, vol. 34 (1803–1807), p. 311; starting time from GCMin (Feb. 4, 1806), vol. 30 (May 29, 1805–).

88. GCRec, vol. 34 (1803–1807), p. 308.

89. Lemuel Deming case, Jan. 19, 1806, GCP. Handwriting analysis reveals that the committee report was drafted by Artemas Ward (cf. Artemas Ward to Henry David Ward, Shrewsbury, Oct. 10, 1796, Artemas Ward Papers, 1747–1953, MHS). Artemas Ward probably had a personal reason for exercising caution in recommending the death penalty. In 1778 his father—also Artemas—headed the council that rejected a stay of execution for Bathsheba Spooner, who, with some medical support, claimed to be pregnant. The senior Ward's council ordered Spooner's death only to learn from her autopsy that her claim was accurate. Deborah Navas, *Murdered by His Wife: A History with Documentation of the Joshua Spooner Murder and Execution of His Wife Bathsheba, Who Was Hanged in Worcester, Massachusetts, 2 July 1778* (Amherst: University of Massachusetts Press, 1999), p. 92.

90. Petition of Denison Robinson et al. on behalf of Ephraim Wheeler, Sept. 26, 1805, GCPNG.

91. Committee report on Wheeler case, n.d., GCPNG. Handwriting analysis reveals that Samuel Dexter drafted the report (cf. Samuel Dexter to Theodore Sedgwick, Boston, May 29, 1806, Sedgwick Papers I, Theodore Sedgwick, MHS). Because Dexter and Ward prepared the Deming report, which is in Ward's hand, we suppose that the same committee of two also prepared the Wheeler report, with Dexter taking his turn at drafting the report.

92. Governor Caleb Strong speech to the legislature, Jan. 13, 1804, *PS,* Jan. 23, 1804, 2:2–3.

93. "An Act Respecting Conditional Pardons," Mar. 7, 1804, *PS,* Apr. 30, 1804, 1:2.

94. Journal of the Senate, vol. 26 (May 1805–March 1806), pp. 356–363, MA.

95. In 1817 the case of Henry Phillips, a murderer, was suspended because the defense counsel petitioned the governor and council arguing that they had come to their decision based on a published trial report that had omitted key information. They later denied Phillips's plea, and he was executed (GCRec, vols. 37, 39, 41, 43, 52). This 1817 case suggests that the governor and council read trial reports, possibly the *Report of the Trial of Ephraim Wheeler,* which had been available since November and was published in Newburyport as well as Stockbridge.

96. *A Concise and Simple Narrative of the Controversy between Thomas Allen, A.M. of Pittsfield and that part of his church and congregation which have lately separated from his pastoral care, and have been incorporated by the legislature of the Commonwealth, into a parish by the name of "Union Parish in the Town of Pittsfield"* (Pittsfield, 1809), p. 42.

97. Tuesday, Feb. 4, 1806, GCMin, vol. 30 (May 29, 1805–).

98. Alan Taylor, "'The Unhappy Stephen Arnold': An Episode of Murder and Penitence in the Early Republic," in Ronald Hoffman, Mechal Sobel, and Fredrika Teute, eds., *Through a Glass Darkly: Reflections on Personal Identity in Early America* (Chapel Hill: University of North Carolina

Press for the Omohundro Institute of Early American History and Culture, 1997), pp. 96–121.

99. "Legislative History of Capital Punishment," 99–100.

100. Cornelia Hughes Dayton states that in eighteenth-century Connecticut the only sexual violence that led to convictions for white men was incest (*Women before the Bar*, p. 233). Anna Clark, in *Women's Silence, Men's Violence: Sexual Assault in England, 1770–1845* (London: Pandora, 1987), chap. 3, reports that whereas men were rarely convicted of raping an adult woman, assaults on children were more often punished, especially if the victim was younger than ten to twelve years old. However, Clark also notes (p. 103) that in 1839 a man was acquitted of the rape of his thirteen-year-old daughter on the grounds that she consented. Yet in an 1817 case that echoes Wheeler's, Clark says that "at the conclusion of the trial of William Townsley for raping his eleven-year-old daughter, Mr. Justice Bayley admitted that the child had proven the assault, but recommended acquittal because the only other corroborating evidence was the mother, who 'in point of law, could not give evidence against her husband . . . for those wise reasons that domestic divisions or family differences might induce her to state an untruth to the prejudice or injury of her husband.' Incest was thus a crime too bound up in the patriarchal family to punish consistently" (ibid.). For an English case where a teenage girl succeeded in her charge of rape, possibly because she could prove her sexual innocence, see Randolph Trumbach, *Sex and the Gender Revolution. Vol. 1: Heterosexuality and the Third Gender in Enlightenment London* (Chicago: University of Chicago Press, 1998), pp. 311–312. See also Patrick J. Connor, "'The Law Should Be Her Protector': The Criminal Prosecution of Rape in Upper Canada, 1791–1850," in Merril D. Smith, ed., *Sex Without Consent: Rape and Sexual Coercion in America* (New York: New York University Press, 2001), pp. 117–118.

101. Copy in GCPNG.

7. THE EXECUTION

1. Sarah Snell Bryant Diary, 1806, Houghton Library, Harvard University, Cambridge, Mass. She wrote her diary entry on the day of the execution

from her home in Cummington, where several of the Odel sisters had lived for more than fifteen years and where Hannah and Ephraim Wheeler also resided at times: "Thursday [Feb. 20] warm—very mudy [*sic*] cloudy—PM rain E Wheeler hung at Lenox—Seth Ford Married."

2. *Narrative,* p. 10.

3. This description rests on the *PS* account of Feb. 24, 1806; *Narrative,* pp. 9, 11; and descriptions of other execution ceremonies of the period. The fact that this was not an exclusively Puritan or Congregational ritual in New England is suggested by a 1791 manual produced by William Smith, the Anglican Rector of Trinity Church, Newport, Rhode Island: *The Convict's Visitor; or Penitential Offices Consisting of Prayers, Lessons, and Meditations, with Suitable Devotions before, and at the Time of Execution* (Newport: Peter Edes [1791]). Smith's guide for ministering to convicts, especially those to be executed, included scripts for the cleric and the convict up to and including execution day. The convict's final words at the gallows were scripted as follows: "Lord Jesus, remember me when thou comest in thy kingdom! Into thy hands, O God, I commend my spirit!" Then, after the signal for execution, the clergyman was to say: "The Lord have mercy upon him, Amen!"

4. The sheriff's role as hangman was evidently common practice in Massachusetts at this time; see Robert A. Gross, "A Disorderly Tradition: Violence and Community in Concord, Massachusetts, 1790–1820," paper delivered at the Institute of Early American History and Culture, Williamsburg, Va., Sept. 19, 1995, pp. 4–5. Wheeler's death warrant ordered the sheriff to "cause" the prisoner's death; and among the records of the expenses generated by the prosecution there is no record of payment to a hangman.

5. These generalizations are based on extensive reading in the literature of crime and executions in Massachusetts; see especially Karen Halttunen, *Murder Most Foul: The Killer and the American Gothic Imagination* (Cambridge, Mass.: Harvard University Press, 1998), chap. 1, p. 19 (for time between sentencing and execution); Daniel A. Cohen, *Pillars of Salt, Monuments of Grace: New England Crime Literature and the Origins of American Popular Culture, 1674–1860* (New York: Oxford University Press, 1993), chaps. 1–5; Louis P. Masur, *Rites of Execution: Capital Punishment and the*

Transformation of American Culture, 1776–1865 (New York: Oxford University Press, 1989), chap. 2; Stuart Banner, *The Death Penalty: An American History* (Cambridge, Mass.: Harvard University Press, 2002), chaps. 1–3. Ritual burial under the gallows is from Nathaniel Ames, *The Diary of Dr. Nathaniel Ames of Dedham, Massachusetts, 1758–1822,* ed. Robert Brand Hanson (Rockport, Me.: Picton Press, 1998), vol. 2, p. 773 (entry of Oct. 7, 1802, regarding Ebenezer Mason).

6. Rollin H. Cooke, "Pittsfield Families," vol. 6, pp. 115–117, in Berkshire Atheneum local history collection, Pittsfield Public Library.

7. U.S. Congress, *Biographical Directory of the United States Congress, 1774–1989,* Kathryn Allamong Jacob and Bruce A. Ragsdale, editors-in-chief (Washington, D.C.: U.S. Government Printing Office, 1989), pp. 1344–45. The *Directory* supplies incorrect information on Larned's term as treasurer.

8. *PS,* Sept. 8, 1804, 3:2; Sept. 22, 1804, 3:2.

9. Ibid., Feb. 11, 1805, p. 2.

10. Bernard Mandeville, *An Enquiry into the Causes of the Frequent Executions at Tyburn* (London, 1725), pp. 20, 24, 25; Samuel Richardson, *Familiar Letters on Important Occasions,* intro. by Brian W. Downs (New York: Dodd, Mead and Co., 1928), letter no. 60, pp. 217–220. This work originally appeared in London and Dublin editions in 1741. In 1755 it went into its sixth edition. An alternate title of this work is *Letters Written to and for Particular Friends, on the most Important Occasions. . . .*

11. Richardson, *Familiar Letters,* pp. 217, 218, 219. According to novelist, playwright, and justice of the peace Henry Fielding, executions were carried out at six-week intervals as of 1751: *An Enquiry into the Causes of the Late Increase of Robbers and Related Writings,* ed. Marvin R. Zirker (Middletown, Conn.: Wesleyan University Press, 1988 [first pub. 1751]), p. 167. Leslie Richardson, "Justice or a Trap? Rape Prosecutions in Fielding's Comedy," American Society for Eighteenth-Century Studies Annual Meeting, April 4, 2002, discusses Fielding's 1730 comedy *Rape Upon Rape; or, the Justice Caught in his Own Trap.*

12. Richardson, *Familiar Letters,* pp. 218–220. Halttunen, *Murder Most*

Foul, pp. 22–23, includes analysis of the ways the New England execution ritual did not fit Foucault's model of the state "inscribing" its power on the suffering individual. Instead, the criminal was supposed to acknowledge the legitimacy of the state, and the execution was intended to overawe the spectators. Michael Ignatieff analyzes eighteenth-century English discussion of capital punishment in *A Just Measure of Pain: The Penitentiary in the Industrial Revolution, 1750–1850* (New York: Pantheon, 1978), chap. 2.

13. Hogarth's print is reproduced in *Hogarth's Graphic Works,* compiled and with annotations by Ronald Paulson (New Haven: Yale University Press, 1965), 1st complete ed., vol. 2 *(The Engravings),* pp. 190, 200–201. According to an observer at a 1776 Tyburn execution, the crowd numbered 40,000, the largest ever. Between 1765 and 1774 London had eight hanging days annually, and in London and Middlesex some 278 persons were executed. See Donna T. Andrew and Randall McGowen, *The Perreaus and Mrs. Rudd: Forgery and Betrayal in Eighteenth-Century London* (Berkeley: University of California Press, 2001), p. 7.

14. [Job Wells], *The Trial of Job Wells of Redburn in the County of Hertford, for a Rape committed on the Body of his own Daughter, Maria Wells, at the Assizes held at Hertford, . . . to which is added, A full Account of his Behaviour under Sentence, and at the Place of Execution. And the Substance of a most Excellent Sermon, on this Occasion. . . .* (London, 1753), pp. 12–14. Henry Fielding noted the difference between London and "the Country" in 1751 in his *Enquiry into the Causes,* p. 168. The same seriousness was observed on Oct. 20, 1744, in a Worcester, Massachusetts, execution, according to an observer, the Sutton clergyman Reverend David Hall (David Hall Diary, MHS).

15. Blackstone quoted in J. M. Beattie, *Crime and the Courts in England, 1660–1800* (Princeton: Princeton University Press, 1986), pp. 556–557; Masur, *Rites of Execution,* pp. 61–63, 65.

16. Sullivan quoted in Thomas Coffin Amory, *Life of James Sullivan with Selections from his Writings* (Boston, 1859), vol. 1, p. 205.

17. [David Dudley Field and Chester Dewey], *A History of the County of Berkshire, Massachusetts; in Two Parts* (Pittsfield, 1829), p. 110. Bly and Rose

claimed that their crimes were political, but contemporary accounts say otherwise. See Hearn, pp. 172–173.

18. William Bentley, *The Diary of William Bentley, D.D., Pastor of the East Church, Salem, Massachusetts* (Gloucester, Mass.: P. Smith, 1962), vol. 2, p. 156 (Aug. 6, 1795). The broadside announcing Pomp's execution, which seems to have been directed toward sailors, was so vulgar and commercial that it included an advertisement for a pawnbroker and a cure for venereal disease: "Dying Confession of Pomp, a negro man, who was executed at Ipswich, on the 6th of August, 1795, for murdering capt. Charles Furbush of Andover, taken from the mouth of the prisoner, and penned by Jonathan Plummer, jun. [Newburyport, 1795] Printed for and sold by Jonathan Plummer, jun. Price 6d, who still continues to carry on his various branches of trifling business—underbeds filled with straw and wheeled to ladies doors—Any person wanting a few dollars at any time may be supplied by leaving a proper adequate in pawn—Wanted 1000 junk bottles. A certain secret disorder cured privately and expeditiously—Love letters in prose and verse furnished on shortest notice—The art of gaining the object beloved reasonably taught—." Early American Imprints, 1st ser., no. 29329.

19. Bentley, *Diary,* vol. 2, p. 170 (Jan. 1, 1796).

20. Gross, "A Disorderly Tradition," p. 3; [Samuel Smith], *Last Words and dying Speech of Samuel Smith, Who was Executed at Concord, in the County of Middlesex, and Commonwealth of Massachusetts, the 26th December, A.D. 1799, for the Crime of Burglary* (Boston, 1799). Smith was the last person executed for burglary in Massachusetts.

21. Quotation from [Nathaniel Coverly, Jr.], *Biography of Mr. Jason Fairbanks and Miss Eliza Fales* (Boston [1801]), col. 4 of broadside; Cohen, *Pillars of Salt, Monuments of Grace,* p. 181.

22. Sullivan in Amory, *Life of James Sullivan,* vol. 1, p. 205.

23. Josiah Quincy, *Remarks on some of the Provisions of the Laws of Massachusetts affecting Poverty, Vice, and Crime; being the general topics of a charge to the Grand Jury of the County of Suffolk, in March Term, 1822* (Cambridge, Mass., 1822), p. 27.

24. Gamaliel Bradford, *State Prisons and the Penitentiary System Vindi-*

cated, with observations on Managing and Conducting these Institutions; drawn principally from experience (Boston, 1821), p. 7.

25. Asa Greene, *Berkshire American,* Nov. 16, 1826, and Aug. 29, 1827, quoted in Richard D. Birdsall, *Berkshire County: A Cultural History* (New Haven: Yale University Press, 1959), p. 289.

26. [Field and Dewey], *History of the County,* p. 111 (by D. D. Field); David Dudley Field, *Warning Against Drunkenness: A Sermon Preached in the City of Middletown, June 20, 1816, the day of the execution of Peter Lung for the murder of his wife, at the request of the sheriff of the county of Middlesex & in accordance with the wishes of the criminal, together with a short sketch of the life & hopeful repentance of said Lung* (Middletown, 1816).

27. Masur, *Rites of Execution,* chaps. 3–5, pp. 95–96; Philip English Mackey, *Hanging in Balance: The Anti-Capital Punishment Movement in New York State, 1776–1861* (New York: Garland, 1982); Timothy Dodge, *Crime and Punishment in New Hampshire, 1812–1914* (New York: P. Lang, 1995), p. 299. In 1837 New Hampshire ended public executions.

28. Quoted in Alan Taylor, "'The Unhappy Stephen Arnold': An Episode of Murder and Penitence in the Early Republic," in Ronald Hoffman, Mechal Sobel, and Fredrika Teute, eds., *Through a Glass Darkly: Reflections on Personal Identity in Early America* (Chapel Hill: University of North Carolina Press for the Omohundro Institute of Early American History and Culture, 1997), pp. 111–112.

29. Richardson, *Familiar Letters,* p. 220.

30. *The Centennial Anniversary of the Dedication of the Old Church on the Hill, Lenox, Mass., June 12, 1906* (Pittsfield: Sun Printing Co., 1908), p. 15.

31. Sketch of Shepard in Franklin Bowditch Dexter, *Biographical Sketches of the Graduates of Yale College: with Annals of the College History* (New York: Holt, 1885–1912), vol. 5 (1792–1805), pp. 84–87; Peter T. Mallary, "The Church on the Hill, Lenox, Massachusetts, 1805," chapter in his *New England Churches and Meetinghouses, 1680–1830,* photographs by Tim Imrie (New York: Vendome Press, 1985), pp. 126–129; Samuel Shepard, "An account of a work of divine grace, in a revival of religion, in the town of Lenox,

State of Massachusetts, in the year 1799, in a letter to the Editors from the Rev. Samuel Shepard, of that town," Lenox, May 7, 1801, in *Connecticut Evangelical Magazine,* October 1801, pp. 136–142. The founding editor of this journal was the Yale-educated Hartford minister Nathan Strong (1748–1816). In 1771 Strong himself had given an execution sermon for Moses Dunbar, who was convicted of treason in Connecticut. Strong edited the journal in the periods 1800–1807 and 1808–1815; Samuel Shepard, *A Sermon Preached in Lenox, Mass., April 30, 1845, at the Celebration of the Fiftieth Anniversary of his Ordination to the work of the Gospel Ministry in said Town.* . . . (Lenox, 1845).

32. William J. Bartlett, *Half-Century Memories* [Lee, Mass., 1894], unpaginated pamphlet.

33. Massachusetts General Court, Journal of the House of Representatives, vol. 26, pp. 194, 210, 312, MA; *Salem Gazette,* Feb. 18, 1806, 3:2.

34. Shepard, *Execution,* p. 3.

35. Dexter, *Biographical Sketches of the Graduates of Yale College* . . . , vol. 5, p. 85.

36. Shepard, *Execution,* p. 3.

37. Ibid., pp. 3, 4.

38. Ibid., pp. 6, 7.

39. Ibid., pp. 9, 10.

40. *Narrative,* p. 8.

41. Shepard, *Execution,* pp. 12–13.

42. Ibid., p. 13.

43. Ibid.

44. Ibid., pp. 13, 14.

45. Ibid. This image of being suspended recalls a terrifying passage in Jonathan Edwards's 1741 sermon, at Enfield, Connecticut, *Sinners in the Hands of an Angry God:* "O sinner! Consider the fearful danger you are in: 'tis a great furnace of wrath, a wide and bottomless pit, full of the fire of wrath, that you are held over in the hand of that God, whose wrath is provoked and incensed as much against you as against many of the damned in hell: you hang by a slender thread, with the flames of divine wrath flashing

about it, and ready every moment to singe it, and burn it asunder." John E. Smith, Harry S. Stout, and Kenneth P. Minkema, eds., *A Jonathan Edwards Reader* (New Haven: Yale University Press, 1995), p. 98. Shepard was a follower of Edwards; see Shepard, *A Sermon Preached in Lenox, Mass., April 30, 1845,* p. 15.

46. Shepard, *Execution,* p. 14.

47. Ibid.

48. Ibid., pp. 15, 16.

49. Ibid., p. 16.

50. *Narrative,* p. 9.

51. Ibid., p. 11.

52. *PS,* Feb. 24, 1806, 3:2.

53. Ibid.

54. Thomas Lawrence Davis, "Aristocrats and Jacobins in Country Towns: Party Formation in Berkshire County, Massachusetts (1775–1816)" (Ph.D. diss., Boston University, 1975), p. 383.

55. [Fred A. Packard], *Report of the Trial of George Bowen for the Murder of Jonathan Jewett, who committed suicide on the 9th of November, 1815, while confined in the common Gaol of the County of Hampshire, under sentence of Death for the Murder of his Father* (Northampton, 1816), pp. 55–56.

56. "To Simon Larned Esqr. Sheriff of our County of Berkshire—Greeting," warrant for executing Ephraim Wheeler, Oct. 16, 1805, GCRec.

57. *PS,* Feb. 24, 1806, 3:2.

58. Gross, "A Disorderly Tradition," p. 4. The sheriff's duties at executions were prescribed in a 1771 statute: see [Massachusetts], *The Civil Officer: or the Whole Duty of Sheriffs, Coroners, Constables and Collectors of Taxes,* 2d ed. (Boston, 1814), p. 42.

59. The specific details of Wheeler's hanging are nowhere recorded. This account is a composite reconstruction based on the methods of hanging and details of the process reported and recorded by [Joseph Drew], *The Life and Confession of Joseph Drew who was Executed at Portland, Maine, July 21, 1808, for the murder of Ebenezer Parker, a deputy sheriff of Cape Elizabeth*

(Northampton, Mass., 1808), p. 7; and V. A. C. Gatrell, *The Hanging Tree: Execution and the English People, 1770–1868* (Oxford: Oxford University Press, 1996), pp. 51–54. Woodcut images of hangings supply significant details; see that of Ebenezer Ball (Castine, Maine [Mass.], 1811), broadside at AAS; Elisha Thomas (Worcester, Mass., 1788), reproduced in Masur, *Rites of Execution*, p. 48; William Huggins and John Mansfield (Worcester, Mass., 1783), reproduced in Cohen, *Pillars of Salt, Monuments of Grace*, p. 128; Wild Robert (England, 1797), reproduced in Gatrell, *The Hanging Tree*, p. 162; and Gross, "A Disorderly Tradition," pp. 3–5. According to Gross, the stocking cap intended to hide Smith's face was knitted by the sheriff's wife, and perhaps Larned's wife also knitted a cap to hide Ephraim's dying agony.

60. *PS*, Feb. 24, 1806, 3:2; [Drew], *Life and Confession*, p. 7. Sources for details used here include: *The Last Words of Ebenezer Mason, who was executed at Dedham, October 7, 1802; for the Murder of William Pitt Allen, His Brother in Law, on the 18th of May 1802. Taken from his own Mouth a few Hours previous to his Execution*, 2d ed. (Dedham, 1802), p. 17. Elijah Waterman, *A Sermon Preached at Windham, November 29th, 1803. Being the day of the Execution of Caleb Adams, for the Murder of Oliver Woodworth. . . . Also A Sketch of the Circumstances of the Birth, Education, and Manner of Caleb's Life, with practical Reflexions, delivered at the place of Execution. By Moses C. Welch, A.M. . . . with an Appendix, Giving an account of the behaviour of the Criminal at his trial, during his confinement, and on the day of Execution* (Windham, 1804), pp. 31, 32. See also Gatrell, *The Hanging Tree*, pp. 51–54.

61. The time is from Simon Larned's Feb. 24, 1806, endorsement on Wheeler's death warrant, "To Simon Larned Esqr.," GCRec. On verso it is endorsed in Simon Larned's handwriting: "Berkshire Ss: 24th February 1806. In obedience to the within Warrant, on Thursday the twentieth day of February current, I took the within named Ephraim Wheeler, from the place of his Confinement to the usual place of Execution, and between the hours of twelve & three oClock in the day time on sd. Day I caused the said Ephraim Wheeler to be hanged by the neck until he was

Dead. Simon Larned Sheriff of Berkshire County." Other details are informed conjectures based on accounts of Massachusetts hangings (including Maine), ca. 1780–1815.

AFTERMATH

1. [Alpheus Livermore and Samuel Angier], *The Trial of Alpheus Livermore and Samuel Angier before the Supreme Judicial Court of the Commonwealth of Massachusetts, upon an indictment for the murder of John Crevay, an Indian, committed November 23, 1813. Containing the evidence at large, the arguments of the Solicitor General, and of the counsel for the prisoners, the charge of the Hon. Judge Sewall to the traverse jury, and his address on pronouncing sentence of death* (Boston, 1813), p. 47.

2. *Narrative*, pp. 9, 10, 11, 12.

3. Ibid., p. 12.

4. Reprinted from *Western Star*, Feb. 22, 1806, in *Narrative*, p. 9.

5. *Narrative*, p. 12. The first four lines follow the last stanza of Sir Willliam Davenant's (1606–1668) poem "To a Mistress Dying": Bartleby.com "Great Books Online," *http://www.bartleby.com/101/302.html.*

6. *PS*, Feb. 24, 1806, 3:2, and *Narrative*, p. 14. The attribution of the piece to the Reverend Thomas Allen comes from *A Concise and Simple Narrative of the Controversy between Thomas Allen, A.M. of Pittsfield and that part of his church and congregation which have lately separated from his pastoral care, and have been incorporated by the legislature of the Commonwealth, into a parish by the name of "Union Parish in the Town of Pittsfield"* (Pittsfield, 1809), pp. 39–43.

7. *PS*, Feb. 24, 1806, 3:2.

8. *Narrative*, pp. 12, 13, 14, 15, 21. Willard's pamphlet was 47 percent devoted to the political controversy, making a twelve-page into a twenty-four-page pamphlet with a blank last page. Willard may have regarded the longer format as more viable commercially.

9. Ibid., p. 23.

10. Ibid., pp. 15, 16, 17, 19. The author was "Timoleon."

11. Ibid., p. 21. Alan Taylor, "'The Unhappy Stephen Arnold': An Epi-

sode of Murder and Penitence in the Early Republic," in Ronald Hoffman, Mechal Sobel, and Frederika J. Teute, eds., *Through a Glass Darkly: Reflections on Personal Identity in Early America* (Chapel Hill: University of North Carolina Press for the Omohundro Institute of Early American History and Culture, 1997), pp. 110–116.

12. *Narrative*, p. 18.

13. Ibid., pp. 14–20.

14. *PS,* March 10, 1806, 3:2–3.

15. See, for example, *Connecticut Journal and Advertiser* (New Haven), March 6, 1806, 3:2; and the *New-York Weekly Museum,* March 8, 1806, 3:2.

16. *National Aegis* (Worcester), March 5, 1806, 2:4. Boston's *Independent Chronicle,* the state's leading Jeffersonian paper, did not mention Wheeler's execution in any of its February through April 1806 issues; neither did another Republican paper, the *Salem Register.*

17. *A Concise and Simple Narrative of the Controversy,* pp. 39–43. This passage first drew the Wheeler case to our attention.

18. Richard D. Birdsall, *Berkshire County: A Cultural History* (New Haven: Yale University Press, 1959), chaps. 3, 4; Christopher Clark, *The Roots of Rural Capitalism: Western Massachusetts, 1780–1860* (Ithaca, N.Y.: Cornell University Press, 1990).

19. Ezra Hutchinson Probate Court Docket no. 3161, March–August 1814, Berkshire County Registry of Probate, Pittsfield, Mass.

20. The names of Hutchinson's attorneys from Records of the SJC for Berkshire County, September term of 1813, consulted at Pittsfield County Court House, since moved to Massachusetts Archives, Boston. This record states that the convict be "hanged by the neck until he is dead—dead—dead." Copied by Joseph Woodbridge, Clerk. This phrase was also used sometimes in eighteenth-century England. The text quotation is from [Ezra Hutchinson], *The Solemn Address and Dying Advice of Ezra Hutchinson, who was executed at Lenox, (Mass.) November 18, 1813, for a rape on the body of Miss Lucy Bates* (Stockbridge, 1813), p. 5.

21. *PS,* Nov. 11, 1813, 3:3.

22. Henry Pyner file, GCRec, 1813, MA. Rape of Harriet Butters, spinster,

Aug. 22, 1813, at Ludlow, *Commonwealth v. Pyner,* SJC for Hampshire County, September term of 1813, executed Nov. 4, 1813. *Hampshire Gazette* (Northampton), Sept. 29, 1813, 3:2; Nov. 11, 1813, 3:3. See also Hearn, p. 196.

23. *PS,* Nov. 11, 1813, mentioned a "rev. Chapman" in connection with the Ezra Hutchinson execution.

24. *PS,* Dec. 1, 1819, 3:4; and Dec. 8, 1819, 3:4.

25. Ibid., Dec. 8, 1819, 3:4; Dr. Asa Greene, in *Berkshire American,* Nov. 16, 1826, and Aug. 29, 1827, quoted in Birdsall, *Berkshire County,* p. 289; [David Dudley Field and Chester Dewey], *A History of the County of Berkshire, Massachusetts; in Two Parts* (Pittsfield, 1829), p. 111 (by D. D. Field); Josiah Quincy, *Remarks on some of the Provisions of the Laws of Massachusetts affecting Poverty, Vice, and Crime; being the general topics of a charge to the Grand Jury of the County of Suffolk, in March Term, 1822* (Cambridge, Mass., 1822), p. 27.

26. Hearn, pp. 210–211.

27. Robert Rantoul, *Memoirs, Speeches, and Writings of Robert Rantoul, Jr.,* ed. Luther Hamilton (Boston, 1854), pp. 426–428.

28. Alan Rogers, "'Under Sentence of Death': The Movement to Abolish Capital Punishment in Massachusetts, 1835–1849," *New England Quarterly* 66 (1993): 45. Rogers reports the deaths of Washington Goode (black, 1849) and Thomas Barrett (Irish, 1845), but he omits Benjamin Cummings (white, 1839). See Hearn, pp. 224–225, 226, 229–230. For reform outlook see Louis P. Masur, *Rites of Execution: Capital Punishment and the Transformation of American Culture, 1776–1865* (New York: Oxford University Press, 1989), pp. 109–110.

29. Massachusetts House of Representatives Document 2575, "Legislative History of Capital Punishment in Massachusetts," (Boston: Commonwealth of Massachusetts, 1959), Appendix C, pp. 100–101; Masur, *Rites of Execution,* pp. 147–148. Gen. 9:6. See also Karen Halttunen, *Murder Most Foul: The Killer and the American Gothic Imagination* (Cambridge, Mass.: Harvard University Press, 1998), chap. 1, esp. pp. 22–30, and chap. 2, esp. pp. 35, 49, 50, 56–58.

30. Berkshire County probate, land, and vital records housed in Pittsfield

and Adams, Massachusetts, include no guardianship, real property, or death records.

31. The purchase by Isaac Odel in 1794 for £20 and the sale for $200 in 1808 to John Persip of the four-acre Cummington parcel are recorded in Hampshire County Registry of Deeds, vol. 10, p. 242, and vol. 36, p. 311, in Northampton, Massachusetts. The abutting twenty-acre parcel in Windsor is recorded in the Berkshire County Registry of Deeds, Pittsfield, Massachusetts.

32. John Percip, William Martin, Michael Pepper deeds recorded in Berkshire County Registry of Deeds, Pittsfield, Massachusetts.

33. *Narrative,* p. 11.

34. The *Vital Records of Hinsdale, Massachusetts, to the Year 1850* (Boston: n.p., 1902), p. 86: "Martin, Lucy, wid., colored, Jan. 5, 1843, a 75 y. 355 d. (Church Rec.)," p. 89 (for Molly Percip). The 1840 Census of Hinsdale lists as "free colored" a household of John Persip, and another of James Martin. (Information from a student of ours, Margaret Harnois.) The next generation of Percip girls retained traditional Odel names, including Elizabeth Percip (identified as a "negress" in 1885), who married Henry Field, the grandson of a slave; and Hannah Persip, who married an ex-slave named Philip Hoose. Nine of their children, including Richard Hoose and Amos D. Hoose of Hinsdale, appear in the records of 1885: Hamilton Child, *Gazetteer of Berkshire County, Mass., 1725–1885: Part First* (Syracuse, 1885), pp. 176, 178. As of 1997 Persips are still found in the Pittsfield telephone directory, and the local American Legion Post, next to the public library and the county courthouse, is named for Charles A. Persip.

35. [Field and Dewey], *History of the County,* pp. 110–111, identifies the race of nonwhite criminals and victims ("blacks," "Indian," "man of colour") but does not so identify Betsy who is "white" by default.

36. On Jan. 1, 1818, a marriage between Charlotte Chase and Ephrahim [*sic*] Wheeler is recorded in the *Vital Records of Sutton, Massachusetts,* p. 229; but we have no evidence that this is the son of Hannah Odel Wheeler who was born in Sutton in 1763. If the Odels still had kin or friends in Hannah's birthplace, however, this 1818 husband might well be the person

we have called Ephraim, Jr. We have been in correspondence with one of this "Ephrahim"'s descendants, a man living in Texas who has supplied us with ca. 1860–1880 photographs of three of "Ephrahim"'s children, possibly the grandchildren of Ephraim and Hannah Odel Wheeler.

37. See Chap. 3, note 4.

38. *Narrative,* pp. 3, 10. A fellow prisoner in Lenox jail also told Heman Willard that Ephraim revealed in a private conversation that his true name was Reuben Haskin, and that before coming to Berkshire County he had taken the name Ephraim Wheeler after assisting in the jailbreak of two Plymouth County convicts who had been sentenced to hang. While Hoskins is a common name in the Rochester region, we found no record of any Reuben Haskin (or Haskins, Hoskins, Hoskin, Hosken) in Plymouth or Bristol counties, and no evidence of a jailbreak by two capital convicts in the years 1783–1786. Sarah Avery, at her mistress's direction, casually assumed a new identity in Vermont in the 1820s to get away from a disreputable family name: *Trial of Joseph Burnham, before the County Court held at Woodstock, in the County of Windsor, June, 1826* (Woodstock, Vt., 1826), pp. 4, 9; for other false identity cases, see Steven C. Bullock, "A Mumper among the Gentle: Tom Bell, Colonial Confidence Man," *William and Mary Quarterly,* 3rd ser., 55 (April 1998): 231–258; Robert A. Gross, "The Confidence Man and the Preacher: The Cultural Politics of Shays's Rebellion," in Robert A. Gross, ed., *In Debt to Shays: The Bicentennial of an Agrarian Rebellion* (Charlottesville: University of Virginia Press for Colonial Society of Massachusetts, 1993), pp. 297–320, 385–386n4. On Burroughs, see *Memoirs of Stephen Burroughs,* 2 vols. (Hanover, N.H.: Benjamin True, 1798; rpt., with an introduction by Philip Gura, Boston: Northeastern University Press, 1998). The best-known case of invented identity may be the sixteenth-century Frenchman known as Martin Guerre, treated in Natalie Davis, *The Return of Martin Guerre* (Cambridge, Mass.: Harvard University Press, 1983), whose notoriety even extended to New London, Connecticut, by the 1760s, when the case was laid out in the local press. Natalie Zemon Davis, "On the Lame—*American Historical Review* Forum: The Return of Martin Guerre," *American Historical Review* 93 (1988): 572n1.

39. Hannah Northrup's marriage to a Mr. Baxter of Boston is cited in Ansel Judd Northrup, *The Northrup-Northrop Genealogy: a Record of the Known Descendants of Joseph Northrup, who came from England in 1637, and was One of the Original Settlers of Milford, Conn., in 1639; with Lists of Northrups and Northrops in the Revolution* (New York: Grafton Press, 1908), p. 45; her twin sisters both married as well. After her father's second marriage the family moved to Monroe County, New York, near Rochester. Susannah Temple, who at the ages of twelve and thirteen was the victim of her father's repeated incest in 1772 and 1773, married John Woods in April 1778 and later gave birth to five children: Major Benjamin Farrar deposition of June 23, 1783, taken by Josiah Deane, in Sarah Temple Divorce Petition to Governor John Hancock, in 1783 divorce case of Stephen Temple, housewright, and Sarah, Supreme Judicial Court, Suffolk County, case 129821 (Reel 49), vol. 795; and *Vital Records of Upton, Massachusetts, to the end of the year 1849* (Worcester, Mass.: F. P. Rice, 1904), pp. 65, 66, 67, 69, 136. Sarah Avery's marriage is reported in Randolph Roth, "The Other Masonic Outrage: The Death and Transfiguration of Joseph Burnham," *Journal of the Early Republic* 14 (1994): 47. Phebe Bailey, the daughter of Asa Bailey and Abigail Abbot Bailey, may also have married. Ann Taves, the editor of [Bailey], *Religion and Domestic Violence in Early New England: The Memoirs of Abigail Abbot Bailey* (Bloomington: Indiana University Press, 1989), on p. 191n133 explains that she was unable to find conclusive evidence of Phebe Bailey's subsequent life, though a nineteenth-century local historian, William Whitcher, asserted that Phebe married and later joined a Shaker community as Phebe B. Huntington.

40. The children of the "black," mixed-race minister Lemuel Haynes, who had married a white woman, became "white" in the nineteenth century. Richard D. Brown, "'Not Only Extreme Poverty, But the Worst Kind of Orphanage': Lemuel Haynes and the Boundaries of Racial Tolerance on the Yankee Frontier, 1770–1820," *New England Quarterly* 61 (1988): 502–518. In the first U.S. Census of 1790, the Haynes household was listed as white (518n).

41. In the first half of the twentieth century it was claimed that Betsy had

a "weak mind." No evidence supported this contention, but it enabled Berkshire residents to distance themselves from the Wheeler legacy. George H. Tucker, *A History of Lenox* (Lenox: Lenox Library Association, 1992; rpt. from galleys of unfinished book, 1935–1936): under "Hangings in Lenox," Tucker discusses Ephraim Wheeler and notes, "There was some doubt as to his guilt, the girl, who was the principal witness against him, being of weak mind" (galley 52-2).

42. "John Whitfield Hulbert," in Rollin H. Cooke, "Pittsfield Families," vol. 5, pp. 176–177, and "Sheffield Cemeteries," vol. 38, p. 46, Berkshire Atheneum, Pittsfield Public Library, Pittsfield, Massachusetts; "John Whitefield Hulbert," U.S. Congress, *Biographical Directory of the United States Congress, 1774–1989,* Kathryn Allamong Jacob and Bruce A. Ragsdale, editors-in-chief (Washington, D.C.: U.S. Government Printing Office, 1989), p. 1229.

43. Genealogical and biographical information from Dewey-Bliss Papers, box 1, folder 2, AAS; "Daniel Dewey," U.S. Congress, *Biographical Directory of the United States Congress,* p. 903.

44. Dewey-Bliss Papers, box 1, AAS; Henry B. Dewey letter to authors, Worcester, Dec. 18, 1999.

45. *Report of the Trial of Dominic Daley and James Halligan for the Murder of Marcus Lyon, before the Supreme Judicial Court . . . April 1806* (Northampton, [1806]); James Russell Trumbull, *History of Northampton, Massachusetts, from the first settlement in 1654* (Northampton, 1902), vol. 2, p. 590. Justice Theodore Sedgwick ordered that the bodies of Daley and Halligan be "anatomized" for the benefit of science rather than buried; a new Massachusetts law permitted this procedure. See also Steven Robert Wilf, "Anatomy and Punishment in Late Eighteenth-Century New York," *Journal of Social History* 22 (1989): 507–530. Cheverus (1768–1836) was named Bishop of Boston in 1808. He moved to France in 1823 and was made cardinal in 1835. Joseph V. Tracy, "Jean-Louis Lefebvre de Cheverus," *Catholic Encyclopedia,* online ed., 1999 [1st ed. 1908]), vol. 3, *www.newadvent.org/cathen/03650a.htm.*

46. Trumbull, *History of Northampton,* vol. 2, p. 590.

47. William G. McLoughlin, *New England Dissent, 1630–1833: The Baptists and the Separation of Church and State* (Cambridge, Mass.: Harvard University Press, 1971), vol. 1, p. 658.

48. "James Sullivan," in *Sibley*, vol. 15 (1761–1763) (1970), pp. 318–319; on ballots, see Thomas Coffin Amory, *Life of James Sullivan with Selections from His Writings* (Boston, 1859), vol. 2, pp. 158–159.

49. [James Sullivan], *An Address to the Electors of Massachusetts* [Boston, 1807].

50. Amory, *Life of James Sullivan*, vol. 2, p. 317.

51. "Simeon Strong," in Franklin Bowditch Dexter, *Biographical Sketches of the Graduates of Yale College with Annals of the College History* (New York, 1896), vol. 2, pp. 437–438. The sentence is recorded in the judgment against Wheeler, GCPNG.

52. Samuel Sewall to Theodore Sedgwick, Marblehead, May 4, 1806, Sedgwick Papers I, Theodore Sedgwick, MHS; Richard E. Welch, Jr., "The Parsons-Sedgwick Feud and the Reform of the Massachusetts Judiciary," *Essex Institute Historical Collections* 92 (April 1956): 171–176.

53. Welch, "The Parsons-Sedgwick Feud," p. 176.

54. Richard E. Welch, Jr., *Theodore Sedgwick, Federalist: A Political Portrait* (Middletown, Conn.: Wesleyan University Press, 1965), pp. 249–250; David Hackett Fischer, *The Revolution of American Conservatism: The Federalist Party in the Era of Jeffersonian Democracy* (New York: Harper and Row, 1965), pp. 13–14.

55. In [Samuel Sewall], *Catalogue of the Library of the late Chief Justice Sewall: to be sold at auction Sep. 2, 1814, at the store of Whitwell & Bond* (Cambridge, Mass., 1814).

56. Samuel Sewall and Nathan Dane, *Communication from the Hon. Samuel Sewall, Esq. and the Hon. Nathan Dane, Esq. accompanied with Several Bills for the Regulation of the State Prison, and an alteration of the Criminal Laws of the Commonwealth* (Boston, 1805), 64 pp.

57. [Livermore and Angier], *Trial of Alpheus Livermore and Samuel Angier*, pp. 47, 48, 50.

58. Welch, "The Parsons-Sedgwick Feud," pp. 171–176.

59. Simon Larned Probate Court Docket, no 3605, Berkshire County Registry of Probate, Pittsfield, Massachusetts. Probated Apr. 7, 1817.

60. There is no will. "Simon Larned," in Rollin H. Cooke, "Pittsfield Families," vol. 6, pp. 115–117, Berkshire Atheneum, Pittsfield Public Library, Pittsfield, Massachusetts.

61. Samuel Shepard, *A Sermon Preached in Lenox, Mass., April 30, 1845 at the Celebration of the fiftieth Anniversary of his Ordination to the Work of the Gospel Ministry in said Town* (Lenox, 1845), p. 26.

62. Ibid., pp. 21, 26.

63. Ibid., p. 16. Shepard is paraphrasing Psalm 31:12: "I am forgotten as a dead man and clean out of mind."

64. Field and Dewey, *History of the County*, pp. 110–111.

65. In Catharine M. Sedgwick to Theodore Sedgwick, April 1, 1804, in Mary E. Dewey, ed., *Life and Letters of Catharine M. Sedgwick* (New York, 1871), pp. 80–81, the fifteen-year-old discusses town politics; Catharine M. Sedgwick and Katharine Sedgwick Minot, eds., *Letters from Charles Sedgwick to His Family and Friends* (Boston, 1870); Samuel Sewall to Theodore Sedgwick, Marblehead, May 4, 1806, Sedgwick Papers I, Theodore Sedgwick, MHS.

66. Mary Michael Welsh, *Catharine Maria Sedgwick: Her Position in the Literature and Thought of Her Time up to 1860* (Washington, D.C.: Catholic University of America, 1937), pp. 72–74, 97, 102; Edward Halsey Foster, *Catharine Maria Sedgwick* (New York: Twayne Publishers, 1974), p. 26; Mary Kelley, ed., *The Power of Her Sympathy: The Autobiography and Journal of Catharine Maria Sedgwick* (Boston: Massachusetts Historical Society, dist. by Northeastern University Press, 1993), p. 21; Dewey, ed., *Life and Letters of Catharine Maria Sedgwick;* "Berkley Jail," in *The Atlantic Souvenir* (Philadelphia, 1832), pp. 13–53, quotes Byron, "None are all evil"; "Daniel Prime," *The Magnolia for 1837* (New York, 1836), pp. 281–311.

67. C. M. Sedgwick, "Daniel Prime," p. 282.

68. Several Prime households in Windsor in 1800: U.S. Census, "Population Schedules of the Second Census of the United States, 1800," Microcopy no. 32 (Washington, D.C.: U.S. National Archives, 1959), Roll 13 (Massachu-

setts: Berkshire County). Kenneth A. Lockridge, *On the Sources of Patriarchal Rage: The Commonplace Books of William Byrd and Thomas Jefferson and the Gendering of Power in the Eighteenth Century* (New York: New York University Press, 1993).

69. *Report of the Trial of Dominic Daley and James Halligan,* pp. 10, 11; C. M. Sedgwick, "Daniel Prime," p. 311. Though greed is a common motive for murder, she may have taken it from Ebenezer Mason's 1802 murder of his brother-in-law, who, Mason said, "had no business there to get my father's farm and my interest into his own hands." *The Last Words of Ebenezer Mason, who was executed at Dedham, October 7, 1802; for the Murder of William Pitt Allen, His Brother in Law, on the 18th of May 1802. Taken from his own Mouth a few Hours previous to his Execution,* 2d ed. (Dedham, 1802), p. 6.

70. C. M. Sedgwick, "Daniel Prime," p. 311.

71. David H. Wood, *Lenox: Massachusetts Shire Town* ([Lenox:] published by the town, 1969), pp. 63–64. Wood referred to Shepard's execution sermon, but to neither the Trial Report nor Wheeler's *Narrative.* He treated the execution ritual as a curiosity.

72. In 1996 David Beasley published a fictionalized retelling of the Wheelers' story in an effort to address family violence issues; see his *Chocolate for the Poor: A Story of Rape in 1805* (Buffalo: Davus, 1996).

73. Shepard, *Execution,* p. 16. Shepard's words recall those of the high-church Anglican of the seventeenth century, John Donne, in his Devotion no. 16, *Complete Poetry and Selected Prose,* ed. John Hayward (London: Nonesuch Library, 1955), p. 537: "How many men that stand at an *execution,* if they would aske, for what dies that man, should heare their own faults condemned, and see themselves executed, by *Atturney?*"

74. Melville's annotation of the list of hangings is in his copy of Field and Dewey, *History of the County of Berkshire,* p. 111, Berkshire Atheneum, Pittsfield Public Library, Pittsfield, Massachusetts. Melville penciled two vertical lines next to the entry for Samuel P. Charles's execution of 1826. Melville's report of Nov. 13, 1849, on the London hanging is in his *Journals,* Northwestern-Newberry ed., texts revised with historical note and annotations by Howard C. Horsford with Lynn Horth (Evanston, Ill.: Northwest-

ern University Press; Chicago: Newberry Library, 1989), in *The Writings of Herman Melville,* vol. 15, p. 17. His comment on "the image of God" is in his review of Francis Parkman's *The Oregon Trail,* which the editors date early March 1849, published in *The Piazza Tales and Other Prose Pieces, 1839–1860,* ed. Harrison Hayford, Alma A. MacDougall, and G. Thomas Tanselle, historical note by Merton M. Sealts, Jr. (Evanston, Ill.: Northwestern University Press; Chicago: Newberry Library, 1987), in *Writings,* vol. 9, p. 232.

ACKNOWLEDGMENTS

———— ▸•◆•◂ ————

Several institutions and many people have helped us with this book, and we are eager to acknowledge their aid. First, we thank the John Simon Guggenheim Memorial Foundation for the fellowship provided to Richard D. Brown, and the University of Connecticut, which supplied him with a sabbatic leave and time released from classroom teaching. At the University of Connecticut, Deans Ross D. MacKinnon (College of Liberal Arts and Sciences) and Charles M. Super (School of Family Studies), as well as Altina L. Waller, chair of the History Department, have consistently supported our research, as has the University of Connecticut Research Foundation. Cyrus E. Zirakzadeh encouraged us to teach the Wheeler case as an experimental undergraduate honors seminar, and the University's Teaching and Learning Institute, headed by Keith Barker, provided assistance. We are grateful to students who participated in the course, especially Michelle Angiolillo, Robert Fluskey, and Margaret Harnois, whose research extended our knowledge. Richard D. Brown also thanks the students of History 211 (The Historian's Craft). Student re-enactments of Wheeler's trial enabled us to grasp the story more fully. Two University of Connecticut graduate students in history, Brian D. Carroll and Robb Haberman, also supplied substantial help. In addition, we appreciate assistance at the University's Homer Babbidge Library, its study carrels, microtext collection, and document delivery service. Many on the library staff helped, particularly David F. Avery, Richard J. Bleiler, T. Patrick McGlamery, and Lynn S. Sweet. Norman D. Stevens kindly connected us with Wendell Minor.

367

We also owe thanks to Massachusetts research libraries and archives. Without their collections and staffs we could not have written this work. At the American Antiquarian Society we particularly thank Georgia B. Barnhill, Joanne D. Chaison, Marie E. Lamoureux, and Theresa Tremblay. Peter Drummey, Nicholas Graham, and Anne E. Bentley of the Massachusetts Historical Society helped in many ways. At the Massachusetts Archives Elizabeth Bouvier (archivist for the Supreme Judicial Court), Michael Comeau, and Bill Milhomme assisted our work repeatedly. Both Jerome E. Anderson at the New England Historic and Genealogical Society and Peter Nonack at the Boston Athenæum went out of their way to help, as did Elise B. Feeley at Northampton's Forbes Library. Henry B. Dewey, Esq., a sixth-generation direct descendant of Daniel Dewey, Esq., also assisted us. We also thank the staffs at the Bristol, Hampshire, Plymouth, and Worcester County Courthouses, where we used the land registries and probate and quarterly court records. In Berkshire County, we used the same bodies of documents in Pittsfield and Adams, as well as court records under the supervision of County Commissioner Ronald E. Kitterman. We were also beneficiaries of town clerks in Cummington, Hinsdale, Lenox, Pittsfield, Rochester (where Helena Brown was especially helpful), Stockbridge, Sutton, and Windsor. Arvilla L. Dyer, former town clerk in Windsor, kindly volunteered to supply information on African Americans in early Berkshire, and William L. Streeter, historian of Cummington, generously shared his knowledge of Cummington records and his own electrostatic copies of Cummington tax and warning-out records. In Sutton, Ben McLaren and Paul F. Holzwarth helped with local records. Marcia P. Silva, of the Lincoln County, Maine, registry of deeds, enabled us to pursue leads at a distance.

Staff at the Pittsfield Public Library, especially Ruth T. Degenhardt, aided us, as did Denis Lesieur, Director of the Lenox Library

Association, Barbara Allen and Polly Pierce of the Stockbridge Library Association, and Sylvia Kennick Brown and Rachel U. Tassone of the Williams College library and art museum, respectively. We are also grateful to Norma Lesser and Anne Everest Wojtkowski and the Berkshire County Historical Association, which invited us to speak on the Wheeler case, and to Susan Eisley and Leni Sternerup for use of the society's library at Herman Melville's Arrowhead, his home in Pittsfield. We thank Helmut Wohl, then a resident family member in the Theodore Sedgwick house in Stockbridge, for his tour of the dwelling and the "Sedgwick Pie" family gravesite in the Stockbridge Cemetery. John and Virginia Demos, of Tyringham, generously shared their home and their ideas as our research was unfolding.

When we presented papers on aspects of the project we benefited from the advice of commentators and fellow panelists, especially Michael Grossberg, Barry Levy, James D. Rice, Alan Rogers, Mary Beth Sievens, and Laurel Thatcher Ulrich. Members of the Massachusetts Supreme Judicial Court Historical Society, particularly James Donnelly, offered helpful ideas. Other experts who offered valuable help include faculty in the University of Connecticut School of Family Studies: Stephen Anderson, Preston Britner, and Ronald Rohner. In addition, Regina Barreca, Sharon Block, Charlotte G. Borst, Daniel Caner, Daniel A. Cohen, Patricia Cline Cohen, Cathy N. Davidson, Thomas Doughton, Robert A. Gross, Karen Halttunen, Tamara K. Hareven, Ruth Herndon, Leon Jackson, Gloria Main, Martha J. McNamara, Leslie Richardson, Rixey Ruffin, Daniel Scott Smith, Suzanne Staubach, Nancy Steenburg, and Robert A. Wells gave us the benefit of their knowledge, as did the anonymous readers for Harvard University Press. Jill Kneerim of the Hill and Barlow Agency, and Aïda Donald, Kathleen McDermott, and Donna Bouvier of Harvard University Press have supplied helpful advice, early and late.

Finally, we are deeply grateful to six extraordinary scholars who

generously read our first draft and provided constructive ideas on everything from bibliography, word choice, and prose strategy to matters of fact and interpretation. Two are colleagues at the University of Connecticut, Cornelia Hughes Dayton and R. Kent Newmyer—who also advised on law and legal procedures, saving us from oversights and errors. We are equally grateful to Lawrence I. Buell, John P. Demos, Alan Taylor, and Laurel Thatcher Ulrich, whose contributions to our study we appreciate more than we can say. For all errors, we are responsible.

Universalism, 25, 59

Upper Canada, 301n47

Upton (Mass.), 132

Vermont, 194, 196

Veterans. *See* American Revolution; French and Indian War; War of 1812

Violence. *See* Family violence; Incest; Murder; Rape

Virginia, 194

Voltaire, 26, 192

Voluntary organizations, 25–28, 30

Walker, Esther Chaffe (Mrs. Robert), 318n38

Walker, Quok, 213

Walker, Robert (justice of the peace), 286, 318n38, 335n76; lack of familiarity of, with capital crimes, 81, 117, 148; physical evidence of rape overlooked by, 80–81, 98, 118, 148, 150, 185; as signer of Wheeler's pardon petition, 221; and Wheeler's altercations with Martin, 119, 130, 144–145, 150, 177, 182; Wheeler's arrest by, 118–120, 126, 148, 150; Wheeler's resentment of, 185; as witness in Wheeler trial, 80–81, 87, 92–94

Ward, Artemas, 204–205, 221, 222, 224, 227, 277, 279, 344n89, 345n91

Ward, Jonathan, 109

"Warning out," 137, 270, 323n16, 327n57; of Wheeler and Odels, 104, 139, 310n66

War of 1812, 279–280

Washington (Mass.), 28, 67

Washington, D.C., 30

Washington, George, 213, 224, 275; as Federalist, 19, 193; and Sedgwick, 9, 48, 49

Watson, Elkanah, 27

Webber, Orrin, 329n20

Webster, Daniel, 338n22

Wells, Job, 113, 236, 251, 307n46, 322n11

Wells, Maria, 322n11

Wells, Robert A., 317n19

West, Rev. Stephen, 15, 23, 196, 277, 335n80;

as capital punishment advocate, 195, 239, 240; execution sermons of, 243

Westermarck, Edward, 319n47

Western Star, The (Stockbridge newspaper), 23, 39, 258–261, 263, 264; Federalist slant of, 20–21, 260. *See also* Willard, Heman

West Stockbridge (Mass.), 17

Wheeler, Betsy, 284; accusations of, as credible, 2, 3, 69, 73, 75, 77, 79–82, 87, 91–94, 97–99, 119, 127, 150, 288; accusations of, as false, 83–88, 94, 121–122, 151, 183, 186–187, 216–217, 222, 230, 251, 256, 272, 288; accusations of rape against Wheeler by, 2, 6, 8, 44, 45, 62, 70–75, 79, 102, 112–113, 118–20, 124, 126, 146–148, 150, 217, 220, 223–224, 231, 258–259, 272, 286; birth of, 175; confiding of rape to Hannah by, 70–72, 94, 98, 115–118, 120, 122, 126, 146; courage of, 103, 111–128, 151, 217, 272, 286; on dying "one way as another," 73, 93, 122–123; Hannah's relationship with, 105, 107, 110, 116, 122–124, 130–131, 145, 147, 269; Hannah's support for, 2, 4, 70–72, 79, 80, 98, 116–118, 122, 126, 130–136, 143, 146, 148, 151, 217, 220, 286; as illiterate, 71, 103, 107, 152, 216, 314n2; lack of evidence of rape of, 7, 80–81, 91, 98, 118, 148, 150, 185, 224, 279, 289; naming of, 104, 138, 177; number of Wheeler's rape attempts on, 45, 72–75, 80, 85–86, 89, 92, 99, 115, 117, 122, 124, 181, 225; petition for Wheeler's pardon by, 4, 128, 152, 189, 190, 215–216, 220, 222, 227–228, 253, 270; "weak mind" claims about, 360n41; Wheeler's relationship with, prior to rape, 110–111, 124, 128; after Wheeler's trial, 269–272; Wheeler's violence toward, 70–74, 77, 80, 92, 94, 99, 102, 111, 115, 118, 120, 125, 126, 146, 287; white appearance of, 70, 109, 269

Wheeler, Ephraim: background of, 2, 16, 28, 44, 157–188, 329n20; case of, as instructive for our time, 285–286; death warrant for, 253–254, 347n4, 354n61; declarations of in-

Wheeler, Hannah Odel *(continued)*
appearance of, 109, 137, 140, 269. *See also*
Odel family; *names of specific Odel family
members*
Wheeler, Isaac (Ephraim's father), 155, 158–
159, 161, 168, 187
Wheeler, Mrs. Isaac (Ephraim's mother), 155,
158–159, 166, 187
Whelpley, William A., 33, 185, 218, 231
Whipple, Samuel, 59
Whitcher, William, 360n39
White(s): Betsy Wheeler's appearance as, 70,
109, 269; Hannah Wheeler's appearance
as, 109, 137, 140, 269; Lemuel Haynes'
children as, 360n40; noncapital punishments for rape by, 195; rape by, 2, 3, 42,
60–66, 102, 190–191, 210, 267, 294n7,
301n47; relative lack of rape convictions
for, 3, 60–61, 190–191. *See also* Race
Whitefield, George, 251
Whiting, William, 128
Whittlesey, Eliphalet, 59
Willard, Heman: ads for trial report by, 45,
112–113, 294n9; as Federalist newspaper
publisher, 20, 27, 258–261, 263; Hutchinson's confession published by, 265; sermons published by, 61; and trial report
genre, 43; trial report on Wheeler by, 3, 43,
96–99; on Hannah Wheeler, 268; on
Wheeler's true name, 359n38; Wheeler's
autobiography told to, 156–157, 231. See
also *Western Star*
Williams College, 24, 65, 196–197, 218, 273
Williamson, Unice, 43
Williamstown (Mass.), 22, 25, 65, 67;

Wheeler family in, 107, 110, 177–178. *See
also* Williams College
Windsor (Mass.): Odel family members living in, 268, 309n66; pardon petitions for
Wheeler from, 4, 219, 221; as upland Berkshire County town, 28, 139; Walker as justice of peace in, 80; as Wheeler's community, 45, 66, 109, 110, 171, 180, 257
Witchcraft, 36–37, 49, 278, 318n30
Wollstonecraft, Mary, 26
Women: crimes against, 24, 58, 300n47; in-
ability of, to testify against their husbands,
72, 98, 118, 131, 134, 152, 310n68, 346n100;
lack of historical documentation about
poor, 134–135, 153–154, 268; obedience
taught to, 105, 111, 113–115, 124, 131, 217,
283. *See also* Divorce petition(s); Incest;
Rape
Wood, David H., 364n71
Wood, John, 321n4
Wood, Susannah Temple, 321n4, 360n39
Woodbridge, Joseph (Berkshire County clerk
of court), 63, 68, 100
Worcester (Mass.), 264, 267, 294n7, 349n14
Worcester County (Mass.), 136–139
Worthington (Mass.), 104, 106, 139, 172, 174–
175, 298n24, 316nn12, 16
Worthington, John, 47
Wright, Dr. Asahel, 80, 94, 181
Wright, Sarah, 50

Yale, 22, 47, 48, 65, 242
York (Maine), 52
Young, Robert, 294n7